IP 90 34—

32 6l

EX

Biblical Tradition in
Blake's Early Prophecies

LESLIE TANNENBAUM

Biblical Tradition in Blake's Early Prophecies: The Great Code of Art

PRINCETON UNIVERSITY PRESS
PRINCETON, NEW JERSEY

Copyright © 1982 by Princeton University Press
Published by Princeton University Press, 41 William St.,
Princeton, New Jersey
In the United Kingdom: Princeton University Press,
Guildford, Surrey

ALL RIGHTS RESERVED
Library of Congress Cataloging in Publication Data will be
found on the last printed page of this book

This book has been composed in Linotype Baskerville

Clothbound editions of Princeton University Press books
are printed on acid-free paper, and binding materials are
chosen for strength and durability

Printed in the United States of America by Princeton
University Press, Princeton, New Jersey

To Paula

Contents

The Old & New Testaments are the Great Code
of Art.
                                    —William Blake

Preface

While this book was in its initial stages, a distinguished colleague asked me how I had the temerity to write about so vast a subject as Blake and the Bible. I responded with a quotation from William Godwin's *The Enquirer*: "When a man writes a book of methodical investigation, he does not write because he understands the subject, but he understands the subject because he has written." I have written because I wanted to understand what Blake meant when he said that the Bible is the Great Code of Art. My investigation of this subject began with three earlier studies: one on the relationship of *The Book of Urizen* to Genesis, and the two others on the biblical context of *The Ghost of Abel*. In these studies I found that Blake was not merely concerned with the Bible itself but was also engaged with critical and exegetical premises and conclusions that had accrued from the past and that were being actively tested and revised in his own time. Indeed, given the enormous exegetical overlay that had been imposed upon the Bible since the time of the church fathers, it would be difficult for someone in Blake's time to be reading, in New Critical fashion, simply "the text itself." Therefore, I discovered, the proper study of Blake's use of the Bible must include a consideration of how Blake's contemporaries and predecessors read the Scriptures, and how this is reflected in Blake's theory and practice. I learned, in short, that we cannot talk meaningfully about Blake and the Bible without talking about Blake and biblical tradition. Over the past few years, therefore, I have been concerned with examining this tradition and its relevance to Blake's ideas about —and exploitation of—prophetic form, biblical pictorialism, biblical typology, biblical history, and the possibilities of re-creating the Bible for his own time. The book I have written contains my present understanding of these issues, particularly in relation to Blake's early prophetic books.

In the course of my investigation, one problem that has especially impressed me is the paucity of background studies necessary for a pursuit of Blake's relationship to the biblical traditions available in his own time. Although there is much information about biblical tradition in the Middle Ages and up through the seventeenth century, and an ever-increasing volume of material on Milton's biblical heritage, there are few helpful studies of eighteenth-century biblical criticism and exegesis. My research has therefore led me to a great deal of primary material and to a variety of secondary sources in disciplines other than literary history or eighteenth-century literary studies. The heavily annotated first chapter of this book reflects this spade work, which I hope will be useful to others who want to explore in more detail Blake's biblical milieu. Those readers who have no curiosity about the sources of biblical tradition that were available to Blake, or who are more interested in getting directly to my argument, may wish to skip the opening chapter.

Onerous as the task of tracing Blake's biblical heritage may be, I have, of course, benefited from the work of other scholars, whom I acknowledge in the first chapter and throughout the book. My task has also been made easier by the libraries that graciously have made their collections available. Research for this book was begun under the most ideal conditions, at the Huntington Library, and I am grateful to its staff for their help as well as for their hospitality. Further research was conducted at the Library of Congress, the Folger Shakespeare Library, the Union Theological Seminary Library, the Jewish Theological Seminary Library, St. Mark's Library of the General Theological Seminary in New York, the New York Public Library, the Krauth Memorial Library of the Lutheran Theological

Seminary in Philadelphia, the Scofield Hill Memorial Library of the Philadelphia College of the Bible, the University of Pennsylvania Library, the Houghton Library, the Andover-Harvard Theological Seminary Library, and the Ohio State University Library. I thank the librarians and staffs of these libraries for their courteous assistance.

I also want to express my gratitude to those institutions that have generously supported the research for and the writing of this book. A fellowship from the Huntington Library allowed me to begin work on this project, and a summer stipend from the National Endowment for the Humanities enabled me to continue my research. Additional support for research came from the Wright State University College of Liberal Arts. A grant from the American Council of Learned Societies provided the uninterrupted time necessary to write a first draft of this book.

I am grateful to the editors of *Blake Studies*, Memphis State University, for permission to reprint as the eighth chapter of this book a revised version of my essay, "Blake's Art of Crypsis: *The Book of Urizen* and Genesis." I also thank the editors at Princeton University Press, Jerry Sherwood and Tam Curry, for their patient and expert help in the preparation of the manuscript for publication.

I am indebted to my colleagues at Ohio State University —Ernest Lockridge, John Gabel, Richard Martin, and Richard D. Altick—for reading and criticizing the final draft of this book. The students in my Blake seminar at Ohio State University in the winter of 1979 were a fit and active audience, providing me with the opportunity to test many of the ideas advanced in this book. Large as my debt is to these people who have kindly and enthusiastically examined the final product, even larger is my obligation to those who have provided aid and inspiration during the years that this book was in progress. I want to thank Stuart Curran and Joseph Anthony Wittreich, Jr. for being a constant support to me in many ways. In the course of writing this book, I have benefited from their knowledge, their encouragement, their advice, their hospitality, and their friendship. I am particularly grateful to them for their generously granting me the use of their home, with its extensive library, which greatly facilitated the completion of the manuscript in its final stage. Lastly, and most importantly, this book is lovingly dedicated to someone whose contribution I cannot even begin to acknowledge.

Textual Note

All citations of Blake's poetry and prose are from *The Poetry and Prose of William Blake*, ed. David V. Erdman, rev. ed. (Garden City, N.Y.: Doubleday, 1970) and are given parenthetically within the text, the numbers indicating, wherever possible, the plate and line(s) of the passage cited. All citations of full-plate illustrations in Blake's illuminated books are from David V. Erdman, ed., *The Illuminated Blake* (Garden City, N.Y.: Doubleday, 1974), which uses the numbering of the plates established in Geoffrey Keynes and Edwin Wolf 2nd, *William Blake's Illuminated Books: A Census* (New York: The Grolier Club, 1953). In parenthetical documentation, the following abbreviations will be used:

MHH	*The Marriage of Heaven and Hell*
DC	*Descriptive Catalogue*
VLJ	*A Vision of the Last Judgment*
J	*Jerusalem*

All citations of the Bible are from the Authorized (King James) Version.

Biblical Tradition in
Blake's Early Prophecies

Introduction

From the very beginning, readers of Blake have been aware that the single most important influence on Blake's life, writings, and art was the Bible. John Thomas Smith, one of Blake's earliest biographers, observed of Blake that the Bible "was every thing with him." Benjamin Heath Malkin noted that the Book of Revelation "may well be supposed to engross much of Mr. Blake's study."[1] Blake himself told Henry Crabb Robinson that "all he knew was in the Bible,"[2] and in his *Laocoön* engraving, he inscribed what was always his main artistic tenet: "The Old & New Testaments are the Great Code of Art" (p. 271). Blake's adherence to this code is evident in the numerous biblical quotations and allusions in his works, in the imprint of the King James Bible on his style, in the patterning of his own mythopoetics upon biblical myth, and in his use of concepts of literary form derived from the Bible. Clearly, Blake expected his readers to recognize the biblical context of his works, especially since much of his work was intended to form the "Bible of Hell" that he promised in *The Marriage of Heaven and Hell* (pl. 24). Despite the satiric tone in which this promise is couched, Blake's canon *was* an intentional imaginative re-creation of the Bible, conditioned by his recognition of traditional interpretations of Scripture and by his own reworking of those interpretations, his reading of the Bible "in its infernal or diabolical sense" (*MHH*, pl. 24). Thus much of the shape and meaning of Blake's work is determined not only by his borrowings from the Bible but also by his borrowings and deviations from traditional uses and interpretations of that book. As Joseph Anthony

3

Mazzeo has pointed out, the Bible usually enters literature through a writer's particular "exegetical framework."[3]

The importance of biblical tradition to Blake's art and thought is attested to by Blake himself and also by his early readers. Blake indicated his familiarity with and respect for biblical commentators when he wrote the following marginal annotation to *An Apology for the Bible*, Robert Watson's attack upon Paine's *The Age of Reason*: "Another Argument [of Paine's] is that all the Commentators on the Bible are Dishonest Designing Knaves who in hopes of a good living adopt the State religion this he has shewn with great force which calls upon His Opponent loudly for an answer. I could name an hundred such" (p. 605). Whether Blake meant that he could name a hundred answers to Paine or a hundred commentators who were not state tricksters, it is clear that he had read the works of biblical exegetes, both knavish and inspired. In a letter to Thomas Butts, Blake lists Boehme and Paracelsus—both of whom wrote biblical commentaries[4]—as important influences on his life (p. 680). Elsewhere he explicitly reveals his knowledge of Swedenborg and the cabbala.[5] Frederick Tatham, Blake's contemporary, further testifies to the breadth of Blake's reading; J. T. Smith maintains that Blake read the Bible in several languages; and Henry Crabb Robinson records Blake's familiarity with the "Spiritual sense" of the Bible and with gnostic doctrine.[6] Swinburne, too, deriving much of his information from Seymour Kirkup, a contemporary of Blake's who was not consulted by Gilchrist, points out Blake's debt to biblical tradition and continually cites the Bible and biblical tradition in his discussion of Blake's works.[7]

Swinburne's knowledge and extensive citation of biblical tradition may seem surprising to some, but even more surprising is the dearth of criticism since Swinburne's time emphasizing Blake's use of biblical tradition—especially in view of the significance of the subject. Of course, there have been scattered references to Blake's use of the Bible and

4

biblical commentaries throughout the works of most Blake scholars, but fuller discussion of Blake's use of biblical tradition properly resumes only in 1947 with Northrop Frye's *Fearful Symmetry*, which presents in one of its chapters a brief but important outline of Blake's indebtedness to the Bible and its traditions.[8] Though certainly not thorough in its examination of the relationship of Blake to biblical tradition, Frye's work suggests some directions for future profitable investigation. For instance, in his discussion of Blake's "contrapuntal symbolism," the blending of Christian and pagan mythology in Blake's works,[9] Frye points to the tradition of syncretism that originated in the writings of the church fathers, was elaborately developed during the Renaissance, and was revived again in the eighteenth century. Similarly, Frye's discussion of language and allegory in Blake's poetry suggests, though it does not mention or develop, Augustinian concepts of rhetoric and poetics that were revived among poets and exegetes in the seventeenth and eighteenth centuries.[10] Appearing almost concurrently with Frye's book, J. G. Davies' discussion of Blake's theology necessarily touches upon biblical tradition. Its main value lies in its discussion of Blake's relationship to Swedenborg and its suggestion of points at which Blake is in accord with orthodox traditions.[11] But Davies overemphasizes the latter and neglects Blake's contact with more radical biblical traditions. While Davies tries too much to put Blake in the mainstream of Christian orthodoxy, M. O. Percival, Désirée Hirst, and Kathleen Raine—following a trend established by Yeats and Ellis—go to the opposite extreme, pressing for an interpretation of Blake that depends on the more esoteric traditions, particularly Neoplatonism and hermeticism.[12] These scholars point out some important instances of Blake's borrowing from arcane traditions, but they err in their overemphasis of the importance of those traditions to Blake and in their lack of historical perspective. They too readily assume Blake's subservience to esoteric traditions, rather than his imaginative exploitation of them, and their studies do not explore the extent to which esoteric traditions became absorbed into more popular biblical traditions and thus were modified in the seventeenth and eighteenth centuries. In this regard, Mark Schorer, Peter Fisher, and Morton Paley have provided a more balanced account, though they are not primarily concerned with biblical tradition.[13]

It is only quite recently that Blake scholars have attempted to explore in any extensive way the central biblical traditions that were readily available to Blake and his contemporaries and to discuss the precise ways in which those traditions affected the form and content of Blake's works. Murray Roston and David B. Morris place Blake within the context of the growing interest in biblical poetics in the eighteenth and early nineteenth centuries. Harold Fisch complements these studies by discussing the impact of the Old Testament upon seventeenth-century literature, briefly noting the continuation of this influence in Blake's poetry.[14] More recently, M. H. Abrams, Florence Sandler, Joseph Anthony Wittreich, and Stuart Curran have begun to provide detailed discussion of Blake's relationship to well-known religious traditions, many of which were current in Milton's time, had persisted into the eighteenth century, and were extensively revived in the heated religious and political atmosphere created by the French Revolution.[15] Abrams and Wittreich focus primarily upon the relation of Blake's later prophecies to traditions surrounding the Book of Revelation, and Sandler discusses the exegetical contexts of Blake's critique of "Milton's Religion" and eighteenth-century Christianity in *Milton*. Curran points out Blake's ties with Gnosticism and deals mainly with its impact on *Jerusalem*.

Building upon the important conclusions and suggestions of these previous works, the study that follows is an attempt to describe the ways in which Blake used biblical tradition to give shape and meaning to his early prophecies. The opening chapters discuss Blake's ideas about the form and content of prophecy in light of biblical commentaries, seventeenth- and eighteenth-century discussions of biblical rhetoric and poetics, and the practice of seventeenth- and eighteenth-century poets who adopted a biblical aesthetic. The remaining chapters explain the biblical context of each of the Lambeth books: *America, Europe, The Song of Los, The Book of Urizen, The Book of Ahania,* and *The Book of Los.* I have restricted my discussion to these works mainly because the size of my subject requires the setting of such a limitation and because the Lambeth books constitute Blake's initial attempt to write a Bible of Hell, an imaginative re-creation of Scripture. They mark a distinct phase in Blake's career, his attempt to emulate the biblical canon by combining a number of disparate books into a coherent and unified vision of human life from the Creation to the Apocalypse. Blake later abandons this project, as he becomes more interested in fusing biblical prophecy with the epic mode, casting the entire vision of the Bible in a single work. Here—in *The Four Zoas, Milton,* and *Jerusalem*—Blake's use of biblical tradition becomes denser and even more complex. I must defer discussion of these works until another time. Many of my conclusions in the present study, however, particularly those of the opening chapters, can and will be applied to works other than the Lambeth prophecies. Throughout this work my aim has been to show what I have discovered in my own reading and teaching of Blake: much of what is apparently obscure in Blake is greatly clarified by a knowledge of his use of the Bible and the biblical traditions that were known to him and his contemporaries.

Blake and Biblical Tradition

An adequate account of eighteenth-century hermeneutics, exegesis, and biblical criticism has yet to be written, if indeed it would be possible to contain this subject in all its variety and complexity in a single study.[1] To fully understand the ways in which the Bible was interpreted in eighteenth-century England, we would need to account for the different forms in which the biblical text and its exegesis were transmitted. These would include printed texts (with or without marginal glosses and critical apparatus), commentaries on all or parts of the Bible, printed sermons, tracts, articles and reviews in periodicals, hymns and liturgies of various denominations, literary studies of the Bible, learned dissertations on biblical subjects, studies of biblical and eastern antiquities, writings of the speculative mythographers, paraphrases of poetic books of the Bible, and poems on biblical subjects; they would also include spoken sermons and works of art, inside and outside the church, that dealt with biblical subjects. Besides dealing with the different forms in which biblical tradition was transmitted, we would also have to account for the variety of religious and irreligious points of view in an age that rivaled Milton's in its proliferation of religious splinter groups and polemical wars.[2] It is not possible within the limitations of this study to give such a full account of eighteenth-century biblical tradition, but I would like to outline briefly the major sources of biblical tradition that would have been available to Blake and his contemporaries. Blake, we shall discover, had a rich and multifarious tradition at his disposal. Some elements of this tradition had a stronger influence than others, but all furnished material for the shaping of his own vision.

The Bible itself was omnipresent, appearing in various forms and translations. Those of Blake's contemporaries who were literate read and owned copies.[3] Furthermore, since the ability of the individual Christian to read the Bible was important to the Protestant faith, the Bible was required reading in charity schools, Sunday schools, and other institutions established to promote literacy.[4] Family Bibles—two editions of which Blake did engravings for— were also very popular, and the practice of serial publication made the Bible available in cheap periodical installments.[5] Many of these Bibles had glosses in the form of the original chapter headings of the Authorized Version and/or notes.[6] Such commentaries were usually eclectic in their use of previous biblical scholarship and more or less literal in their interpretation of the text.[7] Various denominations attempted to produce Bibles that would promote their own points of view, however—through new translations, sectarian annotations applied to the Authorized Version, or both. Anthony Purver, for instance, produced a newly translated Quaker Bible, and the Unitarians issued an edition of the Scriptures that reflected their own beliefs.[8] John Wesley's annotated Bible supplied sound corrections to the Authorized Version of the New Testament, his notes freely borrowed from those older commentaries that suited his point of view.[9]

For the wealthier and more learned reader, there were new scholarly translations of the whole Bible or parts of it, each accompanied by critical and exegetical notes that were based upon what was the beginning of modern biblical scholarship. Robert Lowth's Isaiah, William Newcome's Ezekiel, Benjamin Blayney's Jeremiah and Lamentations, and Thomas Percy's Song of Solomon were the most famous of these productions.[10] Blake was probably familiar at least with Newcome's translation, an edition of which was published by Joseph Johnson. He probably also knew the attempt at a new translation of the Bible by the Catholic scholar, Alexander Geddes, who also published with Johnson and who was versed in the latest German biblical criticism.[11]

Biblical commentaries dealing with the whole Bible or with individual books or passages were available in the form of books, printed sermons, periodicals, and pamphlets. Many of these, intended primarily for the clergy and the learned and wealthier laity, were beyond the financial means of Blake and the larger reading public. But Blake would have read some of them in the bookshops, and their contents would filter down to the public through sermons.[12] Blake could also have received a distillation of these exegetical works from his friend, Henry Fuseli, who had been trained and had briefly served as a Zwinglian minister before he left Switzerland and who maintained an interest in biblical and theological matters throughout his life.[13] Some biblical commentaries were printed in inexpensive editions and became very popular, particularly the commentaries of Thomas Scott and Matthew Henry and the combined commentaries of Patrick, Lowth, Arnald, Whitby, and Lowman.[14] Similarly, the evangelical revival stimulated the reprinting and popularization of works that were originally intended for a more learned audience. For instance, the Society for Promoting Christian Knowledge published a brief introduction to the biblical prophets by John Smith of Campbeltown, which abstracted a great deal of material from Lowth, Newcome, Blayney, Thomas Newton, and Benjamin Kennicott.[15] John Wesley, probably the most prolific popularizer of the century, reprinted in his *Notes on the New Testament* (1764) the notes on Revelation from Johann Albrecht Bengel's *Gnomon of the New Testament* and *Commentary on Revelation*.[16] Robert Lowth's *Lectures on the Sacred Poetry of the Hebrews* was reprinted in monthly installments in the anti-Wesleyan *The Christian's Magazine* in 1767 and was summarized in a chapter on

Hebrew poetry in Hugh Blair's popular *Lectures on Rhetoric and Belles-Lettres* (1783).[17]

In these more accessible and more widely distributed publications we see a phenomenon within eighteenth-century biblical tradition that has not been sufficiently emphasized, the mingling of learned and popular culture, which is even more apparent in the numerous tracts and pamphlets that were so widely published and read during Blake's time. This phenomenon is particularly evident in the pamphlets interpreting biblical phophecy, which reached the height of popularity in the 1790s. Pamphlets on religious subjects had always been a staple of Joseph Johnson's firm, and religious tracts had reached a large circulation through the efforts of the S.P.C.K., the Wesleyans, and the Evangelicals who published the Cheap Repository Tracts. But by far the greatest interest in exegetical issues was promoted by the pamphlets that searched the Scriptures for prophecies of the French Revolution.[18] The 1790s saw not only the publication of interpretations of biblical prophecy by chiliasts and radicals belonging to popular religious tradition but also the citation, publication, and reprinting of earlier and contemporary scholarly works on prophecy, particularly the works of Joseph Mede, Thomas Brightman, Sir Isaac Newton, William Whiston, David Hartley, and Joseph Priestley.[19] This mingling of learned and popular biblical commentary also reached the public through the more general journals of the day as well as through the religious periodicals that were published by the Wesleyans, the Evangelicals, the Dissenters, the Unitarians, and other groups.[20]

Blake's biblical heritage came to him not only in spoken and written form but in visual form as well. As Jean Hagstrum puts it, "Blake read the Bible, but he also *saw* it. The white page came stained with color and scored with line, for Blake's Bible was also the Bible of Raphael, Michelangelo, and the great masters of Western religious art, engraved by such masters as Raimondi."[21] What was true for Blake was also true for his contemporaries. The whole tra-

11

dition of Western art formed a *Biblia Pauperum* for the illiterate and the literate alike. Eighteenth-century Londoners were exposed to the lavish illustrations in Bibles and biblical works (such as the writings of Josephus) that were published in inexpensive fascicles.[22] Those who visited the exhibitions were made aware of contemporary attempts to capture in oil and watercolor the sublimity of the Bible.[23]

Whatever form biblical art appeared in, however, the viewer was given not only a dramatic experience of the living Word but an interpretation as well.[24] Depictions of the Fall, for instance, usually contained visual references to redemption and/or judgment, thus promoting the Christian interpretation of the Old Testament text.[25] There were also traditional extracanonical pictorial subjects and motifs in biblical illustration that were derived from religious doctrines and exegetical tradition. The finding of Abel by Adam and Eve, for instance, is not a scene described in the Genesis text, but it was an extremely popular pictorial subject that was often employed to emphasize the martyred Abel's typological foreshadowing of Christ.[26] Similarly, in illustrations to the Book of Job, iconographic details, such as visible or hidden crosses, depict Job as a type of Christ; and various symbols representing the Law and the Gospel are employed to show that Job's final redemption represents the reconciliation of the Law and the Gospel through Christ.[27]

Blake's own illustrations of Job and the Cain and Abel story amply show his awareness of and his participation in these pictorial traditions that are intimately connected with scriptural exegesis. Interestingly, it is only recently that Blake scholars have discovered that much of what was formerly believed to be Blake's private and idiosyncratic iconography is actually rooted in biblical tradition. Given Blake's awareness of the pictorial manifestations of biblical tradition, it is also quite possible that the more readily accessible prints in the printshops that Blake frequented were primary sources of many ideas that were also being disseminated in popular tracts and learned treatises.[28]

Just as diverse as the forms in which biblical material was disseminated are the ways in which the Bible was interpreted. In Blake's time, the rich exegetical tradition of the past was undergoing a dramatic transformation. This state of transition accounts for the great variety of hermeneutical approaches that we encounter in the eighteenth century. Modern historians correctly emphasize the importance of the growth of the higher criticism in the last decades of the eighteenth century, as seen in the works of Eichhorn, Michaelis, Simon, Herder, Lowth, Ernesti, and Lessing—to name but a few of the contributors to the growth of modern biblical scholarship. Their work was excerpted, summarized, and alluded to in English periodicals and books on biblical subjects.[29] The new biblical criticism was available to and employed by the Romantic poets, as E. S. Shaffer has pointed out, and Blake would have heard about this criticism from Fuseli and possibly through contact with other members of Johnson's circle, such as Priestley and Alexander Geddes.[30] The latest ideas about the biblical text and biblical myth and literary structure would influence or confirm Blake's own perceptions about these matters.

Important as the higher criticism was for the nineteenth century and thereafter, its impact upon the general public of the eighteenth century was not as great as that of the precursors of the new biblical criticism, the deists and the freethinkers.[31] The rationalist attacks upon the Bible as a work of divine inspiration and upon the body of exegetical material in which the Bible was ensconced had begun earlier in the century but were later revived through the reprinting of these earlier works and through the publication of translations of Voltaire, in inexpensive editions, and the works of Paine, Gibbon, and Hume.[32] Spurred by the toppling of the authority of Church and State in France, radicals in the 1790s rehearsed in pamphlets and public meet-

13

ings the criticism of the Bible that grew out of the earlier
deist controversy. This renewal of critical deism received
its greatest impetus from the publication of Paine's *The
Age of Reason* (1794-1795) and Bishop Watson's reply, *An
Apology for the Bible* (1796).[33] Like the Dragon man in
Blake's printing house in hell (*MHH*, 15), the deists cleared
away much of the rubbish of orthodox biblical exegesis
that made the Bible an instrument of State Religion—an
achievement that Blake acknowledges in his marginalia to
Watson's *Apology* and in an incidental remark about Vol-
taire.[34] Blake would freely agree with the contention of
Spinoza, Voltaire, and Paine that much of the Bible is
poetic or imaginative (although he did not share their
valuation of poetry and the imagination), and he shared
the deists' awareness that the Old Testament describes
many barbaric and vicious acts performed in the name of
God.[35] In fact, the tone of raillery used by such writers as
Peter Annet and Voltaire is echoed in Blake's satiric at-
tacks, in *The Marriage* and the Lambeth books, upon or-
thodox readings of the Bible.

Blake of course realized that the battle between the ortho-
dox and the deists was not a heated one and that both sides
were in essential agreement about the authority of reason.
As he states in his annotations to Watson's *Apology*, neither
Paine nor the bishop had seen the Everlasting Gospel (p.
608). The Anglican Church, as well as the old Dissent, had
already absorbed some of the deist influence, and their her-
meneutics had become more rationalistic: biblical narra-
tives were beginning to be regarded as historical in the
modern sense of that term, and the older traditions of bib-
lical allegories and types were eclipsed by a more rational
and abstract system of natural analogy.[36] The older tradi-
tions of allegorical or spiritual interpretation of the Bible
persisted well into the nineteenth century, however, em-
bodied in the works of such writers as Swedenborg, John
Hutchinson, John Dove, George Horne, and Samuel Hors-

ley.[37] Emphasizing the internal sense of the Word, these writers take their place in a long tradition of popular piety with which Blake has clear affinities.

We see the survival of older biblical traditions into the eighteenth century not only in the works of Swedenborg, Horne, and Horsley but in other sources as well. The ideas of Jacob Boehme were echoed in the works of Swedenborg, William Law, and their followers—such as Jacob Duché—but they were also presented firsthand to Blake and his contemporaries in the so-called William Law translation of Boehme's works.[38] Boehme, in turn, was transmitting a wealth of biblical material from the cabbala, the church fathers, and the medieval mystics.[39] Another rich source of biblical material was the biblical criticism of Voltaire, in such works as *The Philosophical Dictionary* and *La Bible enfin expliquée*, which borrowed a great deal from previous biblical scholarship, particularly the massive commentaries of Dom Augustine Calmet, whose biblical dictionary was translated into English, incorporated into English Bible commentaries, and often published in inexpensive form.[40] Through both Voltaire and Calmet, the eighteenth-century reader would receive at thirdhand and secondhand, respectively, a great deal of rabbinic, patristic, and medieval mystical material. Older exegetical traditions, such as that of the Gnostics, were also kept alive in the eighteenth century through Pierre Bayle's *Dictionary*, Isaac de Beausobre's *Critique de Manichée et Manichéisme*, Nathaniel Lardner's *History of Heretics* and *The Credibility of Gospel History*, Gibbon's *Decline and Fall of the Roman Empire*, Johann Lorenz von Mosheim's *Ecclesiastical History*, and Joseph Priestley's works—all of which (except Beausobre) were reprinted and frequently cited in the eighteenth century.[41] An even more familiar source of earlier biblical traditions was the poetry and prose of John Milton, which contained the seventeenth-century heritage of radical dissent, but which also publicized the ideas of such exegetes as Au-

15

gustine, Beza, and Pareus.[42] Furthermore, seventeenth- and eighteenth-century annotations to Milton called attention to these traditions.[43]

While Milton is the most obvious source of seventeenth-century biblical interpretation for Blake, we also have strong evidence of the survival into the late eighteenth century of the radical antinomianism that arose in the 1640s. The tradition was preserved by the Muggletonians, the early Quakers, and the various millenarian groups whose existence became conspicuous during the last three decades of the eighteenth century.[44] William Hamilton Reid, a *ci-devant* radical who wrote a pamphlet condemning his former associates, complained that in the 1790s Sunday field preachers at various locations throughout London attracted not only deists and atheists who came to dispute with Christians but they also attracted "Mystics, Muggletonians, Millennaries, and a variety of eccentric characters of different denominations."[45] Reid mentioned particularly a group of *"Infidel Mystics"* called the Ancient Deists of Hoxton, who between 1776 and 1794 made Hoxton "a kind of vortex" that attracted various radical sects. At their meetings, "human learning was declaimed against, . . . and dreams, visions, and immediate revelations were recommended as a substitute." They reportedly conversed with the dead and with Angels; and when the French Revolution began, these people became interested in revolutionary politics.[46] Blake's affinities with these radical groups and with the antinomian tradition of radical chiliasm and "inner light" hermeneutics that these groups espoused has been noted by Christopher Hill, A. L. Morton, E. P. Thompson, and M. H. Abrams.[47]

Among the sectarians gathered at Hoxton, Reid observed, there were "Alchymists, Astrologers, Calculators, Mystics, Prophets, and Projectors, of every class."[48] Exaggerated as this statement may sound, Reid is pointing out an important cultural phenomenon: the sectarians of the eighteenth century, like their seventeenth-century forebears, were actively involved in or associated with the revival of occult traditions, and in the millenarian ferment in England and France in the late eighteenth century, the English public was exposed to the ideas of some of the more esoteric and mystical religious groups.[49] One possible explanation for this link between esoteric and more popular traditions in the seventeenth and eighteenth centuries is the influence of Boehme, who had employed occult systems and their symbols as metaphors for the process of spiritual regeneration.[50]

But whatever the causes may have been, we find in the late eighteenth century a curious mixture of occultism with religious and political radicalism. At that time, there were two international conferences of mystics, occultists, and alchemists—one at Wilhelmsbad in 1782 and another at Paris in 1784.[51] One group that sent delegates to these conventions, the Avignon Society, was later to receive some publicity in London and in circles that Blake was associated with.[52] The Avignon Society was "only one of many shoots in the lush undergrowth of mystical Masonry in the eighteenth century," and it distinguished itself from Freemasonry and other reform movements by its "increasing tendency to seek true science and true reason in such unlikely places as alchemical lore, cabalistic numerology, mesmerist seances, Swedenborgian spiritualism, and (perhaps most surprising of all) the Scriptures."[53] The society believed in the revolutionary regeneration of the world and derived this belief from the "Holy Word," a system of cabbalistic numerology.[54] This group, whose members called themselves "men of desire" and with whom the followers of Swedenborg refused to be connected,[55] may have been included in Blake's conception of those who follow their desires, the Devils' party of *The Marriage of Heaven and Hell*. Blake, of course, did not have to know of the Avignon Society to be aware of the occult traditions.[56] But the existence of groups like this that espoused a revolutionary Christian mysticism shows that Blake's mingling of radical millenarian beliefs with esoteric systems was a reflection of a similar mingling

17

of different traditions that was taking place generally in his own time.

Less politically radical but equally influential on Blake and his contemporaries were the Wesleyans and the Evangelicals. In response to the aridity of eighteenth-century Anglicanism, whose emphasis upon a comfortable and rational Christianity threatened to make the eighteenth century one of the dreariest periods in the history of theology and the church, enthusiasts like Wesley, Whitefield, and Hannah More rekindled and expanded popular interest not only in religion itself but also in the Bible and its interpretation.[57] The Methodists and Evangelicals promoted an increase in literacy, and hence the reading of biblical material, through their establishment of Sunday schools and through their efforts to make printed matter available to a wider reading public. The Methodist Book Room and the availability of inexpensive books and tracts published by Hannah More, James Lackington, John Wesley, and others helped to make a growing reading public increasingly conversant with biblical matters.[58] Wesley's popularizations of religious works, for instance, included an abridgement of Mosheim's *Ecclesiastical History* and *The Apostolical Fathers*; and Joseph Milner, a member of the Evangelical clergy and opponent of Methodism, published a *History of the Church of Christ*, which contained lengthy treatments of the church fathers.[59]

An interest in the Bible and biblical tradition was also promoted by the Methodists' practice of field preaching, which the Evangelicals also adopted.[60] Whitefield's and Wesley's sermons were seasoned with biblical quotations and biblical and classical scholarship.[61] In opposition to the Anglican "Rabbis," who taught only dry morality and who wrangled over the evidences of the inspiration of the Bible, and against the skepticism of the deists, the religious enthusiasts reclaimed the Bible as the center of Christian life and preached the literal acceptance of Scripture as the living Word of God.[62] Such literalism did not preclude imaginative application of Scripture, which was Whitefield's forte, nor did it exclude exegetical tradition, which Wesley was steeped in.[63]

Blake, of course, acknowledged the contribution of these two men to the promotion of faith and the inspiration of the Bible when he designated them as the two witnesses of Revelation 11 (*Milton*, 22:55-62; 23:1-2). Even though Blake would have had reservations about Whitefield's Calvinism and Wesley's emphasis upon morality—and he certainly would have been aware that Hannah More's tracts were intended to stifle the spirit of revolution—he sided with the enthusiasts against the rationalism of the deists and the established church.[64] Blake also would have been sympathetic to the typological reading of the Bible that the Methodists and Evangelicals promoted.[65]

One of the appeals that the Methodists and the Evangelicals had for both Blake and his contemporaries lay in their contribution to the revival of sacred poetry in the second half of the eighteenth century. The hymns of John and Charles Wesley, as well as the Olney hymns of Cowper and John Newton, were significant not only for their promotion of religious faith and reforms in the liturgy but also for their contribution to the revival of an interest in biblical poetry.[66] Lyrics, dramas, biblical paraphrases, oratorios, eschatological verse, and epics produced during the eighteenth century freely or closely adopted biblical themes, stories, and style.[67] The success of the Ossianic poems, for instance, was due in part to Macpherson's borrowings from the Bible.[68] But more frequently the eighteenth-century reader would encounter literature that was more explicitly derived from the Bible, such as Young's *Poem on the Last Day* (1713), the ninth night of his *Night-Thoughts* (1742-1746), Aaron Hill's *The Creation* (1720), Richard Cumberland's *Calvary; or The Death of Christ* (1792), Klopstock's *Messias* (1748-1773), Gessner's *Der Tod Abels* (1758), and Bodmer's *Noah* (1750).[69] For most of these writers the influence of Milton was as strong as that of the Bible and as is

19

later indicated in Byron's preface to *Cain* (1821), Milton's poetry became so engrafted to the biblical tradition that the distinction between the two traditions is often difficult to maintain.[70]

Both in Milton and in eighteenth-century biblical poetry there is a mingling of biblical and classical influences, with the biblical emphasis predominating. This syncretism, which had become such an important part of poetic tradition since the Renaissance, was also part of biblical tradition, going back to the church fathers and even the Bible itself.[71] As Milton pointed out in *Areopagitica*, Paul quotes passages from the Greek poets, and Eusebius' *Preparatio Evangelica* prepares his hearers for the gospel by presenting "a hoard of heathenish obscenities."[72] Eusebius, in the tenth chapter of that book, discussed Greek borrowings from the Bible, whereas many of the other church fathers found Christian types in pagan history and religion.[73] In the seventeenth century, there was a proliferation of books that drew parallels between the Bible and pagan myth, and the Bible itself was annotated with comments drawn from the pagan classics.[74] As Don Cameron Allen points out, "the search for biblical faces in the gallery of pagan gods and heroes was one of the numerous Christian obsessions of the Renaissance, an obsession that does not fade out even when the sun of the Enlightenment rises."[75] In the eighteenth century, pagan parallels with Scripture were amassed in Wettstein's enormously influential edition of the New Testament, were assiduously collected in Calmet's encyclopedic commentary, and were popularized by Voltaire, who not only borrowed extensively from Calmet but also with equal zeal delved into arcane studies to find pagan analogues to the Bible for the purpose of discrediting that book.[76] Between 1789 and 1795, Gilbert Wakefield published *Silva Critica*, an attempt to unify theological and classical learning by illustrating the Bible "by light borrowed from the philology of Greece and Rome, as a probable method of recommending the books of revelation to scholars."[77] Michaelis' ideas about borrowings of pagan myth in the Bible are summarized in a discursive note to Lowth's *Lectures on the Sacred Poetry of the Hebrews*.[78]

While the orthodox continued to cite pagan analogues of biblical stories and characters to prove the sanctity of the Bible, and while deists and freethinkers drew up the same parallels to promote the opposite conclusion, the growth of oriental studies and a taste for the primitive changed the terms of the argument. The Bible, when compared with the literature and beliefs of the pagans, was vindicated on the basis of aesthetics, philology, psychology, and history, rather than primarily upon the grounds of natural laws or natural analogy.[79] A growing appreciation of cultural relativism and a deeper understanding of the historical significance of myth, as well as an enchantment with things primitive, served to override the deists' protests against the irrationality and barbarism of the Bible and began to remove the ambivalence and defensiveness of the faithful, which was caused by their own narrow rationalism and their adherence to neoclassical canons of taste. Those whose taste for the classics conflicted with their literary appreciation of the Scriptures searched the Bible for passages that did conform, or seemed to conform, to neoclassical norms; or they justified biblical poetics by invoking the aesthetic equivalent of the doctrine of accommodation, maintaining that the writers of the Bible, given the rude times in which they were living, succeeded in achieving the same literary ends as the more sophisticated Greeks and Romans.[80] With increasing frequency toward the end of the century, however, biblical poets, prophets, and apostles came to be admired as oriental bards, whose spontaneity and sublimity linked them with Homer and the Celtic bards, and who were worthy of emulation by modern poets; the inspiration of the Bible was maintained by means of a new awareness of the cultural and psychological importance of biblical and pagan myth. Some of the contributors to this transformation were Sir William Jones, Thomas Blackwell, Robert Lowth, John Dennis,

21

Hugh Blair, John Husbands, Eichhorn, Herder, Michaelis, Coleridge, and Gabler.[81]

Coleridge, Eichhorn, and Herder were responsible for the more sophisticated understanding of myth that emerged at the end of the nineteenth century, but their newly developed syncretism evolved from the more primitive attempts to arrive at a science of mythology that were made by the eighteenth-century speculative mythologists.[82] Among these writers were William Warburton, Andrew Ramsay, Samuel Shuckford, Jacob Bryant, William Owen Pughe, Edward Davies, William Stukeley, Jean Sylvain Bailly, Charles Dupuis, and Francis Wilford.[83] Although most of the mythologists were not directly concerned with the Bible or its traditions, they borrowed from and contributed to biblical tradition in several important ways. Whether defending, attacking, or ignoring biblical revelation, they all drew comparisons between biblical and pagan characters, beliefs, stories, and customs. Many of these parallels were drawn from the church fathers and modern Christian apologists, and some of the eighteenth-century writers—such as Warburton, Bryant, Ramsay, and Shuckford—were actually extending this apologetic tradition. In fact, in the course of the eighteenth century, discussion of pagan myth only gradually became separated from its original theological and polemical context. Furthermore, the method of some of the mythologists was really an extension or application of traditional biblical typology to pagan myth, as is the case with Ramsay's structural approach to comparative religion and Stukeley's researches into Druidism to give empirical validation to traditional Anglo-Israelite typology.[84]

The works of many of the mythologists were well known in their time, going through several editions and being popularized in other publications.[85] Blake himself has explicitly mentioned his familiarity with the mythographers, and modern scholars have detailed some of Blake's borrowings from Bryant, Stukeley, Dupuis, and others.[86] These scholars have emphasized the influence of the mythologists upon Blake's major prophecies, particularly the influence of the studies in northern mythology and Druidism upon Blake's concepts of Druidism and the figure of Albion. Blake's earlier prophecies, however, also bear the stamp of the mythologists, not only in Blake's echoing of their syncretism but also in his use of recondite source material that the mythologists made more accessible to poets and readers. Bryant quotes the Babylonian cosmogony as outlined by Berosus, for instance, which Bryant claims influenced Milton's depiction of chaos in *Paradise Lost* and which Blake borrowed from in his depiction of the Creation in *The Book of Los*.[87] Blake's borrowings from such ancient mythologies were recognized by at least two of his early readers, Crabb Robinson and J.J.G. Wilkinson, the latter objecting to Blake's masking of "Truth under the loose garments of Typical, or even Mythological Representation" that was derived from "the ruins of Ancient and Consummated Churches."[88]

Thus biblical tradition in the eighteenth century consisted of a variety of strands that provided sources of or contexts for Blake's ideas and artistic practice. As we would expect, Blake was frequently attracted to the more imaginative and radical elements of that tradition, but he also adopted, modified and transformed the ideas of more orthodox and conventional schools of thought. Inheriting the influence of a number of exegetical schools, Blake never completely adhered to any of them. He could read the Bible literally or allegorically, depending on his particular purpose. He could maintain, for instance, as the deists did, that the Old Testament is a literal history of Israel's barbarisms (*Annotations to Watson*, p. 604), yet he could also defend an objectionable biblical passage by reading it allegorically.[89] He could employ a traditional typological reading of the Bible but then change the traditional significance of a particular type or else radically extend the tradition by creating his own types. He absorbed earlier and more recent critical ideas about biblical imagery, form, and structure;

23

but he went beyond the neoclassical restraints of even the most ardent apologists for biblical poetry by actually employing biblical poetics more literally and systematically than any of his contemporaries. Like Milton, Blake drew upon biblical tradition to assert in theory and practice the superiority of an aesthetic based upon the Bible, but then —true to the essentially revolutionary aesthetic that he and Milton shared—he transformed the traditions he inherited, including the Milton tradition.[90] Though the Bible was, for Blake, the great code of art, regardless of the sense in which we take the word "code," it was through biblical tradition that Blake deciphered that code, interpreted it, put it into execution, and made it flexible enough to meet the needs of his individual talent.

Prophetic Form:
The "Still Better Order"

If, as Blake insists, the Bible is the great code of art, then we must turn to the Bible for the concept and rationale of biblical form that underlies his prophetic books. But first we must look at Blake's ideas about form, as articulated in his prose writings. In a late illuminated work, "On Homer's Poetry," Blake protests against the concept of an externally imposed unity in a work of art:

> Every Poem must necessarily be a perfect Unity, but why Homers is peculiarly so, I cannot tell: he has told the story of Bellerophon & omitted the Judgment of Paris which is not only a part, but a principal part of Homers subject
>
> But when a Work has Unity it is as much in a Part as in the Whole. the Torso is so much a Unity as the Laocoon.   (p. 267)

In "On Virgil," which is etched on the same plate as Blake's comments on Homer, the form produced by the Aristotelian concept of unity is called "Mathematic Form," as opposed to Gothic, which is "Living Form." Blake's preference for organic form is reiterated, this time with reference to pictorial composition, in his *A Vision of the Last Judgment*, where he says that "All Art is founded" not upon the "General Masses" of a composition, but upon the minute discrimination of the manners, intentions, and characters of individual parts (p. 550). The subordination of the general to the particular, with a reliance upon internal coherence among the parts rather than upon an externally imposed order, was precisely the principle that Blake, like many of his contemporaries, found to be operating in the Bible.[1] In biblical poetry, as Murray Roston has pointed out, form is subordinated to significance, with the basic unit of Hebrew verse being the self-contained distich of parallel lines that embody a concrete and "vividly concise picture," thus leading to particularization and creating form by simple juxtaposition.[2] In the prophetic books of the Bible, the same principle works on a larger scale; particular units are combined to form whole books that are connected through the internal coherence of their parts.

In fact, this principle of internal coherence that informs the prophetic books of the Old Testament, as opposed to the principles of unity, chronology, and symmetry, eluded many of the classically trained eighteenth-century literary critics and biblical exegetes. Even Bishop Lowth, who was the unquestioned authority on biblical poetics and who had produced a highly acclaimed translation of Isaiah, failed to find such a principle operating in the prophetic books of the Old Testament. Lowth, of course, was the discoverer of the principle of parallelism in Hebrew poetry, and thus he established the fact that prophetic poetry consisted of the accumulation of individual distichs.[3] He restricted his definition of prophetic poetry to those verse passages that predict future rewards or punishments.[4] Such poetry, Lowth maintains, does not often display any regularity of form: "In respect to the order, disposition, and symmetry of a perfect poem of the prophetic kind, I do not know of any certain definition which will admit of general application. Naturally free, and of too ardent a spirit to be confined by rule, it is usually guided by the nature of the subject only, and the impulse of divine inspiration."[5] Some of the prophetic poems do display regularity of form, however, and it is only from these that Lowth selects examples, in deference to the neoclassical prejudices of his audience, to show that in the prophetic books of the Bible there are many instances of poems "which may with propriety be classed the most perfect and regular specimens of poetry."[6] Thus

Lowth, acceding to the age's preference for external form,[7] hints at but does not pursue a principle of internal form.

When Lowth looks at the total form of the prophetic books, he again shows his limitations. He observes that the writings of the prophets often contain genres other than prophetic poetry: historical narratives, prose orations, sacred odes, and elegies.[8] But he does not attempt to explain how all of these various forms cohere within a given prophetic book, nor can he find coherence among seemingly disconnected prophecies that are juxtaposed in the writings of the prophets. While in such short works as Joel and Nahum he perceives perspicuity in arrangement, the latter prophecy being "a regular and perfect poem,"[9] the Book of Isaiah, which Lowth considers the greatest of the prophecies, presents some difficulties when he approaches the issue of form:

> Isaiah greatly excells, too, in all the graces of method, order, connexion, and arrangement; though in asserting this we must not forget the nature of the prophetic impulse, which bears away the mind with irresistible violence, and frequently in rapid transitions from near to remote objects, from human to divine: we must also be careful in remarking the limits of particular predictions, since, as they are now extant, they are often improperly connected, without any marks of discrimination; which injudicious arrangement, on some occasions, creates almost insuperable difficulties.[10]

When faced with these difficulties, Lowth falls back upon the opinion of previous commentators, resolving that any incoherence in the writings of the prophets must be attributed to either the irrational nature of the divine afflatus that completely overwhelms the prophet or to the possibility that the prophetic book in question was a collection of individual prophecies that were imperfectly collected by redactors.[11]

One of the chief proponents of the former explanation

27

was Pierre Daniel Huet, and Jean Le Clerc was one who offered the latter explanation. Each advanced his position in order to show "the very excellent disorder in [the Old Testament prophecies] and the absence of all suspicion of human art and reason,"[12] and thus to defend the inspiration of those biblical writings, which was a crucial issue in the eighteenth century. Such explanations, however, provided the very grounds upon which freethinkers could argue against the inspiration of the Bible. Thus the assumption of disorder in the writings of the Old Testament prophets placed the eighteenth-century Christian who, like Blake, desired to defend the Bible unperverted (*Annotations to Watson*, p. 601), in a strait between the rather weak defense of inspiration made by the commentators and the cavils of the deists and freethinkers.

Since Lowth had begun to argue for the presence of art or design in the writings of the Old Testament prophets, he should have gone forward to vindicate the inspiration of the biblical prophets on the basis of their aesthetic integrity and coherence. This, at least, was implied by Thomas Howes, who in "Doubts Concerning the Translation and Notes of the Bishop of London to Isaiah, vindicating Ezekiel, Isaiah, and other Jewish Prophets from Disorder in Arrangement" (1783), castigates Lowth for falling back upon received assumptions and claims to extend the work begun by Lowth. Howes, it should be noted, announced that he was not concerned with proving the inspiration of the Hebrew prophecies; his main purpose was to establish the authenticity and the aesthetic integrity of those works. If, as the deists claimed, some of the prophecies were written after their accomplishment rather than before, Howes is not disturbed. He is content to prove that at least those prophecies were composed shortly after their fulfillment had taken place, while those events were fresh in the writer's memory and were uncorrupted by tradition. By establishing the authenticity of scriptural facts and dates, and thus getting freethinkers to acknowledge the authenticity and antiquity of the contents of the prophetic writings, Howes leaves the freethinkers' "denial of the reality of the prophecies" with "no other effect than to substitute good human testimony for the events in question instead of that which is divine" (p. 116).

While Howes thus claims that his arguments provide reasonings that will be available to all, leaving readers to draw whatever inferences that they can, "consistently with a good conscience at the bar of Reason and Judgment" (p. 117), he reveals throughout his arguments a concern for freeing believing Christians from the spurious arguments of previous biblical commentators, for removing from the prophetic books the attribution of "a disorder [that] seemed to many to render the arrangement unworthy of being ascribed to divine agency," and for making the arguments for the inspiration of the prophets plausible again (p. 211).[13] By asserting that "the best human works approach the nearest to divine" and by showing that the art of the Old Testament prophets is compatible with divine inspiration (p. 269), Howes brings biblical criticism in line with contemporary literary theories of inspiration, natural genius, and poetic grace—thus making the Bible the *locus classicus* of the issue of inspiration vs. mechanical composition, artlessness vs. art.[14] Going beyond Lowth, Howes reconciles these conflicting theories of composition and satisfies the need to believe that inspiration is not inconsistent with art and intelligible form.

Although Howes focuses on Lowth's notes and introduction to his translation of Isaiah, he sees Lowth's error as symptomatic of a larger problem that had existed in biblical tradition from the time of St. Jerome until the eighteenth century—the assumption that the writings of the Hebrew prophets were in a state of disorder, that they were "an irregular jumble of history, poetry and prophecy, as has disgusted some candid christians, and distressed all" (p. 227). The disorder of the prophetic books was so universally assumed that commentators did not attempt to prove it, much less investigate the truth of it, not even Huet, who was "in all other respects a strenuous advocate for the authenticity of the scriptures" (p. 136). He and Le Clerc had provided half an answer to the charge of disorder by maintaining that *"Spiritus propheticus non est spiritus chronologicus"* (p. 137), but neither commentator attempted to ascertain what order was used instead, implying that the prophets used no order at all and that the prophetic writings suffer the fault of not being arranged in the order in which they were communicated. Looking back to biblical tradition for an explanation of a possible alternative method of arrangement, Howes concludes,

> Now, excepting Jerome, not one of the interpreters, down to the translator [Lowth], seem to have had the least idea of the possibility of any better and more reasonable order of arrangement, than that of the *chronologic* order in which the prophecies were *delivered*; but this is by no means true, for there are at least two other kinds of order, and both preferable, viz. that of *historic order* in which the prophecies were accomplished, and also that *oratorical order* which might be thought best suited to the purpose of *persuasion and argumentation*.   (pp. 138-39)

Here Howes extends Jerome's suggestion that there might be a more useful order than chronological order and goes on to maintain that whenever a prophet departs from chronological order of delivery, he does so to "substitute a better order of arrangement, namely, either the order of *historic accomplishment,* or the still better order of oratorical and persuasive *argumentation"* (p. 139).

This "still better order" Howes also calls "poetic arrangement" (p. 293),[15] since he claims to be extending the analysis of biblical poetics begun by Lowth:

> For it has been long conceived, that these prophecies are replete with bold poetic ideas and expressions; the translator [Lowth], with his usual learning and accuracy, has

convinced the public, that they are even composed in a
similar metre to the other antient poetic works of the
Jews: I have only ventured, in pursuance of his example,
to advance one step farther in novelty, by shewing, that
there are equally good reasons to conceive these proph-
ecies to be put together in a connected method and order,
agreeably to such modes of poetic and oratorical arrange-
ment, as were customary in the most antient ages, and this
apparently by the respective authors of each prophetic
work.   (pp. 442-43)

Howes claims that this poetic or oratorical order is better
than the historical order of accomplishment for a number
of reasons. First of all, his arguments for the historical order
are based upon facts of biblical chronology that he has yet
to prove, and he himself admits that we cannot always be
certain of some of these facts (pp. 332-33). Second, when-
ever the prophet claims that a prophecy has been fulfilled
by a specific event, he becomes a fallible interpreter of pre-
vious prophecies rather than the communicator of inspired
truths (pp. 146-47). Finally, the whole purpose of the his-
torical order, in which a prophet cites the fulfillment of an
earlier prophecy made by a previous prophet or by himself,
is to establish the credibility of any predictions that the
prophet may make about the future (pp. 178-79); and
Howes seems to be anxious to deemphasize the predictive
nature of prophecy in order to establish its credibility on
the basis of its rhetorical or visionary function.

The rhetorical function of prophecy as Howes conceives
it is derived from his concept of the character of the
prophet:

Upon the whole then we find, that the Jewish prophets
were members, if I may be allowed the expression, of the
opposition, which subsisted in those days, and they fig-
ured among the leading patriots of their country; who
took very free, yet necessary liberties in criticising and

31

condemning the measures of their kings, nobles, priests and people, both in their private and public capacities; and how unwelcome soever any facts they might foretell, yet they employed sufficient *indicia divinae potentiae* to convince all parties who did not obstinately resist conviction, that the events they foretold would certainly arrive: these temporary and occasional harangues delivered at different times, yet all tending to the same purport, as "Did I not tell you this before? and did I not tell you true?" were afterwards combined by their respective authors into one continued metrical oration of admonition; and entered as *protests*, to be preserved for the instruction of succeeding ages, concerning the obstinacy of kings and the infatuation of the people, notwithstanding the signs of the times.   (pp. 214-15)

These prophets were skilled poets, and the writings of a prophet such as Isaiah, contrary to the claims of Vitringa and Lowth (who adopts Vitringa's position), constitute a carefully organized and original vision, as the title announced in Isaiah 1:1 indicates. As Howes says, it was Isaiah himself, not a redactor, who "so arranged and connected the several prophecies together, that they formed but one whole work of religious and patriotic exhortation, though consisting of various coherent parts; just as Homer and Virgil forged each but one Epic Poem out of various connected episodes" (p. 132).

In order to advance their arguments concerning political and religious policy, the prophets eschewed the "beaten track and vulgar round" of chronological order (p. 140) and adopted either the historian's privilege of placing events immediately after those earlier events and attitudes that caused them, or the poet or orator's method of interrupting the chronological or historical order of events to juxtapose two or more distant events that support a general assertion or theme (p. 149). This oratorical order could also include the citation of the fulfillment of a previous

32

prophecy by an earlier prophet or by the prophet himself in order to establish the veracity of a new prophecy that he was about to make; the juxtaposition of events that show the opposite fates accompanying belief or disbelief, obedience or disobedience; or the gathering of prophecies "concerning similar subjects, or concerning neighboring nations, or similar nations, such as Heathens in distinction from Jews, or concerning similar ranks of persons in the same nation: accordingly they will be found sometimes actually thus to arrange together their prophetic exhortations to the Jewish kings; and in like manner those relative to the priests and prophets, and also those relative to the people at large" (p. 150). These and other methods were employed by the prophets "in order to connect together their several *argumentations*, to avoid confusion, and to render their transition from one subject to another more natural and obvious" (pp. 150-51).

The writings of the prophets, then, are always coherent, using at alternate times either the chronological, historical, or oratorical method of arrangement to create "one continued exhortatory oration or prophetic poem out of the several parts" (p. 152). Moreover, since these prophetic writings are poetic, as has long been allowed by all, there is no reason for readers to be perplexed by the abrupt and bold transitions, which we also find in the lyric poetry of the classical age. Although the Greeks and Romans exhibit greater art and skill in oratory, the writings of the prophets are "venerable specimens of the rude efforts of reason as well as genius in those early ages of composition" (p. 263), exhibiting a degree of perfection that was suitable to the character of the speaker and the audience of those rude times (p. 212). Furthermore, older than the classics, the prophetic books of the Bible contain rhetorical modes that were later adopted by Athens and Rome. According to Howes, the writings of the prophets contain a fusion of genres that were later separated and perfected by the Greeks:

33

The union then in these prophetic works of admonitions and exhortations, concerning moral, religious, civil and historic subjects, all delivered in poetic diction, and in a regular and harmonious arrangement of the words . . . but which the more subtilizing Greeks, in later ages, separated into different species of composition, and adapted to each of them a different, and some peculiar mode of structure proper to it; according as it was of a poetic, or of an oratorical or historic kind; this aboriginal union, I say, here of what was not separated until later ages . . . exhibit no other marks of disorder, than what became at the same time marks of the originality, authenticity, and antiquity of these works in their present form and state.
(pp. 446-47)

The prophets' preference for a nonchronological, episodic order thus anticipates the appearance of the same preference in classical poetry, history, and oratory. A case in point is the prophets' practice of introducing digressions that recapitulate past events:

For not only digressive recapitulations of various occurrences extraneous to the principle subject of history, tho' connected with it, have been admitted by almost all historians, and approved by critics, either for the sake of a convenient mode of information or ornament; but the very essence of that historical arrangement adopted by some, and by Herodotus at least, may be properly said to consist in a series of connected recapitulations of the whole history of different nations. (pp. 297-98)

Horace condemns chronological order as being "but a dull, vulgar and beaten round of order" and commends the use of digression "as a testimony of judgment" (p. 298). Homer "rather recommended than invented such narrative episodes in epic poetry" (p. 299). Howes maintains that the presence of this digressive method, along with poetic diction, in the writings of the early classical orators, was not, as Aristotle believed, an innovation based upon a desire to imitate poetry. Rather, the presence of these qualities in oration, as in history, was a relic from the time when history and oratory were inseparable from poetry (pp. 444-45).

Howes is obviously arguing a position that is antithetical to primitivism, since he is citing the works of more advanced art to remove from the Bible any imputation of artlessness. Yet his citation of prophecy as an Ur-form from which later genres evolved could, for readers who would see Howes' "subtilizing Greeks" in a way that Howes did not intend, be construed as an argument for the superiority of prophetic form. Howes' arguments, then, unintentionally contribute a great deal of precision and methodical thoroughness to the critical discussion of the Bible as primitivist literature, for his work extends Lowth's assertion that the writings of the Hebrew poets were "the only specimens of the primeval and genuine poetry."[16]

Such a primitivist interpretation would be the case for a poet like Blake, who preferred "those Grand Works of the more ancient & consciously & professedly Inspired Men" to the works of "The Stolen and Perverted Writings of Homer & Ovid: of Plato & Cicero" (*Milton*, pl. 1). Howes' insistence upon the radical nature and function of prophecy would also appeal to a poet who identified himself with the Old Testament prophets as a member of "the opposition." Blake would find a principle of form existing in the Bible that was based not on external rules, but on a principle of inner coherence that served the poet-prophet's need to protest against the moral, religious, and political abuses of his time. All genres would provide ammunition for this end, allowing the poet to move freely from one to another according to his particular rhetorical purpose. Taking individual units of history, poetry, or oratory as his working blocks, he was not bound by a chronological or historical order, nor was he obligated to provide transitions between individual units. Meaning and coherence were created through the thematic juxtaposition of individual parts. The poet could juxtapose parts that illustrate the same point or that are addressed to the same people or group of people, or juxtapose parts that show antithetical ideas or points of view, or juxtapose parts that move from general statements to particular applications and vice versa. This inspired and harmoniously ordered rhetoric would go beyond argument to lead the reader to vision, removing the "heavy load of mortality" from the reader who perceives the order and coherence of that rhetoric (p. 265).

There is no direct evidence that Blake read Howes' treatise, which was published in Howes' *Critical Observations on Books, Antient and Modern* (1776-1813), but it is highly probable that Blake heard of Howes' ideas. Joseph Johnson, for whom Blake had been engraving since 1780 and with whose circle Blake was familiar, published in 1785 William Newcome's translation of Ezekiel, which stated Howes' thesis in the preface and excerpted portions of Howes' treatise in the notes.[17] Howes' *Critical Observations* would also be known to Johnson's circle, of which Priestley was a part, since they contained an attack upon Priestley.[18] But even if Blake had no knowledge of Howes, direct or indirect, he would have been aware of many of the principles of prophetic form that were delineated by Howes, for although Howes, as he himself claims, was the only writer to carefully explain the principles of unity underlying the Old Testament prophecies, similar ideas about the structure of prophecy were available in contemporary works on rhetoric and literary criticism, commentaries on the Old Testament prophets, and, most importantly, commentaries on the Book of Revelation, which was universally acknowledged to be the summation and the most perfect embodiment of all biblical prophecy.[19]

Howes was not the only writer to deemphasize the predictive nature of prophecy and insist upon its rhetorical function. Charles Daubuz, in his commentary upon Revelation, maintained that prophecies are written "not to satisfy men's curiosity, but to serve as good Argument," to increase the faith, hope, and patience of Christians; prediction is secondary and serves only to further this end.[20] John Gill observed that the commission of the Old Testament prophets "lay very much in shewing the people, to whom they were sent, their sins and transgressions; to convince them of them; to reprove them for them; to call them to repentence and reformation; or otherwise tell them they would issue in their ruin."[21] Similarly, Fénelon, in his well-known and highly influential *Dialogues on Eloquence in General*, describes the biblical prophets as orators who use bold figures and actions to rouse the audience's passions and direct them toward truth and right action.[22] Fénelon's "true orator," who must necessarily be a poet in order to "imprint things on the hearer's mind" and thus raise his audience to a perception of the truth through the imagination, is echoed by Howes' interchangeable use of the words poetry and oratory.[23] This concept of the prophet as poet and orator is part of the Augustinian tradition, of which Fénelon is the eighteenth-century embodiment, and which finds its expression in the concept of the orator in Milton's prose works.[24] Blake's explicit acknowledgment of this aspect of the prophetic tradition is revealed in *Jerusalem*, where in the introductory "To the Public," prophet, poet, and orator are one.[25]

This emphasis upon the prophet's role as orator led other critics and commentators besides Howes to note and explain the basic fact of prophetic structure, which had been originally pointed out by Jerome—that prophecy did not employ chronological order. As Howes himself was probably aware, Vitringa, in his frequently reprinted rules for interpreting prophecy, stated that the biblical prophets broke chronological order to serve specific oratorical ends:

Yet it is to be observed, that some prophecies, whose context is continued, admit of resumptions, repetitions of sayings, and retrograde leaps and skips, or scattered or detached pieces, belonging to superior times, which are inserted into the context, for the sake of illustrating this

37

or that part of the prophecy; examples of which are in Zech. xiii.7 and in Isa. ch. xl. xli. xlii. . . . To these may also be rightly referred the excursions and digressions, in which the prophets, whilst they really have before their eyes some object of more remote time, suddenly leave it, and by way of excursion turn themselves to men of their own time, or the next; that, from the subject of their prophecy, they may admonish, exhort and convince them; which when they have done, they resume the thread of their prophecy. . . . That interpretation of the word of God, especially of the prophecies, is to be accounted the best, which attends to, pursues, and demonstrates the greatest emphasis of the oration or speech, and the wisdom of the Holy Ghost.[26]

This concept of thematic rather than chronological order in the prophetic books of the Bible is further developed in Samuel White's commentary on Isaiah, in which his outline of the structure of that book shows Isaiah's departures from chronological order to serve particular argumentative ends.[27]

But more frequently than the commentaries on the Old Testament prophecies, the commentaries on Revelation dwelt upon the rhetorical function of nonchronological order. Joseph Mede, whose *Key of the Revelation* (1627) was constantly alluded to, summarized, and quoted in eighteenth-century commentaries, was the first to point out that Revelation abandons chronological order in favor of synchronic order that permits the prophet to expand upon and clarify particular issues.[28] Charles Daubuz, like Howes, finds this method analogous to that of the best historians, "who endeavor to give a full Account of every Matter as they take it in hand, to make a compleat system of the whole, interposing Digressions; and then returning to the principal Matters, by giving such Hints and Transitions as suffice to let us understand to what they belong, and how, as to Point of Time, they come in or end with the rest."[29] Johannes

Albrecht Bengel, whose commentary on Revelation in his famous *Gnomon of the New Testament* (1734) was reprinted in abridged form in John Wesley's *Explanatory Notes Upon the New Testament*, observes:

> Indeed the whole structure of it breathes the art of God, comprizing in the most finished compendium, things to come, many, various; near, intermediate, remote; the greatest, the least; terrible, comfortable; old, new; long, short; and these interwoven together, opposite, composite; relative to each other at a small, at a great distance; and therefore sometimes as it were disappearing, broken off, suspended, and afterwards unexpectedly and most seasonably appearing again. In all its parts it has an admirable variety, with the most exact harmony, beautifully illustrated by those digressions which seem to interrupt it. In this manner does it display the manifold wisdom of God shining in the economy of the church through so many ages.[30]

This concept of prophecy as a rhetorical structure that attempted to represent the wisdom of God by means of a nonlinear, nonrational, or suprarational structure was echoed by Augustan literary theorists who, frequently using Scripture as their model, anticipated Blake's announced preference for Gothic or living form over mathematical form. Seeking freedom from the Aristotelian unity of action, they justified originality of form within poetic tradition by drawing analogies with scriptural writers, whose creative freedom was analogous to the creative freedom of a benevolent deity:

> The handiwork of God was the varied and unsymmetrical model for the poet; moreover, the "beauties of spring" made a "more delightful prospect" than arranged flowers to the beholder, and the freedom of connections and transitions in the poem was analogous to the freedom, the ungeometrical "system" of the universe. "Poeti-

cal Reason," wrote Leonard Welsted (1713) "is not the same as mathematical Reason." The poet was, therefore, in this respect, a creator like God, blending apparent disorder into a new kind of order.[31]

This theory echoes Milton's claim that the orator-poet fulfills his role by "making a creation like to God's," a creation in which harmony is formed out of disharmony.[32]

This godlike creation of unity in diversity was also embodied in the prophet's combining many genres into one work. Howes, of course, was not pointing to this conclusion when he claimed that Old Testament prophecy contained all genres. But his claim, intended for an audience whose taste was essentially neoclassical, was a sophisticated reworking of the traditional belief that the Bible's divine origin was also manifested in the fact that it contained all wisdom. This belief, which was begun "as a defense against the superiority of pagan Greek learning in the Hellenistic world, . . . became, by the time of Isidore of Seville's *Etymologiae*, an imperious claim for Israel's primacy in philosophy, science and poetry, maintained, like the claim for literal historical primacy, well into the eighteenth century."[33] St. Jerome had said that the book of Isaiah contained all rhetoric, ethics, and theology.[34] In the seventeenth century, Tommaso Campanella gave voice to the idea, already current at that time, that "the Jews, or more precisely King David, had invented every possible literary form, and that the pagan poets discovered nothing new."[35]

In the eighteenth century, however, such claims, when applied to the Old Testament prophets, tended to be more moderate. Robert Lowth, in his *Lectures on the Sacred Poetry of the Hebrews*, maintained that the writings of the Hebrew prophets contained not only what he designated prophetic poetry but also historical narrative and "complete poems of different kinds, Odes as well as Elegies."[36] Eichhorn observed a diversity of forms in Ezekiel: fables, narratives, allegories, parables, visions.[37] It is only in the commentaries on the Book of Revelation that we find the same claim that Howes makes—that prophecy is a fusion of all genres.[38]

Within the multiform and nonlinear structure of prophecy, the poet-orator was free to provide multiple perspectives on the same theme or the same event. Eichhorn observed this quality in Ezekiel, opening with a statement that is strikingly similar to Blake's concern with the "minute particulars" of form: "A generally acknowledged character of Ezekiel is, that he minutely distinguishes every thing in its smallest parts. What the more ancient prophets brought together under one single picture, and to which they only hinted, and what they explained with the utmost brevity or shewed only from one side, that he explains and unfolds formally, and represents from all possible sides."[39] In Revelation, given its synchronic pattern that Mede discovered, this multiplicity of points of view is more apparent and was noted by such commentators as Henry Hammond, Philip Doddridge, Richard Hurd, Charles Daubuz, and David Pareus.[40]

Thus the principles of prophetic structure explained by Howes—the emphasis upon the rhetorical function of prophecy, the subordination of chronological order to thematic order, the juxtaposition of episodes without proper transitions, the use of digressions, the combining of various genres, and the use of multiple perspectives—were available in the scattered observations of seventeenth- and eighteenth-century critics and commentators, particularly those who dealt with Revelation. But there were other principles either hinted at or ignored by Howes that were educed by other writers, particularly ideas about the dramatic and visual nature of prophecy.

Almost all of the commentators on biblical poetry in general and prophetic poetry in particular remark upon the boldness of transitions in scriptural writing. Many commentators extend this observation to draw analogies between prophecy and drama. Samuel Horsley, in describing

Isaiah's visionary style, had recourse to a theatrical metaphor: "In prophecy, the curtain (if the expression may be allowed) is often suddenly dropped upon the action that is going on, before it is finished; and the subject is continued in a shifted scene, as it were, of vision. This I take to be a natural consequence of the manner in which futurity was represented, in emblematic pictures, to the imagination of the prophet."[41] This use of the theatrical metaphor and linking of it with the pictorial nature of prophecy are not an innovation on Horsley's part. Aquinas and Donne had called prophets *spectatores*, and within biblical tradition "theatrical metaphors were customarily associated with prophetic vision."[42] John Smith, the seventeenth-century Cambridge Platonist, whose treatise, "Of Prophecy" (1660), was often cited and even reprinted in the eighteenth century, described the prophet as a spectator at a drama. The prophet's imagination, for Smith, was a scene or stage where God's visions were revealed symbolically, "as in a masque," and the prophet's frequent shifting of speaking voice and abrupt transitions could be seen as "*exits* and *intrats* upon this prophetical stage being made as it were in an invisible manner."[43] Milton, in *The Reason of Church Government* and in the preface to *Samson Agonistes*, noted that the sixteenth-century biblical commentator David Pareus perceived in Revelation a dramatic structure, dividing the biblical book "as a Tragedy into Acts distinguished each by a chorus of Heavenly Harpings and Song between."[44] Similarly, Joseph Mede's *Key of the Revelation* describes prophecy as an "Apocalyptick Theatre," wherein various visions are presented.[45] Moreover, Mede, like Horsley, insists upon the pictorial nature of prophecy; but Mede goes on to assert that Revelation is literally a work of composite art, combining pictures and language, since "those visions concerning the Seales were not written by Characters in letters, but being painted by certain shapes, lay hid under some covers of the Seales;

42

which being opened, each of them in its order, appeared not to be read, but to be beheld and viewed."[46]

Although the multimedia form of Revelation, as Mede perceives it, is an obvious prototype of Blake's visionary forms dramatic, it must also be remembered that Revelation and the books of the Old Testament prophets contain emblematic actions performed by the prophets themselves, actions that communicate pictorially the prophet's divine message. In Revelation, St. John himself is a participant in his own vision, performing a significative action by eating the small book, (10:9-10). Blake explicitly states his awareness of this aspect of biblical prophecy when, in the second Memorable Fancy of *The Marriage of Heaven and Hell,* Ezekiel explains that the cause of his eating dung and lying alternately on his right and left sides was "the desire of raising other men to a perception of the infinite" (*MHH,* pl. 13). Fénelon, among others, understood such "figurative actions" to be the effect of divine inspiration.[47] The prophet thus makes his own body the form of his message. Blake's essentially figurative art, which illustrates his prophecies, using the human body to express spiritual states, can be seen as an extension into the plastic arts of the prophet's dramatic use of the human form to shape and reinforce his verbal message.

Blake's use of the principles of prophetic form, as they were understood by his contemporaries, is markedly present in his early prophecies. His episodic narration and his use of abrupt transitions and rapidly shifting scenes are immediately apparent in *America,* for instance, where the scenes constantly shift back, forth, above, and even below the Atlantic; where Orc's speech on plate 8 is followed without any preparation by the war song of Albion's Angel on plate 9, followed by an equally sudden shift to the hills of Atlantis on plate 10. In *Europe,* the song of the sons of Urizen is abruptly followed by Enitharmon's song, without any indication of a change in speaker (4:9-10). The most extreme example of this trait is to be found in *Africa,* where often each line marks a new location in time and space, as Blake traces the transmission of Urizen's law and religion:

> Adam shudderd! Noah faded! black grew the sunny African
> When Rintrah gave Abstract Philosophy to Brama in the East:
> (Night spoke to the Cloud!
> Lo these Human form'd spirits in smiling hipocrisy War
> Against one another; so let them War on; slaves to the eternal Elements)
> Noah shrunk, beneath the waters;
> Abram fled in fires from Chaldea;
> Moses beheld upon Mount Sinai forms of dark delusion.
> (Africa 3:10-17)

Blake also resembles the biblical prophets in his practice of disrupting the chronological sequence of events in his early prophecies. One important method of creating this disruption is, as several critics have pointed out, Blake's use of illustrations to arrest narrative movement. Karl Kroeber notes, for instance, that the illustrations to Urizen militate against any temporal order that may exist in the narrative because of the distinct integrity of each individual plate, which creates a tableau effect, and because many of the illustrations do not illustrate the text in any conventional sense and are not arranged sequentially.[48] Similarly, Jean Hagstrum points out that Blake's works are made up of tableaux in which "the proper movement is . . . both literally and metaphorically, from plate to plate. There is no onward rush of temporal movement."[49]

Hagstrum and W.J.T. Mitchell attribute this effect not only to Blake's use of illustrations but also to his poetic practice, since Blake's poetry, even without the illustrations, disrupts the reader's sense of chronological movement.[50] One verbal technique that Blake uses to achieve this effect is borrowed from Ezekiel and Revelation: the practice of first giving a vision in brief and then elaborating upon it in detail.[51] Thus the events depicted in the preludia to *America* and *Europe* and in Eno's prefatory song in *The Book of Los* are contracted versions of the same events that the ensuing prophecies elaborate upon. In *Europe* there are not one but two treatments of the same events that are simultaneous with the action of the Preludium.[52] And Urizen's speech in Chapter II of *The Book of Urizen* narrates events that are simultaneous with the events of Chapter I. Furthermore, as Mitchell maintains, the first eight chapters of *The Book of Urizen* are really "alternative performances of the same event."[53] This principle of simultaneity, as we have seen, is most apparent in the book of Revelation and was publicized by Mede and the numerous commentators who followed him.

Besides simultaneity, Blake, like the biblical prophets, also uses digressions to disrupt chronological sequence. In *America* Blake temporarily halts the escalating conflict between England and America with a brief description of the history of Atlantis (10:5-10), and in *Europe* a longer digression describes the building of Verulam (10:1-23). In *Africa*, after summarizing the transmission of law and religion in ancient times and before continuing his chronicle into the eighteenth century, Blake offers a flashback that tells the story of Har and Heva's reaction to the effects of that transmission (4:5-12). In *The Book of Ahania* Blake uses digression more fully than in any of the other early prophetic works, with each chapter interrupting the narrative with a digression. Each of the first four chapters stops the action to elaborate upon the creation of a particular element that plays an important part in the narrative present. Chapter I describes the creation of the disk of Urizen (2:23-25), Chapter II the creation of the serpent from whose ribs Urizen makes his bow (3:4-16), Chapter III the creation of the Tree of Mystery (3:55-63), Chapter IV the birth of the arrows of pestilence that torment the crucified Fuzon (4:11-35). In the fifth chapter, Ahania not only describes her

45

present misery and her wanderings, which are simultaneous with the action of Chapters II to IV, but also moves backward in time to describe a condition that predates the action of the poem, Urizen's unfallen state (5:7-38). Besides these flashbacks, *Ahania* also contains a digression that moves forward in time, describing an event that takes place in *The Book of Los*, as Blake mentions that Fuzon's fallen beam will be a pillar of fire to Egypt for five hundred years and then be pounded by Los into the body of the sun (2:44-48).

Blake also follows the prophets in offering within a single work multiple perspectives on a given event or issue. In *America*, for instance, he offers several interpretations of the coming of Orc. In fact, the whole poem is a clash of viewpoints, as the debate between Orc and Albion's Angel in plates 6 to 9 makes evident. Orc, of course, perceives his energies to be joyful and renovative, whereas Albion's Angel perceives them to be destructive and fearsome. On plates 10 to 11, a third point of view is offered by the thirteen angels on their magic seats in the Atlantean hills. *Europe* offers three different visions of the eighteen hundred years of European history: the introduction presents the fairy's perspective, the preludium is the nameless shadowy female's, and the prophecy itself is divided between the English people's and Enitharmon's.[54] Susan Fox maintains that *Europe* is the only prophetic work before *Milton* to present "a layered organization of multiple perspectives," that is, a variety of points of view on the same event, superimposed upon each other. The other prophecies offer different perspectives, but these "perspectives are ordered consecutively and responsively, even when they are perspectives on the same event."[55] *Africa* offers a variety of reactions to Urizen's law, and *Asia* presents three points of view concerning the revolution in Europe: those of the Kings of Asia, Urizen, and Orc. In *The Book of Urizen*, the perspective shifts between the Eternals, Urizen, and Los. Similarly, Ahania's lament at the end of *The Book of Ahania* offers an alternate view of the action of the poem, as does Eno's song at the beginning of *The Book of Los*.

These various perspectives are not only presented by shifts in scene and point of view in Blake's narrative but are also represented by Blake's illustrations, which can contradict each other, contradict perspectives offered in the text, and even offer perspectives that are totally different from any given in the text.[56] All of these possibilities can be seen in *America*, whose fourteen plates that comprise the Prophecy present a "dynamic 'single' visualizable picture—of shifting multiple perspectives."[57] As Erdman points out, plates 6 and 10 offer two contradictory visions of Orc's appearance on the Atlantic: the orthodox vision that sees Orc's appearance as that of Satan dwelling in the abyss (pl. 10), and the vision of the revolutionaries who see Orc as the Christ of the Second Coming and who see that Atlantic not as an abyss but as "a mountain rising above the abyss of nonentity."[58] Similarly, plates 4 and 5 show a contrast between the revolutionaries' vision of the pathetic human reality behind the dragon mask of tyranny and the tyrant's vision that sees only monsters.[59]

Many of the other illustrations to *America* develop these contrary perspectives, but some illustrations offer a third perspective, such as the picture of the children sleeping with the sheep on plate 7, which does not refer to anything mentioned in the text. This illustration, as well as the picture of the children riding a serpent on the bottom of plate 11 (which alludes to the renovative image of the child playing with the asp in Isaiah 11.8), transcends the vision of the Revolution as conflict, which the text and the other illustrations present.[60] More importantly, the outstretched arms and raised knee of Orc in plate 10, repeating the position of Urizen in plate 8, presents a vision that goes beyond the contrary points of view that the two plates represent and reveals the essential similarity between the tyrant and the rebel, thus presenting Blake's critique of the cyclical pattern of tyranny and rebellion that Frye identifies as the Orc

47

Cycle.[61] The design on plate 7 offers not only a perspective that differs from that of many of the other designs but also a vision that contradicts the text to which it is attached. The demonic image of Orc that Albion's Angel conjures up —"Blasphemous Demon, Antichrist," "Lover of wild rebellion, and transgressor of God's Law" (7:5-6)—is juxtaposed against a picture of millennial peace that suggests that Orc's identity and motives are quite the opposite of what the text describes them to be. Plate 14 shows another contrast of perspectives, with the monstrous tree, heavy clouds, and "death-preaching sibyl" contradicting the text's optimistic narration of the resistance of the thirteen colonies to the plagues sent by George III.[62]

Blake's use of verse and illustration to create multiple perspectives in *America* and in his other prophecies, as Erdman suggests, makes his prophecies windows into or promptbooks for a "mental theater" in which the reader achieves imaginative vision.[63] In this perception and in his calling *America* "an acting version of a mural Apocalypse,"[64] Erdman approaches what we now understand to be an important inheritance from the prophetic tradition: the dramatic use of multiple perspectives within the prophetic or apocalyptic theater, which is originally located in the mind of the prophet and which, through the communication of his prophecy, is relocated in the mind of the reader. The Apocalypse and the Old Testament prophecies were understood to be dramas in which different perspectives, rather than different characters, contended with each other.[65] This understanding of the dramatic nature of prophecy was elucidated in Pareus' commentary on Revelation, which "was absorbed into eighteenth-century commentaries on Revelation and treatises on prophecy."[66] Other critics besides Erdman have understood that Blake's "Visionary Forms Dramatic" involve contending perspectives rather than characters, especially since Blake's "characters" represent different points of view rather than fully rounded individuals,[67] but few have understood that this important principle of prophetic structure comes from biblical tradition.

Blake, in his handling of multiple perspectives, also follows prophetic structure within a given prophetic book by using multiple styles and genres that contain these different perspectives and hold them in dynamic tension.[68] The dramatic effect of biblical prophecy is particularly heightened by the prophet's adoption of the dramatist's technique of using "choric devices both to lead an audience toward, and to jostle it into adopting, new perspectives."[69] This dynamic interaction between lyric and other modes in Blake's prophecies is noted by Swinburne, who regards Blake as a poet whose "lyrical faculty had gained and kept a preponderance over all others visible in every scrap of his work" and who states that Blake's "endless myth of oppression and redemption, of revelation and revolt, runs through many forms and spills itself by strange straits and byways among the sands and shallops of prophetic speech."[70] Swinburne observes that in Blake's prophetic books this diversity of styles and forms included "gigantic allegory," epic narrative (in which the poet "passes from the prophetic tripod to the seat of a common singer"), and many examples of Blake's "grand lyrical gift," some of those lyrical passages being "not always unworthy of an Aeschylean chorus . . . each inclusive of some fierce apocalypse or suggestive of some obscure evangel."[71] George Saintsbury, commenting on the variety of rhythms in Blake's verse, notes, "it has been said that more or less regular lyrics occur" in some of the prophetic books,[72] a statement reminiscent of Lowth's commentary on the poetry of the Hebrew prophets. And more recently, Alicia Ostriker perceives in Blake's prophecies "a limited number of distinguishable styles," which include that of "narrative, oratory, lyric, incipient naturalism and the Job-like piling up of rhetorical questions."[73] Ostriker further observes that Blake's works adopt from the Bible "the rhetoric of lamentation, song of praise, pastoral, aphorism, invective."[74]

Thus the mixture of history, oratory, lyric, and other modes that Howes, Lowth, and others perceived in the prophetic books of the Bible is an important structural principle operating in Blake's prophetic books. In *America* we see a number of distinct genres: the song of Orc on plate 6, "The morning comes, the night decays, the watchmen leave their stations" (6:1), is an almost universally recognized set piece,[75] which echoes the watchman's songs in Ezekiel 7:1-15 and Isaiah 21:12; plate 8 contains a prophetic speech by Orc that echoes Esdras, Daniel, and Revelation; plate 9 contains the response of Albion's Angel, which takes the form of a war chant with the repeated refrain, "Sound! sound! my loud war-trumpets & alarm my Thirteen Angels!" There are a number of other rhetorical set pieces, including two recognition speeches, one by the shadowy daughter of Urthona (2:7-17) and the other by Albion's Angel (7:3-7), and the rhetorical questions modeled upon the Book of Job that are spoken by Boston's Angel (11:4-15). *Europe*, which has been called a "collage of techniques" and a "series of set pieces loosely linked together,"[76] exhibits a variety of poetic forms and styles: a fairy's song (iii: 1-6) couched in what Ostriker calls Blake's "middle, expository style,"[77] a lament sung by the nameless shadowy female (1:4-2:16), a bacchic choric song by the sons of Urizen and Enitharmon (4:3-14), Enitharmon's triumphal song (6:1-8:12), a parodic version of an Ovidian metamorphosis (12:15-20), and an aubade sung by Enitharmon (13:9-14:31). *Africa* is a combination of annal and Ovidian fable, the latter being the tale of Har and Heva, whereas *Asia* contains a lament by the Kings of Asia and a prophetic vision that echoes Ezekiel's vision in the vale of dry bones (*Song of Los* 7:31-40). Needless to say, *Africa* and *Asia*, two divergent works that contain divergent forms, constitute a single work, *The Song of Los*, which juxtaposes them and holds them in tension.

Like *America*, *Europe*, and *The Song of Los*, the other Lambeth prophecies are composed in several different styles and genres, although to a lesser degree than those political prophecies. *The Book of Urizen* exhibits variety in its style and meter, but in this work Blake appears to have abandoned his practice of combining oratory and lyric with narrative. There are no lyrical passages, and the only oration, Urizen's parody of prophetic speech on plate 4, is missing from four of the seven extant copies of the prophecy.[78] Blake may have taken this plate out because of a desire to eliminate the declamatory style that is so prevalent in the political prophecies of *America* and *Europe*. *The Book of Ahania* continues Blake's apparent preference for narrative above other modes, but the individual digressions in Chapters I to IV compose a series of individual mythic or emblematic poems placed within a larger mythic action; the book's last chapter, containing Ahania's lament, is primarily lyric. Similarly, there is only one lyric in *The Book of Los*, Eno's lament in free verse (3:1-26), which is followed by narrative in essentially trimeter verse.[79]

This multiplicity of styles and forms is also present in the illustrations to Blake's prophetic books. Not only is there a variety of pictorial styles and genres in the prophetic books but there is a variety of engraving techniques as well.[80] Blake's usual practice in the Lambeth books is to depict in relief etching one or more sharply outlined forms that soar, fall, hover, or dance within a relatively abstract space that is either undefined or represented as such elemental forms as flames, clouds, water, and rocks.[81] Some of Blake's designs, however, particularly the interlinear and marginal designs, contain a cruder delineation of the human form. The figure trapped in a net on plate 12 of *Europe* and the floating female on plate 13 of *Urizen* and on the title page of *Ahania* are three cases in point. On the other hand, Blake also presents designs that locate his figures in a more clearly defined space that minimally places the figures on the ground and often suggests a landscape or an architectural setting, as in the pictures in *America* of two children sleeping beside a sheep (pl. 7) and of the man

51

entering death's door (pl. 12). Some of these designs, such as the frontispiece to *America*, are highly finished, exhibiting the manner and techniques of commercial engraving; whereas other designs, such as plate 8 of *America*, combine these commercial techniques with Blake's characteristic relief etching technique.[82] Blake also uses "white line engraving," as in plate 9 of *America*,[83] a technique that is often combined with Blake's relief etching technique, as in the frontispiece of *Europe*.

Besides containing a variety of styles and engraving techniques, Blake's prophetic books also contain examples of various pictorial genres that were popular in his time. There are several plates, for instance, that even to the most casual observer are strikingly different in style and subject matter from the rest of the designs. These are the "Famine" (pl. 6) and the "Plague" (pl. 7) of *Europe* and the child with the "dog at the wintry door" in *Urizen* (pl. 26). These plates depict scenes from eighteenth-century London, using figures in contemporary dress, and partake of the familiar and sentimental genre pieces of the day, such as those that Blake had executed for Mary Wollstonecraft's translation of Salzmann's *Elements of Morality* and her own *Original Stories from Real Life*.[84] Some of the designs in *Europe* (plates 1, 2, and 11) adopt the content and the idiom of political cartoons.[85]

Other designs in a number of the prophetic books employ what was the most prestigious pictorial form in the eighteenth century, the history painting, which included those paintings in the grand manner that depicted episodes from ancient and modern history, classical mythology, ancient and modern literature, and the Bible.[86] The historical painters, whose works Blake had engraved and whose practice Blake often followed in his own paintings and graphic works, showed "a predilection for large idealized figures, rhetorically grouped configurations, static attitudes and 'morally elevating' events."[87] In the popular thought of his contemporaries, this form was regarded as the pictorial analogue of the epic,[88] and Blake's invocation of the tradition of history painting appears in several of the prophetic books, such as *America,* where plate 1 is an adaptation of a popular biblical subject, Adam and Eve discovering the body of Abel.[89] Plate 8 of *Europe,* with its use of static pose and histrionic gesture, suggests the reunion of Lear and Cordelia, and *King Lear,* of course, was exploited by history painters as a source of sublimity.[90] Another Shakespearean subject, Oberon and Titania, appears on plate 5 of *The Song of Los.*[91] Plate 15 of *Europe,* which suggests a scene from the *Aeneid,* echoes a pose derived from classical statuary that was also adopted by Flaxman.[92] Such echoes of classical sculpture were a staple of the genre, and Blake appears to mock this vogue in plate 21 of *Urizen,* in which Los's misery is underscored by the calmly statuesque attitudes of the figures: Los is depicted as a jealous Hephaestos, Enitharmon as a coy but amorous Venus, and Orc as a Mars in embryo.

Finally, several of Blake's designs belong to the tradition of allegorical paintings or personifications that the eighteenth century inherited from the Renaissance.[93] The most famous example of this tradition in Blake's prophetic books is the frontispiece to *Europe,* which recalls "countless personifications of Mathematics, Architecture and Learning in Western art."[94] Other examples are plate 5 of *Europe,* whose male figure flanked by two females suggests the choice of Hercules, an extremely popular emblematic motif;[95] and plate 8 of *The Song of Los* and plate 5 of *The Book of Los,* both of which are reworkings of Raphael's allegorical picture of Astronomy in the Stanza della Segnatura.

In his combining of different pictorial and poetic genres, as well as in his adoption of the other properties of prophetic form that biblical critics and commentators were also aware of, Blake makes the "still better order" of biblical prophecy the structural model upon which his visionary forms dramatic are built. He found in the Bible a concept of art that is visual, dramatic, and rhetorical, that combines spectacle and confrontation, that acts upon the reader and enjoins the reader to act in response to it. He found that such a concept of art is inherent not only in prophetic form but in prophetic language as well, as the minute particulars of biblical prophecy reinforce the larger structural elements that form Blake's code of art.

The Figurative Language of Scripture and Blake's Composite Art

However novel the combining of visual and verbal art in Blake's prophetic books may have seemed to his contemporaries, it was actually a literal application of theories of prophetic language that most eighteenth-century readers would have been familiar with. As we have seen, Joseph Mede's *Key of the Revelation* introduced the idea that the book with the seven seals contained pictures rather than words.[1] A similar idea was later advanced by Henry Hammond, who stated that the vision of the seven churches in Revelation appeared to St. John in the form of "Symbols or visible Hieroglyphs."[2] Vitringa believed that Isaiah's prophetic inspiration took the form of shifting pictures.[3] Fénelon, in his *Dialogues on Eloquence in General,* included "painting"—the presentation of lively images to the imagination—as one of the three elements in the art of oratory and claimed that the biblical prophets outdid Homer in their skill at such painting.[4] This idea of the pictorial nature of prophecy persisted into the nineteenth century, as can be seen in the sermons of Samuel Horsley, who reiterated the traditional idea that biblical prophecy took the form of "emblematic pictures" that were presented by the Divine Spirit to the prophet's imagination.[5]

From the seventeenth through the nineteenth centuries, words such as "emblems," "impresses," and "hieroglyphs" appeared in discussions of the nature and form of prophetic vision, each term emphasizing the particularly pictorial nature of prophetic utterance.[6] The last of these terms had the widest currency and was often connected to theories about the origin and development of language.[7] The most well-

55

known theory of the relationship between hieroglyphs, prophetic language, and language in general was that propounded in the fourth book of William Warburton's *The Divine Legation of Moses* (1738).[8] Warburton sought to vindicate the language of prophecy from the attacks of the deists by showing the historical basis and hence "the logical propriety of prophetic language and sentiment."[9] The apparently obscure language of the prophets, says Warburton, was the result of God's accommodating His message to man's habits of mind during a time when language was not fully developed. The prophets fashioned their language to the mode of the ancient hieroglyphics, which had originated in Egypt and which were transmitted to all the other ancient nations, including the Hebrews, who had spent so many years in Egypt. These hieroglyphs were the products of nature and necessity rather than choice and artifice, as the rudeness of language in ancient times compelled the Egyptians to use visual signs to communicate abstract ideas. The hieroglyphic mode was thus originally used to reveal rather than conceal information. But when letters were invented, the Egyptians continued to use this method of signification and employed it for the purpose of concealing its sacred mysteries from the eyes of the profane.

Warburton also applied the same pictorial principle to spoken language, stating that a speaker in ancient times would supply the deficiencies of speech through the use of "significative actions" or signs, which among eastern nations were called "the voice of the sign" (Exodus 4:8).[10] We see numerous examples of these actions in the Bible, such as Jeremiah's breaking a potter's vessel (Jeremiah 19) and Ezekiel's weighing the hair of his beard in a balance (Ezekiel 5). Such is the manner in which the prophets instruct their audiences in the will of God. When God wishes to communicate more directly, He condescends to the same mode of instruction by presenting the significative action in the form of vision, as when God bids Jeremiah to regard the rod of the almond tree and the seething pot (Jeremiah

1:11, 1:13).[11] Warburton notes that this way of communicating through action coincides with writing by picture and that the pictorial mode still survives in more sophisticated forms of language. As speech becomes more highly developed, for instance, the significative action evolves into the apologue or fable, "a kind of speech which corresponds, in all respects, to writing by hieroglyphics, each being a symbol of something else understood."[12] As speech further improves, the apologue becomes contracted into the simile, which then becomes further contracted into the metaphor, and finally becomes the epithet. During this evolutionary process, the earlier forms of speech continued to be used, even after more sophisticated modes evolved, and the prophetic books of the Bible contain all these different forms. The important point that Warburton is making about all these different forms of writing is that their common foundation was "a picture or image, presented to the imagination through the eyes and ears" and that the prophetic language of scripture, which follows the "Asiatic Style," is a "speaking hieroglyph."[13]

A corollary of Warburton's theory about the relationship of hieroglyphics to prophetic speech is his idea about the relationship of hieroglyphs to idolatry. Although God condescended to use the pictorial form of communication that the Hebrews learned in Egypt, He expressly forbids them, in the second commandment, to use hieroglyphics. Warburton argues that this is because the hieroglyphics became a source of idolatry and superstition.[14] The pictorial forms of animals that had originally been used by the Egyptians to denote the attributes of Egyptian heroes and deities became in time the actual objects of worship.[15] Thus idolatry resulted from the mistaking of the signifier for the thing signified, a form of literalism that the Egyptian priests came to encourage.[16]

Other eighteenth-century writers presented variations, major and minor, upon Warburton's theory of the pictorial nature of prophecy. Richard Hurd, in the first series of

Warburtonian lectures, *An Introduction to the Study of the Prophecies* (1772), sketches the basic outlines of Warburton's theories.[17] Both Hurd and Warburton, in turn, derived many of their ideas from Charles Daubuz, who in his *Perpetual Commentary on the Revelation of St. John* (1720), also traced the origin of prophetic symbolism to Egyptian hieroglyphics. Stating that the prophecies and visions of the Old and New Testaments use the same "Symbolical Terms, Images, or Types, as were in use amongst the Egyptians and Chaldeans, or other Nations,"[18] Daubuz repeats the popular tradition that Moses introduced letters to the Hebrews in order to wean them from the idolatry that the hieroglyphic symbols tended to promote.[19] God thus eliminated Israel's use of hieroglyphics as a means of communicating wisdom and of indulging their predilection for the pagan arts of divination, but He continued to use the symbolic method of communication, turning what was once a corrupt practice to His own good ends.[20] Thus, in biblical prophecy we see the Holy Ghost acting as a painter, presenting man with a series of pictures or signs.[21]

Daubuz also notes the interplay of visual and verbal elements in the Book of Revelation, comparing that work to emblem books. Just as these books contain visible images or symbols, accompanied by a motto, or literal expression that explains the symbol, "in the same manner the Visions of *St. John* are Emblems, or Prophetical Impresses; having figures exposed to the Sight, and *Motto's* to explain the precise Meaning of the Symbol or Figure, and to determine its Accidents or Attributes according to the Intention of the Holy Ghost."[22] Johann Gottfried Eichhorn noted the presence of the same "show and tell" pattern in Ezekiel,[23] whose prophetic visions, like those in Revelation, contain "giant-forms"[24]—a term that Blake employs to describe his visions (*Jerusalem* 3)—and whose visual luxuriance requires that the reader have the "eye of an eagle" to comprehend the meaning of the whole work.[25]

Many of these ideas concerning the visual nature of prophetic language are extended to the language of the entire Bible by William Jones, who, reading the Scriptures in terms of allegorical tradition, sees the whole Bible as being essentially prophetic in function:

> It being the professed design of the Scripture to teach us such things as we neither see nor know of ourselves, its style and manner must be such as are no where else to be found. It must abound with figurative expressions; it cannot proceed without them: and if we descend to an actual examination of particulars, we find it assisting and leading our faculties forward; by an application of all visible objects to a figurative use; from the glorious orb which shines in the firmament to a grain of seed which is buried in the earth. In this sort of language did our blessed Saviour instruct his hearers; always referring them to such objects as were familiar to their senses, that they might see the propriety and feel the force of his doctrine. This method he observed, not in compliance with any customary speech peculiar to the Eastern people, but consulting the exigence of human nature, which is every where the same.[26]

Refusing to exculpate the oddities of biblical language on the basis of cultural relativity—as Warburton, Hurd, Lowth, and others were doing[27]—Jones argues from very traditional hermeneutical principles, many of which go back to St. Augustine, and makes more radical claims for biblical figuralism than his apparently more learned contemporaries were willing to do. Eschewing their historicism, Jones insists that symbolism is eternal, universal, and biblical in origin. For him "the whole dispensation of God towards man, is by signs, shadows, and figures of visible things";[28] and this form of pictorial communication existed from the very beginning of the world. Adam was educated about life and death through the symbols of the two trees in Eden, and "the whole scenery of paradise was disposed into an hieroglyphical school."[29] Jones goes on to assert, following Augustinian tradition, that symbolism is universal because it transcends differences in nationality and because the language of signs is "the language of the mind; which understands and reasons from the ideas, or images of things, imprinted upon the imagination."[30] Not only is this language the fittest medium of instruction, as the practice of the ancient pagans has attested, but it also has the power of converting the natural man to the spiritual man, and through this power of transfiguration, it gives man "a foretaste of the glorious presence of God."[31] This power is realized only in the Bible, of course, which contains the originals of all signs and symbols, the symbolism of the pagans being either a foreshadowing or perversion of biblical figuralism.[32] Like Warburton, Jones sees idolatry as the attachment to the symbol at the expense of what it signifies.

Within his discussion of the pictorial nature of the language of the Bible, Jones remarks that the Bible, more than any other book, abounds with personifications, which is a point that he borrows from Lowth.[33] Hugh Blair, who also is borrowing from Lowth, states that "the Poetical Figure, which, beyond all others, elevates the Style of Scripture, and gives it a peculiar boldness and sublimity, is Prosopopoeia or Personification."[34] Similarly, Daubuz observes that in many of the prophecies in the Old and New Testaments the prophet himself was a sign,[35] which—as in prosopopoeia—shows the Bible's predilection for communicating divine truths in human form. Thus biblical language is not only pictorial but also strongly predisposed toward a pictorialism that is anthropomorphic.

This constellation of ideas about the pictorial nature of prophetic language, much of which was derived from older traditions, would have been available to Blake mainly through the several editions of the works of Daubuz, Lowth, Fénelon, Jones, Warburton, and Hurd that were published in the eighteenth century, as well as through the citation of those works by other biblical commentators and literary critics. From these ideas Blake would have discovered either the impetus or the theoretical sanction for his decision to cast his prophecies into a form that combines both words and pictures. All the commentators and exegetes agreed that the verbal picture was an important part of the prophet's communicating the word of God. Many also agreed that the bodily gesture and prosopopoeia, the communication of the Word in human form, were prominent features of prophetic discourse. Furthermore, the critics and commentators pointed out that the use of pictorial communication had the authority of antiquity, representing the oldest and —for some commentators—the best method of conveying divine truths since it was a form of communication most like the actual workings of the human mind and least affected by differences in language, time, or custom. The visible signs used by the prophets thus constituted a universal language, available to and employed by all nations but perfected to the highest art by the writers of the Bible.

Because of the Bible's pictorialism, many commentators felt that the use of *visibilia* to communicate information about the invisible or eternal world had both traditional and divine sanction, for this method of communication was believed to be the primary means by which God communicated to man. This belief was in accord with the idea, which had become a commonplace by the time of the Renaissance and which Milton advanced in *Of Education,* that as a result of the Fall divine truths could be communicated to man only through the senses.[36] This blend of Christian and Platonic aesthetics thus asserted that the presentation of sensory images to the imagination aided the intellect in its attempt to reach an apprehension of the deity and that by means of perceiving and interpreting the visual sign man could achieve a knowledge of God or even the state of godhead itself. Daubuz, citing Augustine and Tertullian, notes that prophetic signs or symbols, the significance of which is initially obscure, "give a Lustre to the Divine Oracles, and shew their Sublimeness; so they give a pleasant Sting, and

61

alluring Appetite to a Pious Soul, pushing it on to the Angelical Curiosity of prying into God's Mysteries."[37]

Blake's adherence to this Augustinian aesthetic is most obvious in his stated preference for an art that "rouzes the faculties to act," using *visibilia* that, through the Imagination or "Spiritual Sensation," lead the perceiver to "Visions of Eternity" (pp. 676-77). The "wisest of the Ancients" considered this method to be "fittest for instruction" (p. 676), because it is only through Spiritual Sensation, the stimulation of the imagination to perceive the eternal significance of the signs presented to the senses, that man can transcend his finite or fallen state. Conversely, failure to construe the eternal significance of a sign would constitute idolatry. Or, to put it in Augustinian terms, the inability to perceive the divine significance of signs would constitute enslavement to the world of appearances, the world of the fallen senses, whereas the ability to interpret the sign constitutes freedom.[38]

It is the Bible's promotion of this freedom, its celebration of God as the source of all signification itself, that makes it superior to other books.[39] By employing *sensibilia* to communicate *intelligibilia* (eternal truths),[40] the Bible implies that all of the created world is actually God's language. The idea of the world as God's Book of Nature or Book of Creatures had become a commonplace by the time of the Renaissance.[41] This idea persisted into the eighteenth century, as we can see from William Jones' articulation of it:

> To those who understand it, all nature speaks the same language with revelation: what the one teaches in words the other confirms by signs. . . . If Christ is called the *true bread*, the *true light*, the *true vine*, and the talents or gifts of God's grace are the *true riches*, &c. then the objects of sense, without this their spirit and signification, are in themselves mere image and delusion; and the whole life of man in this world is but a shadow.[42]

Man learns to "read" nature by reading Scripture, which shows how God transforms *visibilia* into signs of the invisible world. Thus all objects of sense have no real significance unless they are perceived to articulate a relationship between the human and the divine. From Augustine's point of view, a stone is simply a stone unless "Jacob sleeps on it in the particular circumstances in which God made him sleep on it in order to make the event a sign."[43] By placing the object in a context that connects man with God, the Bible imaginatively transforms the object, uniting the human perceiver with the object of perception and giving that object both human and divine significance.

Blake enunciates this principle in *The Marriage of Heaven and Hell* when he has Ezekiel state that the God of the Old Testament is the first principle of human perception, the Poetic Genius, or the Imagination (pl. 12). In *All Religions are One* Blake asserts that this process of imaginative significance produces a universal language of symbols that are accommodated to the "dialect" of each particular culture: "thus all sects of Philosophy are from the Poetic Genius adapted to the weaknesses of every individual," and "the Religeons of all Nations are derived from each Nation's different reception of the Poetic Genius which is every where call'd the Spirit of Prophecy" (p. 2).[44] But the Old and New Testaments are "an *original* derivation from the Poetic Genius" (p. 3, italics mine) because their subject is the imaginative process itself. To return to Jacob's pillow, here we have one example among many of the imaginative creation of significance, wherein the subject of the story is not merely the content of Jacob's vision but the actual process of vision itself, which is celebrated and commemorated by the conferring of a name upon the stone that Jacob had rested his head on, Beth-el, the house of the Lord (Genesis 28:18-19). Such metaphoric namings persist throughout the Bible, and in each case the act of conferring metaphoric names upon objects is itself a metaphor for the imaginative transformation of the objects of sense into visible signs that carry divine significance and that celebrate God as the source of this significance.

The pictorialist terms used by biblical commentators and critics inevitably raise the question of the relationship of biblical tradition to the sister-arts tradition and the relationship of both traditions to Blake's concept of the form and language of prophecy. In Blake's time, the theory that poetic language communicates ideas by presenting visual images to the mind was a critical commonplace, however much the idea was denied by certain critics.[45] Equally familiar was the tradition of *ut pictura poesis*, a part of the sister-arts tradition that stressed the parallels between poetry and painting and emphasized the ability of poetry to paint verbal pictures. Three strands of this tradition that Jean Hagstrum sees in Blake's works are the verbal icon, the picture gallery form, and the visualizable personification.[46] The verbal icon is an allusion to or a verbal description of an art object or some other visible product of civilization, the most famous being Homer's description of the shield of Achilles. In the picture gallery form, the poet abandons narrative or linear order in favor of presenting a series of tableaux, sometimes with alternating commentaries or purely "verbal" passages. The "painterly personification," possibly "the most striking characteristic of pre-Romantic pictorialism," was a strongly visualizable form of prosopopoeia.

These three aspects of the *ut pictura* tradition, as well as the impulse of the sister-arts tradition to unite poetry and painting to transcend both modes of expression, can be found in biblical tradition as well. As Hagstrum points out, "prophetic language, like *ut pictura poesis* and the sister arts, unites the verbal and the visual in ways that are strikingly parallel. The God of Israel speaks in visions (Genesis 4:61, Psalms 89:19), and the prophet Nathan (2 Samuel 7:17) addresses David 'according to . . . vision' and 'according to . . . words.' "[47] As we have already seen, this concept of biblical pictorialism was advanced by biblical commentators and critics. They also saw in the Bible the three specific features of the *ut pictura poesis* tradition that Hagstrum emphasizes in Blake. Verbal icons, such as the descriptions of the tabernacle and the priestly vestments in Exodus 26-28 and the chariot of God in the first chapter of Ezekiel, were cited by writers who wanted to stress the pictorial vividness of Scripture.[48] The tableau structure of prophecy, as we have seen, was pointed out by Mede, Vitringa, Hurd, Eichhorn, and Daubuz. Daubuz even compared the structure of Revelation to that of the shield of Achilles and the Tablet of Cebes, two classical progenitors of picture gallery form that had a strong influence within the *ut pictura poesis* tradition.[49] We have also seen that commentators and literary critics alike remarked the predominance of personification as a means of creating vividness and sublimity in the Bible.

Thus it would appear that Blake's illuminated prophecies have their theoretical basis in both biblical and pictorialist tradition. But a closer examination of these theories and of Blake's actual practice shows the influence of biblical tradition to be the most decisive. Although Hagstrum is correct in stressing that in practice Blake used the *ut pictura* and sister-arts traditions to suit his own purposes, his assertion that Blake's essential aims were consonant with those of the tradition is a position that is challenged convincingly by W.J.T. Mitchell. Mitchell argues that although Blake absorbed some of the general practices of the sister-arts tradition, he was highly critical of that tradition. Although Blake uses the verbal icon, picture gallery form, and personification, he does not use them "in a visual or pictorialist manner, as the eighteenth century understood it."[50] Blake's verbal allusions to icons or artifacts, Mitchell states, do not really invite the reader to visualize them or attach any special significance to their visual appearance, nor does Blake make a verbal icon the controlling image of any of

65

his poems. Similarly, his use of picture gallery form differs from that of his contemporaries in that his "gallery" is not made up of pictures, but of visions that "tend to be not visual but synaesthetic, tactile, and phantasmagoric." Furthermore, these visions are not arranged as a series of independent visual works in a gallery but "tend rather to be linked in a dramatic fashion, as the oratory or stream of consciousness of characters who have conflicting visions to express."[51] Finally, Blake's personifications are not really visualizable verbal portraits.[52] Thus showing that Blake rejected pictorialism as the eighteenth century conceived it, a pictorialism that was based upon the doctrine of the imitation of nature, Mitchell suggests that Blake's imagery is derived "from the older and more radical pictorialism of sacred literature, in which language becomes vision and the word is made flesh."[53]

In this last statement, Mitchell points to an awareness of biblical pictorialism that Blake and his contemporaries shared. Contemporary statements about the pictorial qualities of the Bible reveal that the eighteenth century *did* understand pictorialism in Blake's sense, though Blake's contemporaries rarely put such an understanding into practice. Although eighteenth-century critics claimed the same pictorial qualities for the Bible that they saw in their favorite classical models, many were also aware that the power of the Bible's pictorialism lay in its brilliant economy, its startling use of a spare, concrete language to achieve synesthetic effects. Eichhorn, for instance, admires the painterly elaboration of Ezekiel's visions but finds them less aesthetically pleasing than the sparser, more rapidly conceived visions in Isaiah and Revelation.[54] Michaelis finds Ezekiel less sublime than Isaiah for the same reason.[55] Patrick Murdoch stresses the kinesthetic rather than purely visual effects of biblical imagery, as does Hugh Blair, who praises the Bible's use of concise, bold, animated, and rapidly shifting figures that exhibit "bold sublimity" rather than "correct elegance."[56]

In his distinction between the "correctness" of neoclassical norms and the wild freedom of biblical poetry, Blair displays an awareness that there is a difference between the pictorialism that we find in the Bible and that which we find in the *ut pictura* and sister-arts traditions. Other critics also appear to have been aware of this difference, yet, as Vincent Freimarck has noted, they often tended to ignore or minimize it.[57] Take, for instance, the description of the horse in the Book of Job, which Steele greatly admired:

> Hast thou given the horse strength? hast thou clothed his neck in thunder? Canst thou make him afraid as a grasshopper? the glory of his nostrils is terrible. He paweth in the valley, and rejoiceth in his strength: he goeth on to meet the armed men. He mocketh at fear, and is not affrighted; neither turneth he back from the sword. The quiver rattleth against him, the glittering spear and the shield. He swalloweth the ground with fierceness and rage: neither believeth he that it is the sound of the trumpet. He saith among the trumpets, Ha, ha; and he smelleth the battle afar off, the thunder of the captains, and the shouting.   (Job 39:19-25)

Since metaphors, according to most eighteenth-century critics, present a visible picture to the mind of the reader, the test of the perspicuity of a metaphor was its ability to present a distinct picture. If there are too many metaphors crowded together or too many details piled up within a single metaphor, the result will be confusing. Clearly the passage from Job does not meet this standard for perspicuity, yet Steele lavishes his praises upon it, claiming that it is superior to any classical description and that its images "would have given the great wits of antiquity new laws for the sublime, had they been acquainted with these writings."[58] In his discussion of this passage,

> Steele . . . admired a number of rather unorthodox details . . . such as "Hast thou clothed his neck with thunder?" (Job 39:19); "the glory of his nostrils is terrible"

67

(Job 39:20); "he swalloweth the ground" (Job 39:24). In the first of these, "the sacred author, by the bold figure of thunder, not only expresses the shaking of that remarkable beauty in the horse, and the flashes of hair which naturally suggest the idea of lightning; but likewise the violent agitation and force of the neck, which in the oriental languages had been flatly exprest by a metaphor less than this." Here Steele is trying hard to prove that a visual image is produced. But of "the glory of his nostrils is terrible" he is content to say that it is "more strong and concise" than a notable similar line in Virgil, "which yet is the noblest line written without inspiration"; and "he swalloweth the ground" Steele calls "the boldest and noblest of images for swiftness" without attempting to demonstrate its soundness.[59]

What permits Steele to ignore accepted canons of taste is his distinction, implied in the above passage, between a sacred and a secular text. This kind of discrimination permits him to cast aside the prime critical standard of the time, that art must imitate nature. The style of the Bible, he recognizes, is not that of "mortal authors," and in the Job passage the reader is presented with a figure "just as it appears in the eyes of the Creator," that is, a figure that is not pictorial in the commonly accepted sense: "I can not but particularly observe, that whereas the classical poets chiefly endeavoured to paint the outward figure, lineaments, and motions; the sacred poet makes all the beauties to flow from an inward principle in the creature he describes; and thereby gives great spirit and vivacity to his descriptions."[60] This is a view of poetical pictorialism that Blake would obviously approve of and which he clearly endorses in his own practice.

Steele was not the only critic to modify orthodox critical precepts in order to justify the Bible's brilliant deviations from classical norms. Aaron Hill, Hugh Blair, and George Campbell all praised biblical figuralism while at the same time they implicitly or explicitly acknowledged that those figures departed from the pictorial norm.[61] John Husbands, like Steele, uses the analogy of painting in his praise of biblical poetry but casts aside the belief that great poetry must imitate external nature. The Bible, Husbands maintains, presents us with "the language of heaven," which according to Husbands' defense of the Bible as primitivist poetry, turns out to be the language of the passions:

> We may indeed observe in the cadence of certain poetical passages (of the ancient Hebrews) something different from the prosaic style. We may observe certain bold figures and animated expressions never used in bare narrations. Yet still they imitated nature without art, and without study described agreeably things, sentiments and affections. For the strength and energy of the figures and the true sublimity of style are a natural effect of the passions. No wonder therefore that their diction is something more flourished and ornamental, more vigourous and elevated, more proper to paint and set things before our eyes, than plain and ordinary recitals. This sort of poetry is more simple, and at the same time more worthy of the majesty of God, than that which is regular and confined, which must with difficulty express the dictates of the Holy Spirit, and would be apt to give some alloy to the sublimity of the sense.[62]

Thus the Bible is praised for its primitive depiction of internal rather than external nature. The Song of Solomon is great poetry because in it "the lineaments of the mind are beautifully drawn, and the passions themselves painted to the life."[63] The writings of the prophets contain "a divine Enthusiasm, a Fury something more than Poetical," whereby "The Descriptions of the Deity are so lofty, so far superior to any thing that the mind of man, unassisted, cou'd have been able to invent or conceive."[64] Husbands anticipates the expressive theory of biblical poetry advanced by Lowth,[65]

69

who defended the tendency of Hebrew poetry to violate eighteenth-century standards of perspicuity by appealing to the principle of cultural relativity.

Lowth notes that the crowding of metaphors is a violation of Aristotle's edicts about perspicuity but explains that the licentious use of metaphors among the Hebrew poets must be attributed to the "general freedom and boldness" of Oriental writers:[66]

> [Hebrew poetry] is unconstrained, animated, bold and fervid. The Orientals look upon the language of poetry as wholly distinct from that of common life, as calculated for immediately expressing the passions; if, therefore, it were to be reduced to the plain rule and order of reason, if every sentence were arranged with care and study, as if calculated for perspicuity alone, it would no longer be what they intended it, and to call it the language of passion would be the greatest of solecisms.[67]

Noting that Hebrew figures are frequently allusive, sometimes justifiably obscure, Lowth rarely makes any facile statements about their pictorial qualities. Yet behind his criticism of the Bible are the same pictorialist assumptions that he shares with his contemporaries; for instance, he notes that, given the expressive proclivities of Oriental poetics, it is surprising to find in the Hebrew poets "so much purity and so much perspicuity, both in sentiment and language."[68] Balaam's prophecy (Numbers 24:5-9) "abounds in splendid imagery copied immediately from the tablet of Nature,"[69] especially when the translation offered by Lowth is more consciously pictorial than the King James translation:

> In proud array thy tents expand,
> O Israel o'er the subject land:
> As the broad vales in prospect rise,

As gardens by the water spread,
As cedars of majestic size,
That shade the sacred fountain's head.[70]

Commenting on Isaiah 11, which is not pictorial in the conventional sense of that word, Lowth remarks, "the Greek and Latin Poets have painted their golden age in very beautiful colors, but the exquisite imagery of Isaiah stands unequalled and inimitable."[71] Thus Lowth, like several of his contemporaries, modified or ignored the idea that biblical figuralism affected its readers by presenting distinct pictorial images to the imagination. Instead they asserted that the rapidly shifting images, the violent yoking of apparently far-fetched metaphors, and the use of synesthesia (a term which they did not use but whose effects they always noted) imitated not the external world but the process of perception as it takes place either in the divine mind or in the mind of a poet-prophet inflamed with either passion or divine inspiration.

Sometimes the operations of the divine mind, poetic passion, and divine inspiration were equated by eighteenth-century critics. Lowth, for example, identifies prophetic inspiration as "True poetic enthusiasm," the ability of a poet to absorb and effectively express the passions of another. To possess this enthusiasm means "as the ancients would have expressed, 'to be inspired; full of the God': not however, implying that their ardour of mind was imparted by the Gods, but that this ecstatic impulse became the God of the moment."[72] But, as Fénelon asserts (and Lowth would agree), the pagan poets possessed false enthusiasm compared to the true enthusiasm of the biblical prophet, who as poet and true orator was skilled in painting his passions and soaring above himself to "express something divine."[73] John Husbands, who quotes Fénelon's views on the true enthusiasm of the prophets, makes the same point.[74] Here we are close to Isaiah's assertion, as given in *The Marriage of Heaven and Hell,* that "the voice of honest indignation is the voice of God" (pl. 12) and to Blake's address to the public in *Jerusalem,* identifying the "true Orator" as the poet-prophet who imitates the enthusiasm of the ancients by expressing the word of God in "Thunder of Thought, & flames of fierce desire" (3:6).

For Blake, Husbands, Fénelon, and Lowth, then, the divinity and the sublimity of prophetic utterance lay not in its imitation of nature but in its imitation of psychological states. Lowth makes this point most explicitly and deserves extended quotation:

> Poetry is said to consist in imitation: whatever the human mind is able to conceive, it is the province of poetry to imitate; things, places, appearances, natural and artificial, actions, passions, manners, and customs: and since the human intellect is naturally delighted with every species of imitation, that species in particular, which exhibits its own image, which displays and depicts those impulses, inflexions, perturbations and secret emotions, which it perceives and knows in itself, can scarcely fail to delight above every other. . . . When a passion is expressed, the object is clear and distinct at once; the mind is immediately conscious of itself and its own emotions; it feels and suffers in itself a sensation, either the same or similar to that which is described. Hence that sublimity which arises from the vehement agitation of the passions, and the imitation of them, possesses a superior influence over the human mind; whatever is exhibited to it from without, may well be supposed to move and agitate it less than what it internally perceives, of the magnitude and force of which it is previously conscious.[75]

For Lowth, as well as for his contemporaries, many of whom were influenced by his lectures, biblical pictorialism was not based upon the standard of imitating an ideal, generalized Nature—which *was* the standard in the sister-arts and *ut pictura* traditions—but they claimed that the distinctive pictorialism of the Bible nevertheless satisfied Aristotelian precepts by asserting, paradoxically, that the Bible does not present a clear and distinct picture in its figuralism because it presents a true imitation of the mind in a state of excitement. The "clear and distinct" object is created within the mind of the reader by his or her own sympathetic response.

We see, then, that biblical pictorialism, however much it appears to resemble that of the sister-arts tradition, functions independently of that tradition. The ontological status of biblical figuralism was perceived to be entirely different from that of writers or painters in the *ut pictura poesis* tradition. The language of the Bible, as Mitchell reminds us, is the word made flesh, and it expresses neither a facsimile of nature, nor an idealized nature, nor a Platonic Idea. Rather, it is the living expression of the divine pathos, of a God who acts upon and interacts with specific persons at specific times in history; it is the sudden invasion of the eternal upon the temporal, obliterating normal conventions of time and space and causing language to express the sudden dislocation through synesthesia, rapidly shifting images, dramatic rather than pictorial personifications, and a symbolic economy that packs a wealth of significance into a single figure. As the communication of a divine subject to a human subject or subjects, the language of prophecy is both dramatic and highly rhetorical. This kind of rhetoric or poetic is certainly pictorial, but its effects are achieved mainly through the reader's experience of images in motion rather than through his or her contemplation of static pictures; and, as Bloom and Erdman have said of Blake's works, the best analogy would be that of the cinema.[76]

Obviously lacking this analogy, biblical commentators and critics of the seventeenth and eighteenth centuries who apprehended the above-mentioned qualities in the Bible frequently used the analogy of drama or oratory, sometimes both, as we have already seen. These readers came to terms with the uniqueness of biblical figuralism either by attributing that uniqueness to the Oriental style of writing, by

73

positing the idea of psychological mimesis, or by falling back upon more orthodox explanations. Whatever theory they expounded, they all understood that in the Bible they were confronting an aesthetic that defined prophecy as a combination of visual and verbal communication that adhered to laws of language and form that were for the most part alien to the dominant aesthetic norm. In their attempts to justify the Bible in the face of that norm, they inadvertently began to create an aesthetic theory that was to be adopted, refined, elaborated upon, and put into practice by Blake and the other Romantics. Blake, however, unlike the other Romantics, was constantly aware of the biblical roots of his aesthetic and kept that aesthetic firmly grafted to biblical tradition.

Blake's aesthetic was always tied to biblical tradition because his theory of art was centered on the Incarnation, the process whereby the Word becomes flesh; the Incarnation became the central metaphor into which he absorbed and synthesized the theories of biblical exegetes and literary critics. He was able to do this because his conception of the Incarnation was very broadly conceived, equating Christ with the Poetic Genius, or the Imagination, and holding that God acts and is in existing human beings. Thus the prophet not only communicates the Word but he *is* the Word; his very existence is a sign, an indication of the eternal penetrating the temporal. Within his own person, the prophet fuses verbal message and significative action, as the biblical commentators noted and as Blake states in *The Marriage of Heaven and Hell*, where he explains that Isaiah, Ezekiel, and Diogenes all performed these significative actions to raise man to a perception of the infinite. Similarly, in *Milton*, the existence and ministry of Wesley and Whitefield, whom Blake identifies as the two prophetic Witnesses of Revelation, are signs and miracles: "Can you have greater Miracles than these? Men who devote/Their lifes whole comfort to intire scorn & injury & death" (Milton 23:1-2).

Blake equates this fusion of human activity and verbal message with his own "infernal method" of printing: the production of illuminated prophecies that combine visual image and verbal communication to raise man to a perception of the infinite by cleansing the senses and expunging "the notion that man has a body distinct from his soul" (MHH, pl. 14), a notion that is contrary of course to the idea of the Incarnation. The figurative nature of Blake's visual art and his assertion of the primacy of personification, both in theory and practice, are an extension of the same principle. Both in The Marriage and All Religions are One, for instance, Blake sees personification as the manifestation of the Poetic Genius, which is Christ, "the True Man"; and in both works he states that the Poetic Genius is the first principle of perception that gives human form to man himself and to all the objects of his perceptions. To cleanse the doors of perception and perceive the infinite in all things is to totally integrate the senses so as to become Christ's body, the whole man, or the human form divine, and to realize, within the microcosm and the macrocosm, Christ's body as the source of all form and significance.

Blake knew that this teleology and the methods that he used to achieve it originated in the Bible. That the Bible engages all of the senses and, primarily through the figure of Christ, uses those senses to create form and significance is an idea that Blake would have found in Boehme, but it actually goes back to St. Augustine and, ultimately, to St. Paul. In On Christian Doctrine Augustine draws an analogy between language and the Incarnation, stating that just as thought is expressed in sounds "without any deterioration in itself" when we speak, so God became flesh without undergoing any change.[77] Besides its obvious pedagogical function, the analogy also functions as a teleological metaphor: just as the end of language is thought, the end of thought is Christ, and it is only through the Incarnation that both language and the human body acquire any universal and eternal significance. Therefore, the language that comes closest to communicating this significance is that which most closely approximates the form of Christ's body. In other words, when the analogy becomes reality, when language merges with Christ's body and thought merges with Christ, both the speaker and his or her message become the incarnate Word.

Augustine's linking of the Incarnation with rhetoric also appears in his discussion of signs, where he shows that the Bible, through its declaration of the Incarnation, continuously points to Christ as the source of all significance. For Augustine, the process of language itself is a metaphor for the Incarnation, because the Bible engages not only sight and hearing but the other senses as well in order that man's body may be identified with the body of Christ, the true church. This point is strongly implied in the examples that Augustine gives to show how different signs communicate through the different senses. To illustrate visual signs, he cites hand gestures, bodily gestures of actors, banners, and military standards. For aural signs he cites words and musical instruments. But when he discusses the other senses, he uses examples from the life of Christ: the odor of the ointment that his feet were anointed with, the taste of the bread and wine at the Last Supper, the touching of the hem of his garment that healed a diseased woman. These last three examples, as Joseph A. Mazzeo points out, refer to "God's unique power to confer on realities their significance as signs":

> What is striking in these examples from the life of Christ is that they should be drawn from Scripture for precisely those senses which it is most difficult to conceive as possessing value as signs in ordinary human life. Is it the case that the only certain use of such *sensibilia* as

signs can be found in the life of Christ whose every gesture, according to St. Augustine, had some bearing on his mission of revelation? One is inclined to suspect that this may be so, and it would be in harmony with St. Augustine's conviction that only the Divinity can use things as signs in an intrinsic and natural, and not conventional meaning. I suppose some conventional signs adapted to the senses of smell, touch, and taste might have been found if St. Augustine had been willing to imagine a situation which would provide the metacommunicative context for a gesture, an odour or touch acquiring value as a sign. Such a context is of course immediately given in the doctrine of the Incarnation, for no divine act whatever could be meaningless.[78]

For Augustine, then, the Bible's use of language to invoke the five senses and direct those senses toward an apprehension of the Incarnation creates a perfect fusion of form and content. The Bible not only announces that the Word was made flesh but also enacts that very process.

Augustine's idea that through the Incarnation the objects of sense are transformed into signs is developed in more detail by Boehme, who was familiar with Augustinian tradition. Boehme believed that the material world was stamped with the signature of the spiritual world, and he states, in *Mysterium Magnum* (1623), that the objects of sense are part of the natural or sensual language.[79] This language is "the one only holy mental Tongue" (36:45); it was dictated by the holy spirit to the "holy Penmen" of the Bible (35:63) and is understood by birds and beasts. Man understood it before he fell into the material world, at which time the original unified and unifying spirit of the sensual language became fragmented into the spirits of the individual letters of the human alphabet, which is a fallen form of the original holy tongue. The biblical story of Babel is concerned with this loss of the sensual language (35:68).

The human alphabet is thus a fragmented and abstract

form of a language that originally united man with the objects of his perceptions. The consonants of this fallen language represent the observable qualities of sensual perception. The vowels represent that which perceives those qualities and gives them significance, since words cannot be formed without vowels (36:45). The five vowels form the tetragrammaton, "the holy Name of God"; "the Name *Jehova* has nothing in it but only the five Vowels, A, E, I, O, V" (35:49). These vowels are the five senses, "the five holy Languages out of the Name Jehovah, from whence the Holy Spirit speaks" (35:49). The external world, the world of Nature, "is tinctured with the *five* Vowels, so that it becomes full of Joy and Delight" (35:49). When man fell, he became attached to "the external Form" of the letters (i.e., the consonants), the observable properties of the senses, and he forgot the vowels (the five senses) that gave those properties life, significance, and joy (36:45). The senses became divided from each other, and the objects of sense became divided from the active force that perceives them, gives them significance, and unifies them with the perceiver.

This lost unity can be regained only through the Incarnation, which is enacted in each individual when he or she abandons reason and abstract knowledge and realizes the divine origin of the five senses, thus recovering the five vowels of the divine name. This is accomplished through the destruction of the images of the consonants within oneself, to "suffer not one of them at all to have its own Self-Life; not *desiring* to know or will any more of *God*, only and alone what God wills to know in us and through us; and also . . . [to] immerse or resign the Soul's Hunger and Desire . . . into the five Vowels," wherein "the great holy Name of JEOVA or JESUS (viz. the living Word) is manifest" (36:43). Through the reintegration of the fallen senses, the Incarnation is reenacted and humanity is brought again into union; people become "ONE again with one another, *one* People, *one* Tree, *one* Man in Soul and Body" (36:43).

For Boehme, as well as for Paracelsus and Berkeley, the qualities that the mind perceives in the objects of sense inhere not in the objects themselves, but in the mind that perceives them, and Boehme identifies this mind as the divine intellect or Jesus, who represents the process of signification. Jesus' language, the universal language of the senses, is manifested in the Bible, which integrates and unifies the senses with each other and the senses with their objects. The God of the Bible, the Word, is thus a principle of perception, and the subject of the Bible is the attempt of the Word to become flesh, to manifest itself among mankind.[80]

Although the Bible is written in the "holy mental Tongue," as it was dictated by the Holy Spirit, Boehme believes that the Word also manifested itself in the languages of all nations, "according to every Nation's and People's Property; so that every Nation and People does use, or bear forth the same only Word according to its Property" (35:47). This idea is reiterated by Blake in *All Religions are One*, one of his early tractates that identify the Incarnation with the process of perception and the source of all life, order, and significance. Identifying Boehme's concept of the Word as the Poetic Genius or the Spirit of Prophecy, Blake maintains that "all sects of Philosophy are from the Poetic Genius adapted to the weaknesses of every individual" and that "the Religeons of all Nations are derived from each Nation's different reception of the Poetic Genius which is every where call'd the Spirit of Prophecy" (p. 2). Furthermore, in *There is No Natural Religion[b]* Blake more explicitly adopts the Augustinian concept of the five senses deriving divine power through the Incarnation. What Boehme calls Babel, "the external Form and the Division" of the Word (35:47) that resulted from man's attachment to self-will and the material world, Blake identifies as "Reason or the ratio of all we have already known" (p. 2). Blake then states that man can perceive God only by appropriating godlike powers of perception through the enactment of the Incarnation within each individual: "He who sees the

Infinite in all things sees God. He who sees the Ratio only sees himself only. Therefore God becomes as we are, that we may be as he is" (p. 2). Like Boehme and St. Augustine, Blake believed what had become a commonplace in seventeenth-century religious and aesthetic thought—that everything on earth is the Word of God, the book of God's creatures; that as a result of the Fall man lost his ability to understand this divine language; and that the Bible provided the means of regaining that lost language both by presenting sensory phenomena as signs and by representing the deity as the source and the process of signification that is available to everyone through identification with the deity.

This Christological or incarnational rhetoric, wherein all the senses are employed to raise man to vision and thereby to a perception of the infinite through identification with the body of Christ, provides the rationale for the use of synesthesia and a combination of media in any work that purports to be divinely inspired. For, if the Incarnation represents the unity of body and soul, subject and object, the individual and the community (which is traditionally identified as the mystical body of Christ), then this unity is effected and expressed by the complete interdependence and integration of all the bodily senses. This metaphor of the body is expressed in I Corinthians 12, which Augustine paraphrases:

> You can see in our bodies, brothers, how our limbs each have their jobs. The eye sees, it doesn't hear; the ear hears, it doesn't see; the hand works, it doesn't see or hear; the foot walks, it doesn't see or hear or do what the hand does. But if there is health in the one body, and its parts are not quarreling among themselves, the ear does see—with the eye; the eye does hear—with the ear.[81]

Just as within the healthy body each member retains its identity, yet participates in and enjoys the powers of the other members, so do all the members of the Church, which is Christ's body, enjoy each other's gifts in a community of brotherhood and love. Thus, each Christian works miracles because Peter worked miracles, since all members function as part of the whole. This is straight Pauline doctrine that Augustine is elaborating upon, though Paul does not describe the integration of the body of Christ in terms of synesthesia.

Boehme emphasizes the same Pauline doctrine and, like Augustine, uses the language of synesthesia to describe the process of unification. In *Aurora* (1612) Boehme identifies the five senses with the "Five Qualifying or Fountain-Spirits" of God. "As the Members of Man's Body love one another, so do the Spirits also in the *Divine* Power," and when the spirits are unified, there is a joyous co-mingling, whereby each of the senses enjoys the powers of the others: "And so there is nothing else but a *hearty*, loving and friendly Aspect of Seeing, a curious Smelling, a good Relishing or Tasting and lovely Feeling, a gracious, amiable, *blessed* Kissing, a Feeding upon and Drinking of one another, and lovely Walking and *Conversing* together."[82]

Boehme's description of the mingling and gratification of all the senses alludes to the manifold sensual joys described in the Song of Solomon. Boehme also explicitly reinforces this allusion by stating that the union of the five fountain-spirits is the union of the bride and the bridegroom,[83] which is the scriptural metaphor, in Canticles and elsewhere, for the Incarnation and the apocalyptic marriage of Christ and his church. The biblical allusion points to a conception of biblical rhetoric that both Boehme and Augustine advanced: that the union of the members within Christ's body, whereby each of the senses partakes of all the others, is duplicated by the language of the Bible, through the use of synesthesia and the interplay of aural signs and signs that appeal to the other senses. The crowded metaphors, far-fetched analogies, and rapidly-shifting images of biblical poetry all serve to rouse the faculties to act, to create a reintegration of the senses and a reenactment of the Incarnation within the individual and within the Christian community. Thus biblical rhetoric serves its prophetic function by imitating the process that it seeks to instill in its audience, the integration of the individual into the body of Christ.

Since union with Christ is the ultimate goal of Christianity, we find Blake expressing this theme throughout his work—sometimes expressing a fairly orthodox point of view and other times giving the doctrine some radical twists.[84] When, in his annotations to Lavater's *Aphorisms on Man*, Blake writes, "every thing on earth is the word of God" (p. 589), he is reiterating the traditional idea of the world as the Book of Creatures whose significance can only be apprehended through Christ. Besides encountering Boehme's idea of the world as part of the "holy mental Tongue," Blake would have encountered a similar idea in Swedenborg's doctrine of correspondences between natural and spiritual things. Blake's concern with the theme of the Incarnation also appears in *Jerusalem*, where he says that every man is "a Divine Member of the Divine Jesus" (91:30); this echoes the ideas of Augustine, Swedenborg, Boehme, and a host of other theologians and biblical commentators. But Blake's identification of Christ with the Imagination in his early tractates and in his annotations to Berkeley's *Siris* (p. 654) appears to be the unique contribution of Boehme and Swedenborg to his thought,[85] though the idea of Christ as the first principle of perception goes back at least to St. Augustine. From Swedenborg, Blake also received the idea that the function of the imagination was to transform the world of sense into human form, and the idea of the divine humanity: "God is Man & Exists in us & we in him" (*Annotations to Berkeley*, p. 654).[86]

But besides these various doctrinal points surrounding the Incarnation, Blake also appears to be aware of the rhetorical implications of the Incarnation as Augustine and others perceived them. In the climactic plate of the Job series (pl. 17), Blake's main inscription reads, "I have heard thee with the hearing of the Ear but now my Eyes see thee," which is adapted from Job 42:5. This quotation, which describes theophany as a joining of sight and sound, is juxtaposed with a series of quotations in the lower margin taken from John 14, one of the main biblical passages that articulate the union of God, Christ, and Man. Blake quotes most of the following passage:

> And I will pray the Father, and he shall give you another Comforter, that he may abide with you for ever; Even the Spirit of truth; whom the world cannot receive, because it seeth him not, neither knoweth him: but ye know him; for he dwelleth with you, and shall be in you. I will not leave you comfortless: I will come to you. . . . At that day ye shall know that I am in my Father, and ye in me, and I in you. (John 14:16-18, 14:20)

By juxtaposing the quotation from Job with those from John, Blake clearly equates the process of vision—the combined ability to see and hear—with the process of identifying with Christ. In other words, to see and hear God is to become God; the union of the senses within the body of the perceiver imitates the wholeness of Christ's body and effects a union with that body.

The same idea is developed in *The Marriage of Heaven and Hell*, where Blake invokes the theme of Christ's body. Blake's infernal or diabolical interpretation of the passage from John 14 is that the Comforter is Desire, which Reason needs in order to "have Ideas to build on" (pl. 6). Although Blake is satirically mocking the pretensions of those who believe in a philosophy founded upon unaided Reason, he is serious about the idea that it is only through the activation of the senses, by Christ or the Poetic Genius, that true knowledge can be achieved. We see this in the early tractates.

The Incarnation also is the theme of the last "Memorable Fancy" of *The Marriage*, the biblical context of which is I Corinthians 12, the same passage that is so important to

83

Augustine and Boehme. The Pauline context of this last section of *The Marriage* is appropriate, since Blake's final vision describes a conversion experience and since the idea of identification with Christ is essential to the Christian concept of conversion.[87] The Pauline epistle is alluded to in the opening speech by the Devil, for whom the Poetic Genius or Imagination is Christ. The Devil states that membership in Christ's body is effected by the enjoyment, through the senses, of the fruits of one's genius and the genius of others: "The worship of God is. Honouring his gifts in other men each according to his genius. and loving the greatest men best, those who envy or calumniate great men hate God, for there is no other God" (*MHH*, plates 22, 23). Not only can this Devil quote Scripture but he offers an interpretation that, however radical, is true to the spirit of the Pauline doctrine of a Christian community held together by love, in which all members enjoy the gifts of God that each has received. The Devil is a true orator because he shows the Angel that it is only through the body—and not through abstract laws—that God becomes man and man becomes God. Given the Devil's definition of Christ as a man enjoying the fires of genius, acting from impulse and not rules, the Angel signals his conversion by identifying, through the senses, with Christ: he stretches his arms out and embraces the fires of genius. In so doing, he effects a marriage in the sense that Boehme describes it, a union with Christ through the reintegration of the senses. Furthermore, the converted Angel, who is transformed into the prophet Elijah and who befriends the narrator, realizes within the macrocosm the Pauline ideal of the community as the body of Christ. Manifesting and sharing the gifts of prophecy, which Paul considers to be the most important spiritual gift within the Christian community (I Corinthians 14), the newly converted Angel— along with the prophet-narrator—forms part of Christ's body as it is defined by Blake's Devil and St. Paul.

Blake's idea of the union between man and God and

between man and man through the Poetic Genius is most explicitly stated in the *Laocoön* engraving:

The Eternal Body of Man is The IMAGINATION

that is $\left.\begin{array}{l} \text{God himself} \\ \\ \text{The Divine Body} \end{array}\right\}$ [Yeshua] JESUS we are his members

It manifests itself in his Works of Art (In Eternity ALL is Vision). (p. 271)

In the Bible and in all other works of visionary art, then, the senses are engaged through the imagination to enact the process by which they unite in the body of Christ. The Bible is the great code of art because it contains and inculcates the highest form of mimesis, the *imitatio dei*, which for Blake is the imitation of the actual process of vision. This rhetoric of vision that employs all *sensibilia* to transform the reader-viewer-auditor into the body of Christ was implicitly understood by St. Augustine, Boehme, Fénelon, Swedenborg, and Jones; and this rhetoric formed the basis of Blake's composite art.

Sublime Allegory:
Blake's Use of Typology

As we have seen, Blake follows biblical tradition in maintaining that the Bible employs the universal language of symbolism and that the preeminence of the Bible rests upon its recognition of God as the power that transforms *sensibilia* into signs and upon its use of the figure of Jesus, the incarnate Word, as an archetypal symbol of the process of signification. Blake states these ideas explicitly in his *Descriptive Catalogue*: "The antiquities of every Nation under Heaven, is no less sacred than that of the Jews. . . . All had originally one language, and one religion, this was the religion of Jesus, the everlasting Gospel. Antiquity preaches the Gospel of Jesus" (p. 534). Here Blake reiterates much of what he had already said in the early tractates and in *The Marriage of Heaven and Hell*, but the last sentence and the context of these remarks expand upon Blake's concept of the nature of biblical symbolism. As part of Blake's claim of fidelity to fact in his painting, *The Ancient Britons*, the comments above form a critique of eighteenth-century historiography and posit a theory of the relationship of symbolism to history. In addition to making the apparently nonhistorical comment about the presence of the Gospel in all antiquities, Blake castigates the "reasoning historian, turner and twister of causes and consequences, . . . who does not see spiritual agency" and who rejects certain acts because they seem improbable or impossible (p. 534). Blake holds that "Acts themselves alone are history" and that the historian's reasoning and opinions are rubbish (p. 534). If all antiquities speak the language of Jesus—that is, the language of symbolism—then the proper interpretation of history is available to the reader who is conversant with that language. For such a reader, "the history of all times and places is nothing else but improbabilities and impossibilities" (p. 534), which are validated and given significance by the Gospel of Jesus.

Blake is here distinguishing history as *kairos* from history as *chronos*, that is, history as a number of moments containing divine and "intemporal significance"[1] from history based upon clock time. Blake rejects the latter concept, asserting instead that without the presence of spiritual agency history is meaningless and that the Gospel of Jesus provides the principles upon which human history is organized. Throughout his discussion of *The Ancient Britons*, Blake gives a practical application of these principles. Immediately preceding his critique of modern historians, Blake presents an alternative historical method, using the figure of Albion: "The giant Albion, was Patriarch of the Atlantic; he is the Atlas of the Greeks, one of those the Greeks called Titans. The stories of Arthur are the acts of Albion, applied to a Prince of the fifth century, who conquered Europe, and held the Empire of the world in the dark age, which the Romans never again recovered" (p. 534). This application of a paradigmatic figure to different times and places also occurs in other parts of his notes on *The Ancient Britons*: in Blake's assertion that the Hebrew patriarchs were Druids (p. 533), and in his explanation of the significance of the three Britons in his painting. In the former, Blake is anachronistically projecting biblical figures into early British history, and in the latter, he further develops this principle by using a quotation from the Book of Daniel (3:25) to identify the three Britons with the three men cast into the fiery furnace: "and the form of the fourth was like the Son of God" (p. 533).

While Blake's Hebraizing of the Druidic age is most immediately derived from the eighteenth-century mythographers,[2] the practice of the mythographers is part of a tradition that extends back to the Puritans and ultimately the

87

CHAPTER IV

Bible itself. The anachronistic placing of the Hebrew patriarchs in ancient Britain is an extension of the Puritan idea of England as an elect nation or the New Israel, an idea employed by Milton in *Areopagitica*.[3] The rationale for this disregard of chronological order in history is expressed in Blake's concept of history as a series of wondrous acts whose relationship to one another is thematic rather than causal. Such a concept of history juxtaposes events, things, or persons from different time periods in order to relate them to a central theme or paradigm that transcends the world of time and causality. This practice and the historiography that informs it are derived from the Bible and constitute the method of interpretation and literary construction known as typology. Blake's invocation of this biblical tradition in his *Descriptive Catalogue* points to the essentially typological content and structure of Blake's imaginative vision in all his works.

The subject of typology and its use in literature and literary analysis has received a great deal of attention in recent years, but we have no more reached a precise definition of this symbolic system than Blake's contemporaries had. In Blake's time the word "type" was used very loosely, often interchangeably with "prophecy," "emblem," "symbol," "hieroglyph," "allegory," and "figure."[4] Today we can distinguish the different senses in which the term can be applied, but we have not reached a definition of typology upon which all people agree. In its strictest sense, typology involves a relationship between two biblical events, persons, or things that have a reality and a significance in and of themselves but that also share a special relationship in which one event, person, or thing is said to be a type or foreshadowing of the other.[5] To take an example from Blake, in "Samson" from *Poetical Sketches*, the potential deliverer of the Hebrews is depicted as a type of Christ through the representation of Dalila, who sells her lord for gold (p. 434), as a type of Judas; through the emphasis upon Samson's being a Nazarite; and through the rewording of the angel's annunciation of Samson's birth in Judges 13:5 to make it echo the Annunciation in Luke 1:28: "Hail, highly favoured! said he; for lo, thou shalt conceive, and bear a son" (p. 436). Here Blake is employing a conventional interpretation of the Samson story, whereby the Old Testament character is seen as a foreshadowing or promise of Christ.[6] While the Old Testament figure is recognized as having an independent reality, it is also considered to be a shadow (*umbra*) of its New Testament counterpart, which is considered to be the truth (*veritas*) or the fulfillment of the Old Testament figure.[7] In the Pauline Epistles and in the writings of the church fathers, the New Testament figure is considered to be the *forma perfector* and the Old Testament figure the *forma inferior*, much as the sculptor's original model can be said to be said to be inferior to the finished work of art.[8]

This orthodox conception of typology is clear enough, but it is complicated by the fact that typology also has its eschatological applications, whereby some exegetes perceived the New Testament as only a partial fulfillment of Old Testament types and expected the ultimate fulfillment to take place at the apocalypse. These commentators, among whom was St. Augustine, divided typology into three phases: the Old Testament period, which contained figures promising the coming of Christ; the New Testament period up until the coming of Christ, which promised eternal life and the kingdom of heaven; and the period after the coming of Christ, which will contain the realization of the promise of all biblical types.[9]

Thus far we have been looking at typology as a method of biblical exegesis, but it is also a method of literary construction, with the principles of typological exegesis derived from very clear and pronounced uses of typology in the Bible.[10] In The Gospel according to St. Matthew, for instance, Jesus proclaims that Jonah, who spent three days and three nights in the belly of the whale, was a type of the

Son of Man, whose body will remain in the tomb three days and three nights before the Resurrection (Matthew 12:40). Similarly, the brazen serpent raised by Moses in Numbers 21:9 is cited as a type of Christ's crucifixion in John 3:14. But this kind of typological literary structure is also present in the Old Testament, as Lowth points out in his ninth lecture, which is devoted to biblical imagery taken from the sacred history of the Hebrews.[11] There he remarks that one unique feature of Hebrew poetry that distinguishes it from that of other nations is its continued use of allusions to significant events from the past, particularly through images referring to chaos and the Creation, the Flood, the destruction of Sodom, the exodus from Egypt, and the delivery of the Law at Sinai. Although he treats this imagery as metaphor, Lowth recognizes that many of the images that he cites should more properly be called allegory, specifically the "sublimer kind of allegory" employed by the biblical prophets.[12] This sublime or mystical allegory is Lowth's term for what we and his contemporaries recognize as typology.[13] Lowth points out that imagery from sacred history is to be found predominantly in the writings of the prophets, who would, for instance, cite the Exodus as a type of future delivery from present afflictions.[14] Similar uses of typology in the Old Testament have been noted by modern scholars; Auerbach has emphasized the invocation of Moses and Exodus imagery by Old Testament writers as types of the coming messianic age; and A. C. Charity observes that typology and typological thinking are essential to Old Testament theology.[15]

Despite the various conceptions of typology as literary construct and exegetical method that I have thus far described, almost all strict definitions of typology insist upon the historical reality of each of the figures in a typological relationship. Furthermore, since most discussions of typology deal primarily with Christian typology, most critics agree that typology in its strictest sense is Christocentric, having only Christ as its object.[16] This historical and

Christocentric construction supposedly sets limits that would distinguish typology from allegory and prevent typology from becoming an arbitrary method of interpretation. The traditionally loose construction of the Christological significance of typology, however, allows a great deal of latitude in interpretation, for the object of typology is Christ in the widest accepted sense, "the whole Christ," as Jean Daniélou has stated:

> The Christological meaning can be subdivided into as many sections as there are aspects in Christ himself. Christ may be considered either as a historical Person manifested in the events recorded in the Gospel, or living a hidden life in the "sacraments" of the Church which is his body, or as appearing at the parousia at the end of the world and reigning in glory. Further, these three *adventus*, to use a term of St. Augustine's, have more than one side to them. In the historical Christ we may consider either the external actions of his earthly life or the spiritual content of its mysteries. In the mystical Christ, again, we may consider either the collective aspect, which is the whole Church, or the separate members, each of whom has "put on" Christ (Romans 13:14; Galatians 3:27).[17]

Thus, every biblical type points to Christ, who "recapitulates all things in himself."[18]

The insistence on the historicity of each biblical type, like the insistence on the Christocentric nature of all types, does not really set fixed limits upon typology, for history was often read allegorically and the concept of history itself was often expanded to include myth. In the New Testament, we find parallels between two historical events, persons, or things whose connection is made possible only by allegorical interpretation. A case in point is Paul's representation of Sarah as a type of the new Jerusalem, the covenant of the spirit as opposed to that of the flesh, the latter being embodied in the figure of Hagar, the bond-

91

woman (Galatians 4:23-31). Another example is the use of Melchizedek as a type of Christ in the Epistle to the Hebrews (5:6-10, 6:20, 7), where the connection between the two figures is made clear only through allegorization.[19] Much more extreme than either of these two examples from the Bible is the interpretation by the church fathers of Rahab's scarlet thread (Joshua 2:18) as a type of salvation through the blood of Christ.[20] This movement away from a literal to an allegorical conception of history was extended to the point at which pagan history and myth were also incorporated into the typological framework. Paul himself had, through an allusion, drawn a parallel between Aratus' Zeus and Jehovah (Acts 17:28), and the practice of combining pagan and Christian types was employed from the time of the church fathers to the eighteenth century.[21]

We can see this expansion of the boundaries of typology, which is latent in the Bible itself, when we look briefly at the development of typology from its beginnings through the eighteenth century. While the typological method is explicitly present in the New Testament, its popularity as an exegetical instrument received its strongest impetus from St. Augustine, who used it to demonstrate the unity of the Old and New Testaments and to reconcile two dominant but conflicting schools of biblical exegesis: the Alexandrian school, whose Hellenistic tendencies led it to allegorize the Bible to the point of undermining the historicity of biblical narrative, and the Antiochene school, which emphasized the literal sense of the Bible.[22] Through typology Augustine was able to preserve the literal sense of the Scriptures and at the same time retain his interest in Neoplatonism.[23] He could assert that within the Bible *visibilia* are shadows of the divine world but could center that divine world within the figure of Christ, the meeting point of the human and the divine, the historical and the eternal.[24]

Although Augustine did not invent typology, his pro-

92

found and thorough development of this method of exegesis firmly established it as an important part of biblical tradition.[25] As Mazzeo points out, typology operated within and subsumed the traditional fourfold method of allegory that was first formulated by John Cassian and became the exegetical norm in the middle ages:

> The allegorical sense, *sensu stricto*, was the meaning of an Old Testament text applied to Christ or to the church Militant. The tropological or moral sense applied the text to the soul and its virtues. The anagogical sense applied the text to heavenly realities. Thus the psalm, *In exitu Israel de Aegypto*, a favorite example which Dante also uses, might be interpreted as follows: the literal sense is simply a reference to Exodus, the allegorical sense might be to Christ as a true Moses whose death and resurrection have led mankind out of bondage, the moral or tropological sense might be the passage of the soul from sin to virtue, while the anagogical sense might be the passage of the soul from this world to the heavenly hereafter. Obviously, a good deal of exegetical latitude is possible even with Cassian's formula. Nevertheless, the historicity of the method is clear. A historical event from the history of Israel leads to one from the history of Christianity, next to the "history" of the soul in its moral drama, and last to the eschatological reality which sets a term to history.[26]

Of course, allegorical exegesis of a more abstract and nonhistorical nature subsisted alongside typological exegesis; "nevertheless, Christian allegorism remained bound to events in the conviction that sacred history was both a system of events and a system of signs, illuminating analogically both the nature of the human soul and its ultimate destiny in time and beyond."[27]

Thus from the fourth century onward, typology persisted as a part of exegetical tradition and Christian thinking, reinforced by its appearance in sermons, in art, in the

93

chapter headings of the Authorized Version of the Bible, and even in the liturgy.[28] Typology reached its height of popularity during the Reformation, however, when it was invoked to solve a particular exegetical problem. Once the authority of the Catholic church declined and the reading of vernacular translations of the Bible became an integral part of the Protestant scheme of salvation, Protestant reformers felt the need to set limits upon biblical interpretation to ensure the right hearing of the word of God and prevent the excesses of subjective interpretation. And typology provided those limits.[29] Tyndale, Luther, and Calvin employed and encouraged the typological interpretation of the Bible, distinguishing typology, as a method rooted in the literal sense of the Bible, from the more subjective allegorizations associated with the Alexandrian school and with medieval scholasticism.[30]

Although the Reformers thus limited allegorical interpretation of the Bible by insisting upon the historicity of both terms of a biblical analogy, the sixteenth and seventeenth centuries saw an expansion of the ways in which this historicity was applied. More radical Protestants, especially the Puritans in the seventeenth century, who were concerned with justifying their preference for the Old Testament, would often reverse the typological process and Christianize the Old Testament—to the point of disregarding the historicity of Jesus and asserting that Adam was the first Christian.[31] They also began to apply typology to contemporary events, both in the life of the community and in the lives of individuals, though this practice was not invented or employed exclusively by radical Puritans.[32] Following the traditions of saints' lives and the imitation of Christ tradition, individual Christians began to find parallels between their own lives and those of Jesus and other biblical figures.[33] On the communal level, Puritans in England and America perceived themselves as the true inheritors of the biblical covenant, the elect nation, and began to draw parallels between events in the life of the community and the events of biblical history.[34] Not only identifying with the Israel of the Old Testament but also with the New Israel of the millennium, the Puritans extended their typology both backward and forward in time, relating contemporary events to events depicted in the historical books of the Bible as well as to events predicted in the eschatological parts of the Bible.[35] Furthermore, Puritans and other Christians in the seventeenth century made extensive application of biblical typology to pagan history and myth.[36]

All of these looser applications of typology that were developed in the seventeenth century persisted well into the late eighteenth and early nineteenth centuries. The use of pagan types and the application of biblical types to the lives of individuals increased in popularity among English writers, and the political application of typology, although it abated after the Restoration,[37] was revived at the end of the eighteenth century under the impetus of the American and French revolutions.[38] The vitality of the typological tradition is attested to by the fact that Thomas Paine, who attacked typology in *The Age of Reason*, understood its force well enough to employ it in *Common Sense*, where he likened King George to Pharaoh.[39] This continuation—and even the further expansion—of typology and typological thought in the eighteenth century was promoted by the writings of Lowth, Warburton, Volney, Bryant, Price, Hartley, Butler, and virtually every commentator on the Book of Revelation.[40] These and other writers of the time often applied biblical types to contemporary events, but some also recognized and popularized typology as a valid means of thought and expression that could be applied to nonreligious contexts, such as secular interpretations of natural phenomena, human behavior, and history.[41]

Thus we can see in Blake's time the completion of a process that had begun much earlier, the separation of typology from its original exegetical and theological contexts, forming what Paul Korshin has called "abstracted typology," that is, typology that has been "drawn away from the theological field of action, although there may be religious significance in the way in which each [type] is introduced."[42] To be sure, strict typology, which was most elaborately codified in the seventeenth century,[43] continued to be widely used as a method of biblical exegesis in the late eighteenth century,[44] but the very presence of strict typology in Christian education and thought insured the transportation of typology into secular contexts. Within these new contexts, typology persisted as a structure that is recurrent, predictive, and transcendent. Korshin finds this to be particularly true for the development of eighteenth-century fiction, which employed the character type, the individual character who represents a generalized class of humanity that exists everywhere and at all times, whose behavior within the fiction can be predicted by the reader, and whose behavior in the real world is predicted by the fiction.[45] This relationship between the fictive world and a reality beyond the fiction is, for Korshin, a distinguishing characteristic of types, which he describes as signs having a semiotic existence beyond the fictional structure that contains them:

> These figures would qualify semiotically as non-linguistic symbols, which can be shifted from one text to another, always keeping the same approximate significance. . . . Like numbers, they are in a class by themselves, expressed through the medium of language, but usually visual or semiological, working on a plane separate from language. They may be seen as a sort of non-visual iconography.[46]

Lowth makes the same point when he distinguishes Hebrew from pagan uses of images drawn from history, observing that the Hebrew images retain the same meaning regardless of the context in which they are placed, each image designating "a universal or unlimited idea."[47] Like these biblical figures, the figures that belong to abstracted typol-

ogy are distinguished from other kinds of images in that
typological persons, events, and places recur within time
and depend upon the reader's remembering and recogniz-
ing their appearance in past and future contexts: "The cir-
cumstances of abstracted typology have an accepted and
acknowledged history of their own; a writer who uses an
abstracted type could expect—or hope—that some of his
audience would spot the connection."[48]

This idea of typology as a structure that is dependent
upon the principle of recurrence is, according to Joseph A.
Mazzeo, the basis of all fictions that are deliberately con-
structed as allegories. Such fictions

> assume the existence of a central paradigmatic story, of
> a sacred or near-sacred character, set in the past and as-
> sumed to be historical, or which we are asked to believe
> as historical fiction. This story appears as an archetypal
> pattern of the story told in the literal sense of the text,
> and the author, through metaphor and allusion and,
> above all, personification, reminds us of the correspond-
> ence between "then" and "now." The archetypal story is
> the pattern for events of permanent significance repeated
> now in the life of everyman in an individual mode. What
> was once "history," whether in the Bible, Homer, or
> Virgil, has now entered memory, has been detemporal-
> ized, and is relived as fictional event in the actions of the
> protagonist, and as spiritual event in the consciousness of
> the reader. Allegory thus takes account of the historicity
> of the paradigmatic story, its repeatability as a fiction set
> in a new time and place, and the significance of the his-
> tory and its corresponding fiction for an analogous spir-
> itual or psychological event taking place in the conscious-
> ness of the reader.[49]

Thus biblical typology becomes abstracted into a literary
structure based upon the principle of recurrence, derived
from the belief that certain archetypal fictions need to be
retold so as to be applicable to the present.

97

Abstracted typology became not only a literary structure but also a structure of thought that persisted long after the original theological and biblical contexts of typology had been discarded. Referring to the survival of such a typological structure in nineteenth-century American thought and literature, Karl Keller sees this structure as the process by which the facts of everyday life or nature are perceived to be types that proceed from and are organized by a divine antitype:

> From a structuralist point of view, the distinctions are insignificant between the antitype of Winthrop's city upon a hill, Sewell's fulfilled America, Cotton's phenomenalized Christ, Taylor's attention-giving Love-Jesus, Mather's heroic New England, Edwards' will, and Emerson's imperial self. They all get their worlds going . . . by conceiving of a Christ who is the means and the end of all else in their purview.[50]

This looser form of typology is distinguished from mere platonizing because it retains its essentially Christological base, maintaining that things can become signs only through the incarnation of Christ, the "whole Christ," however loosely He is defined: "Things are not merely synecdoches . . . but *made* synecdoches by the force of the strong outpouring of desire from a god-figure on things."[51] More importantly, for American Romantics like Emerson, Thoreau, and Whitman, the antitypal Christ is identified with that which is Christlike in individual men, the ability to create or re-create the world in accord with one's expanded perceptions.[52] At this stage, however, Keller observes, the antitype, completely loosed from its biblical moorings or from any principle of historical recurrence, becomes unworkable because it lapses either into metaphysical fuzziness or egotism, and the failure of typology in nineteenth-century America to extract confidently any universal significance from things is chronicled by Hawthorne, Melville, and Twain.[53]

What began as a theological strategy that was devised and employed to validate the message of the New Testament and to preserve the sanctity and the integrity of the Bible in the face of certain historical pressures developed into a revolutionary polemic, a concept of history, a literary structure, and an epistemology. Of course, orthodox typology also served all of these functions in varying degrees, but the development of typological thought since the age of Augustine saw the abstraction of these functions from their original theological center. Although as literary critics it is important for us to distinguish between strict typology and its looser forms, it is also important for us to recognize that artists in the seventeenth and eighteenth centuries often did not make these distinctions.[54] This is certainly the case with Blake, who uses typology both in its strictest and broadest senses. By defining Christ as the Imagination, Blake adopts as his subject the typological process itself. We can locate precise examples of Blake's strict use of typology in as early a work as *Samson*, as we have already seen, and in as late a work as *The Ghost of Abel*, which invokes the Epistle to Hebrews—a book that is in itself a work of typological exegesis—to draw parallels and emphasize differences between the death of Abel and Christ's atonement.[55] But Blake more frequently employs abstracted typology, in order to show typology to be the means by which the human mind creatively transforms reality.

Typology, for Blake, is synonymous with the creative process itself. The discovery or the creation of signs is a typological process in that all imaginative activity is a re-enactment of the Incarnation, the process whereby the human and the divine merge through the imaginative transformation of the objects of sense into human form. This point Blake states explicitly in the *Laocoön* engraving, where he identifies the Imagination as the Eternal Body of Man, Jesus, of which every person is a member and which manifests itself in works of art (p. 271). Within the Laocoön engraving, Blake presents illustrations of this process, particularly in his typological interpretation of the sculpture itself. For Blake, the Greek statue is a representation of Jehovah and his two sons, Adam and Satan, "as they were copied from the Cherubim of Solomon's Temple by three Rhodians & applied to Natural Fact or. History of Ilium" (p. 270). Blake was aware that the cherubim of Solomon's temple, fashioned according to the pattern that God had implanted in David's mind (I Chronicles 28:12, 28:19), were a type of the cherubim that Moses, whose mind was also implanted with the divine pattern, had erected on the mercy seat when the tabernacle was constructed (Exodus 25:9, 25:17-22). Since the holy of holies in which the cherubim were depicted was, according to the Epistle to the Hebrews, the pattern or type—the Greek Testament uses the word *typos*—of heaven (Hebrews 8:5), the cherubim were understood to represent the inhabitants of heaven, identified by Blake as "The Hosts of Heaven" (p. 271). Furthermore, according to the most widely read and respected Hebrew lexicon of the time, Parkhurst's *Hebrew and English Lexicon* (1762), the cherubim, because they were cast in human form, represent the various divine attributes that were united to man through the Son. Parkhurst explains that the cherubim were instituted at the time of Adam, were preserved by Noah and seen by Ezekiel in his vision of the chariot of God (Ezekiel 1); these sacred emblems not only recur throughout the Old and New Testaments but also appear in pagan history, although in impure form, as the gods of the various heathen nations.[56]

Given this understanding of the cherubim as emblems or types of Christ whose original forms were dictated by God and copied by the artists of all nations, art becomes for Blake the organization of human perception and experience—in the case of the *Laocoön*, the history of Troy—according to a divine pattern or archetype. This archetype is not an abstract Platonic Idea but the human form itself,

the body of Christ, the eternal body of man. Blake empha-
sizes this point by distinguishing the gods of Priam from
those of Greece and Egypt: "The Gods of Priam are the
Cherubim of Moses & Solomon The Hosts of Heaven. The
Gods of Greece & Egypt were Mathematical Diagrams. See
Plato's Works" (*Laocoön*, p. 271). Implicit in these remarks
is the distinction between typology, which always points to
Christ, and allegory, which always points to abstractions—
a topic to which I will return.

Blake's reference to the cherubim further identifies art
with typology because of the Bible's identification of the
temple, in which the cherubim reside, with the body of
Christ (John 2:19, 2:21; Hebrews 10:20). The cherubim are
identified in *The Descriptive Catalogue* as the "wonderful
originals" of Asia that the Greeks and Hertrurians copied
(p. 522). The Greek gods were originally the "Cherubim of
Phoenicia," and the gods of both Greece and Troy are "vi-
sions of the eternal attributes, or divine names" represented
by the cherubim, which were originally part of "jesus the
Saviour, the vine of Eternity" (p. 527). Insofar as they are
separated from the temple, the divine humanity, and be-
come elevated to the status of gods, the cherubim lose their
visionary quality and degenerate into allegory, becoming
destructive to humanity (p. 527). Conversely, when they
are perceived as types of a divine original, the gods of
Priam and of Greece become the servants of man, in that
they are perceived to be "Visions of . . . eternal principles
or characters of human life [that] appear to poets, in all
ages" (p. 527). Their manifestation in classical art—as in
the sculptures of Venus, Minerva, Jupiter, and Apollo—
would be recognized as "representations of God's immortal,
to the mortal perishing organ of sight" (p. 532).

This incarnational principle of art, which asserts that a
spirit and a vision exist only in human form, "organized
and minutely articulated beyond all that the mortal and

101

perishing nature can produce," was recognized by the biblical Prophets and Apostles, who "describe what they saw in Vision as real and existing men whom they saw with their imaginative and immortal organs" (p. 532). Like the real and existing men who appear in the Bible, and like the cherubim of the Asiatic patriarchs, the gods of classical art and literature are modeled upon the only form that spirit can ever take and the only true object of worship, the human form divine, the Imagination, which continually asserts the centrality of man and subsumes all history, all art, and all mythology to this purpose. Even the cherubim, those grand originals, are subservient to man, as Blake asserted early in his career: "Man is the ark of God the mercy seat is above upon the ark cherubims guard it on either side & in the midst is the holy law man is either the ark of God or a phantom of the earth & of the water" (*Annotations to Lavater*, p. 585). As in the Epistle to the Hebrews, the holy of holies and all its appurtenances are types of the whole Christ, the human form divine. Thus, for Blake, all imaginative activity begins and ends with Christ, and all cultural artifacts typologically represent the members of the divine body of God, the human form itself.

The typological process, for Blake, manifests itself not only in the relationship between the work of art and the world of the senses but also in the relationship between artifacts of different cultures and different periods. We see in Blake's identification of the cherubim of Moses and Solomon with the gods of Priam the principles behind the continuity of artistic tradition, and these principles are contained within the Bible. If we recall the obvious fact that the Bible essentially consists of two texts, the Old and the New Testaments, each marking a significantly different era of human history, and if we recall that the New Testament adopts the most significant symbols from the Old Testament in order to interpret, criticize, and transform the form and content of the earlier text—at the same time that it claims both to fulfill and supplant that text—then we can see why Blake believed that all cultures preached the Gospel of Jesus. The Gospel itself is a paradigm of the process by which a new culture creates its own artifacts.

Focusing more specifically on the creation of literature, we can see, as Frank Kermode has suggested, that the intertextuality of the Old and New Testaments is a model for the fictive process itself and that this intertextuality is established by that figural or typological process.[57] Modern biblical scholars, as well as biblical commentators of Blake's time, have been aware that the Gospels were strongly influenced by rabbinical exegesis and that the New Testament evolved out of the interpretation of the Old Testament, containing within itself that interpretation,[58] partially in the form of explicit statement, but also—and most pronouncedly—in the form of symbols. By applying the symbols from a previous text to a new context, the new text establishes its own credibility and reaffirms the value of the older text by repeating a paradigmatic story that both share.[59] In the Old Testament, this paradigmatic story is the *Heilsgeschichte*, the miraculous intervention of God in human history that would culminate in the coming of a Messiah and the union of man and God through the transformation of the world into the kingdom of God.[60] By placing this paradigmatic story in a new context, the New Testament validates and supplants the previous text by claiming to be a more perfect embodiment of the paradigm.[61] The meaning of the paradigm is retained, but its significance is altered by the new context.[62] Thus the New Testament reaffirms the pattern of God's salvific plan in history but changes the terms in which that plan is realized, positing a dispensation of grace in contrast with the dispensation of the law. A case in point is the image of paschal lamb, which in the Old Testament commemorates God's delivery of Israel out of Egypt (Exodus 12), and which in the New Testament is identified with Christ, the true paschal lamb (I Corinthians 5:7), whose sacrifice enacts God's delivery of the new Israel and abolishes the Mosaic

103

law that prescribes the yearly ritual sacrifice of the paschal lamb.

What distinguishes the Bible from other cultural artifacts and makes it a sacred text is, as Frye has pointed out, that its paradigm claims to encompass all of human existence and all of human time.[63] Another distinction, which is actually a corollary of Frye's point, is that the text embodies and encourages a dialectical relationship between itself and history. Through its typological structure, the text is always pointing to and impinging upon realities beyond the text, realities which in turn modify it. Through the use of types, the text itself is a meeting point of human history and the divine reality: it projects forward and backward into history and upward to God, bringing the temporal and the eternal to bear upon the present moment in order to promote faith and call man to a new existence through the realization that the Word is eternally present.[64] Unlike myth, which is essentially conservative in its encouragement of the reader to identify with an established archetype, biblical typology asserts that the types must be constantly renewed in the face of historical change:

> Typology in both Testaments does not exist to inhibit God's speaking any word but a word from a past grown rigid; it is used instead to allow the right hearing of a word which concerns the present and is new. It was thus the call at the Exodus must have struck home to Israel, compared with the ancient 'archetypes'. But when the act of God at the Exodus lost its precarious dependence upon faith and became, or seemed to become, their possession, which nothing could shake or alter, and so itself only an 'archetype', a 'security', preventing the hearing of God's new word and the seeing of his new act, it was thus, in turn that a word of the future was spoken, which would correspond to the past but transcend it. This is how genuine typology works in the Bible always.[65]

104

Thus in Isaiah 43:16-21 the Exodus is invoked and then dismissed in order to proclaim a new act of God:

> Thus saith the Lord, which maketh a way in the sea, and a path in the mighty waters; Which bringeth forth the chariot and horse, the army and the power; they shall lie down together, they shall not rise: they are extinct, they are quenched as tow.
>
> Remember ye not the former things, neither consider the things of old. Behold, I will do a new thing; now it shall spring forth; shall ye not know it? I will even make a way in the wilderness, and rivers in the desert.
>
> (Isaiah 43:16-19)

This new act will eclipse the Exodus at the same time that it depends upon that previous event for man's recognition of the significance of the new act.[66] The Exodus interprets history, making the promised return to Israel a divine event that is consistent with God's past actions; and history interprets the Exodus as a type of a new Exodus, which reaffirms the transforming power of God's acts and invites man to participate in this process of transformation.

The typological structure of the Bible, then, makes the Bible's central theme the creative power of God, who can bring about the miraculous and the totally new at the same time that He insures stability and continuity.[67] This dialectic between transformation and stability, which is expressed through the renewal of the type, begins in the Bible and extends outward into postbiblical history. We see, for instance, that the idea of the covenant and the symbols that express it undergo considerable revisions in the course of the Bible. The Old Testament ends with the failure of Israel to fulfill the terms of the covenant but also promises its eventual fulfillment in the future. This fulfillment is described in terms of the past, but a past that is transcended:

There would be a new Exodus, a new redemption from slavery, and a new entry into the land of promise (Jer. 16:14f); a new covenant and a new law (Jer. 31:31-34). . . . There would be a new Jerusalem (Isa. 21:6; Ezek. 40) and a new David to be God's shepherd over Israel (Jer. 23:5; Ezek. 34:23f) and a new temple where perfect worship would be offered, and from which a perfect law would go forth (Isa. 2:2-4; Ezek. 40-46).[68]

The Old Testament opens up into history and invites an interaction between the text and the external world upon which it impinges. The writers of the New Testament, reacting to a totally different set of historical events, are able to give those events coherence and significance by applying the Old Testament types to the life and ministry of Christ and his Apostles. Thus, as we have already seen, Christ is described by Paul as the new paschal lamb (I Corinthians 5:7), whose appearance in history repeats and transcends the passover of the past. Similarly, through their use of wilderness imagery, the Gospels present the temptation and victory of Christ in the wilderness as a repetition and perfecting of Israel's experience of temptations in the desert of Sinai.[69]

Like the Old Testament, the New Testament in turn invites a renewal of its types through the application of the pattern of Christ's life to the lives of the Apostles in Acts and through its eschatological promise that Christ will appear again within the course of human history.[70] The reader of the New Testament is asked to search the Scriptures in order to rightly understand the appearance of the Word in his own times and in order to make his own life a subfulfillment of the eschatological kingdom of God through the imitation or following of Christ.[71] In effect, the only response that the Bible attempts to elicit is interpretation and action based upon that interpretation, both of which will ensure the renewal within the world of postbiblical history of the types delineated in the Bible, all of which originate and culminate in the figure of Christ.

Thus, according to biblical typology, although the Bible contains the Word, the Word itself is eternal and continually manifests itself in human history. In *A Vision of the Last Judgment* Blake designates this continual renewal of the Word as vision, Imagination or Visionary Fancy:

> The Nature of Visionary Fancy or Imagination is very little Known & the Eternal nature & permanence of its ever Existent Images is considered as less permanent than the things of Vegetative & Generative Nature yet the Oak dies as well as the Lettuce but Its Eternal Image & Individuality never dies. but renews by its seed. just [*as*] ⟨so⟩ the Imaginative Image returns [*according to*] ⟨by⟩ the seed of Contemplative Thought the Writings of the Prophets illustrate these conceptions of the Visionary Fancy by their various sublime & Divine Images as seen in the Worlds of Vision.   (pp. 544-45)

Vision, according to Blake, should be carefully distinguished from allegory or fable:

> Fable or Allegory are a totally distinct & inferior kind of Poetry. Vision or Imagination is a Representation of what Eternally Exists. Really & Unchangeably. . . . The Hebrew Bible & the Gospel of Jesus are not Allegory but Eternal Vision or Imagination of All that Exists.
>   (*VLJ*, p. 544)

Allegory or fable, for Blake, entails the use of *sensibilia* to represent abstract ideas or to emblematize rules of moral conduct, whereas vision, as it is articulated in the Bible, represents the recurrence within time of what eternally exists. And what eternally exists is the Divine Humanity that manifests itself at different times in history in distinctly human forms that constitute his members: "All Things are

107

comprehended in their Eternal Forms in the Divine body of the Saviour the True Vine of Eternity" (*VLJ*, p. 545).

Thus identifying vision with biblical typology, the recurrence within history or myth of figures that point to Christ, Blake celebrates Chaucer as a visionary artist because the Canterbury pilgrims are the embodiment in human form of eternal principles that exist in all ages and all nations, and that even exist in the animal, vegetable, and mineral worlds (*DC*, pp. 523-24). Blake claims that "Visions of these eternal principles or characters of human life appear to poets, in all ages," as he typologically identifies Chaucer's pilgrims with the Greek gods, who are in turn identified with the ancient cherubim of Phoenicia (*DC*, pp. 522, 527) that in the Bible are typologically identified with Christ, as already noted. The Greek gods, like the gods of Priam, are visions that are part of Jesus, the Divine Humanity, and that become destructive to mankind when they are separated from him and become idolized as gods (p. 527).

But the problem is that in the fallen world these imaginative visions invariably do become separated from their divine origin, as they are appropriated by those who would promote empire and tyranny. At this point they degenerate into allegory, as their human significance is obscured by the abstractions that are attached to them. When the types become thus encrusted by orthodoxy or become part of state policy, it is the visionary artist's task to liberate or redeem the types by embodying them in a new art object; and by liberating or redeeming the type, the artist redeems man as well. This is precisely what Chaucer accomplishes by taking the same types that were embodied in the works of the Greeks and applying them to medieval England. Like the Prophets and the Apostles of the Bible, he represented "what [he] saw in Vision as real and existing men whom [he] saw with [his] imaginative and immortal organs" (*DC*, p. 532).

This principle of the redemption of the type, which has its origin in biblical tradition, lies at the very core of

Blake's aesthetic and is nowhere more dramatically and explicitly stated than in *The Marriage of Heaven and Hell.* That work achieves its goal, as well as its structural unity, by following a common practice that occurs in the Bible and biblical exegesis, the juxtaposition of analogous types. The enumeration in Hebrews 11 of Old Testament heroes of faith who are types of Christ is the most obvious example of this device. Similarly, in Isaiah 51 the promise of a return from the Babylonian captivity (51:11) is juxtaposed against the eschatological promise of a re-creation of Eden out of the wilderness (51:3), the myth of Jahweh slaying a sea monster before the Creation (51:9), and the parting of the Red Sea (51:10)—all of which depict God's saving acts as the creation of order out of chaos.[72] A Christian exegete would add to Isaiah's types Christ's victory over Satan in the wilderness, since the Gospels themselves employ Exodus typology to explain the significance of the Temptation,[73] and he would further add the binding of Satan in Revelation.[74]

Similarly, in *The Marriage of Heaven and Hell,* from the opening Argument to the concluding *A Song of Liberty,* the reader is presented, both in the text and the illustrations, with different manifestations of a single paradigmatic story. That story is a tale of usurpation, initially stated in the Argument's narrative about the just man being driven into the wilds by the sneaking villain, which suggests both the fall of Adam and Esau's loss of his birthright but which is deliberately vague because it presents the paradigm that is to appear in more familiar and specific forms in the rest of *The Marriage.* The expulsion of Satan in *Paradise Lost*—which is both mentioned in the text and illustrated in plate 5; the imprisonment of Ugolino in Dante's *Inferno,* which is illustrated on plate 16; the overthrow of the Titans, "the Giants who formed this world into its sensual existence" (pl. 16); and the expulsion of the newborn child by the starry king in *A Song of Liberty* are all analogous versions of the biblical story of Jacob's stealing

109

Esau's birthright. In the Bible, Esau is also called Edom, and Jacob is called Israel, and they are both the eponymous founders of the two nations mentioned in Isaiah 34 and 35. By citing these two biblical passages and by declaring that "Now is the dominion of Edom, & the return of Adam into Paradise" (pl. 3), Blake makes Adam a type of Esau and places all of the types used in *The Marriage* within the context of the fall of man and the promise of restoration at the apocalypse.[75]

These types also conform to two of Blake's more historical and didactic narratives in *The Marriage*: his recounting of the origin of religion as the usurpation of the poets' authority by the priesthood (pl. 11), and Isaiah's tale of the triumph of literalism over poetic perception in biblical interpretation, whereby all nations become subject to the God of Israel (plates 12 and 13). These last two narratives not only adumbrate the type but also explain the rationale for Blake's encyclopedic inclusion of all these types in *The Marriage*. All the poetic tales to which Blake alludes have fallen into the hands of the orthodox and have degenerated into allegories—fables or validating myths that serve the ends of those in power, the members of the Angels' party. In other words, these myths are types that have been divorced or abstracted from their origin, the human imagination or the Poetic Genius, the original source of all types, of which they form a part and from which they originally derived their power and significance. By thus becoming signs that have become detached from that which they signify, the types have become the objects of idolatry and the cause of slavery, in accordance with the Augustinian concept of slavery as adherence to the sign instead of that which is signified.[76] By forgetting the Poetic Genius, from whence all signs come and to which they all refer, man causes the Poetic Genius to lose its hegemony.

In order to redeem the types and man as well, Blake presents all of these types that embody a common paradigm in order to neutralize whatever power each type in its isolation may possess as a vehicle of political or moral abstraction. Acutely aware of the conceit and bigotry of members of the Angels' party who, like Swedenborg, sanctify their own validating myths by claiming originality (plates 21 and 22), Blake adopts the deists' strategy of demolishing that claim through the enumeration of analogous myths. He thus deprives each individual myth of any *a priori* moral, religious, or political sanction. Like the deists, he is content to have his readers recognize that even the stories of the Bible are imaginary tales. In fact, this is precisely Blake's point. By forcing his readers to recognize all of those types as products of the imagination, he is snatching those myths out of the hands of the priests, the tyrants, and the bigots and is returning them to their rightful home, the human breast, wherein all deities reside. Destroying the sanctity of each individual type by getting the reader to perceive the imaginative consistency of all of the types, Blake makes an important step toward the redemption of the type.

Had Blake been content to stop here, *The Marriage of Heaven and Hell* would have been an earlier, though somewhat cryptic version of *The Age of Reason*, which, incidentally, Blake admired for its iconoclasm.[77] He was not willing, however, to tear down the God of orthodoxy in order to erect the deists' god. At the same time that he deprives each type of its local signification, he affirms the validity of the types by placing them in a new context that gives them new significance. He places these types within an eschatological fictional framework, which is in itself a fiction of renewal, a vision of the world turned upside down, wherein all inequities are corrected—the desert blooms, empire is turned into a wasteland, the crooked road is made straight, as is prophesied in Isaiah 34 and 35. Thus, by proclaiming the dominion of Edom, Blake creates the same kind of inversion by giving positive value to Esau, who for the orthodox readers of the Bible is a type of the reprobate as opposed to the elect Jacob. Furthermore, the

111

basis of this reversal is Blake's application of the biblical type to contemporary history. Building upon the traditional typological identification of England as the New Israel, Blake applies the prophecy of Isaiah 63 to the French Revolution. The chapter in Isaiah describes the *Dies Irae* as the coming of God out of Edom, a country to the southeast of Israel, and Blake easily identifies revolutionary France, which lies to the southeast of England,[78] as a manifestation of Edom, clothed in the wrath of God, returning to reclaim his birthright. By thus applying the type of Esau, Blake reaffirms the validity of the type as a means of giving significance to human events and reinterprets the type of Esau not in terms of moral categories but in terms of the contrary forces of Reason and Energy. In fact, according to Blake's interpretation, the repression or imprisonment that the types depict is caused by the very forces that would rob the types of their life and validity: abstract reason and the code of morality that it promulgates.

Blake's identification of Edom with Christ reinforces the Christocentric nature of all of the types in *The Marriage of Heaven and Hell*, for it is through Christ, the Poetic Genius, that the redemption of the type—and thus man as well—is made possible. The essentially Christocentric nature of Blake's typology, as well as his radical Christology, is more directly revealed in three different parts of *The Marriage*. In the section that begins with "The Giants who formed this world into its sensual existence" (plates 16 and 17), Blake affirms his belief that the Incarnation is a continuous process and that all of humanity constitutes the body of Christ when he proclaims that "God only Acts & Is, in existing beings or Men." This idea is also expressed, as well as illustrated, in the second "Memorable Fancy," where God is embodied in Isaiah's "voice of honest indignation" and in the significative actions of Isaiah, Ezekiel, Diogenes, and the American Indians (plates 12 and 13). Finally, the point is reiterated in the last "Memorable Fancy," when the Devil in the flame of fire informs an angel that "there is no other God" but He who is incarnated through His gifts to all men, "each according to his genius," especially the greatest men—Jesus being preeminent among these (plates 22-24). Here, as in the other two sections that express this theme, Blake is invoking and interpreting doctrines concerning Christ's body that are expressed in I Corinthians 12-13 and I Peter 4:7-11. Building upon these passages, which state that Jesus Christ is glorified through his gifts to all men and that the mystical body of Christ consists of men exercising their various spiritual gifts and uniting in bonds of Christian charity, Blake radically extends these ideas by asserting that the following of one's genius and the loving of others who follow their genius is a typological fulfillment of the union between man and God that the Bible promises and typifies through the images of the Incarnation and the mystical body of Christ.

In the last "Memorable Fancy" of *The Marriage*, this fulfillment is illustrated by the conversion of the Angel, as I pointed out in the previous chapter. There I also noted that the Angel's conversion was effected by his imitation of Christ. In the context of the present discussion, it is clear that the Angel's conversion, which finds its figural expression in the renewal of a type, the prophet Elijah, points to the fact that Blake's typology—like much of typological tradition itself—is intimately connected with the imitation of Christ tradition. We can see this relationship even more clearly when we compare Blake's vision of the Angel's conversion with the idea of conversion as stated by a writer who more explicitly concerns himself with the imitation of Christ, Jacob Duché, whose sermons were influenced by Boehme and Swedenborg and were probably read by Blake.[79]

Like Blake, Duché uses the image of fire to describe the agency that effects conversion. Duché identifies charity with energy, through which the divine image embodies itself in and redeems nature; this energy is derived from Christ, the Sun of Righteousness, compared to which human reason is

113

merely a "little taper."[80] This energy is also described as the "Heavenly Fire" that has the "salutary efficacy" of opening and unifying the fallen senses of man, thereby effecting "the marriage of the Lamb."[81] Like Boehme, whose influence is apparent here, Duché uses synesthesia and a quotation from the Song of Solomon to describe the marriage of the Lamb as the co-mingling of the senses. Such a marriage takes place when the hearts of the regenerate become "spiritual altars, with the righteous person of CHRIST engraved upon them by the finger of GOD, flaming with the fires of Heavenly Love," when the individual has "spiritually embraced" these fires.[82]

Only those who undergo this process can be considered truly righteous, but before the process can take place, true righteousness must be distinguished from false concepts of righteousness and morality. Those who are to be redeemed must realize that "none, but the truly Regenerate Christian, acting under the immediate influence of the DIVINE SPIRIT, can properly be called a moral man"; that the only principle of morality is "the LOVE OF GOD shed abroad in the human heart by his holy SPIRIT";[83] that the prophets were sent by God to communicate God's disapproval of the very ordinances He had instituted;[84] that "Types and ceremonies and outward ordinances of the Law are taken from the objects of temporal nature, which are, at best, but shadowy representations of Eternal Truth";[85] that evangelical righteousness is found "only in the Incarnate Word of God";[86] and that the Divine Image must be continually re-created so as to manifest itself within man and within the external world.[87] Clearly, this realization and the accompanying conversion experience take place in the last "Memorable Fancy" of *The Marriage of Heaven and Hell*, with the Angel being educated in the ways of true righteousness by the Devil, who informs him that Christ was a true prophet in his defiance of the Law and that Christ was all virtue because he acted from impulse and not rules. Recognizing these truths, the Angel embraces the divine energy, the fire of true righteousness, thus re-creating the divine image and converting the shadowy types to truth.

It is important to see that the conversion described in this last "Memorable Fancy" consists of an interpretation of a text and an action based upon that interpretation. The text may contain the Word of God, but it is a typological reading of the text that, as Charity puts it, "allows the right hearing of a word which concerns the present and is new."[88] The disagreement between the Angel and the Devil centers around the issue of the sense in which Christ is a fulfillment of the Law; or, to put it another way, it is a disagreement about the nature of types. The Angel represents the point of view of the "historical Christian," who sees Christ as product, the end-result of an historical process that represented the perfecting and fulfillment of the Law at a particular moment in history. When he asserts that God is One, he means that the Son, like the Father, is wholly Other and that both type and antitype, the Mosaic Law and Christ, are identical. The Devil, on the other hand, sees the type as representative of a process that continues throughout human history, the perpetual communion between man and God, as described by Duché:

Under the Old Testament, this blessed intercourse was understood and felt by patriarchs and prophets, through the outward means of sacrifices, types, and various ceremonies and ordinances; all predictive and expressive of a certain Redeeming Process, which "in the fulness of time," was to be accomplished for human nature, in the person of a suffering and triumphant MESSIAH. Under the New Testament, it broke forth, with meridian lustre, in the incarnation, the nativity, life and conversation, sufferings, death, resurrection and ascension of the BLESSED JESUS; in whose sacred person the divine and human natures were most happily united, to the end, that as the SON OF MAN, and the SON OF GOD, he

115

might communicate to every Son of Man that should receive his testimony, and believe in his Name, and the power of becoming a SON OF GOD, John i. 12.[89]

According to this point of view, Jesus both fulfills and transcends the Law by effecting the purpose of the Law, the union of man and God. Rather than achieving salvation for mankind, the historical Jesus was a type, a subfulfillment of the redemption of fallen man and nature, a testimony to God's continued presence in history. Through Jesus, God became man to show the process whereby man may become God, to show that "the real Christian can only be supported by the immediate perpetual inspiration of the Holy Ghost,"[90] that regeneration must be accomplished by the continual re-creation of the divine image in man.[91]

According to Blake, the historical Jesus whose incarnation, life, and death is recorded in the Gospels, is a type, a manifestation of the process known as Christ, the continual re-creation of God in human form. Internally, this process takes place continually in the human soul through the imitation of Christ, through the opening of the soul to the fires of divine inspiration—just as the Angel embraces the flame of fire. Externally, the process of incarnation is expressed through the renewal of the type, the articulation in human form of a divine event that conforms with yet transcends similar events in the past. Hence Blake's Angel is transformed into Elijah, whose reappearance is predicted in the last books of the Old and New Testaments (Malachi 4:5 and Revelation 11:3). Undergoing the apocalyptic baptism by fire predicted in Isaiah 4:4 and Luke 3:16, the Angel, in his transformation, subsumes the Old Testament Elijah and comprehends in a single figure the two witnesses of Revelation, Elijah from the Old Testament and John the Baptist from the New Testament (since the Angel was baptized with the Holy Ghost by Christ himself as John predicted). His appearance heralds the apocalyptic revolution that takes place in *A Song of Liberty*. By cleansing the doors of perception and reenacting the Incarnation, the converted Angel functions as a surrogate for and a type of Blake's ideal reader, who not only can understand the significance of typology but also knows how to act upon it.

Given the nature of Blake's symbolism, it appears to be more than a coincidence that Blake's calling his visionary art a "Sublime Allegory" should recall Lowth's use of a similar expression—a "sublimer kind of allegory"—to describe biblical typology.[92] For, like biblical types, Blake's figures are historical realities or at least fictions intended to be considered as historical realities. They all point to other fictions or historical realities rather than intellectual abstractions, and they all have a prefigurative or postfigurative content. They all are freely combined with biblical figures, pagan figures, figures from national history, and figures from yesterday's news.[93] They all are used prophetically to bring the past and the predicted future to bear upon a situation located in the present. They all, Blake insists, must be continually re-created in the world of time and space, though they derive from, point to, and are part of one eternal form—Christ or the human form divine. Thus, in accord with the traditional practice of writers and exegetes, and with our modern understanding of the term, they are all types.

Blake's use of typology had important aesthetic consequences for him, theoretically and practically. On a practical level, types provided him with an intellectual shorthand that would permit a direct apprehension of complex ideas and attitudes. This is especially true when Blake combines in a single character a number of types. For instance, Los in *The Book of Urizen* represents Jehovah, Adam, Abraham, Apollo, Hephaestus, Jeremiah, Laius, and Jupiter[94] —though not all necessarily at one given moment in the poem. Similarly, the Guardian of the secret codes in *Europe* embodies Nebuchadnezzar and Lycaon. Also, like biblical figures, Blake's characters are often corporate personalities, representing both individuals and classes of individuals, much as someone like Esau or Edom is both a person and a nation.[95] In each case, Blake, like Dante, achieves a style analogous to that of the Bible in that his works become *polysemous*, possessing multiple significations.[96]

The reader who perceives the imaginative unity of Blake's types as they appear in each poem perceives the richness of significance with which Blake has invested his figures and thus the richness of meaning that his poems contain. In this way, Blake adheres to Augustine's aesthetic of using figuralism to rouse the reader's faculties and raise the reader to vision. Augustine praised the eloquence of the biblical prophets, who employed "a useful and helpful obscurity for the purpose of exercising and sharpening, as it were, the minds of the readers and of destroying fastidiousness and stimulating the desire to learn, concealing their intention in such a way that the minds of the impious are either converted to piety or excluded from the mysteries of the faith."[97] Blake echoes these sentiments in his letter to Trusler: "What is Grand is necessarily obscure to Weak men. That which can be made Explicit to the Idiot is not worth my care. The wisest of the Ancients consider'd what is not too Explicit as the fittest for Instruction, because it rouzes the faculties to act."[98] Blake's types are necessarily obscure to those who do not understand typology and its application, but for those who do, the recognition of Blake's types endows those readers with prophetic vision, the perception of the infinite in all things through an understanding of the interconnectedness of past, present, and future.

The formal consequences of Blake's use of typology include the use of an atemporal and thematic ordering of events, the use of the *psychomachia*, and the preponderance of personification.[99] Since, as we have already seen, typology posits a vertical view of history in which events are not related to each other chronologically or progressively but thematically, any fiction that employs typology would tend to express that view in a form that divorces those events from any chronological matrix. Thus, for instance, Milton employs an atemporal, thematic arrangement of events in "On the Morning of Christ's Nativity" and deemphasizes any chronological connection between the events related in the last two books of *Paradise Lost*,[100] both of which are typological fictions. In these works, as in Blake's prophecies, time remains fixed and all events are perceived to be contemporaneous; past, present, and future are fused through the perception of those events as repetitions of a single paradigmatic event. Furthermore, this atemporality is often enhanced by the use of a pattern that Boyd Berry sees in *Paradise Lost*:

> *Paradise Lost* unfolds in much the manner of Puritan theology. Both are processes of self-revelation, self-analysis, and self-elaboration. The first five lines of the poem articulate the whole theme, much as early, short statements of Puritan belief had; they form part of a slightly larger unit of twenty-six lines which do the same thing at greater length. And the poem eddies out from this central thematic statement, unfolding the implications in larger and larger cycles, moving gradually toward that point where the "doctrines" developed in the first part may be applied pragmatically by characters and the reader to events in this world. To put it another way, the poem unfolds and displays the nature of the divine impulse, a movement of release outward into creative multiplicity and then a movement back toward God who shall again in the last days be "all in all."[101]

This pattern, as we have seen, has its roots in biblical prophecy, as in the books of Ezekiel and Revelation, where prophetic statement is followed by symbolic elaboration. Such a pattern is also clearly evident in Blake's early prophecies, where an opening action, Argument, or Preludium is followed by events that repeat or elaborate upon an initial action or theme that contains the essential "doctrine" of

119

that work. For instance, all of the events of *The Book of Urizen* amplify and modify the initial event of the prophecy, Urizen's withdrawal from Eternity;[102] and the Prophecy of *America* elaborates upon the narration of Orc's revival in the Preludium.

Since typological events are repetitions within time of paradigmatic events that are located outside of chronological time, those typological events become analogues of spiritual or psychological events that take place in the mind of the reader, and typological fictions will therefore usually take the form of a *psychomachia*, "the portrayal of critical events and conflicts of the soul as external occurrences."[103] The biblical basis of this aesthetic is the imitation of Christ tradition, wherein the human soul is expected to reenact literally the Incarnation. Similarly, if external events are meant to represent events taking place in human consciousness, then those external events must be taken as personifications of the events of consciousness. We see this, for example, in *The Book of Urizen*, which represents a *psychomachia*, a crisis in human consciousness, whose characters and actions are personifications of particular modes of consciousness.

Besides conditioning the form and content of Blake's prophecies, typology also informs Blake's attitudes toward tradition and the individual talent. If all art is typological in form and content, representing what eternally exists, then the development of the arts is retrospective and cumulative rather than progressive. According to Anthony Collins, it proceeds in the same manner that revelation proceeds: "For if we consider the various *revelations*, and *changes* in religion, whereof we have any tolerable history, in their beginning, we shall find them for the most part to be grafted on some old stock, or founded on some preceding *revelations*, which they were either to supply, or fulfill, or retrieve from corrupt glosses, innovations, and traditions, with which by time they were encumbered."[104] Similarly, for Blake a new work of art could not go beyond the work of its predecessors, but it could perfect the vision that they contained by purging the predecessors' works of the encumbrances of time and custom. Thus Blake makes the following claim in his *Public Address*: "To recover Art has been the business of my life to the Florentine Original & if possible to go beyond that Original" (p. 569). Here "going beyond" the Florentine means going back to the original source of inspiration—the Imagination itself, whose eternal forms are continually embodied in works of genius. Insofar as these works contain those forms, they may be said to represent "the extent of the human mind":

> Milton, Shakespeare, Michael Angelo, Rafael, the finest specimens of Ancient Sculpture and Painting, and Architecture, Gothic, Grecian, Hindoo and Egyptian are the extent of the human mind. The human mind cannot go beyond the gift of God, the Holy Ghost. To suppose that Art can go beyond the finest specimens of Art that are now in the world, is not knowing what Art is; it is being blind to the gifts of the spirit. (*DC*, p. 535)

Like biblical types, inspired works of art are merely manifestations within the physical world of what has always existed, and to assume that one can go beyond (that is, improve upon) the great works of art is the equivalent of placing a greater emphasis upon the type than upon that which it signifies, to keep the vehicle and throw away the tenor. To thus adhere to the outward form at the expense of the inner process that animates it, to assume that the ultimate goal is the perfection of the art object, is to miss the point of all art. For Blake, "art is a vehicle for vision rather than an object of perception," and all great art is of equal value insofar as it releases vision for the perceiver.[105] Therefore if a new work of art can be said to perfect the work of previous artists, it does so only in the sense that the antitype perfects the type; that is, in that it renews what was already present in the previous work—its visionary power—by applying its form and content to a new historical situation. Through interpretation and re-creation of previous visionary works of art, which is achieved by copying the images of previous artists and setting them in a new context, the artist ensures the rekindling of the visionary power that informs those previous works, asserting through the renewal of those images the continual process whereby the Word is made flesh and man becomes God. Through this simultaneously retrogressive and progressive vision of the creative process, Blake creates the conditions by which the perceiver of the art object can enact his own redemption, achieve prophetic vision, and thus realize the goal that Moses, Christ, and Milton had sought: the conversion of all the Lord's people into prophets.

The object of Blake's sublime allegory, then, like that of typology, is conversion, which is expressed in the art object by the process of imaginative transformation and which is expressed in the Bible by the reiteration of God's transforming power. As A. C. Charity observes: "by its very nature, the biblical tradition of typology fastens on one event of conversion with the aim of effecting another."[106] Whether they portray man's union with God or his separation from God, biblical types, when applied to the historical events, transform them into divine events by asserting the operation of spiritual agency; and these transformations are analogues for similar transformations that are to take place in the reader's consciousness. Blake's types, like those in the Bible and in Dante, require "an active and dramatic" reading of the text, whereby "the reader sees himself and sees through himself, whereby the reader is changed."[107] The reader is to become, as the Epistle of James demands, a doer, not a hearer of the Word (James 1:22), who, according to Duché's discourse on this passage, realizes that biblical types represent not only historical realities but also internal states of consciousness and that redemption is possible only through this realization and the realization that the transforming power of divine Righteousness lies within the human breast.[108] What Duché identifies as the universal

Righteousness, available to all mankind, whereby the Divine Image is re-created in man and all mankind becomes part of the body of Christ, Blake identifies as the Imagination, the process whereby God becomes man and man becomes God.

In Blake's early prophecies, the Lambeth books, published in 1794 and 1795, we see the typological process at work, as Blake seeks to re-create the Bible so as to make it applicable to his own time and thereby redeem the time by re-creating and thus redeeming the paradigmatic events depicted in the Bible from (to repeat Anthony Collins' words) "corrupt glosses, innovations and traditions." This is the rationale underlying Blake's concept of the Bible of Hell that he promises in *The Marriage of Heaven and Hell*, a promise that he initially fulfills in *America, Europe, The Song of Los, The Book of Urizen, The Book of Ahania,* and *The Book of Los.* All of these works were written with the intention of renewing the vision of the Bible in order to cleanse the doors of perception and raise Blake's audience to a perception of the infinite. Given the Christocentric nature of this process whereby the senses are activated and integrated into the body of Christ, the human imagination, it is not surprising to find that in the Lambeth books, the most persistent theme is that of the sacred marriage, adumbrated by various types of Christ and the bride or types of their contraries, the beast and the harlot. Through these and through other types, taken from the Bible, Milton, Spenser, pagan myth, and contemporary history, Blake's early prophecies reveal the extent of the human mind and depict its struggle to reclaim the vision embodied in the great code of art.

America: "The Doors
of Marriage Are Open"

In *America* Blake depicts the American Revolution as a
prelude to the apocalypse, and the apocalyptic tone and
imagery of the poem lead us to assume automatically that
his main sources are Daniel and Revelation. However,
while the influence of these two books is clearly present, the
structure, symbolism, and mythology of *America* are drawn
from other biblical sources to which Blake had a strong
attachment. In Blake's well-known letter of 12 September
1800 to John Flaxman, which contains a poetic autobiogra-
phy—Blake's "lot upon Earth" and his "lot in the Heav-
ens"—in the form of a list of persons and events that in-
fluenced his life and thought, the only two biblical writers
that he mentions are Isaiah and Ezra, the latter being the
Esdras of the Apocrypha rather than the canonical Ezra
(p. 680, line 6). Why these two figures had such a formative
influence on him Blake does not say, but his first prophecy
(at least the first to be so named) bears a strong stamp of
that influence. From the eschatological passages in Isaiah,
Blake adopted a dialectical structure for his own poem, and
he followed Isaiah in employing the figures of Esau and
Jacob in an historical myth that embodied that dialectic.
Similarly, Blake drew upon the apocryphal Second Book of
Esdras (also called IV Esdras and the Ezra Apocalypse) for
the main plot and some of the major symbols, images, and
themes of *America*. Like Isaiah, Ezra uses the story of Esau
and Jacob as a central historical myth. Both biblical writers
represent the culmination of history with the symbol of the
divine or apocalyptic marriage.

This symbol of apocalyptic marriage received its fullest

124

articulation in the Song of Solomon, the work of another biblical author whom Blake explicitly acknowledges as an important influence. In his letter of 23 August 1799 to Dr. Trusler, Blake cites Solomon's works as exemplars of visionary art, noting that Solomon was one of "the wisest of the Ancients [who] considerd what is not too Explicit as the fittest for Instruction because it rouzes the faculties to act" (p. 676). Here Blake is alluding in part to the allegorical interpretation of the Song of Songs, and in *America* Blake builds upon this interpretation, fusing the erotic imagery from Canticles with the images, myths, and symbols from Ezra and Isaiah to describe the American Revolution as the first stirrings in his own time of a universal passion that could be satisfied only by the apocalyptic marriage of the human and the divine.

The main apocalyptic passages in Isaiah that Blake draws upon in *America* are those mentioned in the "Argument" of *The Marriage of Heaven and Hell*:

> Now is the dominion of Edom, & the return of Adam into Paradise; see Isaiah xxxiv & XXXV Chap:
> Without Contraries is no progression. Attraction and Repulsion, Reason and Energy, Love and Hate, are necessary to Human existence. (*MHH*, pl. 3)

These two biblical chapters, plus Isaiah 63, to which the "dominion of Edom" alludes,[1] contain the themes and symbols developed in *A Song of Liberty*, whose apocalyptic vision of the American Revolution Blake greatly expands in *America*. Both works form a gloss, as it were, upon the biblical passages in question, perceiving Isaiah's prophetic symbolism as the mythopoetic form of the doctrine of contraries.

Chapter 34 of Isaiah describes the pouring forth of God's vindictive fury upon Idumea (Edom), while chapter 35 announces God's promised restoration of Zion, which the chapter heading of the Authorized Version glosses as "the joyful flourishing of Christ's Kingdom." From Isaiah 34

125

Blake derives much of the imagery of apocalyptic destruction in *America*. The bloody sword "bathed in Heaven" (34:5-6) and the soaking of the land in blood (34:7) are echoed in the bloody clouds arising from the Atlantic (*America* 4:2-6), in the American coast "glowing with blood from Albions fiery Prince" (*America* 3:5), and in Orc's staining the temple with his "beams of blood" (*America* 5:6-7). Isaiah's images of meteors, fire, brimstone, and smoke that descend upon Edom (34:4, 34:8-10) thoroughly pervade Blake's prophecy, where fires and clouds of smoke arise from rebel and tyrant alike. In the opening of "A Prophecy," "the Guardian Prince of Albion burns in his nightly tent," sending fires glowing across the Atlantic (*America* 3:1-2) and showering meteors on England (3:16). The Atlantic sends forth "raging Fires" (*America* 4:3) reminiscent of the streams of burning pitch in Isaiah 34:9. Orc is a burning comet (*America* 5:2) who burns

> towards America,
> In black smoke thunders and loud winds rejoicing in its
> terror
> Breaking in smoky wreaths from the wild deep, &
> gath'ring thick
> In flames as of a furnace on the land from North to
> South.
>
> (*America* 12:9-12)

Isaiah further prophesies that the nobles of Edom shall be replaced by wild birds and beasts of prey—the cormorant, the bittern, the raven, the vulture, and the owl (34:11-12, 34:15)—"and thorns shall come up in her palaces, nettles and brambles in the fortresses thereof: and it shall be a habitation of dragons, and a court for owls" (34:13). This prophecy is alluded to in the very beginning of *America*, where Blake with an ironic literalness mentions the "dragon form" of Albion's Angel in 3:15, and in the illustration to plate 4. Furthermore, Albion's kingdom is possessed by lions and wolves (*America* 7:2, 9:2, 9:27), an eagle devours a female corpse in the headpiece to plate 13, and thorny growths appear in the tailpiece of plate 16.

As Blake indicates with the colon that separates the citation of Isaiah and the doctrine of contraries on plate 3 of *The Marriage of Heaven and Hell,* Isaiah 35 contains images that represent the contrary of the chapter that precedes it; the blossoming of the chosen Zion is contrasted to the desolation of the outcast Edom. Against the transformation of Edom into a wilderness in Isaiah 34, Isaiah 35 posits the joyful blossoming of the wilderness (35:1-2), which is echoed in *America* by Orc's proclaiming that the deserts will blossom through the destruction of Urizen's "ten commands" (8:3-8). Against the maiming of nature and the obscuring of the skies, when the heavens are "rolled together as a scroll" (34:4), Isaiah 35 promises the healing of nature and the opening of vision: "Then the eyes of the blind shall be opened, and the ears of the deaf shall be unstopped" (35:5). This promise is alluded to in Orc's enjoining the freed slave to "look up into the heavens & laugh in the bright air" *(America* 6:7) and in the liberated populace's singing of "a fresher morning" and "a clear & cloudless night" (6:13-14). Their song echoes the songs of "everlasting joy" that the Lord's ransomed will sing in Isaiah 35:10. The beasts of prey that possess the land in Isaiah 34:11-15 are withdrawn in Isaiah's promise of redemption for Zion: "No lion shall be there, nor any ravenous beast shall go up thereon, it shall not be found there; but the redeemed shall walk there" (35:9). This promise is reiterated in Orc's proclaiming in *America,* as he does in *A Song of Liberty.* "For Empire is no more, and now the Lion & Wolf shall cease" *(America* 6:15, *MHH,* pl. 27).

The two chapters in Isaiah carefully image the contrary processes of destruction and creation, damnation and salvation, darkening and illumination. But they also articulate, through the contrasted fates of Israel and Edom, a prophetic mythology of opposing forces in history. Throughout biblical history Edom was the inveterate enemy of Israel,

127

and Isaiah's prophecy refers not only to the historical Edom but also to Edom as a symbol of all of the enemies of Israel, or, in its Christian context, all the enemies of the true church.[2] The enmity between Edom and Israel stems from the rivalry between Esau and Jacob, the respective progenitors of these nations. The name "Edom," which is Hebrew for "red," refers both to Esau, who received the name for selling his birthright for red pottage (Genesis 25:30), and to the nation that descended from this dispossessed son of Isaac whose inheritance was a wilderness. Although Esau and Jacob were eventually reconciled (Genesis 33), the old enmity was later revived when the Edomites refused to allow the Israelites to pass through their land on the way to Canaan (Numbers 20:14-21). Thereafter the intense bitterness between both nations persisted, and the Bible continually mentions the faults of the Edomites and their offenses against Israel. In the writings of the prophets, Edom is an anathema; God's wrath is pronounced upon that nation for its crimes, particularly for its gloating over the fall of Jerusalem and its participation in the plunder of that city (Obadiah 10-14; Ezekiel 25:12-14, 35:1-15; Amos 1:11-12; Joel 3:19).[3]

It is this post-exilic rancor against Edom that informs the thirty-fourth chapter of Isaiah and the prophet's proclamation of God's avenging Edom's wrongs in chapter 63:

> Who is this that cometh from Edom, with dyed garments from Bozrah? this that is glorious in his apparel, travelling in the greatness of his strength? I that speak in righteousness, mighty to save. Wherefore art thou red in thine apparel, and thy garments like him that treadeth the winevat? I have trodden the winepress alone; and of the people there was none with me: for I will tread them in mine anger, and trample them in my fury; and their blood shall be sprinkled upon my garments, and I will stain all my raiment.   (63:1-3)

Taking Edom as a symbol of the profane (Hebrews 12:16) and as a symbol of the persecutor (Obadiah 10-14),[4] Christian exegetes have interpreted this passage as the description of Christ's victory over his enemies.[5] Edom is thereby identified with the Antichrist, whose longstanding enmity with God finds appropriate analogy in the ancient feud that persisted between the descendants of Esau and Jacob up until the destruction of Edom. Thus Isaiah 34 and 35 mythologize Old Testament history, establishing Edom as the symbol of the enemies of God, the outcast descendants of Esau who continually defy God, and who mock and persecute the righteous.

This, at any rate, is the orthodox reading of Isaiah's prophecies. Blake, however, had another reading in mind when he adopted Isaiah's symbolism to articulate the shape and significance of contemporary history. Perceiving ambiguities that are already present in the Bible, and drawing upon Swedenborg's interpretation of the meaning of Edom, Blake employed both the myth of the feuding brothers and the contrary interpretations of that myth to articulate a dialectical vision of history in *America*. While the Edomites are generally an object of scorn among the writers of the Bible, Edom was also said to be renowned for its wise men (Obadiah 8; Jeremiah 49:7), and the Bible states that Edom was the home of God:[6] "Lord, when thou wentest out of Seir, when thou marchedst out of the field of Edom, the earth trembled, and the heavens dropped, the clouds also dropped water" (Judges 5:4).[7]

These details would mitigate and perhaps even contradict the generally harsh view of Edom that the Bible inculcates. Further ambiguity about the meaning of Edom could be derived from the blessing that Isaac confers upon Esau after learning that Jacob had robbed Esau of his birthright: "And by thy sword shalt thou live, and shalt serve thy brother: and it shall come to pass when thou shalt have the dominion, that thou shalt break his yoke from off thy neck"

129

(Genesis 27:40). This could be interpreted as a prediction of the successful revolt of the Edomites against Solomon (I Kings 11:14-22, 25) or of a future apocalyptic event. Blake's reference to the arrival of the "dominion of Edom" (*MHH*, pl. 3) clearly shows the latter interpretation, which connects this passage from Genesis with Isaiah 63. This apocalyptic reading, as Kathleen Raine has pointed out, Blake borrowed from Swedenborg, who interprets Isaac's blessing of Esau as the promised restoration to Edom of the birthright that Jacob has stolen from him. For Swedenborg, Edom's dominion meant the liberation of "the essential good" that had long remained hidden:

> By Edom above all is represented "the Lord's divine human principle as to the natural and corporeal." The reinstating of Edom, therefore, meant for Blake, as it did for Swedenborg, a reinstatement of the bodily man in the Divine Humanity of Jesus.
>
> The dominion of Edom is Swedenborg's "New Heaven," the reign of the Divine Humanity. But also, since it reinstates corporeal humanity, it is said to be "the return of Adam to Paradise."[8]

Raine further points out that the traditional reading of Isaiah 63 was that "Jesus was to enter his Kingdom by way of Edom,"[9] which was probably an extension of the Old Testament references to God's coming out of Edom. Thus Blake had ample exposure to an alternative tradition that saw Edom not as a symbol of the Antichrist, but as the very opposite.

Blake articulates this countertradition in mythic terms in the "Argument" of *The Marriage of Heaven and Hell* and in *A Song of Liberty*, which concludes that work. The conflict between the eponymous brothers is developed in the Argument's myth of the "just man" being driven into barren climes by the usurping villain who "left the paths of ease." Here the Genesis story, its thematic extension

130

throughout the Old Testament, and its symbolic interpretation by Isaiah are invoked to give poetic form to the concept of the contraries that Blake develops in *The Marriage*. The crafty Jacob is the villain who illustrates the proverb of hell: "the weak in courage is strong in cunning" (*MHH* 9:49). He represents one side of Blake's contraries, the "restrainer or reason" that "usurps its place & governs the unwilling" (*MHH*, pl. 5). Esau represents the principle of energy or desire that has been restrained or deprived of its birthright, the condition that Blake proclaims to have ended with the "dominion of Edom" announced in the "Argument." This event is more fully described in *A Song of Liberty*, where Blake borrows images from Isaiah 34 and 35 to reiterate the biblical myth. The falling of the host of heaven described in Isaiah 34:4 receives a dialectical interpretation: the falling fires, ostensibly an expression of divine wrath, instead of devastating the earth, revitalize it. Similarly, the outcast Orc, who is hurled out of heaven, reclaims his birthright by declaring the birth of a new heaven and a new earth, a new morning in which the beasts of the wilderness (the raven, the wolf, and the lion) are banished and human potential is released, as in Isaiah 35. While the orthodox would read Isaiah 34 and 35 as the crushing of the outcast Edom and the glorification of the chosen Israel, *The Marriage* presents an infernal reading of those two chapters, similar to the Devils' reading of *Paradise Lost* (*MHH*, pls. 5-6). According to this reading, the host of heaven in Isaiah 34 fall down not to wreak punishment upon Edom but to revitalize it. It is not Edom that is cast out, but rather the forces that would oppress it. The old heaven falls to become a wilderness while Edom is reborn upon its ashes. In such an interpretation the roles of the damned Edom and the chosen Israel are reversed.

This interpretation of the myth of Edom is developed more fully in *America*, where Orc's rise marks the stirring of Edom to reclaim his birthright, to reinstate the divine

131

humanity, whose dispossession by the heirs of the crafty Jacob has been described in *The Marriage* and is reiterated by Boston's Angel:

> Why trembles honesty and like a murderer,
> Why seeks he refuge from the frowns of his immortal
>   station!
> Must the generous tremble & leave his joy, to the idle:
>   to the pestilence!
> That mock him? who commanded this? what God?
>   what Angel!
> To keep the gen'rous from experience till the ungenerous
> Are unrestrained performers of the energies of nature;
> Till pity is become a trade, and generosity a science,
> That men get rich by, & the sand desert is giv'n to the
>   strong
> What God is he, writes laws of peace, & clothes him in
>   a tempest
> What pitying Angel lusts for tears, and fans himself
>   with sighs
> What crawling villain preaches abstinence & wraps
>   himself
> In fat of lambs? no more I follow, no more obedience
>   pay.
>
> *(America* 11:4-15)

In *America* Orc is more explicitly identified with Esau or Edom than in *A Song of Liberty*: he is the "red Orc" (*America* 1:1), a "hairy youth" (1:11) with "hairy shoulders" (2:2), and his appearance identifies him with the names ("Esau" meaning "hairy" and "Edom" meaning "red") and the physical attributes of his biblical prototype, who at his birth "came out red, all over like a hairy garment" (Genesis 25:25). And just as the heirs of the dispossessed Esau lived in caves (Jeremiah 49:16; Obadiah 3), the disinherited child of Blake's prophecy is imprisoned in caverns (*America* 1:18). Finally, Orc's breaking out of his Edomite caverns and his inspiring the American Revolu-

132

tion parallels the description in Isaiah 63 of the descent out of Edom of a Messiah clothed in red who brings not peace but a sword.

Consonant with Blake's dialectical vision, Orc is perceived as such only by the Americans, permitting them, like the saved in Isaiah 35, to become strengthened in courage, to regain clarity of vision, and to become free of error. They see the bended bow and the chain (*America* 3:7) descending from Albion, as well as the dragon form of Albion's wrathful prince. Burning with Orc's indignant fires, the thirteen Angels of America perceive the usurpation of their rights and refuse further obedience to Albion's Angel. He, on the other hand, remains true to the orthodox perception of Edom and sees Orc as the traditional enemy of God, as the Antichrist, the red dragon who stands ready to devour the offspring of the woman clothed with the sun (Revelation 12:4):

> Art thou not Orc; who serpent-form'd
> Stands at the gate of Enitharmon to devour her children;
> Blasphemous Demon, Antichrist, hater of Dignities;
> Lover of wild rebellion, and transgresser of Gods Law;
> Why dost thou come to Angels eyes in this terrific form?
>
> (*America* 7:3-7)

To the Americans this speech can be nothing less than tremendously ironic, since it is Albion's Angel whom they see in the "terrific form" of a dragon, the form of the Antichrist in Revelation. This dialectic is further underscored by Blake's distribution of fire and cloud symbolism on both sides of the Atlantic. While Orc burns with revolutionary energy, Albion's tyrant is equally energetic in his wrath.

Thus from the dialectic that he perceived in Isaiah 34 and 35—the opposition of Edom and Israel, the damned and the saved, destruction and creation, obscurity and clarity, wilderness and garden—Blake portrayed the American Revolution as a battle of contraries; and the dominion of Edom, particularly as articulated in Isaiah 63, appears to be

no more than the free play of these contraries.[10] Although
Blake obviously stacks his cards in favor of the revolution-
aries, neither side in and of itself is given absolute value.
Albion's Angel, tyrant that he is, is not the same character
as Urizen, though he is surely Urizen's agent. Through the
fire of his wrath he reveals his own error; exposing his
dragon form while calling Orc the Antichrist clearly reveals
that error. The important point here is the willingness of
Albion's Angel to act, to enter into his anger, and thus
openly reveal his position. If Orc is given positive value in
America, it is only insofar as he creates the potential for an
apocalypse by the release of imprisoned energies. His fires
give heat but no light (*America* 4:11); they are easily
quenched by Urizen's tears, revealing that they do not yet
provide the illumination necessary to overcome the force
of Urizen's stony laws.

Blake's portrayal of Orc as a demonic Messiah is devel-
oped through his fusing of Orc's obvious satanic trappings
with a tightly woven fabric of allusions that associate Orc
with Christ. Besides Blake's invocation of a tradition that
associates the Edomlike Orc with the warrior Christ of
Isaiah 63, Blake employs traditional iconography in the
opening plates of *America* to reinforce that association. The
breach in the wall in the frontispiece belongs to a long-
standing pictorial tradition in which the breach signified
various events of Christ's life: the broken wall symbolizes
the breach between man and God as a result of the Fall,
a breach to be healed by Christ.[11] The chained angel in
the frontispiece symbolizes the chained Orc's latent but still
imprisoned potential of fulfilling this Christlike function.

This association of the chained Orc with Christ is even
further strengthened by the illustration at the top of the
Preludium, which is derived from another traditional pic-
torial motif: the discovery of Abel's body by Adam and
Eve.[12] Lucas Van Leyden's engraving of the subject, with
which Blake was probably familiar, may have been Blake's
most immediate source. Blake's transformation of the dead

Abel into the figure of Orc crucified on a rock has its roots in the typological tradition, which sees the martyred Abel as a foreshadowing of Christ.[13] Blake's use of this tradition is deliberately ambiguous, however. The figure on the lower left corner bears a strong resemblance to Fuseli's picture of Cain designed for Lavater's *Physiognomy*.[14] The contracted form and its enclosure beneath the roots suggest that this figure, like the chained figure above, is equally victimized. Add to this detail both the statement in the text that Orc is imprisoned in caverns and the picture of Orc emerging from the ground in plate 2, and we are left with the problem of which figure in plate 1 is Orc—the martyred Christlike Abel or the wretched criminal Cain? From the ensuing prophecy, it becomes obvious that Orc is represented by both figures; he is both rebel and redeemer. In this design Blake appears to be deliberately questioning traditional categories; both the Cain and Abel figures are equally imprisoned by the same fallen nature, symbolized by the writhing vegetable forms below the ground and the heavily loaded symbol of the tree above ground. Both are imprisoned by the categories of Reason and the code of vindictive justice that separates the guilty from the innocent. From this design it appears that a vision of Christ as a passive victim and his enemies as active criminals is a fallen vision that must be transcended through a reconception of the nature of Christ and the nature of redemption.

Blake sees in the American Revolution the possibility of such a reconception and identifies the spirit behind the revolt with the messianic promise of a world redeemed from the bondage of the Law. Orc is given the burden of this messianic promise, and America's role in the redemptive process is articulated through Blake's adaptation of themes and symbols from the Second Book of Esdras. In chapter 13 of that book, Ezra has a dream in which there arises from the sea a man who "waxed strong with the thousands of Heaven" and whose voice takes the form of flames that burn all who hear him. A multitude of men

135

gather against this man, attempting to subdue him, but he graves himself a great mountain and flies up to it. His opponents, though they are "sore afraid," continue to pursue him. He defeats them, however, using no other instrument of warfare than his own mouth, from which fires, sparks, and tempests fly. He then comes down the mountain and gathers together another multitude, this time a "peaceable" one (2 Esdras 13:1-12).

Ezra awakens and asks the angel Uriel for an interpretation of the vision and is told that the dream foretells the coming of the Messiah, whose appearance shall astonish the earth, first causing nations to fight each other. The Son will then ascend to be declared, and the people hearing his voice shall leave fighting each other to make war against him:

> But he shall stand upon the top of the mount Sion. And Sion shall come, and shall be shewed to all men, being prepared and builded, like as thou sawest the hill graven without hands. And this my Son shall rebuke the wicked inventions of those nations, which for their wicked life are fallen into the tempest; and shall lay before them their evil thoughts, and the torments wherewith they shall begin to be tormented, which are like unto a flame: and he shall destroy them without labour by the law which is like unto fire. And whereas thou sawest that he gathered another peaceable multitude unto him; those are the ten tribes, which were carried away prisoners out of their own land in the time of Osea the king, whom Salmanasar the king of Assyria led away captive, and he carried them over the waters, and so came they into another land.   (2 Esdras 13:35-40)

But these ten tribes, wishing no longer to stay among the heathen, seek out a further country, where "never mankind dwelt" and where they could keep their own statutes. They cross over the Euphrates, as God holds back the wa-

136

ters until they have passed through, and travel for a year
and a half until they reach a region called Arsareth. There
they will dwell until "the latter time," when God will again
make a path through the Euphrates and gather to himself
the ten lost tribes, along with the faithful remnant of those
who had remained in Palestine (2 Esdras 13:41-50).

It is upon this vision and its interpretation that Blake
mounts his myth of Orc's rise and his fomenting of the
American Revolution. Orc, like the Son of God in Ezra's
vision, arises from the sea in flames (*America* 4:7-10) and
announces his presence upon a mountain (in the illustra-
tion and text of plate 6), provoking war and inspiring op-
position against himself with his fiery words. The Prince
of Albion and his host arise to oppose Orc and are smitten
by the flames, but the Americans—though not as peaceable
as the loyal multitude in Ezra—take Orc's counsel and are
liberated by his message.

The American colonies are identified with the lost tribes
of Israel, through Blake's adoption in *America* of the bibli-
cal version of the Atlantis myth. Just as the captives of
Salmanasar had fled "over the waters" to "another land,"
so the Americans had left the tyranny of England, crossing
a body of water to an uninhabited region. And as Blake's
contemporaries were aware, Ezra's captives not only must
have traveled over the Atlantic Ocean but probably settled
in the middle of it. Francis Lee, in his well-known "Dis-
sertation on the Second Book of Esdras," had observed that
the land to which the captives made an eighteen-month
march, "if we allow them to travel by very easy Marches at
the rate of Eight or Ten Miles a Day, cannot have any-
where a Subsistence but in the *Atlantic* Ocean, with the
Old or New Atlantis."[15] This is where Blake situates the
thirteen angels or ruling spirits of the American colonies,
apparently identifying Ezra's land of Arsareth with the
"Atlantean hills." Like Ezra's exiled tribes, the thirteen
angels "return" at the hearing of the voice of the man risen
in flames from the sea. They, along with the faithful rem-

137

nant in England—those who are inspired rather than tormented by Orc's fires—anticipate a general rebirth. This identification of Orc with the Son of God, and the thirteen colonies with the true followers of the Son, is reinforced by Blake's description of the thirteen angels casting off their robes (*America* 12:1-6), which likens them to the multitude who have "put off the mortal clothing and put on the immortal" to crown the Son on Mount Sion in 2 Esdras 2:42-45. Finally, the image of the drying of the sea to permit the return of the lost tribes, which in turn is an allusion to Isaiah 11:15-16, is echoed in Orc's proclaiming that with the stamping out of the law the deeps will "shrink to their fountains" (*America* 8:8).

Blake's invocation of the book of Esdras, in addition to identifying America with the lost tribes of Israel, identifies Albion's Prince and Urizen with the forces of tyranny that the coming of the Son shall abolish. In the eleventh chapter of his book, Ezra has a vision of an eagle who came up from the sea and who "spread her wings over all the earth" (2 Esdras 11:2), which, as Uriel explains, is the fourth kingdom mentioned in Daniel 7:7 but hitherto unexplained. The beast is interpreted and rebuked by the Son of God:

> Art thou not it that remainest of the four beasts, whom I made to reign in my world, that the end of their times might come through them? And the fourth came, and overcame all the beasts that were past, and had power over the world with great fearfulness, and over the whole compass of the earth with much wicked oppression; and so long time dwelt upon the earth with deceit. For the earth hast thou not judged with truth. For thou hast afflicted the meek, thou hast hurt the peaceable, thou hast loved liars, and destroyed the dwellings of them that brought forth fruit, and hast cast down the walls of such as did thee no harm. Therefore is thy wrongful dealing come up unto the Highest, and thy pride unto the Mighty. The Highest also hath looked

upon the proud times, and, behold, they are ended, and his abominations are fulfilled.   (2 Esdras 11:39-44)

Like the beast rising from the sea in Daniel and Revelation (13:1), the eagle would be interpreted by Christians as the Antichrist.

In *America* the wrathful Prince of Albion, seeing the discomfiture of the thirteen Governors and the British soldiers by Orc's fires, "burnt outstretchd on wings of wrath cov'ring / The eastern sky, spreading his awful wings across the heavens" (*America* 13:11-12), thus assuming the form of Ezra's eagle. Similarly, at the end of *America*, the self-pitying Urizen reacts to the recoiling of the plagues upon Albion by assuming the same eagle form—"his jealous wings wav'd over the deep" (*America* 16:6)—symbolizing the lack of completion of the apocalyptic promise of the American Revolution. True to Blake's dialectical vision, Albion's Angel, who, as we have seen, also represents the Antichrist in his taking on the form of a dragon, echoes the rhetorical question that the Son of God asks in 2 Esdras: "Art thou not Orc . . . Blasphemous Demon, Antichrist, hater of Dignities?" (*America* 7:3-5). The fact that both the Son of God and the eagle rise from the sea in Ezra makes Orc's significance initially ambiguous, adding to the dialectic in *America*. While accusations are hurled from both sides of the Atlantic, the weight of Blake's allusions to the Antichrist falls more heavily upon the British side.

In addition to drawing on the Ezra Apocalypse for the outline of this mythic construction of the American Revolution, Blake employs Ezra's symbols and images to create the strong note of apocalyptic expectation that pervades his prophecy. A sense of urgency, expressed by the scribe's unremitting search for manifestations of the divine will, is the keynote of the Ezra Apocalypse. Besides the familiar apocalyptic symbols of the sword, fires, clouds, and scales of justice (illustrated in plate 5 of *America*)—which are also present in the Old Testament prophets and in Revelation—

Blake borrows Ezra's womb symbolism, which dominates the apocryphal book and creates its intense apocalyptic pressure. Ezra, when asking how long he must wait for the righting of present injustices upon earth, receives the following answer from Uriel:

> So he answered me, and said, Go thy way to a woman with child, and ask of her when she hath fulfilled her nine months, if her womb may keep the birth any longer within her. Then said I, No, Lord, that can she not.
>
> And he said unto me, In the grave the chambers of souls are like the womb of a woman: for like as a woman that travaileth maketh haste to escape the necessity of the travail: even so do these places haste to deliver those things that are committed unto them.
>
> (2 Esdras 4:40-42)

In this image of the earth as a womb waiting to deliver up its dead, time and space are fused in the interpretation of history as the gestation period of the apocalypse. The later the age, the fuller the womb becomes, and the greater the sense of impending delivery.

The concept of time as a womb is reiterated through Ezra's questionings of the workings of God's providence and is given mythic specificity in the image of the birth of Jacob and Esau:

> Then answered I and said, What shall be the parting asunder of the times? or when shall be the end of the first, and the beginning of it that followeth?
>
> And he said unto me, From Abraham unto Isaac, when Jacob and Esau were born of him, Jacob's hand held first the heel of Esau. For Esau is the end of the world, and Jacob is the beginning of it that followeth. The hand of man is betwixt the heel and the hand: other question, Esdras, ask thou not.　　　　(2 Esdras 6:7-10)

This investing of the myth of Esau and Jacob with apocalyptic meaning echoes the prophecy of the destruction of

140

Edom in Isaiah 34 and the rebirth of Zion in Isaiah 35. Here Ezra follows traditional symbolism in associating the infant Esau with the corrupt past age and Jacob with the new holy age, a symbolism that Blake obviously reverses by having the red Orc proclaim the new age.

It is to this birth of a new age that Albion's Angel refers when he says to Orc, "the harlot womb oft opened in vain / Heaves in enormous circles, now the times are return'd upon thee, / Devourer of thy parent, now thy unutterable torment renews . . . / Ah terrible birth! a young one bursting!" (*America* 9:18-20, 22). Orc the Eternal Serpent is reborn to devour his parent, time, devouring his mother like the hell hounds that gnaw the entrails of Milton's Sin (*Paradise Lost* II:790-802). From the tyrant's point of view, time or history is equated with the harlot or with Sin because it breeds numerous abortive rebellions against the tyrant's rule. Orc is particularly threatening because he has the potential to demolish time and return the world to Eternity, thus depriving the tyrant of the medium necessary for his power, the world of finite time and space.

The new birth that terrifies Albion's Angel is an equal torment to the "shadowy daughter of Urthona," of the "Preludium" to *America*, in whose womb the birth is conceived. Her rape by Orc reiterates the association of Orc with the Messiah: the erotic and natal imagery of the Preludium suggest the Incarnation, since Orc's embrace of the woman signifies his taking on an earthly form, the infusion of earth or nature with apocalyptic energy. The womb that he seizes is "panting" and "struggling" as a woman in childbirth, and the daughter of Urthona smiles her "firstborn smile." At last, seeing the "terrible boy" who has brought this joy, the woman recognizes the significance of both Orc and the event in which she is an actor: "Thou art the image of God who dwells in darkness of Africa; / And thou art fall'n to give me life in regions of dark death" (2:8-9).

Orc is called the image of God who dwells in Africa, the

concept of God become flesh, because according to Sweden-borg's *The Last Judgment*, which Blake quotes in his annotations to Swedenborg's *Divine Love and Divine Wisdom*, "the Gentiles, particularly the Africans . . . entertain an Idea of God as of a Man, and say that no one can have any other Idea of God" (p. 593). Orc's embrace is a threat and a torment to the woman, who is the matrix of time and history, because as a potential Messiah, Orc's begetting himself upon her presages the destruction of time and the renewal of Eternity: "O what limb rending pains I feel. thy fire & my frost / Mingle in howling pains, in furrows by thy lightnings rent; / This is eternal death; and this the torment long foretold" (*America* 1:15-17).

The event has been foretold not only by the accumulated associations of Orc with Christ but also by the significance of the "fourteen suns" that mark the day on which Orc makes his assault (*America* 1:2). In the Bible, fourteen suns signify the fourteenth day of the first month, on which begins Passover, the feast celebrating the delivery of Israel from bondage in Egypt (Numbers 9:3, 9:5, 28:16). Furthermore, and more importantly, the number fourteen is used to divide the epochs of biblical history leading up to the birth of Jesus: "So all the generations from Abraham to David are fourteen generations; and from David until the carrying away into Babylon are fourteen generations; and from the carrying away into Babylon unto Christ are fourteen generations" (Matthew 1:17). Reading "fourteen suns" as a pun, we can interpret Orc's reappearance as a new epoch fraught with divine significance—or, as Albion's Angel would have it, a reopening of the harlot's womb that had been opened in vain numerous times before. Orc's fierce embrace of the daughter of Urthona is thus both a rape and a birth, signifying the penetration of Eternity into time, or the Word again made flesh. The rekindling of Orc's fires on earth portends a final consummation in both the apocalyptic and erotic sense of that word.

This mingling throughout *America* of erotic imagery

with the themes of the apocalypse and the Incarnation, forming the imaginative center of Blake's concept of the American Revolution, is hardly Blake's invention. These themes and images are contained in different parts of Isaiah and Esdras, and they find a unified and coherent articulation in the Song of Songs and in the interpretive tradition surrounding that book, which Blake invokes repeatedly throughout his prophecy. Indeed, the Ezra Apocalypse, from which Blake borrows so heavily, also employs images from Canticles and invokes the allegorical interpretation of that book that by Blake's time would be taken for granted.

From the time of its entering the canon, the Song of Solomon's openly erotic and apparently disconnected love lyrics presented problems to religious exegetes, who usually solved those problems by allegorizing the text.[16] There arose various and often conflicting allegorical interpretations of the Song of Songs, but the essential outline of this tradition that subsisted into Blake's time may be summarized as follows:

> The prophets of the Old Testament represented the covenant between Yahweh and Israel in the desert of the Exodus as being a marriage covenant. But this union was only the figure of a more perfect union which was to take place at the end of time, in the New Exodus: "I will lead her into the desert and I will speak to her heart" (Osee II:11, 16). Now the Canticle of Canticles is for certain exegetes the prophecy of this future marriage, the epithalamion of the eschatological wedding of the Lamb described in the Apocalypse: "I saw the New Jerusalem coming down from heaven, prepared as a bride adorned for her husband" (21:2). The New Testament shows us this eschatological marriage as fulfilled by the Incarnation of the Word in which He contracted an indissoluble alliance with human nature (John III:29). This marriage will be finally realized when the Bridegroom returns at

the end of time and the souls of the just form a wedding escort to go forth to meet Him (Matt. XXV: 1-3).

But between its inauguration and its completion at the Parousia, the marriage of Christ and the Church continues—and does so in her sacramental life.[17]

Just as the church saw the Song of Songs as an internalized allegory of the apocalyptic marriage, medieval devotional writers freely adopted the erotic imagery of that book to interpret the divine marriage not as an external event taking place at the end of human history, but as an internal event capable of taking place within the individual soul in the present.[18] Thus the sacred marriage depicted in the Song of Songs was understood to have prophetic significance. According to tradition the marriage takes place on three occasions: (1) in the past, at the Incarnation, (2) in the future, at the Apocalypse, and (3) in the present, in the regeneration of the individual soul—"the intimate joining of all the faculties of the 'soule and body; sense and affections, and all active powers' with the spiritual Bridegroom."[19] This concept of the marriage as the process of integration is underscored in Boehme's and Duché's citations of the Song of Solomon in their descriptions of the process of regeneration.

The tendency to regard the Song of Songs as a prophetic book that links past, present, and future in a unified and unifying vision of God's relationship to man was reinforced by a related but less popular line of interpretation that saw the biblical book as an historical allegory. This interpretation was advanced by the Targum, or Chaldee Paraphrase, which read the Song of Songs as an allegorical history of God's dealings with Israel, from the Exodus to the coming of the Messiah.[20] R. Saadias Gaon, Ibn Ezra, and other Jewish commentators continued to read Canticles as an historico-prophetic allegory.[21] Christian exegetes, such as Aponius (who is quoted by the Venerable Bede) and Nicholas De Lyra, adopted this tradition by substituting the Christian church for the Jewish nation and thereby reading the Song of Songs as an allegory of God's dealings with the church from its beginning until the Last Judgment.[22] The seventeenth-century commentaries of John Cocceius and Thomas Brightman saw the Canticles as an allegorical history of the church that paralleled the structure and content of the Book of Revelation.[23]

The allegorical interpretation of Canticles is present in the Second Book of Ezra, with the prophet drawing upon images from that book to develop his apocalyptic vision. Ezra describes Israel as a lily among the flowers (5:24), alluding to the image of the bride in the Song of Songs 2:1, and as a dove (5:26), which describes the bride throughout the Song of Songs. The image of the bride and its relation to the Incarnation is mentioned explicitly in 2 Esdras 7:26-44, where the appearance of the bride heralds the coming of Christ.[24]

Although some of Blake's contemporaries began to adopt a literal reading of the Song of Songs, seeing the book as a prothalamium or an epithalamium celebrating Solomon's marriage to Pharaoh's daughter, the allegorical view persisted into the late eighteenth century, sometimes existing side by side with the literal view.[25] When John Bland published his dramatic paraphrase of Canticles in 1750 and called it "A Sacred Drama. To be perform'd at *Jerusalem,* during the Millennium Sabbath,"[26] he was expressing a traditional vision of the biblical book that was already familiar to his readers. Milton had called the Song of Songs a "Divine pastoral Drama,"[27] "which is generally beleev'd even in the jolliest expressions to figure the spousals of the Church with Christ [and which] sings of a thousand raptures between those two lovely ones farre on the hither side of carnall enjoyment."[28] Blake, like many of the seventeenth-century paraphrasers of the Song of Songs, would have discounted Milton's chastened interpretation of those nuptial joys, playing freely with the latitude permitted in the Reformation's interpretation of the "Church" as the individual

Christian.[29] As Northrop Frye has observed, Blake saw the Song of Songs as "neither as voluptuous Orientale nor a chilly allegory" but a combination of the two: "The Christian interpretation of it [Canticles] as an allegory of Christ's love for his Church is really Blake's, if the frankly sexual aspect of the imagery is not too hurriedly passed over."[30]

This interpretive tradition accounts for one of the most striking features of Blake's treatment of the American Revolution—his conceiving of that historical event in erotic terms. As we have seen, he had ample precedent in the traditions that saw Canticles as prophetic history and that interpreted the Christian pattern of history as the movement toward the apocalyptic marriage.[31] If a prophetic view of history is a view that deals with the love relationship between Christ and his church, the apocalyptic consummation of that relationship is anticipated through sexual imagery that expresses the church's arousal to a fever pitch of longing for union with the Bridegroom.

In *America* the Incarnation and the promised apocalyptic marriage are necessarily presented in erotic images to show the reawakening of this holy lust that has too long been repressed by false religion and political tyranny. The true climax of *America* is the proclamation that "the doors of marriage are open" (15:19), an allusion to the Song of Songs:

> I sleep, but my heart waketh: it is the voice of my beloved that knocketh, saying, Open to me, my sister, my love, my dove, my undefiled: for my head is filled with dew, and my locks with the drops of the night. . . .
>
> My beloved put in his hand by the hole of the door, and my bowels were moved for him.
>
> (Song of Solomon 5:2, 5:4)

The female spirits of Albion, freed from the "bonds of religion" by the energies of Orc, "feel the nerves of youth renew, and desires of ancient times, / Over their pale limbs as a vine when the tender grape appears" (15:25-26). This image of the grapevine, repeated in the illustration at the bottom of plate 15, is another allusion to the Song of Songs: "Let us get up early to the vineyards; let us see if the vine flourish, whether the tender grape appear, and the pomegranates bud forth: there will I give thee my loves" (Song of Solomon 7:12). Blake's use of vine imagery to describe the women's bodies in *America* 15:25-26 and the illustration to plate 15, where female nudes mingle with a cluster of grapes and a nude whose arms and feet trail off into vines, echoes the verse in Song of Songs 7:8, "thy breasts shall be as clusters of the vine."

Thus, while Orc is described in *America* as Christ coming down with a sword, he is also Christ the Bridegroom (Christ is also represented as both in Revelation), a god who is both wrathful and loving.[32] This identity is established in the Preludium by means of allusions to the Song of Songs. The shadowy daughter of Urthona is described as a "Dark virgin" (1:11), for example, and thus assumes the physical attributes of the bride in the Song of Songs: "I am black, but comely, O ye daughters of Jerusalem, as the tents of Kedar, as the curtains of Solomon" (Song of Solomon 1:5). Orc's cry to the dark woman, "my red eyes seek to behold thy face" (1:19-20), echoes the bridegroom's plaint in Song of Solomon 2:14, "O my dove, that art in the clefts of the rock, in the secret places of the stairs, let me see thy countenance, let me hear thy voice." After Orc essays his fierce embrace, the woman exclaims, "I know thee, I have found thee, & I will not let thee go" (2:7), recalling the bride's words in Song of Solomon 3:4, "I found him whom my soul loveth: I held him, and would not let him go, until I had brought him into my mother's house, and into the chamber of her that conceived me."

The allusions to the Song of Songs that identify the daughter of Urthona with the bride of Christ not only carry the theme of the apocalyptic marriage but also reinforce the theme of the Incarnation that I have already

147

noted. As Blake's painting of the black madonna reveals,[33] he was well aware of the tradition that associates the bride in the Song of Songs with the Virgin. This renders Orc's embrace of the dark virgin a symbol of the Incarnation, the wedding of the Word and the flesh that is acknowledged in the daughter of Urthona's recognition speech (2:7-17). Like the Virgin, the shadowy female is the matrix of history, whose impregnation by the fires of Orc portends the entering of the divine into human events. She trembles at the possibility that through the incarnation of Orc the Word will be permanently made flesh and the final mystical marriage will be consummated. Emphasizing two of the occasions on which the marriage takes place, the past Incarnation and the promised Apocalypse, the Preludium points to the possibility that the marriage will take place in the present, that is, through the Revolution, and thereby typologically unify past, present, and future in a single prophetic action.

It is the failure of the Revolution to complete the pattern, to bridge the past and the future by renewing the biblical type in the present, that causes the stern bard in the Preludium to throw down his harp (2:18-19). His despair expresses the same impatience to hasten the Apocalypse that we encounter in the book of Esdras. Yet the prophecy itself is dominated by a note of joyous expectation, a feeling of optimism that is unique in Blake's early prophecies. And this note of optimism is reinforced by repeated allusions to the Song of Songs. Orc's proclamation of the coming of morning, for instance, echoes the anticipation of daybreak in the Song of Songs:

> The morning comes, the night decays, the watchmen leave their stations; (*America* 6:1)

> The Sun has left his blackness, & has found a fresher morning; (*America* 6:13)

> The times are ended; shadows pass the morning gins to break. (*America* 8:2)

Until the day break, and the shadows flee away, turn, my beloved, and be thou like a roe or a young hart upon the mountains of Bether. (Song of Solomon 2:17)

Until the day break, and the shadows flee away, I will get me to the mountain. (Song of Solomon 4:6)

The image of the fleeing hart appears in the designs of plates 15 and 16, underscoring the hope that the morning will actually break in Europe. The picture in the Preludium (pl. 2) of Orc emerging from the ground, along with the grapevines on either side of him, recalls the budding of the vines in Song of Songs 7:12, and Orc's calling the slave to run out into the field (6:6) alludes to the lover's call to go into the field in Song of Songs 7:11.

The picture of the child being instructed beneath the tree in the illustration to plate 14, as well as the pictures of children beneath a tree in plates 1 and 7, refers to the following passage in the Song of Songs: "Who is this that cometh up from the wilderness, leaning upon her beloved? I raised thee up under the apple tree: there thy mother brought thee forth; there she brought thee forth that bare thee" (8:5). The interpretive tradition surrounding this passage explains the symmetry of those three designs in *America*:

> In the last chapter of the Canticles one reads that man was born beneath a tree, where he was reared by his mother, Eve. As Luis de Granada and others wrote, this tree was none other than the interdicted Tree of Paradise. Not only was man raised there, his flesh was the very branching (or rather, withering) of its root. In this single metaphor the symmetry of God's plan of redemption was manifest: man lost his favored position "beneath the tree," and beneath a tree it was regained, "namely beneath the tree of the Cross."[34]

Plate 14 illustrates the theme of the Fall, with the child being nurtured by the priestess of Apollo, who is initiating him into the world of fallen nature. As David Erdman has pointed out, the sibyl's purpose is to cut off the child's perceptions of the infinite: "Her thumb and fingers demonstrate that life is but a span. From her womb speaks a lean but eloquent serpent, one of the monsters of error that breed in the womb of Moral virtue."[35]

Erdman also calls attention to the similarity between this kind of instruction and the instruction of the chained Orc by the shadowy daughter of Urthona in 1:1.[36] The illustration to that bleak plate carries the same motif of the child under a tree, and the iconographical linking of the chained Orc with Abel reinforces the traditional concept of fallen man being raised under the Tree of Knowledge by his mother, Eve. Although this illustration and that on plate 14 use the motif from the Song of Songs to carry the theme of the Fall, the illustration on plate 7 uses the same motif of children under a tree to develop the contrary concept that the motif implies, the concept of salvation beneath the tree. In the latter design a new nature and nurture is promised by the figure of the ram—a symbol of Christ—and the rays of sunlight (in copy M), whose benevolent power is further indicated by the budding grapevine that is beginning to appear beneath the tree.

This design, as Kathleen Raine suggests, alludes to another passage in the Song of Songs:[37] "Tell me, O thou whom my soul loveth, where thou feedest, where thou makest thy flock to rest at noon: for why should I be as one that turneth aside by the flocks of thy companions" (Song of Solomon 1:7). The design thus illustrates the repose with the Bridegroom that the bride longs for, the church's deliverance from its afflictions. This design is set in dialectical tension with the designs on plates 1 and 14, creating a feeling of optimistic anticipation that through the American Revolution man will cast off his false nature/nurture and will be raised up under God's grace.

Although this promise is not fulfilled in *America*, the

150

imagery from Canticles makes Blake's prophecy tremble
with hope even to the very end of that work. Even though
the last plate describes the quenching of Orc's fires by
Urizen's tears of jealousy, the text tells us that the fires will
be rekindled in twelve years, and the doors of perception in
Europe—"the doors of marriage"—have been melted open
by the fires of Orc. The colophon heightens this optimism
by holding forth a last image of the bride, a lily among the
thorns (Song of Solomon 2:2), echoing the bridegroom's
longing for consummation with the bride. The image of
Urizen's temporary and ineffectual quenching of Orc's fires
is drawn from what is perhaps the most famous passage in
Canticles:

> Set me as a seal upon thine heart, as a seal upon thine
> arm: for love is strong as death; jealousy is cruel as the
> grave: the coals thereof are coals of fire, which hath a
> most vehement flame. Many waters cannot quench love,
> neither can the floods drown it.   (8:6-7)

Orc, whose energies are "strong as jealousy" (2:1), is identi-
fied as a type of Christ, the principle of love or (to use
Duché's terms) the heavenly fire of true Righteousness that
promises the obliteration of the laws of jealousy, opens the
doors of marriage and causes the world to hunger for the
coming consummation.

Europe:
The Bride and the Harlot

Whereas *America* is primarily concerned with the arrival of Orc as the apocalyptic bridegroom, *Europe* presents a more detailed examination of the condition of the bride. In the latter prophecy, which deals with the events in Europe subsequent to the American Revolution, Blake continues to work within the context of the apocalyptic marriage, but he expands this prophetic symbol by invoking its biblical antithesis, the separation between God and the harlot. The Old Testament prophets depicted the promise of redemption in terms of the marriage metaphor, but they also castigated Israel's falling away from God by describing her as the whore who fornicates with other gods or nations (Ezekiel 16:15-36, 23:1-21; Isaiah 1:21; Hosea 4:12-19). Thus the Bible contains a dialectical female mythos that parallels the dialectical male figures of Esau and Jacob, Christ and the Antichrist.

This dialectic is of course most dramatically developed in Revelation, where the Whore of Babylon must be overthrown before the bride, Jerusalem, can be revealed. Yet it is present in the wisdom literature as well as in the prophetic books of the Bible. In the Book of Proverbs and in the apocryphal books of Ecclesiasticus and the Wisdom of Solomon, Wisdom is represented as the bride, the consort of God, the part of man that unites him with God, and in Proverbs her rival for man's affections is the harlot, who represents all that is opposed to divine vision and wisdom. The harlot's usurpation of the bride's position in man's heart thus symbolizes man's fallen condition, and the process of redemption therefore requires the identification and casting off of the harlot so that the bride may regain her rightful position.

This female mythos also appears in Book I of Spenser's *The Faerie Queene*, as the opposition between Una and Duessa, and in other works by Spenser. And Blake shares Spenser's interest in the two female figures, as we can see in *Europe* where he invokes both Spenser and the biblical tradition of which Spenser partakes to embody in mythic form eighteen hundred years of European history, which Blake depicts as a period in which the harlot reigns. The harlot is represented in Blake's prophecy by Enitharmon, who is set in opposition to another female figure, the "nameless shadowy female" of the Preludium, who has the attributes of the biblical figure of Wisdom. Enitharmon is also contrasted to her rebellious daughter, Oothoon, whose cries for open and generous love in *Visions of the Daughters of Albion* and whose desire to give up "womans secrecy" in *Europe* (14:22) liken her to the women of Albion in *America* and Wisdom in the Book of Proverbs. Enitharmon represents, among other things, Nature and the biblical harlot; but Blake's interpretation of the nature of her harlotry is unusual in that her most important activity is her promulgation of a religion of chastity, which perverts human energies through the creation of a chivalric ideal and a theology based on power rather than love.

The harlot's influence had been so pervasive that it even touched the mind of one of England's greatest poet-prophets, John Milton, whose *On the Morning of Christ's Nativity* subverted its own prophetic intention by embracing her ideology. Blake seizes upon this contaminated vision of the birth of Christ, an event that was, after all, the ideological foundation of European civilization, as being symptomatic of Europe's malaise. Blake exposes Milton's errors by recreating *The Nativity Ode*, casting it into the form of true prophecy; he achieves this form by placing Milton's work within the context of biblical tradition.

Europe, the product of this recasting, is closely patterned

153

upon Milton's *Nativity Ode*, in terms of thematic content, symbols, and structure.[1] The introductory verses (plate iii) and the Preludium of *Europe* parallel the introductory verses of Milton's poem, for instance, in that both introductions announce the theme of the Incarnation.[2] The next parallel, and the most obvious one, is that of the opening of Milton's Hymn with the opening of Blake's "A Prophecy," where the "deep of winter" (3:1) in which Orc descends echoes the "Winter wild" of Christ's nativity in Milton's Hymn.[3] Milton then describes the reign of peace at Christ's birth, the reaction of the natural world, and the attendant music of created nature that accompanies the event (lines 32-148). Similarly, Blake shows the cessation of war at Orc's descent (3:4-7), the response of the natural world—of Los (3:9-14), the sons of Urizen (4:3-9), and Enitharmon (4:10-14)—accompanied by the music of the sons of Urizen. Milton's descent of Justice (line 141) is paralleled by the descent of Enitharmon (4:17). The transitional stanza in Milton's poem, which telescopes the intervening time between the first and second coming of Christ (lines 149-164), appears in *Europe* as the lines mentioning the eighteen hundred years of Enitharmon's sleep that separate the two events (9:1-5). The routing of the pagan deities, which forms the next major structural division in Milton's poem, is echoed by two movements in Blake's: the fall of Albion's angelic band (9:6-13:8) and the moonlight revels of Enitharmon's fairy band, the latter being an expansion of the fairy revels mentioned in stanza xxvi of Milton's *Nativity Ode*. Both poems end with the breaking forth of light that emanates from the newborn child and the description of the child and his attendant host in military images: chariots and armed angels.

Within these structural parallels, however, Blake works important variations upon Milton's poem. These variations both illuminate and criticize Milton's vision in order to apply that vision to the crisis that Blake perceived to be facing his own age. As we examine the parallels and divergences more closely, we shall see that Blake's reading of Milton's *Nativity Ode* and his revision of that work were attempts to place both Milton and the state of modern Europe in their true biblical context.

The four stanzas that form the prelude to Milton's Hymn in *On the Morning of Christ's Nativity* announce the occasion of the poem, the poet's muse, and his theme. It is the morning of Christ's birth, the moment when eternity entered time, when Christ "laid aside" his "glorious Form," "Forsook the Courts of everlasting Day / And chose with us a darksome House of mortal Clay" (lines 8-14). The phrase "chose with us," which can be interpreted to mean "chose as we have chosen," links the Incarnation with the Fall, suggesting that Christ, as the second Adam, initially repeats the pattern of the first Adam by choosing mortality, and conversely, that Adam could have shared Christ's divinity had he not chosen to fall. This linking of Christ with fallen man is further emphasized by Milton's description of the Incarnation as the enveloping of eternal light by darkness, which is "a complete reversal of the traditional Christian representation of Christ's birth as a sudden illumination of a world that has been darkened by sin since Eden."[4] This reversal has the effect of telescoping time in Milton's poem, since the metaphor emphasizes Christ's human nature, which he shares with mankind not just at one point in history but at all times.[5]

Yet, paradoxically, Milton emphasizes Christ's bond with humanity in order to point out a significant difference: Christ chose to fall in full consciousness of what he was doing and in order to point the way to redemption: "That he our deadly forfeit should release, / And with his Father work us a perpetual peace" (lines 6-7). Or, as Blake would put it, "God becomes as we are, that we may be as he is" (*There is NO Natural Religion* [b], p. 2). Here Milton's use of the same act to distinguish two different states of consciousness anticipates the theme in *Paradise Regained* of one man's disobedience redeemed by a greater man's

155

obedience. The implication of Milton's complex metaphor is that if man, like Christ, is in fact a potentially divine being that has chosen mortality, the only thing that prevents him from achieving his divinity is his lack of consciousness or vision. Such a lack, for a modern Christian, can only be accounted for by a perverseness on his part, since the pattern of incarnation and redemption has been revealed in the past through Christ's entering human history. But man chooses to remain, in Jacob Boehme's phrase, an historical Christian,[6] perceiving Christ's actions through the lens of his fallen, time-bound consciousness. This obstinacy, as we shall see, is the essential point of Milton's *Nativity Ode* as Blake reads it, and it is this kind of fallen consciousness that Milton initially seeks to overcome in the opening of the *Nativity Ode* by manipulating the reader's sense of time to make the birth of Christ an event taking place in the reader's present time.

The reading of Milton's poem that I have just outlined is the one that Blake inculcates in the opening of *Europe*, as he builds upon and extends Milton's metaphor of the "darksome house of mortal clay" that Christ and man choose to dwell in. The preface to *Europe* opens with the metaphor of the body as a house within which "cavern'd Man" dwells and in which he willfully chooses to remain. Like Milton, Blake employs images of light and darkness, extending the metaphor of the darkened house by describing the senses as windows that admit the light of eternity, the "everlasting Day" that Milton's Christ forsakes. The ears admit the music of the spheres, an allusion to the symbol that dominates the first part of the Hymn in Milton's *Nativity Ode*; the tongue tastes the fruit of the "eternal vine"; and the eyes "see small portions of the eternal world that ever groweth" (iii:1-4). In this catalogue of the windows that open up to eternity, Blake significantly diverges from Milton by proclaiming the sense of touch, man's sexuality, as the means of redemption—in opposition to the visual and auditory senses, particularly the latter,

156

that the rest of Milton's poem relies upon to image man's return to eternity. Thus while Blake follows Milton in emphasizing the Incarnation as an eternally recurring event within the life of every man and in stressing the perversity of man's refusing to follow the pattern of redemption revealed by Christ, he significantly disagrees with Milton about the conformation of this pattern. It is because of Milton's concept of the Atonement as elucidated in the *Nativity Ode* that Blake invokes that poem to describe the condition of modern Europe.

This essential point of disagreement with Milton—and the orthodox notions upon which Milton's theology relies— is most fully developed in Blake's preface and in the Preludium to *Europe*, through Blake's response to Milton's invocation of the Christian muse in the *Nativity Ode*. The "Heav'nly Muse" whose "sacred vein" produces Milton's "humble ode" is a complex of Renaissance ideas and attitudes about divinely inspired poetry that are personified in a single figure. This figure synthesizes the pagan muse of astronomy with the biblical personification of Wisdom (or "Sapience," as Spenser called her in his *Hymne of Heavenlie Beautie*) that appears in Proverbs, The Wisdom of Solomon, and Ecclesiasticus. The new muse was first introduced to the literary world by Du Bartas' *L'Uranie*,[7] and the tradition surrounding her was invoked by Spenser in *The Teares of the Muses, Complaints*, and *An Hymne of Heavenlie Beautie*.

Milton, of course, was to expound more fully upon this tradition in his inductions to the first, third, seventh, and ninth books of *Paradise Lost*. The Christian muse, as the inspirer of divine poetry, possessed and instilled in the inspired poet not only a knowledge of the natural operations of the entire created universe but also a knowledge of the heavenly hierarchy and the workings of Divine Providence.[8] But even more than this, the muse is identified as the power through which the universe was created and is maintained:

> Both heauen and earth obey vnto her will,
> And all the creatures which they both containe:
> For of her fulnesse which the world doth fill,
> They all partake, and do in state remaine,
> As thir great Maker did at first ordaine,
> Through obseruation of her high beheast,
> By which they first were made, and still increast.
> (An Hymne of Heavenlie Beautie, lines 197-203)

> Thou from the first
> Wast present, and with mighty wings outspread
> Dove-like satst brooding on the vast Abyss
> And mad'st it pregnant.
> (Paradise Lost I: 19-22)

As Milton's image of the dove implies, the muse was often described in language that associated her with the Holy Ghost. She was also described in erotic terms, as "The soueraine dearling of the *Deity*" who sits in his bosom (*An Hymne of Heavenlie Beautie*, lines 183-84).

Whether she is called Urania, Sapience, or simply the Heavenly Muse, this traditional figure derives almost all of her attributes from the personification of Wisdom in the Bible and the Apocrypha. There Wisdom is described as the beloved of God, possessed by Him before the Creation (Proverbs 8:22-26), and a participant in the genesis of the universe:

> When he prepared the heavens, I was there: when he set a compass upon the face of the depth: When he established the clouds above: when he strengthened the fountains of the deep; When he gave to the sea his decree, that the waters should not pass his commandent: when he appointed the foundations of the earth: Then I was by him, as one brought up with him: and I was daily his delight, rejoicing always before him.
> (Proverbs 8:27-30)

Wisdom, in fact, is identified as the very force behind that creation: "The Lord by wisdom hath founded the earth; by understanding hath he established the heavens. By his knowledge the depths are broken up, and the clouds drop down the dew" (Proverbs 3:19-20). As such, she is the source of all knowledge both human and divine (Wisdom of Solomon 7:17-22). She is the personification of divine inspiration:

> For she is the breath of the power of God, and a pure influence flowing from the glory of the Almighty: therefore can no defiled thing fall into her. For she is the brightness of the everlasting light, the unspotted mirror of the power of God, and the image of his goodness. And being but one, she can do all things: and remaining in herself, she maketh all things new: and in all ages entering into holy souls, she maketh them friends of God, and Prophets. (Wisdom of Solomon 7:25-27)

She bestows the gift of eloquence, "For wisdom opened the mouth of the dumb, and made the tongues of them that cannot speak eloquent" (Wisdom of Solomon 10:21).

In Ecclesiasticus, Wisdom, besides containing most of the above-mentioned attributes, also is imaged as the voice of God residing in the cloud that rises from the altar in the tabernacle (Ecclesiasticus 24:1-15). Milton alludes to this image of Wisdom's voice rising from the altar when he requests of his muse, "join thy voice unto the Angel Choir, / From out his secret Altar toucht with hallow'd fire" (lines 27-28). All the divine powers and attributes of the biblical figure of Wisdom belong to the traditional muse invoked in Milton's *Nativity Ode*. By invoking the muse, Milton clearly reveals his intention to be that of elevating himself, his poem, and his readers to a perception of the infinite. He wants the heavenly gift that is bestowed upon those who are found to be worthy followers of Spenser's Sapience:

159

[She] letteth them her louely face to see,
Wherof such wondrous pleasures they conceaue,
And swcct contentment, that it doth bereaue,
Their soule of sense, through infinite delight,
And them transport from flesh into the spright.

In which they see such admirable things,
As carries them into an extasy,
And heare such heauenly notes, and carolings,
Of Gods high praise, that filles the brasen sky,
And feele such joy and pleasure inwardly,
That maketh them all worldly cares forget,
And onely thinke on that before them sct.

(Hymne of Heauenlie Beautie, lines 255-66)

This is clearly what Milton seeks and achieves in the first part of the Hymn. But his muse intends much more than the mystic raptures of the individual soul; she is also concerned with the deliverance of all of mankind from the chains of sin and mortality—hence the cessation of the vision of the heavenly spheres and the focus on the idolatries that must be destroyed before universal redemption can be achieved.

Compared to the high aspirations of Milton's muse, Blake's use of a fairy to dictate *Europe* seems trivial. Moreover, this fairy belongs to that band of "yellow-skirted *Fays*" that are banished as false oracles by the infant Christ (lines 235-36), a point to which I will return. Blake appears to be intentionally deflating Milton's muse, for the muse of *Europe* affords no solemn strains but rather sings of the joys of the material world:

If you will feed me on love-thoughts, & give me now
  and then
A cup of sparkling poetic fancies; so when I am tipsie,
I'll sing to you to this soft lute; and shew you all alive
The world, when every particle of dust breathes forth
  its joy.

(i:15-18)

160

The poetic fancy upon which Blake's fairy feeds is precisely the fancy that, Milton speculates, might bring back the Golden Age if that fancy continued to be enwrapped with the holy song of the angel chorus (lines 133-35). Milton abandons this aspect of his muse, recalling that wisest Fate says that this cannot be so until man's redemption is worked out within the world of time and space; he recalls the dissonances that must be removed before universal harmony can become permanent. Blake, in his preface to *Europe*, embraces what Milton in the process of the *Nativity Ode* reluctantly abandons—both the fays and the poetic fancy.[9] Milton's angel choir is replaced by every particle of dust breathing forth its joy, and the secret altar touched with hallowed fire is replaced by the clouds of incense arising from the plucked flowers. The plucking of the flowers, with its sexual connotations, is posited against the concept of chastity that is implied by Milton's secret altar, which Blake interprets as the inaccessible female organ of generation.[10]

Blake's criticism of Milton's muse is present not only in the preface, which Blake includes in only two versions of *Europe*, but also in the Preludium. There the nameless shadowy female is none other than the Christian muse, whom Blake shows to be in a fallen state.[11] The preface helps establish the context for this identification through the fairy's mocking statement about man's unwillingness to escape his fallen condition: "For stolen joys are sweet, & bread eaten in secret pleasant" (i:6). This is an allusion to the appeal of the harlot, the enemy of Wisdom, in the Book of Proverbs: "Stolen waters are sweet, and bread eaten in secret is pleasant" (Proverbs 9:17).[12] Since mankind has accepted this call, Wisdom has been rejected and is represented as such in Blake's Preludium.

The context of allusions to the biblical books in which the figure of Wisdom appears is further developed in other plates at the beginning of *Europe*, which thereby identify the shadowy female with the Christian muse. The famous frontispiece of *Europe* derives its central symbol, the compass, from a speech that Wisdom makes in Proverbs: "When he prepared the heavens, I was there: when he set a compass upon the face of the depth" (Proverbs 8:27). The picture that forms the headpiece of the Preludium, which depicts assassins who are waiting to ambush a pilgrim, represents those who have turned away from Wisdom and who say, "Come with us, let us lay wait for blood, let us lurk privily for the innocent without cause. . . . So are the ways of every one that is greedy of gain; which taketh away the life of the owners thereof" (Proverbs 1:11, 1:19). The images of Wisdom as a tree of life in Proverbs 3:18 and as a fruit-bearing tree whose roots come from God (Ecclesiasticus 1:16-20, 24:17-19) are echoed in the shadowy female's saying, "My roots are brandish'd in the heavens. my fruits in earth beneath" (1:8). Just as Wisdom is the inspiration of God that is poured forth into every living thing (Wisdom of Solomon 7:25-27), so the nameless shadowy female produces fires of inspiration from her bosom that are stamped into earthly form by Enitharmon (2:9-10). Finally, the voice of the female in Blake's poem, like the voice of Wisdom in Ecclesiasticus—and like Milton's muse—is identified with the cloud that arises from the altar, for when the voice of Blake's female ceases, she rolls her shady clouds into the secret place (i.e., the holy of holies in Ecclesiasticus 24, Milton's "secret altar").[13]

Besides these biblical associations with Wisdom that identify the shadowy female with the Christian muse, there are allusions to other literary traditions that reinforce this identity. The shadowy female's lament that "the red sun and moon, / And all the overflowing stars rain down prolific pains" of death and destruction (1:14-15) likens her to Spenser's Urania, who uses the same imagery—borrowed from The Wisdom of Solomon (14:22)—of pestilence poured down from the stars to describe the blindness and ignorance that infects mortal minds, imprisons man in the fallen world by debasing those "mindes of men borne heauenlie" (*Teares of the Muses*, lines 481-98). Both women gaze up to heaven and both lament fallen man's bestial condition (*Teares*, lines 528-34; *Europe* 2:1-11). An even stronger connection with Spenser's Urania is shown by Blake's modeling his entire Preludium upon the genre in which Spenser's Urania appears, the complaint. Like all the muses in Spenser's poem, Blake's shadowy female laments the fallen world's neglect of her and the sad case in which fallen man now finds himself as a result of his refusal to seek her divine benefits.

Yet unlike Spenser's Urania, who has withdrawn to become pure contemplation, Blake's figure of the Christian muse has fallen from her original purity. Her snaky hair likens her to Megaera or to Milton's Sin, as she was portrayed in a cartoon by Gillray.[14] She no longer represents knowledge of all things both human and divine; rather, she has been reduced to Newtonian science, as exhibited by her counting the stars, an activity that is significant both literally and metaphorically. Not only does the female represent the debasement of heavenly knowledge to that which is measurable but she represents the debasement of earthly knowledge as well, since the stars are a biblical metaphor for the generations of man (see Genesis 15:5). She numbers the generations of man, drawing from the stars the energy or power of the souls that Enitharmon stamps with earthly form, and her only knowledge is that of the pains of the cyclical repetition of generation and decay.

This latter aspect of her character is further reinforced by allusions to another one of Spenser's complaints, *The Ruines of Time*, from which Blake borrowed his symbol of Verulam in "A Prophecy." Spenser's representation of the fallen city of Verulam as a lamenting female spirit is echoed by Blake's shadowy female. Like Blake's female, the spirit in Spenser's poem is nameless; the renewing generations of man have caused her name to vanish, her place not to be found. Singing the *ubi sunt* theme, she recalls the mighty kings and nobles, devouring and devoured, who constitute

163

the nightmare of history. As a *genius loci*, Spenser's spirit represents the historical consciousness of her race: the glory of Verulam, which in Roman times rivaled that of London, has disappeared along with the generations of heroes who contributed to her greatness. In Blake's poem, the female image of faded glory is fallen not because Verulam has been destroyed, but because it has been maintained by the science of Bacon, Newton, and Locke. In "A Prophecy" the erecting of Verulam becomes a symbol of the incarnation of fallen man, answering the questions that the shadowy female asks before her silence: "And who shall bind the infinite with an eternal band? / To compass it with swaddling bands? and who shall cherish it / With milk and honey?" (2:13-15). To man's fallen mind, the infinite becomes bound in the serpent folds of time (10:16) and knowledge is reduced to an awareness of death and desolation. Given the present state of heavenly and earthly wisdom, the shadowy female does not want to be awakened to life by Enitharmon because her awareness of man's fallen condition is too painful.

Thus Blake represents the Christian muse as the fallen consciousness of history that cannot see beyond the cycles of birth and death, the endless incarnations of spirit into flesh. She is forced to obey Newton's laws and watch the fires of inspiration become stamped into the forms of death and decay. Like Wisdom in the Book of Proverbs and like Urania in *Teares of the Muses*, she laments that her name is becoming forgotten among men, who perversely prefer to retain their fallen condition. At the end of her complaint, she looks forward to the time when either her name will be completely blotted out or she will be present at a new creation, echoing the passages in Proverbs and the Book of Job (38:9) that refer to her participation in the Mosaic creation. She questions whether the latest incarnation of Orc will break through the swaddling bands and open the fallen world to the infinite or whether this will be another finite revolution, another instance (to use the

Angels' terms) of "the harlot womb oft opened in vain" (*America* 9:18). Remaining in doubt and disgusted with the fallen world, she withdraws her oracular clouds back into the tabernacle, "the secret place" (2:18).

This last image in the Preludium, the secret place, corresponds to the secret altar that is the last image in Milton's Proem to the *Nativity Ode*, but in Milton, instead of being withdrawn inward, the clouds of prophecy come out to join the angel choir. Milton's celebration is thus Blake's lament. Milton's muse will sing of the promise of the Incarnation, but she reappears in Blake's poem as a fading hag who has seen too many incarnations to be impressed by the latest one that is about to take place in Europe. Rather than rushing to greet the new incarnation, she collapses into secrecy and self-communion. The traditional Christian muse, Blake is saying, has lost her power. Fallen man has been closed to inspiration, and both art and life have suffered. The muse's withdrawing into the secret place, read as a sexual metaphor, implies that the once beloved of God who used to play continually before Him has become a victim of the religion of chastity; she is divorced not only from man but from God as well. Her powers of integrating the human and the divine have diminished.

Although seeing Milton as a potential prophet who points to the need for man's reclaiming his divinity through vision, Blake's preface and Preludium imply that the way to vision provided by Milton's muse is no longer viable. That muse has fallen, and, Blake will go on to say, Milton himself has contributed to that fall, for Milton made the error of confusing divine inspiration with moral virtue. His lumping of the fairies and the pagan deities in the same category was an oversimplification. These fairies are capable of the errors of those deities, but they are also capable of leading man back to divinity—they are beyond the moral categories to which Milton assigns them. The young Milton is impetuous to push forward the time of the apocalypse, but he yields to the admonitions of "wisest Fate" and thus collapses a vision that could very well have ushered in the Golden Age. He lacks the maturity of a prophetic figure like Ezra, who would use his whole being if necessary to persuade God to hasten the promised end.[15]

As "A Prophecy" parallels and comments upon Milton's Hymn, Blake further develops these ideas about Milton's errors. In contrast to the birth of Christ, Blake depicts the birth of Orc. In both poems the event takes place during a time of peace, but this peace, Blake shows, is really "the great war of ignorance," the "great plagues" that fools and idolators call peace (Wisdom of Solomon 14:22). In Milton's poem, Nature assumes a mantle of chastity to sympathize with her maker (lines 32-34); she refrains from wantoning with the Sun, "her lusty Paramour" (line 36), and appears to be ready to abdicate when she hears the musical response to the divine event (lines 101-108). In Blake's reworking of the poem, the birth of Orc-Christ has the opposite effect. Nature becomes chaste, but it is not out of any sense of obedience to the new Master, but because through the Incarnation she has bound the sexual energy that he possesses. Rather than looking forward to the end of her reign, Enitharmon, who represents Nature in Blake's poem, employs her chastity as a means of asserting dominion. Like Nature, Lucifer in Milton's poem is subdued by the birth of Christ (lines 74-76); but in Blake's poem, Lucifer is "Urizen unloos'd from chains" who "Glows like a meteor in the distant north" (3:11-12) and exerts his powers over the natural world.[16] His sons respond to the birth of Orc with a demonic chorus that parodies the angelic chorus of Milton's Hymn. In contrast to the freely mingling strings and "Divinely-warbled voice" (line 96) in Milton's poem, the sons of Urizen create a forced harmony by binding the warbling joys of life to their loud strings (4:3-6). The sons of Urizen are counterparts to Milton's "sons of morning" (line 119), and both allude to the time "when the morning stars sang together, and all the sons of God shouted for joy" (Job 38:7). Blake's stars do not sing the powers of a benevolent Creator, however, but rather celebrate their own power, the "lucky hours" (4:9) of joy that man attributes to the stars that represent time and Milton's "wisest Fate."

Milton's globe of circular light that contains the singing chorus of angels is replaced in Blake's poem by the demonic Orc surrounded in a whirling globe of flaming stars, which echo the "Globe of fiery Seraphim" that surround Satan in *Paradise Lost* (II:512). Once bound, the incarnate Orc becomes Enitharmon's "lusty paramour" as she descends into his red light, a unilateral kind of relationship that suggests what D. H. Lawrence was later to call sex in the head. The heavens do not sing a song of celestial harmony, but rather extol the dominion of the female will, which will cause Europe to be ravaged with war for eighteen hundred years. Nature falls into a sleep and delegates her powers to priests and kings, represented in the heavenly chorus by Rintrah and Palamabron. Nature, rather than doffing her gaudy attire, actually dresses her train, calling forth the subordinate deities who will destroy all joy and create discord on earth. Instead of harmony and light, the birth of Orc produces darkness and discord, the "night of Enitharmon's joy" (6:1). The pagan ceremonies and oracles are established rather than destroyed by the great event, as Enitharmon, who is Blake's equivalent of Milton's "Heav'n's Queen and Mother both" (line 201), begins her reign rather than loses her following. Enitharmon's regents, Rintrah and Palamabron, are represented in imagery that likens them to the pagan deities that decline in Milton's poem. Palamabron, the horned priest, suggests the ram's form of Hammon, who "shrinks his horn" in Milton's poem (line 203). Rintrah, "Prince of the sun" (8:9), is Milton's Apollo (lines 176-78), here gaining rather than losing his powers.

Rather than heralding a transformation of the fallen world, the incarnation of Orc-Christ consolidates Nature's hegemony through a refinement upon paganism: the religion of chastity and war that Christian priests and kings

167

were to promulgate in Europe for eighteen hundred years. The admonition of wisest Fate in Milton's poem, who requires redemption on the bitter cross before the fallen world is transformed, is the actual cause of the existence of eighteen hundred years of "those ychain'd in sleep" (line 155). With the birth of the Christian dispensation, it is not the dragon who is circumscribed, but man himself.

For Blake, then, as we have seen in his answer to Milton's music of the spheres, the birth of Christ—as the orthodox have interpreted it—increases rather than diminishes the powers of the pagan deities. The old errors of paganism, along with the new ones introduced by Christianity, become a consolidated body of error. This concept is developed further in the second part of "A Prophecy," which parallels the rout of the pagan deities in the *Nativity Ode*. At the opening of the second part of the poem, the previous incarnation of Orc (in *America*) has caused the shadows to flee, in a rhetorical echo of the opening of "A Prophecy," where the troops flee like shadows, smitten with their own plagues. These shadows, Albion's Angels, are like the sinners in the first chapter of Proverbs (illustrated on plate 1 of *Europe*) whose crimes will recoil upon them (1:18). Just as the fallen angels at the beginning of *Paradise Lost* arise from the lake of fire and build Pandemonium, so the Angels of Albion arise from the ruins of the council hall as stars rise from the great salt lake and follow their fiery king to the Serpent Temple of Verulam (10:1-5).

This action reverses the section of Milton's poem on the rout of the pagan oracles. Here Typhon, who in Milton's poem no longer dares abide after Christ's nativity (lines 224-26), asserts his serpentine sway. Verulam symbolizes the infinite becoming trapped in the finite serpent form (Typhon), the transformation of the God who pities into a devouring flame (Moloch); man, rather than Milton's pagan nymphs (line 188), is banished to the forest. With these pagan symbols Blake makes the assertion that fallen "man became an Angel; / Heaven a mighty circle turning;

God a tyrant crown'd" (10:22-23), which is exactly the theological situation of Milton's poem. The dumb oracles that no longer issue from the arched roof in the *Nativity Ode* (lines 173-75) are revived in *Europe*. Moloch is erected in the form of Albion's Angel on the Stone of Night, who calls for the sacrifice of the young of Albion to the religion of war and chastity, a sacrifice that is also depicted in the cannibalism of plate 6. The hearth in plate 6 and the gravestone-door of plate 7 suggest the "consecrated Earth" and "holy Hearth" (lines 189-90), where the Lars and Lemures now preside over the sacrifices of war.

Thus, according to Blake, the old errors give way to new ones, as the cyclical process of history continues. Europe, at the end of eighteen hundred years is still in the Iron Age, rather than moving toward any Golden Age. Just as Milton had adopted images from Ovid and the Bible to anticipate the return of the earth to a Golden Age, Blake uses images from the same sources to show Europe's decline. In contrast to Milton's emphasis upon the Mosaic creation and Ovid's myth of the Golden Age, Blake uses imagery from the apocalyptic literature of the Bible and from Ovid's description of the decline into the Iron Age. This decline is particularly reinforced by Blake's figure of the Guardian of the secret codes, who is an adaptation of Ovid's Lycaon and of the biblical figure of Nebuchadnezzar. Lycaon, who is cited by Ovid's Jupiter as a particularly gruesome example of the depravity of the fallen age, tried to prove Jupiter's divinity through a murder attempt and through tempting Jupiter to eat human flesh. As a punishment for these crimes, Lycaon was transformed into a wolf: "His mantle, now his Hide, with rugged hairs / Cleaves to his back, a famish'd face he bears."[17] Blake's Guardian suffers the same fate; his wig and "furr'd robes" cling to him and become flesh, and like Lycaon, he flees into the wilderness (12:15-20). The themes of tempting God and cannibalism that are developed in Ovid's poem, and which are reiterated in other parts of *Europe*, are appropriate to Blake's condemna-

169

tion of the Newtonian science and the materialism that tempts God and turns man into a beast. Ovid's image of the tyrant turned into a beast has its biblical equivalent in the figure of Nebuchadnezzar, who in the Book of Daniel also tempts God continually and who assumes a bestial form that will not be removed until seven times pass over him—a period that symbolizes the seven trumpets of the Apocalypse. Urizen's brazen book (11:3) is the same book of threatening laws of brass that Ovid claims was absent during the Golden Age. In the Iron Age, according to Ovid, the earth is divided, a theme echoed in Blake by the dividing of the eternal forests (10:18) and by the picture (on the frontispiece) of Urizen with a compass.[18]

The cause of Europe's failure to transcend this fallen condition was its adherence to the complex of beliefs and attitudes symbolized by Enitharmon's sleep: the religion of chastity, the concept of chivalry that arose from that religion, the militaristic concept of atonement, and the deification of Nature. These are errors that Blake perceives to be present in Milton's *Nativity Ode*; *Europe* maintains that Christ's birth did not abolish the pagan idols, but rather erected new ones, symbolized by Enitharmon:

> Not long after Jesus a "coy mistress" began to make her appearance, inspiring a code of love which was inseparably connected with a code of war. Such axioms as "None but the brave deserve the fair" usually mean by "fair" a statuesque, aloof and rather stupid beauty, who has little animation or friendliness or a capacity for companionship, but is, like most divinities, an unwearied poseur. The fallen Enitharmon in Blake is typically the mistress of chivalry, spiritually inviolate because wrapped up in herself in a way which makes devotion to her a teasing mockery of love, a frustration of life to be expressed in murder.[19]

Blake was aware that the feud between Christianity and the pagan world did not revolve around the commitment to a code of war and the subordination of the individual to the state, which he saw to be errors espoused by the classics: "The Classics, it is the Classics! & not Goths nor Monks, that Desolate Europe with Wars" (*On Homer's Poetry*, p. 267). Blake had only to look at Virgil's fourth eclogue, a major source of Milton's *Nativity Ode*, to see how the "political ideal of domination under a heroic Messiah"[20] was congenial to both Christian and pagan alike. The continuation of this ideology from the classical epic into the Christian epic and Christian romance testified that the pagan oracles had indeed not ceased.

Blake's reading of Milton would have made him acutely aware that Milton himself had succumbed to this error by embracing the concept of heroism, with its ascetic and chivalric ideals, that was really an extension of the pagan errors that he claimed to oppose. These errors were particularly pronounced in passages in which Milton dedicated himself as an inspired poet. In *An Apology for Smectymnuus*, Milton describes his aspirations to write heroic verse, identifying the poet with the moral virtues represented by the hero. He says that the poet "ought him selfe to bee a true Poem, that is, a composition, and patterne of the best and honourablest things; not presuming to sing high praises of heroick men, or famous Cities, unlesse he have in himselfe the experience and the practice of all that which is praise-worthy."[21] Describing the early influences of medieval romance upon his young mind, Milton penetrates the central ideology of Christian heroic poetry that Blake was later to criticize:

I betook me among those lofty Fables and Romances, which recount in solemne canto's the deeds of Knighthood founded by our victorious Kings; & from hence had in renowne over all Christendome. There I read it in the oath of every Knight, that he should defend to the expence of his best blood, or of his life, if it so befell him, the honour and chastity of Virgin or Matron. From

171

whence even then I learnt what a noble vertue chastity
sure must be, to the defence of which so many worthies
by such a deare adventure of themselves had sworne.[22]

Milton goes on to indicate that he does not advocate the
literal taking up of arms among modern Christians, and
his opposition to war is strongly apparent in *Paradise Lost*
and *Paradise Regained*, but it was an oversight on his part
to ignore the fact that the murderous impulses that lead to
corporeal war are inherent in his promotion of a religion
of chastity.

In the "Sixth Elegy," in which he discusses the *Nativity
Ode* that he is in the process of composing, Milton again
voices his dedication to poetry in terms of the same heroic
ideal. First he playfully praises the poetry of love and wine
that accompanies those who received the favors of Bacchus,
Apollo, and Ceres. But he says (in Thomas Warton's Eng-
lish paraphrase) that

> he who sings of wars, and Jove, pious heroes, and leaders
> exalted to demigods, the decrees of heaven, and the pro-
> found realms of hell, must follow the frugal precepts of
> the Samian sage, must quaff the pellucid stream from the
> beechen cup, or from the pure fountain. To this philoso-
> phy belong, chaste and blameless youth, severe manners,
> and unspotted hands. . . . For in truth, a poet is sacred;
> he is the priest of heaven, and his bosom conceives, and
> his mouth utters, the hidden god.[23]

Here Milton sets the religious context of the interest in
heroic poetry that he announced in the *Vacation Exercise*,
and his following these sentiments with a mention of the
Nativity Ode in the "Sixth Elegy" must be interpreted as
his presenting the *Ode* as a first poetic essay in that direc-
tion.[24] The elegy's pattern of movement from revelry to
chastened sobriety, from Bacchus to Christ, is repeated in
the Ode's movement from celebratory joy to heroic virtue.

Milton's heroic image of Christ as a "dreaded infant"

who vanquishes the pagan gods reveals the theological basis of Milton's heroic ideal. As Florence Sandler has observed, the *Nativity Ode* "may well be the most explicit statement in English literature of the *Christus Victor* theory of the Atonement."[25] This theory of atonement achieved through Christ's victory over sin and death has its origin in Old Testament images of Jahweh as a man of war who defeats his enemies, and ultimately it derives from traditions surrounding the gods of Canaan. Blake, of course, did not have to know about Canaanite practices to be critical of this heroic theory of atonement, which he later exposed in his vision of the last seven churches as "the Male-Females, the Dragon Forms / Religion hid in War" (*Milton* 37:42-43).[26]

In *Europe* Blake's position is dramatically brought home through the illustrations on plates 5 and 11. Plate 5 depicts an heroic warrior king, perhaps "pious Aeneas," one of Milton's "pious heroes" or "leaders exalted to demigods," whose piety is testified to by the two angels on either side of him—not unlike Gloucester surrounded by the two bishops in Shakespeare's *Richard the Third*. If the satiric point of this illustration is not sufficiently clear to the viewer, he merely has to turn a few pages to find the same two angels attending a fat, bat-winged bishop seated in judgment on a cloud. This second illustration unveils the reality behind the chivalrous image of plate 5 and thus undercuts any value attached to the heroic image. This is Milton's dreadful judge who "in middle Air shall spread his throne" (line 164). He represents the decree of wisest Fate in the *Nativity Ode* that pronounces a delay of universal redemption until the Great Battle between God and Satan is won on the bitter cross, through which Christ gains the power to descend with the same thunder and clang that accompanied the giving of the law on Sinai.

In other words, Christ the Judge and Christ the warrior are one and the same, and both are subject to an externally imposed law of redemption that continues rather than ends the cycles of history. This false concept of atonement is later corrected by Milton, when he is reincarnated in Blake's poem, *Milton*, and confronts Satan:

> Satan! my Spectre! I know my power thee to annihilate
> And be a greater in thy place, & be thy Tabernacle
> A covering for thee to do thy will, till one greater comes
> And smites me as I smote thee & becomes my covering.
>
> *(Milton* 38:29-32)

Thus while Christ subdues Typhon in Milton's *Nativity Ode* (line 226), "a greater than Typhon may prove to be only a greater Typhon!"[27] The heroic ideal that cemented the religious and political order of Europe for eighteen hundred years is exposed by Blake as an error that defeats the very purposes that it was established to achieve—man's transcendence of the world of sin and death.

Blake not only shows Milton's pagan idols to be very much alive and articulate but he has more to say about those yellow-skirted Fays that Milton so reluctantly bids goodbye at the end of the section on the rout of the pagan deities in his *Nativity Ode*. Milton merely mentions the end of their moonlight revels: "And the yellow-skirted *Fays* / Fly after the Night-Steeds, leaving their Moon-lov'd maze" (lines 235-36). Although the magic of these lines renders the fairies attractive, they, like the rather harmless nymphs who mourn "in twilight shade of tangled thickets" (line 188), must ultimately dissolve in the light of the Sun, that is, must perish in the light of Christian truth.[28] Blake implies an understanding of Milton's lingering attraction for these beautiful creatures that are consigned to the same fate as the pagan demons. In describing the sports of night within Enitharmon's crystal house, Blake is identifying those Fays in Milton's poem as the spirits of Nature that operate within the fallen world. The crystal house is the created universe; it corresponds to the concentric crystalline spheres of Ptolemaic astronomy in Milton's poem (line 125). By lingering upon these creatures at greater length than Milton does, Blake suggests that Milton may have dismissed them too summarily.

Blake was careful to distinguish the elemental spirits from the heathen gods, the latter being more completely abstracted from their origin in the human breast.[29] In *Europe* Enitharmon's sleep signals the supplanting of the genii or fairies by the pagan deities, which further separates man from Nature and thereby makes Nature the mysterious Other—symbolized in pagan religion by the Queen of Heaven and in the chivalric code by the *belle dame sans merci*—that makes man a passive recipient of sense impressions. When Enitharmon is revived after eighteen hundred years, she is still the Queen of Heaven, but she is rendered somewhat more attractive; she summons up an enchanting moonlight vision of Nature that is reminiscent of the joyous music at the beginning of Milton's Hymn: "for All were forth at sport beneath the solemn moon / Waking the stars of Urizen with their immortal songs, / That nature felt thro' all her pores the enormous revelry" (14:32-34). Her song is attractive, despite her mistaking totally the significance of Orc's reappearance, despite her continued commitment to secrecy, and despite her lack of consciousness of the amount of time that has elapsed. Her song is bathed in a self-indulgent and self-deluded reverie, wherein lies her danger. She is trapped in a time warp and becomes melancholy and eventually horrified as some of her children (Antamon, Oothoon, and Orc) rebel. She cannot escape the cycles of history, as is witnessed by her persistence in seeing Orc as a god who renews her each morning with his red light.

Orc's light, however, promises something else entirely; his actions carry symbolic significance that reveals Enitharmon's condition. Beholding the coming of morning, Orc

> Shot from the heights of Enitharmon;
> And in the vineyards of red France appear'd the light
>   of his fury.

175

The sun glow'd fiery red!
The furious terrors flew around!
On golden chariots raging, with red wheels dropping
  with blood;
The Lions lash their wrathful tails!
The Tigers couch upon the prey & suck the ruddy tide:
And Enitharmon groans & cries in anguish and dismay.

                                                    (15:1-8)

The imagery of the raging chariots decked in flames and blood is taken from Nahum's prophecy of the chariot of God's wrath that will be unleashed on Nineveh (Nahum 2:3-4, 3:2-3). The allusion indicates the eschatological significance of Orc's action and also reveals Enitharmon to be like the "well-favored harlot" who bears the brunt of God's anger. Like the harlot, Enitharmon is "the mistress of witchcrafts, that selleth nations through her whoredoms and families through her witchcrafts" (Nahum 3:4). The irony in Blake is that such whoredoms and witchcrafts are the practices resulting from the religion of chastity—an irony that is perhaps derived in part from a literal reading of Isaiah's ironic name for the most famous harlot and sorceress in the Bible, the "virgin daughter of Babylon" (47:1). The similarity between this harlot, the harlot in Nahum, and the Great Whore in Revelation is an easy one to see and one upon which biblical commentators have continually remarked.[30] In this role of harlot-enchantress, Enitharmon represents for Blake the state of imaginative torpor that causes war. She is an extended personification of Milton's wisest Fate, who denies the redemptive power of fancy.

Although Enitharmon is identified as the harlot, her crystal world is not given the kind of moral value that Milton imposes upon his fairies' world. In fact, Blake's elaboration of this world goes so far as to assert that the fairy world is the source of inspiration for whatever is imaginative in the musical vision in the first part of Milton's Hymn. Enitharmon's world is a dream world gone stale, however, because, like Milton's concept of fancy, it has become contaminated by Reason. Thus Blake represents this world as a vision of earthly paradise that is aware, like the Angels of Albion, of its own morbidity and that seeks renewal through the energies of Orc; hence Enitharmon's cry:

> Orc! smile upon my children!
> Smile son of my afflictions.
> Arise O Orc and give our mountains joy of thy red light.
>   (14:29-31)

At the crisis of European history that Blake is depicting, Nature needs to be re-created, either to begin a new cycle of history or to return to the Golden Age that Milton's and Virgil's nativity poems prophesy.

In the *Nativity Ode*, Milton himself understands that Nature must be re-created in order to effect the return to the Golden Age, but in perceiving re-created Nature as Nature chastened, purified of all earthly sensuality, he must necessarily reject fairy fancy as a means of achieving the Golden Age in favor of the decrees of wisest Fate. What Milton fails to understand is that wisest Fate and the vision of a chaste Nature are one and the same, that the concept of chastity will continue to prevent the achievement of the Golden Age that the poet most desires, thus keeping man locked in time and dependent upon an externally imposed act of providence to redeem a sense of sin that is entirely self-created. By separating fancy from the workings of divine providence, casting out revelation through the senses and embracing the thunderous laws delivered on Sinai, Milton implicitly denies the efficacy of imaginative vision and thus turns fancy into the kind of malignant preciosity that we see in Enitharmon's world.

Fancy then becomes the chaste abstraction that is so ardently extolled in William Collins' "Ode on the Poetical Character."[31] There, Milton's fancy, identified with the

177

Christian muse—and with the biblical figure of Wisdom—wears a girdle of chastity, and Truth is prudishly clothed in a "sunny vest" (line 45). In Collins' chilly allegory, the "dangerous Passions" are "kept aloof" (line 41) during the creation of the magical girdle, and the act of creation is celebrated by the dance of the "shadowy tribes of Mind" (line 47), an ironically appropriate image recalling the "holy shadows" of Enitharmon (13:18) that are elaborated upon in *Europe*, the products of the moralizing imagination. Like Enitharmon, Milton's muse is a mockery of God's lusty paramour who is celebrated in the Song of Songs and the Wisdom books of the Bible. For Blake, this muse is the antithesis of the bride, the Great Whore herself.

Milton's reaction to the possibility of a Golden Age at Christ's birth was typical of his age—he withdrew from the possibility because he mistrusted any force that would so possess his fancy. He thus rejects fancy in favor of Christian Truth, withdraws from the heavenly music and replaces it with the clang of Sinai and the groans of defeated gods. Like an inverted Thel, Milton withdraws from entering the earthly paradise, that is, from imaginatively re-creating the Golden Age. Such sweets he rejects in favor of the bitterness of Christ's Passion and the Second Coming, unaware that clinging to an externally imposed law of atonement is yet another trap for the imaginative man.

The whole movement of the *Nativity Ode* from fancy to truth—a gloss easily deducible from the movement of the "Sixth Elegy"—locks Milton into categories with which he does not appear to be content, as the nostalgic look at the departing nymphs and fairies will testify. Such categories ultimately defeat his attempt to escape from classical to Christian art. In the *Nativity Ode*, the Father is Destiny; He is the decree of wisest Fate that atonement will be achieved by some far-off future act of force in which man will have little part. The Son is a ratio of the five senses, a Christian warrior whose battle for truth and chastity must reject the world of the senses and the world of fairy fancy.

Milton's Holy Ghost is a vacuum, because in banishing all the fairies and genii, Milton has banished inspiration. Failing to create a space for the sensual pleasures and for the Imagination, Milton's error was that of abstracting rather than identifying the power of fancy and the part that it plays in man's redemption.

Milton, of course, came to know better as he matured, and Blake was very aware of this. In *Tetrachordon*, Milton does create space for sensuality, providing an important source for Blake's conception of Beulah and employing, significantly enough, allusions to God's sporting with Wisdom and to Solomon's sensual marriage song;

> No mortall nature can endure either in the actions of Religion, or study of wisdome, without sometime slackning the cords of intense thought and labour: which lest we should think faulty, God himself conceals us not his own recreations before the world was built; *I was,* saith the eternall wisdome, *dayly his delight, playing alwayes before him.* . . . We cannot therefore alwayes be contemplative, or pragmaticall abroad, but have need of som delightfull intermissions, wherin the enlarg'd soul may leav off a while her severe schooling; and like a glad youth in wandring vacancy, may keep her hollidaies to joy and harmles pastime. . . . wisest *Salomon* among his gravest Proverbs countenances a kinde of ravishment and erring fondnes in the entertainment of wedded leisures; and in the Song of Songs, which is generally beleev'd, even in the jolliest expressions to figure the spousals of the Church with Christ, sings of a thousand raptures between those two lovely ones farre on the hither side of carnall enjoyment.[32]

Blake was also aware that in *Paradise Regained* Milton articulated a vision of redemption that rejected the "bitter cross" and the conceptions of atonement surrounding it.[33] In *Europe*, however, Blake is responding to a work that reflects the early Milton's attachment to dominant cultural

179

values and treating that work as a symptom of a great cultural malaise. Milton's separation of fancy from truth and his opting for the latter at the expense of the former reflect a literary trend against which Blake was strongly reacting, as evidenced in Blake's selecting a fairy rather than the traditional Christian muse as the muse of *Europe*. This choice reflects Blake's avowed desire, expressed in his early "An Imitation of Spenser" (pp. 412-13), that Apollo's beams of truth wash his earthly mind so "that wisdom may descend in fairy dreams" (line 5), an echo of Gray's invocation, in *The Bard*, of Spenser's "truth severe, by fairy fiction drest,"[34] which Blake illustrated literally by depicting the two figures of truth severe and fairy fiction standing side by side as Spenser creates his fairies.[35]

Blake's desire to wed the products of the fancy with truth or wisdom by selecting the fairies of Albion as his muse reflects the movement in the eighteenth century toward a mythopoeic poetry that celebrates the power of the imagination to reach greater truths than reason can.[36] The adherents of this poetic looked back to Spenser and other Elizabethan poets, all of whom embraced the notion of the poet as *vates*, or seer, and who were involved in the process of "making the classics more prophetic and the Bible more poetic."[37] This tradition of divine poetry that sought to supplant the influence of the classics with a poetic understanding and use of the Bible reached its fullest expression in Renaissance England in the work of Milton. This ideology completely informs the *Nativity Ode*, from Milton's selection of the Christian muse to the very structure of the poem, which entails the movement from pagan falsehood to Christian truth. The problem in this poem is that the tradition appears to have ossified, because, unlike Spenser, Milton has separated fairy fancy from truth severe. Milton, who begins the *Nativity Ode* with a description of the inner process of vision, superimposes Christian morality upon that vision, making the poem rather distant and abstract. The chilly world of Enitharmon's crystal house, which represents fairy fiction that has become separated from truth, becomes Blake's apt commentary upon Milton's cold pastoral.[38] This separation merely reflects the course of literary history between the time of Milton and Blake, a course that Blake and his contemporaries attempt to reverse.

In *Europe* Blake seizes upon the *Nativity Ode* as an expression of the concept of Christ Triumphant, as a poem that marks a watershed in Milton's life—his first attempt at divine poetry—and as an example of divine vision corrupted by the very idolatry that it seeks to destroy. Since the older Milton never went back to correct the errors of that poem, Blake attempts to do so, and in so doing, he corrects the errors of Western thought that prevent Milton's poem from being the work of prophecy that it was intended to be. Blake replaces the traditional Christian muse, who has been contaminated by the classics and the ideologies underlying them, with the fairies or genii that animate the natural world. Milton's form is antithetical, creating sharp distinctions between harmony and disharmony, darkness and light, error and truth.[39] Blake offers instead a circuitous form that explores the same actions from two different perspectives, showing a conflict of those perspectives rather than moral categories. Milton's form, despite its innovations, is derived from the classical ode,[40] whereas Blake's form is modeled upon Revelation. By recasting the *Nativity Ode* in the form of a prophecy, Blake acknowledges Milton's original intention, and he fulfills that intention by restoring the biblical context that the original poem lacked.

Blake expands upon the fairy world because of the importance he attached to the clarification of the Imagination's role in the redemptive process. Enitharmon is fallen not because she is sensual and therefore evil, but because she advocates the secret and exclusive enjoyment of desire and thus represents a state of imaginative stagnation that must be overcome in order that fallen man may reclaim the divine vision and, through that vision, his own divinity.

181

Blake seeks to accomplish this not through violence, but through the articulation of the errors that she represents.

Such an exposure of error is the primary function of prophecy, as Blake follows the strategy of Revelation, revealing the body of error so that the body of truth can replace it.[41] The prophetic context of Milton's *Nativity Ode* and of the events described in *Europe* is established by the allusions to Nahum at the end of *Europe*. Through these allusions to the biblical prophet, Europe is likened to Nineveh, which has become dominated by the female will, represented in Nahum by the enchantress-harlot and by the queen, whose fall provides a striking parallel to that of the queen of France: "And Huzzab shall be led away captive, she shall be brought up, and her maids shall lead her as with the voice of doves, tabering upon their breasts" (Nahum 2:7). Enitharmon, who is similarly discomfited by the descent of Orc into France, is an amalgamation of both female figures.[42] She is set in contrast to the lamenting figure in the Preludium, her advocacy of stolen joys linking her to the harlot who is the foil to Wisdom in Proverbs. Her heavenly crystal palace is like the harlot's house and like the crystal palace of Antichristian Rome in Spenser's apocalyptic *Visions of Bellay* (lines 15-28). In Blake's poem, Enitharmon's celestial edifice finds its earthly equivalent in the Serpent Temple at Verulam, whose zodiac symbolism reinforces this identity.

The temple is presided over by Enitharmon's regents, Rintrah and Palamabron, both of whom are defined by allusions to Nahum. Palamabron, the horned priest who skips upon the mountains, is a parody of the bringer of deliverance in Nahum: "Behold upon the mountains the feet of him that bringeth good tidings, that publisheth peace!" (Nahum 1:15). Rintrah the king, whose progeny is an innumerable race of lions, is like the king of Assyria whose young lions will be devoured by the Lord's anger (2:11-13). Both figures, as well as the guardian of Albion, mirror the wicked counselor in Nahum 1:11, who is defined by Poole as "one whose counsels and projects are without any regard to right and equity, who by injustices and oppressions, who by frauds and deceits, by blood and slaughter, designs his own greatness, and the ruin of his neighbours."[43] Albion's Angel and the Guardian of the secret codes, the equivalents of Rintrah and Palamabron in the political allegory, also fall under this definition.

Through the biblical contexts established by Nahum and Proverbs, Blake represents the history of Europe as a consolidation of errors, which is represented in the Bible by the harlot and the harlot's house and which finds its symbolic equivalents in the Serpent Temple, Enitharmon's crystal palace, and Enitharmon herself. Ultimately they are all subsumed under the concept of Babylon as articulated in Revelation, where Babylon signifies Rome.[44] The Serpent Temple, established in the city of Verulam, which rivaled its southern neighbor, London, in Roman times, parallels the northern city of Babylon from which the exiled Ezekiel looked south toward Jerusalem (Ezekiel 20:46).

In the Bible, the harlotry of Babylon is a metaphor for idolatry, which is manifested in *Europe* as the product of the harlot's love of secret joys—which at Christ's birth becomes transmuted into the religion of chastity, the chivalric code, and into the code of war resulting from the previous two errors. In the political allegory of *Europe*, these errors become consolidated in the representation of the Guardian of the secret codes as Nebuchadnezzar-Lycaon transformed into a beast, a type of those who tempt God through tyranny, violence, or experimentation and whose angelic form is that of Newton. Both the beast and Newton herald the crack of doom that descends upon Europe.

In response to Milton's vision of the banishing of the pagan oracles, which heralds a diminution of error in the *Nativity Ode*, Blake presents an alternative vision, based upon Revelation, of history as the growth and consolidation of error that awaits to be overturned by the descent of

183

Orc's bloody chariot of wrath. Blake's prognosis for the future, however, is bleak; the emphasis upon the strife of blood in the last line indicates that in 1794, as Blake would assert in 1798, "The Beast & the Whore rule without control" (*Annotations to Watson*, p. 601).

The Song of Los:
Enslavement to the Elements

As David Erdman has suggested, the two lyrics that make
up *The Song of Los* form a prologue and epilogue to the
other two illuminated historical prophecies.[1] *Africa* ends
with the first line of "A Prophecy" in *America*, and *Asia*
begins with the howl that rises up from Orc's appearance
in *Europe*. In terms of structure and content, however, the
two songs also form a self-contained unit that places Blake's
prophecies about contemporary events within the frame-
work of biblical history and epitomizes the pattern of that
history.[2] Both African and Asian continents are represented
as symbolic or spiritual states in Blake rather than merely
geographic entities, and that symbolism is derived from the
Bible. The Scriptures never mention the continent of Af-
rica but represent it primarily through Egypt; and Blake
asserts in *The Book of Urizen* that Africa was formerly
called Egypt (28:9-10). Similarly, Asia, besides being the
continent occupied by the Hebrew people, is frequently rep-
resented in biblical history and prophecy by the eastern
enemies of Israel, particularly the Chaldeans, Babylonians,
and Assyrians. In the New Testament the name "Asia" ac-
tually appears and is used to refer to the Roman province
of Asia Minor.

According to popular tradition, Egypt was the source of
all the civilized arts and sciences that were later adopted
by both the Jewish and classical worlds. Egypt was thus the
heartland (as Blake's "heart-formed Africa" [*Africa* 3:3]
puns) of abstract law and philosophy, as well as state reli-
gion. Asia, on the other hand, was the area in which Paul
did his most important work (see Acts 18:9f., 19), the loca-

185

tion of the seven churches addressed by St. John in Revelation, and, most importantly, the location of Patmos, the island upon which the culminating vision of the Bible was revealed. Thus Blake uses the two continents as symbols that define the movement of biblical history, starting in Africa with the origin of the Mosaic law and ending in Asia with the abrogation of the law and the apocalyptic birth of a new dispensation.

The key to this movement lies in a biblical allusion in *Africa*:

> (Night spoke to the Cloud!
> Lo these Human form'd spirits in smiling hipocrisy War
> Against one another; so let them War on; slaves to the
> eternal Elements.)
>
> (3:12-14)

The last phrase, "slaves to the eternal Elements," echoes a passage in the Epistle to the Galatians, where Paul preaches Christ's deliverance of both Jew and Gentile from the bondage of the law through the analogy of an heir who is waiting to be adopted and who is hence granted the freedom accorded to a son:

> Now I say, That the heir, as long as he is a child, differeth nothing from a servant, though he be lord of all; But is under tutors and governors until the time appointed of the father. Even so we, when we were children, were in bondage under the elements of the world.
>
> (Galatians 4:1-3)

These elements, which in the Bible mean rules of law,[3] take on a double meaning in Blake, referring both to the elements of the law and the natural elements that enslave those who adhere to abstract law, abstract philosophy, and natural religion. Blake's catalogue of the continued bondage to the law even after the coming of Christ reiterates Paul's complaint: "But now, after that ye have known God, or rather are known of God, how turn ye again to the weak and beggarly elements, whereunto ye desire again to be in bondage?" (Galatians 4:9).

History, up until the eighteenth century, consists of the persistent attempts of mankind to alleviate the problems of sin and suffering through the perfection of a system of externally imposed laws, leaving the world, like Jerusalem in Paul's time, in a state of civil and religious bondage (Galatians 4:25). Besides the externally imposed laws of pagan Rome, Jerusalem is imprisoned from within by the laws delivered from Mount Sinai (Galatians 4:25). *Asia* employs this image of Jerusalem in bondage, besieged and oppressed by king and priest, and projects the liberation of Jerusalem not through faith, as in Galatians, but through the revolutionary energies of Orc, whose appearance precipitates the destruction of Urizen's books of law.

In *Africa* Blake outlines the transmission of civilization, employing a theory that had been advanced by John Marsham and John Spencer in the seventeenth century and that was popularized through Warburton's *The Divine Legation of Moses.*[4] According to Warburton, "the Egyptians were the first people who perfected civil-policy, and established religion" (I, 70),[5] and it is they who began state religion by introducing the idea that laws were divinely inspired: "The FIRST step the Legislator took, was to pretend a Mission and revelation from some God, by whose command and direction he had framed the Policy he would establish. Thus *Amasis* and *Mneves*, lawgivers of the *Egyptians* (from whence this custom spread over *Greece* and *Asia*) pretended to receive their laws from *Mercury*" (I, 174).

Warburton continues with a catalogue of legislators and their pretended sources of inspiration, a list that may very well have been the source of Blake's catalogue, since Warburton includes many of the names mentioned in *Africa*. Those legislators, Warburton goes on to say, claimed divine revelation *"not only to beget a veneration for their laws, but likewise to establish the opinion of the superintendency of the Gods over human affairs"* (I, 176). To this end the Egyptians not only inculcated natural religion—the belief that God is and that He rewards the faithful and punishes the unfaithful—but they also established the Mysteries, through which they promoted the doctrine of future rewards and punishments that would befall the individual after death. Trismegistus, "the great Hero and Lawgiver of the old Egyptians" (I, 497), was well versed in these arts, as was Pythagoras. Plato traveled to Egypt and was initiated into the mysteries of the priesthood (I, 449), and other Greeks adopted Egyptian doctrines and practices, which they then spread to the rest of the world. Moses, according to the Bible, "was learned in all the wisdom of the Egyptians" (Acts 7:22), which Warburton interprets to mean *"that Moses was consummate in the science of Legislation"* (II, 316). "The *Mosaic Religion* was a REPUBLICATION of *natural Religion* to the Jews" (II, 65), which Blake perceived to be "forms of dark delusion" (*Africa* 3:17).

According to Blake, Moses delivered Israel from the bondage of Egypt only to impose upon his people the bondage of moral and ceremonial law, which he had actually taken from the Egyptians. Similarly, the Gospel, which claims to liberate mankind from the bondage of the Mosaic law, perpetuates that bondage insofar as it supports moral law and the doctrine of future rewards and punishments. In *Africa* Jesus hears Oothoon, who in *Visions of the Daughters of Albion* is Blake's equivalent of the woman taken in adultery, but He takes from wretched Theotormon a Gospel of jealousy that would condemn rather than forgive the sinner (3:22-24). The eighteen hundred years of dissemination and the perfection of the philosophy and religion of Egypt reinforces Blake's theme of man's perverse and continued self-enslavement to the elements, which are the laws or systems of thought that sacrifice the individual and his or her energies—symbolized by the chaining of Promethean Orc (3:21)—to the state or to some abstract concept of the Good.

In *Africa* Blake's catalogue of the dissemination of abstract law and philosophy is followed by the myth of Har and Heva (4:5-12), whose fleeing and shrinking into reptile form is taken from the story of Cadmus and Harmonia in Books III and IV of Ovid's *Metamorphoses*. Having killed the giant serpent of Mars by spearing its neck against an oak tree, Cadmus hears a voice proclaiming, "Why dost thou thus with secret Pleasure see, / Insulting Man! what thou thyself shall be?"[6] Cadmus then sows the teeth of the dragon from which grow a band of warriors who begin to fight among themselves. The five survivors of this battle help him to build the city of Thebes. The city flourishes, and Cadmus marries Harmonia, the daughter of Mars and Venus. Their progeny, however, suffer severe misfortunes, which cause Cadmus and Harmonia to flee, feeling that their ill fortune was attached to Thebes. When they arrive in Illyria, Cadmus despairs that the snake he had killed was holy and that his fate has been the result of some divine act of vengeance. He prays to be transformed into a serpent, a prayer granted to both him and his wife.

Blake's extended allusion to this myth at the end of his catalogue of the transmitters of the law is immediately relevant because, according to Warburton, Cadmus and Harmonia spread Egyptian lore to Greece, from whence it was transmitted to Europe (I, 170). According to popular allegorical tradition, Cadmus' slaying of the dragon represented the virtuous man overcoming sin,[7] and his spearing of the serpent's head has obvious affinities with the promise of bruising the serpent's head in Genesis 3:15. Blake, however, points out the irony that would accompany the full application of this allegorical picture of the Christian warrior, by depicting in *Africa* the point at which Cadmus is transformed into that which he had fought. Cadmus was also reputed to be the one who introduced the alphabet to the world, replacing the Egyptian hieroglyphs with letters.[8] The teeth of the slain serpent, which Cadmus had sown,

189

represent, according to Erasmus, the seeds of wrangling and discord, the adherence to the letter rather than the spirit that was the cause of so much civil and religious strife.[9]

These meanings surrounding the myth of Cadmus make him an apt symbol of the law's attempt to overcome the unruly elements of life—or the irrational—by means of an externally imposed force or order. The Cadmus myth, through its pattern of a man vanquishing a serpent to found a city and then becoming a serpent himself, epitomizes the cyclical concept of history, which was also represented by the symbol of the serpent, "image of [the] infinite / Shut up in finite revolutions" (*Europe* 10:21-22). Blake's source of Har and Heva also contributes to the theme of the triumph of the law in *Africa*, in that Ovid's *Metamorphoses*, according to Warburton, is a popular history of providence that shows the punishments imposed by the gods for impiety (I, 443).[10]

Blake's use of Har and Heva makes *Africa*, like the Epistle to the Galatians, address itself not only to the pagans but to those under the biblical dispensation as well by combining the myth of Cadmus with that of the biblical Flood. The pattern of flight and diminution in stature, also present in the myth of Noah, links the pagan and biblical myths, and Blake emphasizes the connection between them through the repetition of the word "shrunk": Har and Heva "shrunk / Into two narrow doleful forms" (4:7-8), and "Noah shrunk, beneath the waters" (3:15) when Brama received abstract philosophy from Rintrah. Here Blake is employing the Flood as metaphor, since the event depopulated the world of the race of giants mentioned in Genesis 6:4. The flight of Har and Heva from war and lust, like the escape engineered for Noah by a God who would destroy sin by destroying the sinners, symbolizes the panic underlying the impulse to create laws, the "closing and restraining" (4:15) of the senses that lead to the diminution of man. This theme of the diminution of man, the shrinking of man from his original divinity, is reiterated at the

end of *Africa* by another biblical allusion to the myth of
the Flood: the fallen angels "on the desarts of Africa"
(4:20), which is taken from Genesis 6 and the Book of
Enoch. The fallen angels are the Watchers or "sons of God"
who fell when they lusted after "the daughters of men"
(Genesis 6:2) and who lived on earth and propagated a race
of giants (Enoch 6-7).[11] Like the shrinking of Noah, their
fall represents a stage of man's fall into the world of
Generation.

In the myths of Cadmus and Noah, whether the reaction
to what is perceived as evil is one of armed combat or flight,
the error lies in the externalization and separation of a por-
tion of the human psyche, thereby causing the diminution
of man through the further separation of man and the ob-
jects of his perceptions. Thus, as Noah and Cadmus shrunk,
"all the vast of Nature shrunk" (4:11). As man's senses
shrink, so do the objects of his perceptions, a reciprocity
between the perceiver and what is perceived that is empha-
sized in *Africa* by the metamorphosis of Cadmus into the
snake he opposes and by the parallel between the binding
of Orc on Mount Atlas (3:21) and the binding of the sons
of Har to earth by their fallen perceptions (4:14).

In *Africa*, which forms the first of the sequence of politi-
cal prophecies, Blake's emphasis upon the Flood as a symbol
of the Fall explains why each of these prophecies is named
after a continent. According to biblical tradition, after the
Flood, the three sons of Noah each became the possessor of
the continents of Africa, Asia, and Europe.[12] This theory,
according to Simon Patrick, "hath made some so bold as
to say that there were other People in America, who were not
drown'd by the Flood" and that there is a "Neck of Land
not yet discovered" or lost during a flood or earthquake
that joins America to Europe or Asia.[13] Blake, in his politi-
cal prophecies, was indeed so bold as to say that America
was separated from Europe during the Flood, that the un-
discovered land bridge—Atlantis—is still visible to immor-
tal organs of sight that have not been flooded over by

191

Urizen's laws, and that America is the only one of the original four continents untouched by this flood. Thus *Africa* ends with a description of the effects of the Flood on the sons of Har (who are types of the sons of Noah) and the three continents that they inhabit, while it also looks forward to America, the fourth and the only unfallen continent, from which the attempted reversal of the effects of the Flood will begin.

At the end of *Africa*, the Flood, which Blake has been representing as an ongoing typological event that continues from the time of Noah until the eighteenth century, reaches its culmination in the forming of the philosophy of the five senses (4:16), which is the modern manifestation of the law and the natural religion published by Egypt that binds man to the earth and makes him a slave to the elements. Supposedly having reached the limit of its fall, through the consolidation of Egyptian teaching, the world awaits a new revelation, which is symbolized with ironic ambiguity by images taken from Exodus. The clouds that rolled upon Sinai when God appeared to the Israelites to deliver the law to Moses (Exodus 19:16) appear upon the Alps around the feet of two new prophets, Rousseau and Voltaire. As inspirers of the American and French revolutions, these two philosopher-prophets are potentially new Moses figures who will deliver Europe from the Egypt of civil and religious bondage. Yet doubt is cast upon this newly approaching theophany through its juxtaposition with three other heavenly visitations. The same clouds roll around the vegetative gods that died on the mountains of Assyria—Blake's deceased gods on Lebanon (4:19)—and that were prophesied against in Jeremiah 22:20.[14] The clouds also roll around the fallen sons of God whose visitation upon earth precipitated the Flood. The other symbol from Exodus that gives equivocal value to the newly arriving dispensation is the burning of the Prince of Albion in his nightly tent, which echoes the nightly visitations of the Lord in the form of a fire that burns within the tabernacle (Exodus 40:38). The presence of the Prince within the tabernacle, the abode of the priests, reminds us that the state religion of Egypt was reestablished under the Mosaic dispensation, a dispensation that pretended to liberate Israel from that bondage. These concluding allusions, which link contemporary events with the antediluvian, Mosaic, and prophetic periods of Old Testament history—all within the framework of the revelation on Mount Sinai and Israel's wandering in the desert— imply that eighteen hundred years of history have been repeating the pattern of the Fall and wandering in the wilderness without a promise of a return to Eden. The consolidation of all these images that epitomize the pattern of history, however, along with the consolidation of Egyptian teaching into the philosophy of the five senses, holds out the possibility that the body of error will finally be revealed and that the return envisioned in Revelation will take place.

The promise of an apocalyptic return to a prelapsarian state is held out in *Asia*, where Blake depicts the demise of the kings of Asia, who are represented as a consolidation of Israel's enemies in the Old Testament and the worshipers of the Great Whore in the New Testament. The kings are described in spider imagery that alludes to Isaiah's prophecy against those who commit iniquities that separate man from God: "They hatch cockatrice's eggs, and weave the spider's web . . . their works are works of iniquity, and the act of violence is in their hands" (Isaiah 59:5-6). Through their tyranny, the kings of Asia do indeed hatch a cockatrice's egg, since their oppressions precipitate the emergence of Orc in the form of a serpent.

In their reaction to Orc's "thought-creating fires" (6:6), the Asian monarchs cry "in bitterness of soul" (6:8) and proceed to issue a lament that parodies the rhetoric of Job, who cries, "I will complain in the bitterness of my soul," and breaks forth into a complaint in the form of a series of rhetorical questions (Job 7:11-21). In marked contrast to Job, who seeks mercy from an apparently arbitrary God,

193

the kings of Asia seek to justify their arbitrary use of power, using the bogus excuse of teaching man salvation, "the path / That leads from the gates of the Grave" (7:7-8). Yet the last phrase belies their intentions, alluding to the lament of Hezekiah, the king of Judah who fell deathly ill during the attempt of an Asian king, Sennacherib, to mount a siege upon Jerusalem: "I said in the cutting off of my days, I shall go to the gates of the grave" (Isaiah 38:10). Hezekiah is here tempted to despair because of his own illness and because of the heretical taunts of the Assyrian invader. His salvation comes not from the Asian king, but from the ministrations to his body and spirit by Isaiah, who prophesies that God will deliver Jerusalem out of the hands of Sennacherib (2 Kings 20:6). Similarly, in *Asia*, the Asians' calling for the siege of the city "that the pride of the heart may fail" (7:3) alludes to the self-abasement of Hezekiah and the inhabitants of Jerusalem to forestall the Assyrian siege: "Hezekiah humbled himself for the pride of his heart, both he and the inhabitants of Jerusalem, so that the wrath of the Lord came not upon them in the days of Hezekiah" (2 Chronicles 32:26).

Another allusion in *Asia* to the Assyrian king's attempt to lay a siege upon Jerusalem occurs in the "heaps of smoking ruins" (6:21) that the kings' counselors call for, which refers to Sennacherib's power "to lay waste defenced cities into ruinous heaps" (Isaiah 37:26),[15] a power that, in Isaiah's taunting prophecy, reveals Sennacherib to be merely a tool of God. A third allusion in *Asia* to the siege of Jerusalem by the Asian enemies of Israel occurs in the threat of cutting bread off from the city (7:1), which refers to the absence of bread in Jerusalem when it was besieged by the Chaldeans and the Babylonians. Ezekiel, in his prophecy addressed to Jerusalem, warns the inhabitants of the impending Chaldean siege, wherein the inhabitants "may want bread and water" (Ezekiel 4:17). Jeremiah, who was imprisoned in Jerusalem during the Chaldean siege, is

194

in danger of starvation because "there is no more bread in the city" (38:9). Neither is there bread in Jerusalem during the siege by the Babylonians under Nebuchadnezzar (Jeremiah 52:6).

Ezekiel's prophecies are the source of other allusions in the song of the kings of Asia. The famine and pestilence that the kings call for is prophesied in Ezekiel 5:12-17. In the same chapter, Ezekiel's burning a third part of his hair (5:2) symbolizes the "fires in the City" (*Asia* 6:20) that the admonishers of men in *Asia* call for. The Asian kings' desire "To restrain! to dismay! to thin! / The inhabitants of mountain and plain" (6:11-12) echoes Ezekiel's prophecy of impending destruction "to the mountains, and to the hills, to the rivers and to the valleys" of Israel (Ezekiel 6:3). Out of this destruction by the enemies of Israel, a remnant will be saved who will obey: "And they shall know that I am the Lord, and that I have not said in vain that I would do this evil unto them" (Ezekiel 6:10). This sentiment is recalled in the desire of the Asians to decimate the city through famine "that the remnant may learn to obey" (7:2). Here Blake is clearly drawing an ironic parallel between the Old Testament God and the Asian tyrants.

Besides being identified with the enemies of Jerusalem in the Old Testament, Blake's kings of Asia, through allusions to Revelation, are also identified with the enemies of the church in the New Testament. The Asian monarchs who sing of "the day, of full-feeding prosperity / And the night of delicious songs" (6:13-14) and "the night of prosperity & wantonness" (6:22) are the "kings of the earth" in Revelation who pay homage to the Whore of Babylon, "who have committed fornication and lived deliciously with her" (18:9) and who "are waxed rich through the abundance of her delicacies" (Revelation 18:3). Through these allusions to Revelation 18, wherein John recites the kings' lament over fallen Babylon, Blake underscores the plaintive nature of the Asian kings' song, for the obvious answer to their tormented questionings in *Asia* is "no." The unnamed city whose downfall they bitterly envision is, ironically, not Jerusalem, but Babylon.

The cause of the kings of Asia is a lost one, at least until Urizen adopts it. In response to their lament, Urizen attempts to aid them by spreading his wings over Judea and Jerusalem in imitation of Sennacherib, whose coming Isaiah prophesies: "and the stretching out of his wings shall fill the breadth of thy land, O Immanuel" (Isaiah 8:8). Like Sennacherib, however, Urizen fails; he attempts to quench Orc's fires as he had done in *America,* but the fires from the French Revolution cause his books of law to melt (7:14-15). He makes a last desperate attempt to assert his sway over Judea, a land that from the appearance of Adam and Noah (7:20-23) seems dead enough to tolerate his reassuming his "ancient place" (7:18), but the fires of Orc reach even there, causing a general resurrection of Israel's dead.

Just as Urizen is here described in a symbol that associates him with Sennacherib, the Asian invader, so Orc is described in an image that likens him to Hezekiah, the defender of Jerusalem. Orc's appearance on the Alps "like a serpent of fiery flame" (7:28) recalls Isaiah's image of Hezekiah as a "fiery flying serpent" that will smite the Philistines (Isaiah 14:29). King though he was, Hezekiah was an iconoclast and a religious reformer who "rebelled against the king of Assyria, and served him not" (2 Kings 18:7). Yet it is the very ambiguity of Blake's summoning the image of Orc as a king that casts doubt on the efficacy of Orc's revolt.

Further doubt is cast by links between images describing Orc and two major symbols of Israel's wandering in the wilderness. First, Orc's rising "like a pillar of fire above the Alps" (7:27) likens him to the pillar of fire that led Israel through the wilderness. The pillar emerges from the spot upon which Voltaire and Rousseau stood in *Africa* and thus represents the new exodus from the bondage of law that

Blake anticipated at the end of that poem. Second, the image of the fiery serpent refers not only to Hezekiah but also to the brazen serpent, the "fiery serpent" that Moses set up on a pole to save those Israelites that were bitten by the serpents of the desert (Numbers 21:6-9). In the subsequent history of the Jews in the Old Testament, this brazen serpent was then worshiped as an idol, a practice destroyed by Hezekiah when he "brake in pieces the brasen serpent that Moses had made" (2 Kings 18:4).

In the context of biblical imagery, however, Hezekiah himself becomes a fiery serpent, as Isaiah depicts him in his prophecy against the Philistines (Isaiah 14:29). Blake here returns to the myth of Cadmus that he developed in *Africa*, linking *Asia* with its companion poem through the pattern of the man who destroys the serpent only to become a serpent himself, thus emblematizing the cycles of fallen history. Ovid's story of Cadmus is also suggested by the illustration on plate 6, where the cave formed by the overhanging trees resembles the cave overgrown with branches in which the great serpent of Ares dwells.[16]

The significance of this symbolism is deepened by the description of Christ himself, the most obvious and important victor over the serpent in biblical myth, in terms of the brazen serpent: "And as Moses lifted up the serpent in the wilderness, even so must the Son of man be lifted up: That whosoever believeth in him should not perish, but have eternal life" (John 3.14-15). The potential for the creation of a new idolatry through an adherence to the letter of the Gospel, which Blake sees as being realized in the eighteen hundred years of history, is all too apparent in Calvin's interpretation of the lifting up of the Son of man as the lifting up of the doctrine of the Gospel.[17] A more popular interpretation of this passage from John sees the lifting up of Christ as a reference to the crucifixion and thus links the image of the brazen serpent with that of Christ on the cross, the Old Testament image being a type of the

197

Atonement. Given Blake's abhorrence of the orthodox conception of atonement, the idolatry implicit in this symbolic relationship is obvious.

Through his gathering of symbols from pagan myth and from the Bible, Blake questions whether the revolution in Europe will lead the world beyond the previous cycles of history. Orc the iconoclast and liberator is rendered through Blake's similes as a potentially new icon and tyrant. Further ambiguity is created by the lines, "The sullen Earth / Shrunk!" (7:29-30), which link Orc's rise with the shrinking of man and nature in *Africa*. Does this shrinking portend greater bondage? Or does it signify the departure of the first earth and the first heaven so that a new heaven and earth can appear, as in Revelation 21:1? The latter seems to be the case, since Blake shows Orc's appearance to cause a general resurrection, modeled upon Ezekiel's vision of the resurrection in the vale of dry bones (Ezekiel 37): "Forth from the dead dust rattling bones to bones / Join: shaking convuls'd the shivring clay breathes" (7:31-32). The concluding stanza returns to ambiguity, however, with the sexual imagery surrounding Blake's personified figure of the Grave as a womb suggesting both the delivering up of the dead, as in 2 Esdras 4:40-42, and the filling up of her womb with new death—the victims of the French Revolution and the wars emerging from it. Along with the milk and the "glandous wine" (7:38), blood flows in the joyous ecstasy that accompanies Orc's appearance in Asia. At most, Blake is here showing a vision of the earth reborn; he certainly does not show the descent of the bride, Jerusalem, and her consummation with the bridegroom. The allusion of the last line of *Asia* ("Urizen wept") to John 11:35 ("Jesus wept"), whose context is the raising of Lazarus, suggests, like the allusion to the vale of dry bones, that at most Blake is pointing to the resurrection of an earthly Jerusalem rather than the descent of the heavenly city.

The idea that the French Revolution may lead to the establishment of a renovated earth is reinforced by the full-

page illustration on plate 8, the last plate in almost all
copies of *The Song of Los*. This design is Blake's reworking
of Raphael's painting of *Astronomy*, which is in the Stanza
della Segnatura. Raphael's work depicts a female form, sur-
rounded by two cherubs and leaning over a huge globe
that dominates the painting. This allegorical figure has
been interpreted as "the beginning of the universe, with
Philosophy studying the globe of the cosmos, or as Astron-
omy contemplating the universe."[18] Blake's substitution of
Los as the contemplator of the globe reveals Blake's inten-
tion of showing the supplanting of philosophy and New-
tonian science by the Imagination. The abstract philosophy
whose development is traced in *Africa* gives way to inspira-
tion as Blake enacts a principle that he sets forth in the
Descriptive Catalogue: "There are always these two classes
of the learned sages, the poetical and the philosophical. . . .
Let the philosopher always be the servant and scholar of
inspiration and all will be happy" (p. 528). In opposition
to the creation of the fallen universe by the philosophy of
the five senses, Los has re-created the universe, pounding it
into form with his prophetic hammer. As Erdman suggests,
the red globe created by Los "may represent the material
sun, or history, or the corporeal war which Los is forging
into vision."[19]

This picture of Los, as I have already noted, represents
a movement in *Asia* that is contrary to the movement de-
picted in *Africa*. The red globe of Los that forms the last
plate of *The Song of Los* stands in opposition to the globe
of Urizen, inscribed with hieroglyphics, that appears on the
first plate (the frontispiece) of this book.[20] This earlier
plate, Blake's rendition of the true vision of Philosophy or
Astronomy, shows a figure kneeling beneath rather than
above the globe—representing enslavement by rather than
mastery of the form—and leaning over an altar in a pose
suggestive of Noah's sacrifice, performed by Urizen in grati-
tude for the floods of abstraction that are to be detailed in
Africa.[21] This illustration depicts man's enslavement to the

199

elements, which began in Egypt, as the hieroglyphs suggest, whereas the contrary illustration shows the beginnings of man's liberation from the elements. Los's globe, as Erdman interprets it, has been "purged . . . of the runes of Urizenic mystery" and represents a stage in the movement of Los's re-creation of the universe into human form.[22] The two contrary illustrations reflect a vision that is both dialectic and progressive, suggesting the movement of biblical history from enslavement in Africa to liberation in Asia, from the founding of abstract philosophy and law in Egypt to the victory of prophecy over that law on Patmos. While that victory is not complete, the reader is at least left with a picture of Los performing the same historical function as John of Patmos, keeping the divine vision in time of trouble.[23]

The Book of Urizen:
Blake's Inverted Genesis

The Book of Urizen is the Genesis of "The Bible of Hell"
that Blake promised in *The Marriage of Heaven and Hell*.
In this first articulation of a cosmogonic myth, his own
vision of the Creation and the Fall, Blake, like the narrator
in *The Marriage* who promises a devils' Bible, reads the
Bible "in its infernal or diabolical sense." By satirizing
Genesis, he attacks orthodox theology and philosophy,
which he believes to be the true causes of the Fall.

Blake develops his prophetic invective by using the struc-
tural and thematic patterns of Genesis to present a sus-
tained satiric interpretation of that book, an interpretation
that is deeply indebted to the literary and exegetical tradi-
tions surrounding the first book of the Bible. Exploiting
these traditions and literary patterns, Blake transforms the
first three chapters of Genesis into a coherent and dramatic
narrative that condenses all that is contained in that book.
Thus Blake conceals his art through crypsis: he transposes,
condenses, and often inverts the material in his source. In-
deed, he inverts the entire book of Genesis by invoking
Revelation, developing his irony through parallels between
the first and last books of the Bible. Through his "infernal
method" of etching "apparent surfaces away" and throwing
the essential structure into relief (*MHH*, pl. 14), Blake
makes Genesis the plate from which his inverted image is
pulled.

In its treatment of the Creation and the Fall, *The Book
of Urizen* follows the pattern that Blake saw in Genesis 1-3,
a pattern described in his illuminated manuscript copy of
this biblical book (1826-1827):

(p. 667)

In *Urizen*, chapters I-III describe the creation of the natural man, covering Urizen's fall from Eternity and his transformation into a clod of clay. Chapters IV-V contain the story of Los's fall into self-division, whereby the division of the sexes occurs. And chapters VI-IX describe the nature of sexual love, through Los's relationship to Enitharmon, and the fall into generation and death, through the events beginning with the birth of Orc. The Tree of Knowledge does not overtly appear within the narrative, but it is illustrated on the title page and is echoed by visual and verbal images within the text.[2] The Tree of Life, however, does not appear at all. Its function as the symbol of eternal life is given to the Eternals and the figure in flames on plate 3.[3] Eternal life is not represented as a tree because the images of vegetation in *Urizen* carry negative meanings. Neither the Tree of Life nor the Tree of Knowledge has the central narrative significance that each has in Genesis because, for Blake, forsaking the Tree of Life and eating the fruit of the Tree of Knowledge are implied in the events of Genesis that precede the temptation of Eve.

By locating the Fall in the creation of the world and the division of the sexes, Blake is drawing upon the Genesis exegetical tradition. The concept of the Creation as the Fall belongs to the Gnostic tradition.[4] The second stage of the Fall in *The Book of Urizen*, the division of the sexes, suggests that Blake was familiar with Philo's interpretation of Adam's fall. According to Philo's allegorical exegesis, Adam's fall began when he fell asleep; Adam symbolizes the rational soul, and his sleep symbolizes the relaxation of the mind's attention, whereby Eve, the physical senses, was created.[5] In *Urizen*, the sleep of Urizen provokes Los's creation of the five fallen senses, an act that results in Los's fall and the creation of Enitharmon, the counterpart of Eve.

Blake's conception of the Creation-Fall as the act of two separate masculine agents is derived from the two narrative strands in Genesis. The opening chapters of the Bible contain "two independent and varying accounts of the Creation lying side by side, each of which had its own peculiar style and was complete in itself,"[6] and each of which was distinguished by the different name God is called: "Elohim" in the first creation account (1-2:4a) and "Jahweh" in the second (2:4b-23).[7] These two distinct narrative accounts and names embody two different conceptions of the Creator: the Elohim is a generic name ("Judges"), whereas Jahweh is a proper name; the Elohim is a concept, and Jahweh a person. The style of the Elohist creation is "precise, repetitive, and largely abstract, and its austere description of the Creation seems prosaic besides J's [the Jahwist's] striking anthropomorphisms."[8] In the latter account, which is "vivid and pictorial," Jahweh, rather than being "described anthropomorphically . . . is revealed by his shortcomings to be more human than divine."[9]

From these distinctions, Blake derives his conception of Urizen and Los. Urizen initiates the Creation-Fall by the process of abstraction; Los completes the Creation by hammering it into human form. Urizen's character emerges from the pedantic and remote narrative style of the Elohist creation, and his narcissism is that of the Elohim, who creates man in his own image (1:26). Los's character is derived from the more poetic Jahwist account, which describes the Creator as a Promethean craftsman, who brings form out of the crude dust of the earth. Los also is identified with the Jahwist's Adam, who divides into male and female, but so is Urizen, who, like Adam, falls into a deep sleep. This double identification with Adam occurs because both Los and Urizen are fragmented parts of fallen or natural man.

By asserting that the God of the Creation is self-divided, Blake's creation myth resolves the apparent contradictions of the two creation accounts in Genesis. The poet's shifting of Adam's sleep from Genesis 2 into the equivalent of Genesis 1 (chapters I-III of *Urizen*) and his assigning of this sleep to Urizen serve an important structural and thematic function. Urizen's sleep is a dramatic device that allows Blake to move from the Elohist to the Jahwist creation account and to explain the nature of these two distinct creators. In Chapter III of *Urizen*, Urizen's creation, the Elohist creation of Genesis 1, has reached an impasse. An abstract god creates an abstract world, inhabited by an abstract man. Urizen, having become a clod of clay (6:10), falls into a deep sleep because he has reached the limit of his creative potential. The Elohim of Genesis creates a complete world; but like Urizen's black globe, this world is abstract, remote, lifeless. Blake's major attack on the Elohim can be seen in the identification of the creator with his creation. Los is introduced to humanize Urizen's abstract creation and Urizen himself, just as the Jahweh of Genesis 2 humanizes the god of Genesis 1 and his creations. Like Jahweh, Los gives form to the crude material of the earth, but Blake creates a dramatic continuity between Genesis 1 and 2 by making Urizen-Elohim the creator of the clay with which Los-Jahweh must work.

In this reinterpretation of the dual creation accounts of Genesis, Blake reverses the conventional interpretation of the nature of the Elohim and Jahweh. Traditionally the Elohim is considered to be a benevolent deity and Jahweh is considered to be a malevolent god.[10] The Elohim's benevolence is derived from his existence as an idealized abstraction. Jahweh's malevolence is a result of his anthropomorphic nature: he has human limitations and is prone to fits of jealousy and envy. Blake's reading of Genesis, however, attacks this orthodox preference for an abstract deity, this equation of God with an abstract goodness.

The basis of Blake's interpretation of the two deities is aesthetic rather than traditionally moralistic, and thus his reading of Genesis is symbolic rather than literal. The remote, abstract, and prosaic style with which the Elohist creation is described is a direct indication of the nature of the Elohim and the kind of mind that perceives him. An abstract, apathetic god cannot be benevolent, because benevolence is an expression of pathos, of deep feeling and concern. This belief is expressed in one of Blake's *Songs of Innocence*:

> For Mercy has a human heart
> Pity, a human face:
> And Love, the human form divine,
> And Peace, the human dress.
>
> ("The Divine Image," p. 12)

In the counterpart to this poem in *Songs of Experience*, "The Human Abstract," Blake asserts not only that an abstract deity cannot be benevolent but that such a deity is actually malevolent. Jealousy and cruelty are the direct results of a commitment to an abstract Good and divine apathy.

Blake therefore favors the anthropomorphic Jahweh precisely because of his human qualities. Jahweh is given positive value through the poetic style in which he is described, which shows him to be both human and divine. The depiction of Jahweh as a creator who works with his hands fuses the creator with his creation by making God an artist who gives the creation human form. This anthropomorphic perception of God makes divine benevolence possible by humanizing God and deifying man, joining the human and the divine through poetic vision. For Blake, Jehovah (the earlier, conventional pronunciation of Jahweh) represents desire, energy, and inspiration. This conception is stated in

205

The Marriage of Heaven and Hell, plate 6, where Jehovah is "no other than he, who dwells in flaming fire." The Elohim, on the other hand, represents the god of abstract law, the god of jealousy and the natural world. Blake was explicit about this point when he told Henry Crabb Robinson that the Elohim, not Jehovah, created the material world and when he depicted this god of nature in a large color print of 1795 entitled, "Elohim Creating Adam."[11] This deity's associations with materialism and abstract laws of good and evil are emphasized in that picture by the snake that is wound around Adam's body. This motif of a snake wrapped around a figure appears in plate 6 of *Urizen*, at the conclusion of Blake's version of the Elohist creation. Urizen is the direct embodiment of the Elohim and remains so throughout the book. Los represents Jehovah until he falls in Chapter V of *Urizen*.

The fall of Los-Jehovah is a necessary event in Blake's interpretation of Genesis. Given his conception of the Elohim and Jehovah, we can see that he is confronted with a problem in his source. Until Genesis 2:17, Jehovah is shown to be a benevolent and humane creator. With the prohibition of the Tree of Knowledge, however, he becomes irascible and jealous. Not only the God of the second creation account, he is also the God of the Fall. But since Blake gives all the attributes of a malevolent deity to Elohim, he must account for the changes in Jehovah's character. He does this in his version of Genesis 2-3 (chapters IV-IX of *Urizen*), by having Los-Jehovah appropriate to himself, through a fall, the characteristics of Elohim-Urizen. Here Blake draws upon what immediately follows the prohibition of the tree in Genesis, the creation of Eve (2:18-25); and thus Los becomes the self-divided Adam.

In both Genesis and *Urizen* the motive for this self-division is pity. God pities Adam because Adam is alone (2:18), and Los pities Urizen because Urizen has successfully effected his own isolation from Eternity with Los's help.

206

However admirable Jehovah may be, however inspired his activity, he is working with corrupt materials and is forging a mirror image out of a fallen part of himself. His pity for Adam's loneliness is really self-pity because Adam's isolation is a mirror of his own isolation. The creation of Eve is an expedient that avoids the essential issue, the separation of Jehovah and Adam. Rather than working to heal this breach between the two sides of his being, Jehovah falls into self-pity. The self-divided Adam is a reflection of Jehovah's capitulation to the material world and the power of the Elohim. Thus Los-Jehovah becomes the self-divided Adam in Blake's version of Genesis. Through Los's fall, Urizen-Elohim emerges again and dominates Blake's version of the events of Genesis 3, which in the Bible are still dominated by Jehovah.

For Blake, then, Genesis is the story of the division of the Elohim and Jehovah, the conflict between them, and the victory of the Elohim. The triumph of the Elohim over Jehovah represents the triumph of justice over mercy. This conflict between justice and mercy in Blake's rendition of the Creation and the Fall is drawn from the Genesis tradition. Blake's most immediate source would be, of course, the debate between the Father and the Son in Book III of *Paradise Lost*:

The real key to the episode [in Book III of *Paradise Lost*] is to be found . . . in the long-standing tradition of the debate of the four daughters of God. This . . . had its origins in the rabbinic tractates, where God's foreknowledge of the Fall and its consequences was reconciled with His omnipotence by the invention of a dispute between His four daughters, Love, Truth, Righteousness, and Peace. During the course of their argument, which took place before Adam's creation, Love and Righteousness urged that Man should be created, Truth and Peace that he should not. Later versions of the legend reduced the

207

disputants to two, giving the objections of Truth and Peace to the *Torah* and the counter-arguments of Love and Righteousness to God. In both versions of the legend the dispute was finally settled by God's decision that His love of goodness outweighed His hatred of sin, that His mercy was greater than His vengefulness. The medieval Christian treatments of the subject transferred the debate to some occasion after the fall and realigned the four contestants so that Peace and Love (Mercy) defended Man while Truth and Righteousness (Justice) accused him. The controversy now concerned the advisability not of creating Man but of saving him, and its purpose was to reconcile not God's omnipotence with His omniscience but His justice with His benevolence. Further, it was resolved by the Son's offer to satisfy the claims of Justice by dying on Man's behalf rather than by an arbitrary decision on the part of the Father.

By the Renaissance this medieval version of the legend had developed along the same lines as the rabbinic, that is, the four conflicting parties were reduced to two, Justice and Mercy.[12]

In *Paradise Lost* Milton was anxious to deemphasize the allegorical basis of the debate in order to minimize the Father's vindictiveness and to show that mercy and justice are attributes of a unified God. At the opening of the debate, the Father announces: ". . . in Mercy and Justice both, / Through Heav'n and Earth, so shall my glory excel, / But Mercy first and last shall brightest shine" (III. 132-34). Milton was working against a tradition that was very well-established, however,[13] and he himself felt its influence when he originally planned, in the Cambridge Manuscript, a drama based on the theme of the Fall. In the second list of characters for this drama, Milton includes the figures of Justice, Mercy, Wisdom, and Heavenly Love. He planned to have these figures engage in the traditional debate, as his third draft reveals:

Justice		debating what should become of man
Mercie	}	if he fall
Wisdome		

Apparently, Wisdom was to arbitrate between the other two figures. The plan for the debate is abandoned in Milton's fourth draft, "Adam unparadiz'd," but Justice persuades Adam that his punishment is just, and Mercy offers comfort through the promise of redemption.[14]

Blake no doubt read these original drafts and was aware of the tradition behind the debate in Book III of *Paradise Lost*.[15] In his own renditions of this debate, Blake adhered more closely to the biblical tradition, exalting the Son (Mercy) at the expense of the Father (Justice). This can best be seen in *The Ghost of Abel*, in which Blake reaffirms and extends the tradition by shifting the debate from the Fall to the murder of Abel, making Abel's ghost the voice of Justice (ultimately Satan and the Elohim) and Jehovah the voice of Mercy (Christ). Through the cries for revenge of Abel's ghost, Blake asserts that the abstract justice of the Father is a mask of jealousy, vindictiveness, and lust for blood. Rather than attempting to reconcile Justice and Mercy, as Milton does, Blake resolves the conflict, having Jehovah outwit the Elohim by offering himself as a sacrifice. Here Blake extends the tradition by further exalting the Son at the Father's expense. The Son will redeem not only man, but the Father as well. Through Jehovah's sacrifice the Elohim will himself "go to Eternal Death / In Self Annihilation even till Satan self-subdud Put Off Satan" (*The Ghost of Abel* 2:19-20).[16]

Although Blake makes significant changes in the tradition, the debate is resolved with the traditional triumph of Mercy—a redemptive pattern maintained in *The Ghost of Abel*. Earlier, in *The Book of Urizen*, this redemptive resolution of the conflict between Justice and Mercy was ironically reversed. Because Blake combines the Creation with the Fall, his vision of the heavenly debate inverts both the

209

rabbinic and Christian sources. In the rabbinic source, the creation of man is the victory of love and righteousness over the Torah (the Law); in *Urizen* the creation of fallen man is the triumph of Urizen's One Law. Through this reversal, Blake is saying that God's omnipotence and his foreknowledge of the Fall cannot be reconciled. There is no getting around the fact that God is creating a fallen world. The rabbinical concept of an internal debate in which God suppresses a part of himself merely indicates that the creation was not the work of a fully integrated being. This disintegration of the divine psyche is also emphasized in Blake's reversal of the traditional Christian debate over man's salvation. With the triumph of Justice over Mercy, Blake is asserting that the world was created by a fragmented, imperfect being for the sole purpose of accusing man of sin.

For Blake the heavenly debate takes place neither before the Fall, as in *Paradise Lost,* nor after the Fall, as in earlier versions of the legend. The debate is coexistent with the Fall and the Creation of the fallen world. That creation is the direct expression of the psychic conflict and its resolution. In this conflict, not only is Justice triumphant but the very creation of Justice, abstract law, and the concept of sin precipitate the debate. The separation of Justice from Mercy and the absolute refusal of the perpetrator of Justice to be reconciled with Mercy insure the triumph of Justice and the psychic fragmentation that creates the fallen world. Blake thus turns the heavenly debate tradition on end. Rather than redeeming the fallen world, the debate creates it. Instead of using the heavenly debate to reconcile divine Justice with divine Mercy, and to remove from God any imputation of inconsistency or arbitrariness, Blake uses the debate to affirm the arbitrary and perverse nature of the creator of the fallen world.

Although the narrative pattern in *Urizen* parallels the first three chapters of Genesis as Blake interpreted them, the symbolic and thematic elements in Blake's poem indicate that Blake is using the accounts of the Creation and

210

the Fall to sum up the entire book of Genesis, as well as to foreshadow the events of Exodus. This is evident in the first lines of the poem: "Lo, a shadow of horror is risen / In Eternity" (3:1). This opening sentence alludes to Genesis 15:12: "And when the sun was going down, a deep sleep fell upon Abram; and, lo, a horror of great darkness fell upon him." This is how God appears to Abraham in a dream that prophesies Israel's four-hundred-year sojourn in Egypt. The opening lines of the poem not only associate Urizen with the God of Abraham, a God of deep sleep and nightmare visions, but also foretell the outcome of Urizen's revolt from Eternity. This prophecy of the Egyptian captivity is fulfilled in the last chapter of *Urizen*, where the fallen world is identified as Egypt (28:10). There the events of Exodus are foreshadowed by the flight of Fuzon. Again, Blake ironically inverts his source. The "chosen" people, the followers of Urizen, are delivered into slavery, while the "damned" escape with the fiery Fuzon. This division of Urizen's children reflects the same division between the chosen and the reprobate that forms one of the organizing themes of Genesis—a theme expressed in that book, as in *Urizen*, by the archetype of the divided brothers.

By interpreting Genesis 1-3 as a conflict between the Elohim and Jehovah, Blake thematically unifies those chapters with the entire book of Genesis, making the self-divided God of the Creation and Fall the archetype of a series of fraternal conflicts that begin immediately after the Fall with the story of Cain and Abel. The structural and thematic significance of the divided brothers in Genesis can be seen in the following commentary on the character of Jacob:

> Crafty, patient, fearful, faint yet pursuing, he might be said to be the embodiment of the real Israel, the Israel of history and the prophets, continually sinning and suffering, yet ever seeking the birthright and the blessing. One might almost say that the Yahwist has set out to show why

211

the scripture had said, "Jacob have I loved, and Esau have I hated" (Mal 1:2, 3). From the point of view of the natural man, Esau is a far more attractive character, generous and impulsive, quick to forget an injury, but for the Yahwist he is in the line of descent represented by Cain and Ishmael, the line of nature as opposed to the line of grace. Cain and Abel, Ishmael and Isaac, Esau and Jacob, represent the two streams the Yahwist keeps always before him as he develops his theme.[17]

If we reverse the orthodox categories of "nature" and "grace," as Blake does in *Urizen*, we have a vision of Genesis that Blake clearly had in mind. For Blake, the energetic Esau represents the line of inspiration, and "crafty" Jacob, the line of nature. Jacob possesses "the cunning of weak and tame minds. which have power to resist energy, according to the proverb, the weak in courage is strong in cunning" (*MHH*, pl. 16). Urizen, like Jacob, Abel, and Isaac, is of the Angels' party, "the line of grace." These figures represent, for Blake, the line of nature, those who are identified with the Elohim. Los, like Esau, Cain, and Ishmael, is one of "the damned," the man of energy and inspiration typified by Jehovah, "who dwells in flaming fire" (*MHH*, pl. 6). *The Book of Urizen* thus synthesizes four major narratives of Genesis by associating Urizen and Los with these divided brothers who reflect the conflict between the Elohim and Jehovah.

Blake's early use of this archetype can be seen in the Argument of *The Marriage of Heaven and Hell*, which is a reworking of the Esau and Jacob story. With Jacob as the villain who drives the just man Esau "into barren climes,"[18] the Argument presents Esau, or Edom, as he is also called, as the man of energy who is deprived of his birthright and whose restoration is announced in the succeeding plate, where a voice proclaims, "Now is the dominion of Edom, & the return of Adam into Paradise" (*MHH*, pl. 3). Urizen, like the usurping villain, "left the paths of ease, / To walk in perilous paths" (*MHH* 2:14-15). In his fall, Urizen drives Los out of Eternity, depriving him of his birthright as it were, and making him the just man raging in the wilds, a prophet howling in the wilderness. Thus Blake's interpretation of the rivalry between Jacob and Esau presents a pattern that reappears in his account of Genesis 1-3.

Blake's later use of this archetype to represent the self-divided God of Genesis can be seen in *The Ghost of Abel*, where the heavenly debate tradition is invoked to emphasize the significance of the conflict. *The Book of Urizen* not only reverses the redemptive pattern of the tradition that it shares with the former but also incorporates and inverts narrative and thematic elements of Genesis 4 that appear in *The Ghost of Abel* and in Blake's other interpretations of the Cain and Abel story. In the illustrated Genesis manuscript, as in *The Ghost of Abel*, the biblical narrative is given a redemptive construction: "Chapter IV   How Generation & Death took possession of the Natural Man & of the Forgiveness of Sins written on the Murderers Forehead" (p. 667). This interpretation did not suit Blake's purpose in *Urizen*, which was to emphasize the Fall. In *Urizen* Los-Cain actually saves Urizen-Abel, but bears Cain's punishment without any promise of redemption. Like Cain in *The Ghost of Abel*, Los is subdued by the vindictive and jealous nature of the Elohim. The picture of Cain haunted by the ghost of Abel in Blake's paintings of "The Body of Abel Found by Adam and Eve"[19] resembles the howling Los on plate 7 of *Urizen*. Both Cain and Los, stopping their ears, have the same facial expression and have flames shooting from behind them. Although Cain is attempting to flee his torment, both Cain and Los ultimately share the same fate. Cain escapes to the land of Nod, but he cannot escape his enslavement to the Elohim until Jehovah redeems him. Cain's city will be founded upon human sacrifice: "Cains City built with Human Blood" (*The Ghost of Abel* 2:17). Similarly, the world of Generation is built upon human sacrifice, Los's chaining of Orc.

These human sacrifices are demanded by the Elohim, who is embodied in the ghost of Abel and in Urizen. In *The Ghost of Abel*, the voice of Abel's ghost, the voice of the Elohim, and the voice of Satan are unified in a single figure, the Accuser who is at war with Jehovah, the principle of Mercy:

> I will have Human Blood & not the blood of Bulls or Goats
> And no Atonement O Jehovah the Elohim live on Sacrifice
> Of Men: hence I am God of Men: Thou Human O Jehovah.
>
> (2:13-15)

Urizen as Abel-Elohim-Satan thrives on human sacrifice and thus awakens from his sleep only when the sacrificed Orc cries out. As the vindictive Accuser, Urizen denies atonement in the original sense of that word, the unity of man and God. To maintain his power he is committed to the perpetuation of sin rather than to its forgiveness.

One of the symbols of Urizen's world, "the Dog at the wintry door" (25:2), illustrated on plate 26, is derived from the image of sin in Genesis 4:7. God tells the angry Cain, whose offering has been refused: "If thou doest well, shalt thou not be accepted? and if thou doest not well, sin lieth at the door. And unto thee shall be his desire, and thou shalt rule over him."[20] In Blake's ironic treatment of the Old Testament God, it is Urizen who rules over the beast of sin that lies at the door. But Los, like Cain, succumbs to this beast. By pitying Urizen, Los exchanges his newborn child for the dog at the wintry door,[21] sacrificing the joys of energy in an assent to Urizen's concept of sin. The ironic parallel between Los's sacrifice of Orc and the story of Abraham and Isaac again shows that Blake's version of Genesis intentionally excludes all the redemptive elements that are in his source. For Blake, the substitution of the lamb for Isaac begins the defeat of the Elohim and the movement toward regeneration through the Lamb of God.[22] The sacrifice of Orc is an ironic reversal of that movement.

Because of Orc's identification with Isaac, the Isaac-Ishmael parallel to Urizen and Los is not strongly developed in *The Book of Urizen*. The parallel is implied, however, in the archetype of the divided brothers. The principal cause of the division of the three pairs of brothers in Genesis is jealousy, the desire for an exclusive position of power or an exclusive relationship. God's favoring of Abel's offering and his exclusion of Cain cause a rivalry that ends in murder. Ishmael and Isaac, Esau and Jacob, are rivals for a "birthright" that grants an exclusive relationship with God. In these two pairs of divided brothers, jealousy divides not only them, but the parents as well. Sarah and Hagar are jealous rivals because of the claims of their sons to a birthright and because of their own desire for an exclusive relationship with Abraham. Isaac's love for Esau divides him from Rebekah, who favors Jacob. In *Urizen*, Los and Urizen are divided by jealousy: Urizen's desire for an exclusive holiness.

The Book of Urizen thus emphasizes what is a constant theme in Blake's reading of Genesis: the destructive jealousy that is caused by the Old Testament God. This theme of divisive jealousy was noted by a seventeenth-century exegete, Peter Allix, whose commentary on Genesis was reprinted in Blake's time. Tracing the repeated pattern of divisions caused by jealousy in Genesis, Allix points out that this pattern provides the dominant theme of Genesis and the rest of the Old Testament as well: "the spirit of distinction, and the spirit of jealousy, kept in the bosom of his people, ought to be well considered by those that desire to know the genius of God's laws, and the original causes of all the transactions related by *Moses*, and by the other sacred authors."[23]

This interrelationship between jealousy and division is evident throughout Genesis. Besides the three pairs of divided brothers, there is the schism between Joseph and the

215

other sons of Jacob, caused by Jacob's favoring Joseph with a coat of many colors. Similarly, Noah separates his sons by blessing Shem and Japheth and by cursing Canaan to be a slave to his brothers (9:25-27).[24] By dividing their children, the patriarchs of Genesis reflect the behavior of the divine father. God's jealousy of the people of Babel, who attempt to achieve divinity, causes him to separate them. This division is echoed in *Urizen*, when Urizen spreads his net of religion:

> And their thirty cities divided
> In form of a human heart
> No more could they rise at will
> In the infinite void, but bound down
> To earth by their narrowing perceptions.
>
> (25:43-47)

> The remaining sons of Urizen
> Beheld their brethren shrink together
> Beneath the Net of Urizen;
> Perswasion was in vain,
> For the ears of the inhabitants
> Were wither'd, & deafen'd, & cold.
> And their eyes could not discern,
> Their brethren of other cities.
>
> (28:11-18)

Like the Old Testament God, Urizen maintains his exclusive divinity by dividing himself from others and by keeping others divided among themselves.

The spreading of the net of religion is not only Blake's version of the Babel story but is actually a synthesis of Babel and Noah's flood. Since the water symbolizes matter, Blake interpreted the Flood as the entrapment of man in the physical world, the closing of man's infinite senses in a finite body. In his description of Verulam in *Europe*, Blake uses the Flood to describe the time "when the five senses whelm'd / In the deluge o'er the earth-born man" (10:10-

216

11). The same passage describes the formation of finite space in terms of the Flood:

> then all the eternal forests were divided
> Into earths rolling in circles of space, that like an
>   ocean rush'd
> And overwhelmed all except this finite wall of flesh.
>
> (10:18-20)

The last line of *Urizen* uses a similar image of the deluge to describe the fallen world: "And the salt ocean rolled englob'd" (28:23). As in *Europe*, Blake uses the Flood story of Genesis to describe the Fall.

Like Genesis, *Urizen* contains two accounts of a deluge. Urizen's creation of water in 4:20-21 parallels the creation of the primal waters in Genesis 1:1. Urizen's tears of pity that form the net of religion (25:5-22) are the counterpart of Noah's flood in Genesis 6-7. In the Bible the Deluge follows the Fall as the second major catastrophe that changes the whole nature of the world. Similarly, the formation of the net of religion is the second major destructive act of Urizen. The Genesis Flood and Urizen's net both account for the disappearance of giants from the face of the earth—a motif used in both books as a metaphor for the loss of a close relationship between the human and the divine. In Genesis the giants are produced by the intermarriage of the sons of God and the daughters of men (6:2-4); they occupy an intermediate position between Eternity and the world of Generation. The children of Urizen are in the same position: they are of giant stature, and their senses are not completely shrunken up. Like the Flood, Urizen's tears are prompted by the disobedience of the inhabitants of the earth. The formation of Urizen's net is described in water images:

> And he wept, & he called it Pity
> And his tears flowed down on the winds

217

Cold he wander'd on high, over their cities
In weeping & pain & woe!
And where-ever he wanderd in sorrows
Upon the aged heavens
A cold shadow follow'd behind him
Like a spiders web, moist, cold, & dim.

(25:3-10)

In Genesis the giant race is completely annihilated by the Flood, and the world is repopulated by men of smaller stature. In *Urizen* the giants shrink up beneath Urizen's net, continuing a process that began with Urizen's fall: "And in reptile forms shrinking together / Of seven feet stature they remaind" (25:37-38). The main difference between Blake's use of the Flood and the Flood story in Genesis is that Blake gives the Deluge and the primal waters of Genesis 1 equal catastrophic significance.

Whereas the Bible makes the Fall and the Flood two chronologically separate events that carry similar themes, Blake combines both events in a continuous narrative, making the Flood part of the Fall. This fusion of the Flood story with the Fall may have its source in Genesis exegetical tradition. *Song of Songs Rabba* uses the Flood story's theme of the shrinking of man's stature to describe Adam's fall: "Before Adam sinned he could listen to the divine utterance upright and without being afraid, but after he sinned, when he heard the divine voice he was frightened and hid himself. . . . R. Aibu said: on that occasion Adam's stature was lessened and reduced to a hundred cubits."[25] Thus the spreading of Urizen's net connects the Fall not only with the story of the tower of Babel but also with the Genesis story of the Flood.

Another motif that *The Book of Urizen* adopts from Genesis is that of naming. When God creates the day, night, and heaven, he also names them: "And God called the light Day, and the darkness he called Night" (1:5); "And God called the firmament Heaven" (1:8). Since Genesis is a book of origins, these namings and the use of the verb "to call" proliferate throughout the book. Through this activity of assigning names, the authors of Genesis are using language to reproduce the creative power of God. To give something a name is to call it into existence by incorporating it into a language and thus into consciousness. Thus the Babylonian account of the creation expressed the original nonexistence of heaven by the phrase "the heaven was not yet named."[26]

The concept of naming as a divine activity, expressed in the Genesis exegetical tradition, had its origin in primitive religion[27] and persisted in Hebraic and Christian thought. According to Chrysostom, Augustine, and the rabbinical commentaries, one of the attributes of Adam's prelapsarian perfection was his ability to name the animals.[28] Because of the divine power attributed to the assigning of names, naming is a sacred event in Genesis. Since the act of naming originates with God, man's participation in this act expresses his intimate relationship with the Deity. When, in Genesis 4:25, Eve bears Adam another son, she "called his name Seth: For God, said she, hath appointed me another seed instead of Abel, whom Cain slew." Each time that Jacob has a vision, he gives a name to the site of that vision:

> And Jacob called the name of the place Peniel: for I have seen God face to face, and my life is preserved.
>
> (32:30)
>
> And Jacob called the name of the place where God spake with him, Beth-el. (35:15)

Through these acts, man acknowledges God's care and celebrates God as the source of all creative activity.

Namings in Genesis express God's benevolence and his intimate involvement with man. The namings that take place in *Urizen* carry exactly the opposite meaning. Each

219

naming proclaims a further separation between the human and the divine; each calls into existence another error, a new bane rather than a new blessing. In the opening of the poem, Urizen's self-creation—his separation from Eternity —is such a radical departure from the known that the Eternals hardly know how to account for it. They are not sure what to name it:

> . . . what Demon
> Hath form'd this abominable void
> This soul-shudd'ring vacuum?—Some said
> "It is Urizen," But unknown, abstracted
> Brooding secret, the dark power hid.
>
> (3:3-7)

In lines 27-35 Blake shifts to Urizen's point of view and confirms his identity for the reader, but Urizen's identity is not positively acknowledged by the Eternals until Chapter II:

> The sound of a trumpet the heavens
> Awoke & vast clouds of blood roll'd
> Round the dim rocks of Urizen, so nam'd
> That solitary one in Immensity.
>
> (3:40-43)

This final naming of Urizen is delayed in order to depict the process by which such a traumatic change comes into consciousness. Through this delayed naming and Urizen's labors, we experience the pangs of a mind giving birth to a new concept. The same process is expressed when Los gives birth to Enitharmon (13:52-19:1). At the end of this protracted birth, "They call'd her Pity, and fled" (19:1). The birth of these two major errors is followed by a succession of errors whose creation is also revealed by namings. When the Eternals spread a tent to separate Eternity from the fallen world they wove a woof "and called it Science" (19:9). Upon seeing the inability of his children to keep his laws, Urizen "wept, & he called it Pity" (25:3); and, when these tears formed a net "all calld it, The Net of Religion" (25:22). After Urizen's children shrunk up under the net, they "form'd laws of prudence, and call'd them / The eternal laws of God" (28:6-7). When Fuzon and his brothers escaped from the fallen world, "They called it Egypt, & left it" (28:22).

The namings in *Urizen* describe a perverted creation: things that should never exist are called into being. The namings, instead of celebrating life, creation, and divine benevolence, express the traumatic eruption of death, destruction, and an antagonism between the human and the divine. And as an inversion of divine creativity, these namings in *Urizen* echo those of Revelation in which destructive forces are called into existence to undo the creation:

> And I looked, and behold a pale horse: and his name that sat in him was Death, and Hell followed with him.
>
> (6:8)

> And the name of the star is called Wormwood: and the third part of the waters became wormwood.   (8:11)

> And they had a king over them, which is the angel of the bottomless pit, whose name in the Hebrew tongue is Abaddon, but in the Greek tongue hath his name Apollyon.   (9:11)

Urizen echoes the rhetoric of the last passage:

> And the thirty cities remaind
> Surrounded by salt floods, now call'd
> Africa: its name was then Egypt.
>
> (28:8-10)

The identification of the fallen world as Egypt in this passage and in 28:22 is derived from Revelation:

> And their dead bodies shall lie in the street of the great city, which spiritually is called Sodom and Egypt, where also our Lord was crucified.   (11:8)

This identification is underscored in plate 28 of *Urizen* by the small figure of a corpse lying below the colophon.

Revelation is fused with Genesis here because the corpse also echoes the last image in Genesis, Joseph's body: "and they embalmed him, and he was put in a coffin in Egypt" (50:26). The dead Joseph parallels the crucified Christ as the symbolic death of Mercy in the fallen world, Egypt. Just before it tells of Joseph's death, the Bible reiterates his commitment to the forgiveness of sins. When Jacob died, Joseph's brothers feared that Joseph would avenge himself on them; but Joseph forgave them, refusing to identify himself with the God of Justice: "And Joseph said unto them, Fear not: for am I in the place of God?" (50:19). Although he prophesies that his bones will eventually be taken out of Egypt (50:25), Joseph's death symbolizes the bondage of the fallen world, just as the allusion to Egypt in Revelation 11:8 emphasizes the crucifixion from the point of view of the fallen world—the victory of death and vindictive judgment.

Through this fusion of Revelation and Genesis, Blake is representing Genesis as an inverted Apocalypse. The victory of Justice over Mercy is underscored throughout *Urizen* by allusions to the Last Judgment. Urizen's abstraction of the contraries of life into laws of Good and Evil is reflected in the archetype of the divided brothers, the "chosen" and the "damned"—an archetype that contains the main organizing theme of Genesis. By combining this theme with images from Revelation, Blake is implying that the Last Judgment, as the orthodox see it, is coexistent with the Creation, that the separation of the saved and the damned has already taken place. The picture of Urizen on the title page shows him seated with the Book of Judgment in front of him. He is transcribing the names of the saved and the damned into the Book of Life and the Book of Death, which lie on either side of him.[29] The figure on the right in plate 6, the figures on plates 9 and 12, the central figure on plate 15 and the figure of Grodna on plate 24 are all taken from Michelangelo's *Last Judgment*.[30] Through these allusions, Blake asserts that Urizen's promise of "futurity"—of future reward for the obedient and damnation for the recalcitrant—is a sham that actually creates and preserves the fallen world. The Last Judgment took place at the Creation, and the saved—the followers of Urizen's religion—were already condemned to hell, which was the fallen world itself. The creation of the fallen world is an inverted image of the creation of the new Jerusalem.

By satirizing Genesis as an inverted Apocalypse, Blake attacks its theological rationale, what modern scholars have called the *Heilsgeschichte* or salvation history: "The post-exilic editors who gave the Pentateuch its final form intended the collection of traditions of which Gen. is composed to serve as an explanation of God's choice of Israel and of his purpose in choosing her."[31] Blake's comprehension of this narrative strategy in the Old Testament is expressed in *The Marriage of Heaven and Hell*. Ezekiel, in plates 12 and 13, attacks all literal interpretations of the Old Testament because of the exclusive, nationalistic bias that may easily be gleaned from those books. Taken literally, Genesis is a justification of the Angels' party. It is an account of God's attempt to create a species of beings who will obey him and of his eventual success in finding a chosen few among the largely disobedient creation. Genesis begins with an act of disobedience and reiterates that theme in order to establish Israel's claim to an exclusive relationship with God through Abraham's obedience.[32] Blake attacks the literalists' interpretation of Genesis, ironically pointing out the inconsistencies that the rhetorical aim of Genesis produces. In order to glorify obedience, God creates man with a strong proclivity for doing otherwise. Given God's objective, his creation has only negative value: he creates a race of disobedient men; and furthermore, he tempts man to disobey and then punishes him. The divine will must be self-divided: it wants man to obey, but also wants him to disobey. As further evidence of God's self-division, we see that there are actually two different creators in Genesis 1 and 2. This god's perverse and self-divided nature is also seen in his behavior throughout the rest of the book of Genesis. He creates a jealous rivalry between two brothers that culminates in murder and then punishes the murderer. After admitting that his creation is faulty and destroying it, he remains dissatisfied with those of his creations that he has elected to save. He finally succeeds in finding the obedience that he has been seeking by testing the willingness of a man to murder his own son. Through his concept of an exclusive holiness, he creates jealousy, hatred, and bloodshed while he claims to detest these evils. Finally, when he finds his chosen people he delivers them into the bondage of Egypt. Rather than creating order out of chaos, the God of the Old Testament creates greater chaos. His work in Genesis is an anti-creation.

CHAPTER IX

The Book of Ahania:
Moses Fell and Asia Arose

Just as in *The Book of Urizen* Blake develops a consistent
satire upon Genesis, so in *The Book of Ahania*, dealing
with the biblical events from the beginning of Moses' min-
istry to the possession of the promised land of Canaan, he
continues his Bible of Hell by satirizing the remainder of
the Pentateuch. He accomplishes this through an even
greater compression of events and reliance upon biblical
themes and symbols to epitomize and interpret the books of
Exodus, Leviticus, Numbers, and Deuteronomy. These
books, according to Blake, relate the story of a failed revolu-
tion, the futile attempt of Moses to liberate the fallen
world. Blake perceives the last four books of the Pentateuch
as recording Israel's escape from the bondage of Egypt or
Africa (Blake uses the names interchangeably) into the
bondage of Asia, which includes both the laws of Sinai and
the idolatries of Canaan.[1] Although Blake of course de-
viates from his source by perceiving Sinai and Canaan as
the two sides of a coin, his reading of the essential move-
ment of events is clearly encouraged by the biblical text
itself. In the Bible, Moses is commanded by God to deliver
Israel from what is essentially the political bondage of
Egypt—in Exodus God is at war with Pharaoh and not
with the gods of Egypt—and to create out of a mixed multi-
tude of people a nation of priests who will enter into and
keep the covenant of the living God. This stiff-necked peo-
ple appears to be unmoved by God's gifts, however, and
even after many trials and temptations in which they are
constantly given evidence of God's power to save and de-
stroy, even after the forty years of wandering in the wilder-

225

ness, they succumb to idolatry at the first opportunity when they arrive in Moab, just outside of Canaan (Numbers 25:1-3). Furthermore, when God tells Moses of his approaching death, he also tells him that Israel will break the covenant and "go a whoring" after the gods of Canaan (Deuteronomy 31:16). This will happen despite Moses' frequent admonitions against idolatry, particularly the worship of Molech. Thus Israel abandons the political bondage of Egypt for the religious bondage of Canaan. Blake's reworking of this scheme in *Ahania*, where the bondage of the Mosaic law is as sinister as the bondage of Egypt, anticipates the findings of modern biblical scholarship by perceiving that Mosaic religion absorbed much from the Canaanite religion that it opposed,[2] just as in *The Song of Los* Blake stated that Israel had absorbed much of Egyptian culture.

This tendency of a revolutionary movement to become like the tyranny that it so strenuously opposes is most tellingly and economically expressed in one line, the proclamation that Fuzon makes after he believes that he has successfully defeated Urizen: "I am God. said he, eldest of things!" (3:38). Here the rebel has become the tyrant, expressing in his own words the fall that immediately ensues; his victory has been turned to defeat because he has assimilated his foe.

In his rapid rise and fall, Fuzon is a remote and pathetic character, hardly the charismatic image of Moses that we encounter in the Pentateuch. When we recall, however, that much of Moses' power derives from his passion for establishing the Law, expressed most strongly in the extended exhortations that form the book of Deuteronomy, it becomes clear that Fuzon aptly represents Blake's concept of the spiritual form of Moses. Unlike Orc, who represents the energies that animate the world of Generation, Fuzon-Moses represents the passion for justice, the spirit of righteousness that quickly expends its vitality as it takes the form of doctrines, laws, and codes of living. He is depicted as such in the opening of *Ahania*, where Blake combines allusions to *Paradise Lost* and Deuteronomy to evoke the image of righteous indignation, the passion for justice that led Moses to slay the Egyptian who was smiting the Hebrew (Exodus 2:11-12) and to defend the daughters of Jethro from the shepherds who would drive them away from the well (Exodus 2:16-17), and that receives symbolic form as the burning bush in Moses' first theophany and as the fires that form the law on Mount Sinai. Blake's image of this fiery zeal is Fuzon's flaming chariot and the globe of wrath that Fuzon forms:

Fuzon, on a chariot iron-wing'd
On spiked flames rose; his hot visage
Flam'd furious! sparkles his hair & beard
Shot down his wide bosom and shoulders.
On clouds of smoke rages his chariot
And his right hand burns red in its cloud
Moulding into a vast globe, his wrath
As the thunder-stone is moulded.
Son of Urizens silent burnings.

(2:1-9)

The last line emphasizes Blake's allusions in this passage to Christ's putting on the Father's wrath in book six of *Paradise Lost*:

But whom thou hat'st, I hate, and can put on
Thy terrors, as I put thy mildness on,
Image of thee in all things.

(*PL* VI.734-36)

Fuzon's chariot is an echo of the "Chariot of Paternal Deity, / Flashing thick flames" (VI.750-51) with which Christ subdues the rebel angels on the third day of the battle in heaven. The globe that Fuzon forms in his right hand "As the thunder-stone is moulded" (2:8) is reminiscent of the Son's "right hand / Grasping ten thousand Thunders" (VI.835-36) with which he smites the rebel host. Milton's

227

imagery here is drawn from the Bible, as he acknowledges in *An Apology for Smectymnuus*, where he uses the same chariot imagery to describe "the invincible warrior Zeal," whose fiery chariot Milton likens to the one seen by Ezekiel and St. John. Here again Milton associates the image with that of Christ putting on the Father's wrath, using it in this context to justify the expression of righteous indignation against "the perverse and fraudulent seducers."[3] This justification of the voice of honest indignation as the voice of God and the description of the glorious chariot in *Paradise Lost* are passages that Blake most likely had in mind when he described Fuzon's indignant attack upon Urizen's usurped authority.

Although the Miltonic allusions in Blake's opening lines identify Fuzon as an inspired iconoclast and associate Urizen—and by extension, the Old Testament God—with Satan, Blake's imagery, in the context of the events surrounding the exodus of Israel, emphasizes the ambiguity of Fuzon's revolt and foreshadows his defeat. The rushing forth of Fuzon's chariot also recalls Moses' description in Deuteronomy of the establishment of the Law: "The Lord came from Sinai, and rose up from Seir unto them; he shined forth from mount Paran, and he came with ten thousands of saints: from his right hand went a fiery law for them" (Deuteronomy 33:2). Seir is Edom, and this is the same image of a wrathful God coming out of Edom that Isaiah uses (63:1) and that Blake had applied to Orc in *America*. The image of the fiery law in God's right hand, however, which is Fuzon's fiery globe in *Ahania*, casts doubt upon the efficacy of Fuzon's revolt, because we know that the fiery law will become petrified into stone tablets, that the living passion for righteousness and justice will become embodied in laws that will only promote self-righteousness and complacency. Similarly, the iron wings of Fuzon's chariot echo the "chariots of iron" of the Canaanites in Joshua 17:16 and 17:18, thus foreshadowing the hardening of Fuzon's fiery zeal into Canaanite idolatry.

The Book of Ahania thus opens with the beginning of Moses' ministry, emphasizing Moses' role as a religious reformer. The basis of Fuzon's revolt is his refusal to accept a god that he cannot meet face to face:

> Shall we worship this Demon of smoke,
> Said Fuzon, this abstract non-entity
> This cloudy God seated on waters
> Now seen, now obscur'd; King of sorrow?
>
> (2:10-13)

Alluding to the God of Genesis, whose spirit "moved upon the face of the waters" (Genesis 1:2), and the God of Exodus, who revealed himself to the Hebrews in clouds of smoke upon Mount Sinai (Exodus 19:16-20; 20:18-21), Fuzon's speech recalls both Moses' desire to see God face to face—a desire that is never satisfied (Exodus 33:18-23)—and the people's desire for a human mediator rather than any direct confrontation with the God revealed in the smoke on Sinai: "And all the people saw the thunderings, and the lightnings, and the noise of the trumpet, and the mountain smoking: and when the people saw it, they removed, and stood afar off. And they said unto Moses, 'Speak thou with us, and we will hear: but let not God speak with us, lest we die" (Exodus 20:18-19).

The prophet's desire to experience directly the living God and the people's willingness to experience vicariously the prophet's theophanic experience create the central tensions that lead to Fuzon's downfall. The prophet attains the awareness that God acts and is in human beings, but his desire to communicate that information to men of little faith leads to temptations of priestcraft. Moses' intense awareness of and exasperation over this problem is most strongly expressed in his reaction to Joshua's request that he forbid Eldad and Medad from prophesying in the camp: "And Moses said unto him, Enviest thou for my sake? would God that all the Lord's people were prophets, and that the Lord would put his spirit upon them" (Numbers 11:29).

229

The whole impulse behind Moses' legislation was to promote the manifestation of a hidden god among a people who would accept only outward signs of the divinity. The hungry beam produced by Fuzon's throwing his globe of wrath at an abstract god symbolizes this desire to force the deity to manifest himself in humanly recognizable terms. Hurled at an abstract god of creation, who opposes the flaming beam with the abstract form of a disc, Fuzon's religious zeal creates the concept of sin. Fuzon-Moses' impulse to promote righteousness forces the rejection of unformed desires, identified as Ahania, who springs from Urizen's wounded loins like Venus from the castrated Uranus. Blake's parallel to pagan myth is significant in that Ahania thus becomes associated with the Venuslike Canaanite goddess Ashtaroth, to whom the Hebrews were to stray in reaction to the stringent demands of righteousness imposed by the God of Moses.[4]

Although the impulse to righteousness produces these dire consequences, the Mosaic desire to produce a nation of prophets who would embody within themselves the living God also served as an impetus for the rise of Jewish civilization, from the announcement on Sinai to the fall of Jerusalem, a period of about five hundred years.[5] Hence, Blake's mythologizing Fuzon's energies:

> But the fiery beam of Fuzon
> Was a pillar of fire to Egypt
> Five hundred years wandring on earth
> Till Los siezd it and beat in a mass
> With the body of the sun.

$$(2:44\text{-}48)$$

In other words, Moses provided an alternative to Egyptian bondage until the Babylonian captivity, at which point the faith in the possibility of establishing a Jewish polity, a nation of priests or prophets, ceased.

The first chapter of *Ahania*, then, deals with the commission of Moses as the prophet of a religion of righteousness,

230

using biblical imagery to develop the inner significance of that event. Similarly, the rest of *The Book of Ahania* deals with the internal significance of the last four books of the Pentateuch by symbolically representing the main events and themes of those books. Chapter II covers the events beginning with the subjugation of Pharaoh and ending with the arrival at Sinai. Chapter III deals with the establishment of the Law on Sinai. Chapter IV covers the forty years of Israel's wandering in the wilderness, and Chapter V deals with the possession of Canaan, Moses' farewell speeches, and the lament over the dead Moses. The central theme developed throughout is, quite simply, the failure of laws and institutions, no matter how revolutionary in origin, either to ameliorate the effects of the Fall or deliver up the paradisiacal dream of a land flowing with milk and honey.

Most of the second chapter of *Ahania* is concerned with Urizen's preparations for retaliating against Fuzon, and particular attention is devoted to the formation of Urizen's bow, which is made from the ribs of a giant serpent that Urizen had both generated and destroyed. The symbolic significance of this bow underscores the irony of Fuzon's revolt and defeat. Blake's elaboration of the birth and death of the serpent is a capsule history of the rise and fall of Egypt. The birth of the serpent is described in images associated with the fertilization of the Nile, a subject that Blake had engraved for Darwin's *Botanical Garden*:[6]

> For his dire Contemplations
> Rush'd down like floods from his mountains
> In torrents of mud settling thick
> With Eggs of unnatural production
> Forthwith hatching.

(3:7-11)

The "enormous dread Serpent" (3:13) that is part of this brood recalls Josephus' observation about Egypt's fame for producing a vast number of serpents, some of which "are

231

worse than others in power and mischief, and an unusual fierceness of sight."[7] These are, for Blake, the reptiles of the mind produced by the man who never alters his opinion; they are also perhaps the cockatrice eggs that evil people hatch, according to Isaiah 59:5. More importantly, the giant serpent appears in Isaiah as the symbol for a powerful enemy of Israel that Isaiah prophesies against, asserting that the Lord "shall slay the dragon," which is also called leviathan and a serpent, the words being used interchangeably in this passage (Isaiah 27:1).[8] Later in Isaiah this image is applied more specifically to Egypt, which is identified as Rahab the dragon (Isaiah 51:9). Similarly, according to biblical commentators, leviathan and the dragons in Psalm 74:13-14 are symbols of Pharaoh and Egypt.[9] In Ezekiel's prophecy against Egypt, too, Pharaoh is called "the great dragon that lieth in the midst of his rivers" (Ezekiel 29:3), and Milton adopts this image of Pharaoh as a "River-dragon" when he describes Adam's vision of Moses' defeat of the king of Egypt (PL XII.190-99).

Urizen's defeat of this beast thus represents the defeat of Pharaoh by the God of the Old Testament, and Urizen's using the ribs and the poison of this "lust form'd monster" (3:27) to defeat Fuzon with the poisoned rock that becomes Mount Sinai works out in mythopoetic terms an idea that Blake developed in *Asia*: that Moses did not liberate Israel from Egypt but rather absorbed the arts of Egypt when he attempted to establish the code of laws on Mount Sinai. Urizen, the god of abstractions, creates and destroys both Pharaoh and prophet at his own whim, apparently the puppetmaster of the sacred drama being enacted below. Here Blake appears to be reacting to one of the most disturbing elements of the exodus story, God's hardening of Pharaoh's heart, His claiming credit for Pharaoh's continual refusals to respond to Moses' displays of God's powers.[10] The whole series of incidents surrounding the plagues of Egypt have a contrived aspect to them, with Moses and Pharaoh as pawns in a game whose only purpose is to aggrandize the being that manipulates both of them. The defeat of Fuzon with Urizen's poisoned boulder is also an ironic commentary upon the song of Moses in Deuteronomy 32, where the controlling metaphor repeated throughout is that of the Lord as a rock. As in *The Book of Urizen*, Blake is attacking the notion of a god whose main attribute is his devotion to the abstract concepts of justice, and the defeat of Fuzon-Moses is implicit in Fuzon's desire to be more just than the tyrant that he opposes.

The third chapter of *Ahania* describes the formation of the Tree of Mystery and the crucifixion of Fuzon upon it. Here Blake is symbolically representing and commenting upon an essential theme of the last four books of the Pentateuch: the establishment of the priesthood of the Levites. By enacting ceremonial laws along with the moral law, Moses had consolidated priestcraft, the establishment of mediators between man and God based upon the belief that certain aspects of life could be separated out as being exclusively holy. This belief, according to Warburton and others, was begun by the Egyptians who initiated the pagan mysteries, wherein the esoteric and exoteric knowledge of the divine became separated.[11] Blake symbolized this belief by means of the Tree of Mystery, which represents not only the interdicted Tree of Knowledge in Genesis and the cross on which Christ was crucified[12] but also the complex of pagan beliefs and practices that the Jewish and Christian dispensations claimed to oppose. The repressive and destructive nature of the tree is emphasized by Blake's selecting a symbol employed in *Paradise Lost*. As scholars have frequently noted, Urizen's tree is the banyan tree from which Milton has Adam and Eve pluck the fig leaves to cover their shame.[13] Here the theme of repression is obviously appropriate to Blake's message in *Ahania*. The fact that the tree forms its own forest links it with references in the Pentateuch to the sacred groves wherein the forbidden pagan mysteries were performed.[14] Given this biblical context, the crucifixion of Fuzon upon the Tree of Mystery signifies the sacrifice of Fuzon-Moses' prophetic energies to the essentially pagan bondage of ceremonial law. Here Blake briefly summarizes the inner significance of those elaborate and often tedious details in the last four books of Moses that outline the creation of the tabernacle, the construction of priestly vestments, the observance of certain holy days, and the administration of numerous kinds of sacrifices.

The issue of sacrifice obviously becomes the central concern of Blake's third chapter, since the crucifixion of Fuzon raises the theme of the Atonement. Blake is partially working within the whole typological tradition that sees Moses as a type of Christ. The raising of the brazen serpent in the wilderness (Numbers 21:6-9) is, as I have already noted, considered to be a foreshadowing of the crucifixion of Christ (John 3:14-15).[15] Furthermore, the New Testament interprets Moses' proclamation that the Lord will raise up a prophet like unto Moses (Deuteronomy 18:15) as a prophecy of the coming of Christ (Acts 3:22). The Epistle to the Hebrews deals extensively with the typology of Moses in order to develop the theme of Christ's atonement as an extension and an abolition of the sacrifices initiated by Moses. Establishing Jesus as "the Apostle and High Priest of our profession" (Hebrews 3:1), this epistle likens him to Moses only to assert that he "was counted worthy of more glory than Moses" (3:3) and that the admission of only those who believed into the promised land of Canaan was a typical foreshadowing of the salvation available only to those who believe in Christ (Hebrews 3:8-19). Moses is also likened to Jesus in "Esteeming the reproach of Christ greater riches than the treasures in Egypt" (Hebrews 11:26). But the most important use of comparison between Moses and Christ occurs in chapter nine of Hebrews, where the epistle shows the theological basis of Christ's sacrifice to lie in the propitiatory sacrifices established by Moses. While under the old Mosaic dispensation, the blood of bulls and goats was offered as purification for sins every year on the

Day of Atonement, such a ceremony purified only the body but not the conscience. Christ, however, represents a more perfect sacrifice because "neither by the blood of goats and calves, but by his own blood he entered in once into the holy place, having obtained eternal redemption for us" (Hebrews 9:12).

The Epistle to the Hebrews does not say why God requires such a sacrifice to begin with, but Blake's depiction of Fuzon-Moses in imitation of Christ's Passion points to and criticizes the rationale underlying this demand for blood atonement. Urizen's nailing "the corse of his first begotten / On the accursed Tree of MYSTERY" (4:5-6) not only looks ahead to the sacrifice of God's "first-begotten" (Hebrews 1:6) described in the New Testament but also looks back to the source of this demand for the blood of the firstborn. Here Blake exhibits an awareness of one of the major themes in the last four Mosaic books, which is introduced by the sacrifice of the firstborn children of the Egyptians to the wrath of the God of Exodus, while the Hebrews offered the blood of the passover lamb as a substitute (Exodus 12:21-27). The significance of this act is emphasized at great length in the following chapter of Exodus:

> And the Lord spake unto Moses, saying, Sanctify unto me all the firstborn, whatsoever openeth the womb among the children of Israel, both of man and beast: it is mine. . . .

> And it shall be when the Lord shall bring thee into the land of the Canaanites, as he sware unto thee and to thy fathers, and shall give it to thee, That thou shalt set apart unto the Lord all that open the matrix, and every firstling that cometh of a beast which thou hast; the males shall be the Lord's. And every firstling of an ass thou shalt redeem with a lamb; and if thou wilt not redeem it, then thou shalt break his neck: and all the firstborn of man among thy children shalt thou redeem.

> And it shall be when thy son asketh thee in time to

235

come, saying, what is this? that thou shalt say unto him, By strength of hand the Lord brought us out of Egypt, from the house of bondage: And it came to pass, when Pharaoh would hardly let us go, that the Lord slew all the firstborn in the land of Egypt, both the firstborn of man, and the firstborn of beast; therefore I sacrifice to the Lord all that openeth the matrix, being males; but all the firstborn of my children I redeem.

(Exodus 13:1-2, 13:11-15)

This offering of the firstborn of Egypt at the time of the exodus and then the firstborn of animals in ceremonial practice as a redemption of the firstborn of the Israelites, coupled with the frequent injunction within the Pentateuch against the sacrificing of children to Molech (Leviticus 18:21, 20:1-5; Deuteronomy 12:31)—an apparently strong temptation among the Israelites—shows the practice of substitution of the Egyptians and beasts for the firstborn of Israel to be a concession to the Canaanite practice of sacrificing children to appease the deity.

Therefore, Urizen's crucifixion of his firstborn in Blake's version of the Pentateuch points to the Canaanite origins of the Mosaic ceremonial law and the ransom theory of atonement that is developed in the New Testament, an idea that Blake probably derived from Jacob Bryant.[16] Although Moses substituted the sacrifice of beasts for human sacrifice, in doing so he still gave credence to the Canaanite belief that the firstborn should be sacrificed to the deity. In the Book of Numbers there is a further refinement upon this theology, wherein the Levites, the tribe to which Aaron belonged and which was concerned with maintaining the tabernacle, were dedicated as a substitute for the firstborn, all other firstborn males being permitted to be redeemed with a payment of money (Numbers 3:11-13, 8:16-19). This convenient justification of the power and prestige of a priestly class, a group of people who regard themselves as being exclusively holy, subverts Moses' original intention of

building a nation of priests, and this subversion is implied
in Blake's image of Fuzon-Moses being nailed to the Tree
of Mystery. But Blake's most important point is that,
viewed in light of the pagan origins of the ransom theory
of atonement, the sacrifice of the Son in the New Testa-
ment is a throwback to rather than a refinement upon
Canaanite theology.

Thus Blake represents the establishment of the Law
upon Sinai, the building of the tabernacle, and the estab-
lishment of a separate class of priests as the beginning of the
Canaanite or Asian hegemony, whose actual birth is an-
nounced in Chapter IV: "then Asia / Arose in the pendu-
lous deep" (4:41-42). This describes the point at which the
Israelites finally enter the land of Canaan. But the events
that precede this, the forty years between the proclaim-
ing of the Law on Sinai and the arrival of Israel in Canaan,
occupy most of Chapter IV. The arrows of pestilence that
fly for forty years around the corpse of Fuzon represent the
torments of the Israelites in the wilderness. Here Blake is
ironically depicting the fulfillment of the avowed purpose
of Israel's forty-year journey. The arrows of pestilence are
the punishments promised to idolators in Deuteronomy
32:23-24: "I will heap mischiefs upon them; I will spend
mine arrows upon them. They shall be burnt with hunger,
and devoured with burning heat, and with bitter destruc-
tion: I will also set the teeth of beasts upon them, with the
poison of serpents of the dust." Supposedly a future threat
or admonition offered to Israel before it entered the prom-
ised land, this passage actually recounts the torments that
Israel had just undergone. This painful tribulation was vis-
ited upon the Hebrews because of their refusal to believe
that they would be able to overcome the sons of Anak and
possess the land of Canaan: "Because all those men which
have seen my glory, and my miracles, which I did in Egypt
and in the wilderness, and have tempted me now these ten
times, and have not hearkened to my voice; Surely they
shall not see the land which I sware unto their fathers,

neither shall any of them that provoked me see it" (Numbers 14:22-23). Israel will wander for forty years so that this generation of unbelievers will die out: "But as for you, your carcasses, they shall fall in this wilderness. And your children shall wander in the wilderness forty years, and bear your whoredoms, until your carcasses be wasted in the wilderness" (Numbers 14:32-33).

Blake employs this same image of bones falling in the wilderness to depict the formation of a new generation that is deemed worthy to enter the promised land. He talks of the "hurtling bones" (4:24) that Los forms into the new generation that will constitute the civilization of Asia. Blake, however, reminds us that the condemned recalcitrants were created, selected, and nurtured by the God that would now destroy them; he depicts these bones as arising out of the scurf on the surface of a white lake that was produced by the melting of Urizen's "Nerves of Joy" (4:13-21). The white lake is manna, a substance "like coriander seed, white" (Exodus 16:31), with which the Israelites were nurtured in the wilderness. Here Blake obviously satirizes the so-called benevolence of this nurturing, making the white lake produce noxious gases and pestilence:

The clouds of disease hover'd wide
Around the Immortal in torment
Perching around the hurtling bones
Disease on disease, shape on shape,
Winged screaming in blood & torment.

(4:22-26)

This imagery also suggests the ritual sacrifices wherein animals were slaughtered and dismembered, as described in the first chapter of Leviticus.

The tortured and tormented fragments of life that the Israelites are reduced to during their trial in the wilderness are saved from falling into nonentity, just as the fallen Urizen was saved in *The Book of Urizen* by Los's casting his "forg'd nets of iron" (4:29) around the bones:

The shapes screaming flutter'd vain
Some combin'd into muscles & glands
Some organs for craving and lust
Most remain'd on the tormented void:
Urizens army of horrors.

(4:31-35)

This new generation of Israelites formed from the bones is
a parody of the "exceeding great army" that Ezekiel proph-
esies into life in his vision of the vale of dry bones (Ezekiel
37:1-10), where God promises to revive his fallen and frag-
mented people and deliver them into the land of Israel.
In *Ahania*, however, Los's prophetic activity only serves to
produce a new form of fallen life, as Africa, whose birth is
described in *Urizen* and whose demise is described in the
second chapter of *Ahania*, is supplanted by Asia. The har-
dening of the skulls of Urizen's sons and daughters and
their proclivity to "reptilize upon the Earth" (4:43) further
indicates that this new generation and new continent pro-
duced under the Mosaic dispensation was not significantly
different from the world of Africa, in which the inhabitants
of the cities shrunk into reptile forms under Urizen's net
of religion (*Urizen* 25:37). The similarity between Egypt-
Africa and Asia reflects the Mosaic account of the genera-
tion that enters into the promised land, who in their eager-
ness to follow the gods of Canaan do not seem to have
benefited from their wilderness experience. Whether we
look upon it from an angelic or a demonic point of view,
the trial in the wilderness failed to produce its intended
aim.

The lament of Ahania that forms the fifth chapter of
Ahania is a coda to the previous four chapters and func-
tions in Blake's poem in much the same way the book of
Deuteronomy functions in the Pentateuch. The fifth book
of Moses consists almost entirely of three long orations by
Moses, the famous Song of Moses, and Moses' blessing of
the tribes—all of which are delivered on the plains of Moab

before Moses' death and before Israel crosses the River Jordan at the end of their forty years of wandering. These pieces of oration that form Moses' farewell address interrupt the narrative flow of the exodus story, which is then briefly concluded in the last two chapters of Deuteronomy with the death of Moses.

Deuteronomy, which means "second law," is Moses' attempt to renew the covenant, as established on Mount Sinai, for the new generation of Israelites who are about to enter Canaan. Although he recapitulates many of the laws and traditions from the three preceding Mosaic books, Moses' central concern is that of exhorting the Israelites to maintain the covenant in the face of future trials and temptations. In accordance with this purpose, the running theme throughout Moses' orations is God's love for his people, a love that is both jealous and exclusive and that seeks to separate Israel from the heathen nations:

> For thou art a holy people unto the Lord thy God: the Lord thy God hath chosen thee to be a special people unto himself, above all people that are upon the face of the earth. The Lord did not set his love upon you, nor choose you, because ye were more in number than any people; for ye were the fewest of all people: But because the Lord loved you, and because he would keep the oath which he had sworn unto your fathers, hath the Lord brought you out with a mighty hand, and redeemed you out of the house of bondmen, from the hand of Pharaoh king of Egypt. Know therefore that the Lord thy God, he is God, the faithful God, which keepeth the covenant and mercy with them that love him and keep his commandments to a thousand generations; And repayeth them and hate them that hate him to their face, to destroy them: he will not be slack to him that hateth him, he will repay him to his face.   (Deuteronomy 7:6-10)

This paternalistic love, which causes God to chasten Israel as a father chastens his son (Deuteronomy 8:5), demands absolute love and obedience from the beloved;[17] and the rewards and punishments attending the compliance or refusal to comply with these conditions are mentioned throughout Moses' orations, culminating in the powerful recitation of blessings and curses in chapters 27 and 28. Whereas the rewards for keeping the covenant are those of material prosperity, the punishment for breaking it is total destruction.

The tensions created by Moses' hortatory rhetoric are heightened for all postexilic readers by predictions that Israel will in fact break the covenant, both in the immediate and in the distant future, as Deuteronomy 28:36-69 alludes to the destruction of the northern kingdom by the Assyrians in 721 B.C. and to the Babylonian captivity of 587 B.C.,[18] and Deuteronomy 31:16-17 recounts God's telling Moses of the general apostasy that will occur immediately after his death: "and this people will rise up, and go a whoring after the gods of the strangers of the land, whither they go to be among them, and will forsake me, and break my covenant which I have made with them" (31:16). This collapse into idolatry prompts God to inspire the Song of Moses (Deuteronomy 32) in which Moses pours forth prophetic indignation at the failure of Israel to keep the covenant. Voicing God's anger, Moses proclaims: "And he said, I will hide my face from them, I will see what their end shall be: for they are a very froward generation, children in whom is no faith. They have moved me to jealousy with that which is not God" (Deuteronomy 32:20-21). Moses' song is rendered all the more pathetic by his being told on the same day he delivers it that he will ascend Mount Nebo to behold the land of Canaan and die upon the mountain, never to enter the promised land (Deuteronomy 32:48-52). Moses then blesses the tribes of Israel (Deuteronomy 33) and, in the last chapter of Deuteronomy, ascends Mount Nebo and dies. The book ends with a brief elegy over Moses.

Deuteronomy, then, is primarily a coda that serves to give

point to the entire collection of traditions that have come to be known as the Pentateuch. The major concern of the last book of Moses is the maintaining of the covenant in the face of Israel's frequent and inevitable defections from that covenant. Moses, in light of his immediate objectives of establishing the covenant and delivering Israel into a land of milk and honey, was a failure. The people would not keep the laws and continued to worship idols; nor was Canaan to be a land of milk and honey, the El Dorado so tantalizingly described by Moses. Israel suffered hardship and deprivation in acquiring and maintaining that land. Blake, in his ironic counterpart to Deuteronomy deals with this failure in terms of the traditional metaphor for the covenant, the marriage of the bridegroom (God) with the bride (Israel). The metaphor is only implied in Deuteronomy, by the mention of Israel's defection to idolatry in terms of a wife playing the harlot who goes "a whoring" after strange gods (Deuteronomy 31:16), but it figures strongly in the Song of Solomon, Psalm 45, and the prophets, particularly Hosea and Lamentations. This last book is alluded to in the first chapter of *Ahania*, where Urizen's hiding and casting out of Ahania echoes the following verse: "How hath the Lord covered the daughter of Zion with a cloud in his anger, and cast down from heaven unto earth the beauty of Israel" (Lamentations 2:1). Through the lament of Ahania, the outcast bride of Urizen, which combines allusions to the Song of Songs and Psalm 45 with allusions to Deuteronomy, Blake explains the failure of Moses to establish the covenant by showing that the achievement of such a covenant was impossible in the first place.

Ahania, the mysterious female who eludes simple allegorical explanation, represents all that Urizen, the Old Testament God, desires. She is the Wisdom or Sapientia,[19] who "was daily his delight, rejoicing always before him" (Proverbs 8:30), and whom he possessed "in the beginning of his way, before his works of old" (Proverbs 8:22), that is, before the Creation. Ahania alludes to these former times when she asks:

> Where the joy of my morning hour
> Where the sons of eternity, singing
> To awake bright Urizen, my king!

(5:5-7)

This complex allusion refers to the time "When the morning stars sang together, and all the sons of God shouted for joy" (Job 38:7), an event that Job may not have witnessed but the divine Wisdom certainly did.

Urizen's former giving of Ahania's "happy soul / To the sons of eternal joy" (5:15-16) refers to the time when Wisdom's "delights were with the sons of men" (Proverbs 8:31). Ahania also represents the community of love with which the God of the Old Testament seeks to be attached, the beautiful bride so ardently described in the Song of Solomon and Psalm 45. Ahania's mention of the former times when Urizen arose to "the mountain sport" and "the bliss of eternal valleys" (5:8-9) refers to the moments of gratified desire experienced by the bride and bridegroom in Solomon's song.[20] Similarly, Ahania's longing for the former times of bliss when her odors were "Bursting on winds" (5:25) refers to the bride's request that the winds blow upon her garden so that "the spices thereof may flow out" and the bridegroom "come into his garden, and eat his pleasant fruits" (Song of Solomon 4:16). Urizen's prelapsarian ability to take the "daughters of life" into Ahania's chambers of love (5:17-18) alludes to the king's receiving the bride and her virgin companions in Psalm 45: "She shall be brought unto the king in raiment of needlework: the virgins her companions that follow her shall be brought unto thee. With gladness and rejoicing shall they be brought: they shall enter into the king's palace" (Psalm 45:14-15). Finally, Ahania represents the promise of a restored paradise, a promised land flowing with milk and honey, to which she

243

alludes when she speaks of her "ripe figs and rich pomegranates" (5:26), the fruits that the returning spies of Moses bring back from Canaan (Numbers 13:23). Other images of joyous fertility that she uses recall the blessings of abundance promised to the obedient in Deuteronomy.

As the object of Urizen's love, Ahania is fallen, because Urizen's love is a jealous love, an exclusive love that is held in reserve until the time of the fulfilling of the covenant by a certain elect group of people. Given this condition, Ahania is invisible because she is not permitted to manifest herself, becoming like the "dark secret love" that destroys the rose ("The Sick Rose," line 7), a source of pestilence:

> She fell down a faint shadow wandring
> In chaos and circling dark Urizen,
> As the moon anguishd circles the earth;
> Hopeless! abhorrd! a death-shadow,
> Unseen, unbodied, unknown,
> The mother of Pestilence.

> (2:38-43)

Her lament at the end of Blake's prophecy centers around her despair at not being able to manifest herself either in the fallen world or in Urizen's presence. While the racalcitrant Israelites are forced to wander in the desert, the outcast Ahania must wander through chaos and through the fallen world. When Israel enters the promised land of Canaan, however, indicated in Blake's poem by the rise of Asia, Ahania's wanderings do not cease, clearly indicating that the original promise of Moses has not been fulfilled. Looking down upon the earth below, Ahania describes her own condition and the condition of the fallen world in images taken from the punishments promised to those who break the covenant in Deuteronomy. Ahania's vision of the fallen world as a wasteland (4:56-61) shows the fulfillment of God's promise to lay waste the land of Canaan, just as he had done to Sodom and Gomorrah, Admah and

Zeboim (Deuteronomy 29:23). Similarly, Ahania's complaint that she cannot see, touch, or hear Urizen, reveals her condition to be that with which God threatens the recalcitrant Israelites in the Song of Moses and elsewhere in Deuteronomy: "and I will forsake them, and I will hide my face from them" (Deuteronomy 31:17).[21] When Ahania describes the former joys of which she has been deprived, she employs images borrowed from Moses' promises of rewards for the obedient. The causing of Ahania's joy from her "soft cloud of dew to fall / In showers of life on his harvests" (5:13-14) echoes both Isaiah's image of the Lord in repose "like a cloud of dew in the heat of harvest" (Isaiah 18:4) and the promise of fecundating dew from heaven in Deuteronomy (33:13, 33:28).

It may also be that Blake intends Ahania's clearly erotic use of this image to be an ironic commentary upon the opening of Moses' song: "My doctrine shall drop as the rain, my speech shall distil as the dew" (Deuteronomy 32:2). She also takes a negative image from Moses' song and asserts it as a positive value: that of being "Swell'd with ripeness & fat with fatness" (5:24). This repeats an image of excess and complacency that Moses employs to castigate the backsliding Israelites: "But Jeshurun waxed fat, and kicked: thou art waxen fat, thou art grown thick, thou art covered with fatness; then he forsook God which made him, and lightly esteemed the Rock of his salvation"[22] (Deuteronomy 32:15). Similarly, Ahania's ivory bed (5:4) is the luxurious ivory bed that Amos condemns (Amos 6:4). Ahania is clearly opposing the values of generosity and excess to the restraining doctrines of the fallen Urizen, as is also witnessed by her use of imagery of the chamber. Here Blake is playing upon a triple meaning that is implicit in the Bible's use of the marriage metaphor, with the chamber representing the bridal chamber, the bride's pudendum, and the sanctuary of the temple. Within this context, the placement of the veil before the holy of holies wherein only the priests may enter became for Blake an apt symbol of jealousy and repression (*Jerusalem* 69:44).[23]

Ahania's desire for the inclusive, rather than exclusive, love that she shared with Urizen is expressed in her references to the time when Urizen gave her happy soul to the sons of eternal joy and brought the daughters of love into her chamber (5:15-18). The Levitical sacrifice of the firstborn and the sacrifice of first fruits of the harvest described in Deuteronomy 26 are transmitted by Ahania into erotic terms, becoming the eternal "babes of bliss" on her beds and the outpouring of her ripe figs and pomegranates that sport and sing about Urizen's feet (5:19-28). Here Blake transmutes the traditional interpretation of the sacrifices instituted by Moses as types of the spiritual sacrifices made in heaven;[24] the birth and sacrifice of the babes of bliss and the outpouring of first fruits are the eternal exchange of the joys of love freely given and received in a sexual embrace.

The sexual imagery is continued in the next two stanzas, which describe Urizen's former pouring forth the seed of eternal science as openly and generously as the sun pours forth its light and his returning home to Ahania in the evening, awakening the birth of her "mother-joys" (5:29-38). Here Blake's imagery is borrowed from the surprisingly pagan opening of Psalm 19,[25] which describes the pouring forth of the knowledge and glory of God from the heavens in terms of the sun: "Which is a bridegroom coming out of his chamber, and rejoiceth as a strong man to run a race. His going forth is from the end of the heaven, and his circuit unto the ends of it: and there is nothing hid from the heat thereof" (Psalm 19:5-6).

In contrast to this openly shared joy, the outcast Ahania shares the fate of Oothoon, whose open and generous love was also considered to be sin. She laments her removal from the bridal chambers to the top of mountains—the location of both the Sinaitic covenant and the altars erected to the pagan idols:

But now alone over rocks, mountains
Cast out from thy lovely bosom:
Cruel jealousy! selfish fear!
Self-destroying: how can delight,
Renew in these chains of darkness
Where bones of beasts are strown
On the bleak and snowy mountains
Where bones from the birth are buried
Before they see the light.

(5:39-47)

The "chains of darkness" is a reference to the punishment
of the rebel angels of Genesis 6 who lusted after the daugh-
ters of men; God cast them into hell "and delivered them
into chains of darkness, to be reserved unto judgment" (2
Peter 2:4). This association underscores Urizen's rejection
of Ahania's love as something unholy and his condemning
her to the hell of frustrated desire. The joyful mutual sacri-
fices of love are replaced by the bones of the beasts that are
sacrificed on mountains—recalling the detailed descriptions
of animal sacrifice that occur in the recitation of the cere-
monial laws. The bones of birth buried before they see the
light refer to the stillborn babes of bliss that are the result
of Ahania's rejection by Urizen and the promulgation of
the law. The sacrifice of the unborn infant joys also sug-
gests the sacrifice of children to Molech, thus combining
the Sinaitic dispensation with the idolatry of Canaan in the
last lines of the poem. Blake may also be alluding to a case
of metaphoric infanticide: the Jewish tradition of instruct-
ing children in the Torah by beginning with Leviticus,
which ironically, opens with a detailing of animal sacri-
fice.[26] Finally, the burial of the bones also suggests the death
of Moses before he can enter the promised land and the
abortion of his own desire for a community that would
flourish under God's care in a restored paradise.

Such an abortion is the result of the Mosaic law and Ca-
naanite idolatry, which according to Blake are one and the

same in that they both separate man from the objects of his perceptions and cause him to become enslaved by a deified Other. The promulgation of mystery by the promoters of religion causes man to worship the sign at the expense of that which it signifies. This theme is embodied in the very form of *Ahania*, with each of the chapters, except the last one, dwelling upon particular signs that have become abstracted from the all-creative Imagination and that signify the very process of abstraction. Urizen's shield, his bow, the Tree of Mystery, and the arrows of pestilence are all fragmented parts of the imagination that are created by Urizen's tyranny and that are the instruments of that tyranny.

Ostensibly, Blake's description of the formation of each of these forms of error parodies the technique of epic digression. In each case, Blake interrupts the narrative action to describe the formation of a particular symbol that plays an important role in the narrative present, much as, for example, Homer interrupts the narrative of Penelope's fetching of Odysseus' bow in book XXI of *The Odyssey* to relate the story of how Odysseus acquired the bow. As in Homer, the digressions in *Ahania* flatten past and present into a series of events that are continually experienced in the narrative present.[27] This technique is essentially classical and has no analogue in biblical narrative, yet after each of these digressions Blake adds an element that is essentially biblical: he suddenly thrusts beyond the fiction's narrative present into the reader's present. Chapter I ends with the birth of sin and the future pounding of Fuzon's fire into the body of the sun; Mount Sinai is created at the end of Chapter II; the end of Chapter III attests to the survival of the Tree of Mystery to the present day; and the end of Chapter IV sees the birth of Asia and a shift to the present tense to describe the continual reptilization upon earth of Urizen's children. Through this technique, Blake is parodying the priestly teleology of the Pentateuch, which is expressed by the interruption of narrative in order to thrust the narrative into the reader's time and explain the existence of a particular religious or social institution. For instance, the story of the birth of Eve is concluded with an explanation of the institution of marriage (Genesis 2:24), and the narrative of Exodus is interrupted to explain the origin of Passover and its presence in the reader's own time (Exodus 12:24-27).

Thus in each of the first four chapters of *Ahania*, Blake creates the illusion of a unified and flattened fictional surface, only to disrupt that surface at the end of each chapter by describing the sudden intrusion of the fiction upon the reader's reality. In each of these disruptions, the reader is suddenly made conscious of the narrative as fiction at the same time that he is made aware that the fiction has been imposed upon reality. In each chapter, Blake combines pagan and biblical narrative techniques that work together for the same end: to show the creation of a fiction and the abstraction of that fiction from its poetic context to serve the ends of priestcraft. The process itself suggests the creation of the tabernacle and its appurtenances as they are so minutely described in Exodus 25-28.

The final chapter of *The Book of Ahania* abandons parody for pure prophetic song, commenting upon the process taking place in the first four chapters by revealing a prelapsarian past that the other chapters failed to take into account and by revealing a strong sense of a present that has become painfully separated from that past. Moreover, the imagery of the harvest and of erotic love-play that is used to describe this fictional prelapsarian past make that past seem much more like the reader's present reality, or at least like reality as he or she would desire it to be. The images of sacrifice and death that have become literal realities in the first four chapters are replaced, in Ahania's vision of the past, by metaphors whereby death and ritual sacrifice are perceived as types of the self-annihilation of sexual love, the offering of the first fruits of desire to one's beloved. In short, the prelapsarian past embodies the conversion of realities into metaphors, while the fallen present embodies the hardening of metaphors into realities. The attachment of the fallen world to these signs that have become abstracted from the imaginative process that they should signify is perfectly realized by the highly emblematic form of the first four chapters, which, like an emblem book, present verbal pictures, although without the obligatory visual image at the head of each chapter. The almost obsessive detailing of all of these verbal emblems, in a form that combines pagan and biblical narrative techniques, mirrors the attachment to pagan idols and Levitical rituals that caused the failure of Moses' desire to see all the Lord's people become prophets.

The Book of Los: Los Agonistes

Like *The Book of Urizen, The Book of Los* derives its narrative content from Genesis. Here Blake depicts more fully the formation of the sun, and in so doing, makes *The Book of Los*, as Northrop Frye observes, intersect *The Book of Urizen* in much the same way that the J creation narrative intersects the E narrative in the first two chapters of Genesis.[1] Thus in this prophecy Blake appears to diverge from the pattern established in *Urizen* and *Ahania*, where he developed parallels to specific parts of the Bible. While it is true that *The Book of Los* draws its narrative from Genesis, its thematic content is taken from the Book of Judges, with Blake's prophecy exploring the problems presented by Los's role as potential deliverer and awakener of the fallen world. This thematic connection is most strongly established by allusions and parallels linking Los with the most popular figure from Judges, Samson; and it is through Samson and his biblical and pagan counterparts that Blake links the theme from Judges with the content drawn from Genesis.

The narrative of *The Book of Los* actually hinges upon an exegetical problem in Genesis. On the first day of creation, God creates light, separates it from the darkness, and thus establishes day and night; but it is not until the fourth day that the sun is created. This delay in the creation of the heavenly bodies has perplexed many, and Voltaire was certainly not the first to observe, "It is inconceivable that there should be a morning and an evening before there was a sun."[2] The *philosophe* attributes this confusion to a popular error among the ancients that held that the light was merely diffused in the air before the rising and the setting of the sun, the celestial body merely serving to impel the light more strongly. Other explanations were offered by Milton and the biblical exegetes. Most medieval and Renaissance commentators believed that although the light created on the first day was diffused, it was finally embodied in the concrete form of the sun on the fourth day.[3] Milton, like some of the church fathers, including Augustine, maintained that the light created on the first day was of a superior, more spiritual quality than the light that was embodied in the form of the sun.[4]

As for the presence of day and night on the first day without the presence of the sun, there were several solutions. Milton, like some medieval and Renaissance commentators, held that the essential light was embodied in a cloud.[5] Other solutions were that day and night were effected by means of a miracle, by means of the westward movement of this primeval light, or by the dilation of light during the day and the contraction of light at night.[6] This last explanation is the one that Blake adopts in *The Book of Los*, where the illuminating flames of Eternity—which create light and darkness by expansion and contraction—are Blake's equivalent of the primeval light of Genesis 1:3, and the globe that Los creates is the sun of Genesis 1:16.[7] Like the earlier biblical commentators and like Milton, Blake conceives the material form that light finally assumes to be an inferior source of light, the infinite fires of Eternity withdrawing from Los when he creates the sun:

> But no light, for the Deep fled away
> On all sides, and left an unform'd
> Dark vacuity.

> (5:48-50)

As in *Paradise Lost*, there is a threefold gradation of divine, elemental, and solar light in *The Book of Los*,[8] with Los's fall gradually reducing the ability of that light to expand and contract. At the beginning of *The Book of Los*, the divine or eternal light is represented as "flames of desire / . . . living flames / Intelligent, organiz'd" (3:27-29), which contract into spheres because of Los's repressed wrath (3:33-49, 4:1-3), giving neither heat nor light. But when Los expends his wrath, falls, and then begins to organize himself into finite form, creating the four elements in the process, the infinite fires expand again and are poured forth in the form of elemental light:

> Then Light first began; from the fires
> Beams, conducted by fluid so pure
> Flow'd around the Immense.
>
> (5:10-12)

This light, flowing down from "those infinite fires" (5:27), still partakes of the light of Eternity; but when Los seizes the light and the heat from those eternal fires and pounds them into the form of the sun, he makes that light a solid without fluctuation and binds the process of darkness and illumination to the mechanical pattern of the Newtonian universe, the same dull round of the sun's diurnal movement. Not only is this light inferior to the light of Eternity that has fled away but it is finally eclipsed by the rock that forms from Urizen's brain and by the four rivers of Eden that flow from his heart (5:52-55).

Although Blake thus draws upon traditional explanations of the apparent discrepancies between the work of the first day and that of the fourth day of creation in Genesis, he goes beyond these explanations by depicting the work of the fourth day as an attempt to rectify the situation created by the first day's work, which for Blake was the separation of Urizen from Eternity. For Blake, the divine light of Eternity, like the organs that perceive it, freely contracts and expands:

> Earth was not: nor globes of attraction
> The will of the Immortal expanded
> Or contracted his all flexible senses.
> Death was not, but eternal life sprung.
>
> (*Urizen* 3:36-39)

253

In Eno's song at the opening of *The Book of Los*, this lais-sez-faire principle of energy is transmuted into psychologi-cal or moral terms. Eno, a sibyl-like character whose name is possibly derived from "enow," the archaic form of "enough," and thus represents the principle of satiety, de-scribes the prelapsarian state as the expansion and contrac-tion of desire in a perpetual rhythm of arousal and satiety. Before the Fall, what we now call traditional vices were merely different forms of energy that sought expression. When Covet was allowed to be poured full, it expended itself in action and ceased to be Covet, breaking its locks and bars and sleeping with open doors (1:20-21). Similarly, when "Thin-lip'd Envy" was fed with the fat of lambs, he burst forth into song and rejoiced at the rich man's fortune; "Bristled Wrath," when satisfied, was modulated by the softer texture of the lamb that befriended him; and Wan-tonness became civilized, perceiving his object as a "true love" and from that love producing a race of superior beings (1:22-26). Thus, by expending themselves in action, so-called vices become the contrary virtues with which they were traditionally paired: Covet becomes generosity, Envy becomes brotherly love, Wrath becomes meekness, and Wantonness becomes chastity in marriage, the consumma-tion of "true love."[9]

Urizen seeks to freeze this free movement of energy into moral categories to achieve a "solid without fluctuation" (*Urizen* 4:11), thus separating the desires and the states pro-duced by their expenditure into the respective categories of virtues and vices. This attempt to effect a permanent sep-aration of energy and calm is, for Blake, the separation of light and darkness described in Genesis 1:4. While the Bi-ble intends this separation to indicate the beginning of God's imposition of order upon chaos, Blake perceives this separation to be the essential cause of chaos; Urizen's sepa-ration from the fires of Eternity causes him to become, like the earth in Genesis 1:2, without form and void. It is then that the "flames of desire" that run through heaven and earth, which in Eternity are a vital and creative force, become "arm'd / With destruction & plagues" (3:29-30) to the dark shadow that Urizen has become.

Whereas Urizen begins the separation of light and darkness, creating the primeval chaos, Los the eternal prophet also becomes separated from the fires of Eternity; and it becomes his task in the course of *The Book of Los* to assume the role of the spirit of God that moves upon the face of the deep and give form to the chaos that was created by Urizen's fall. This role does not come easily to Los, however, and he becomes lost in the unformed chaos created by Urizen, eventually struggling to rise upon the waters and assume his creative task. When Los is initially bound in a chain and compelled to watch Urizen's shadow, his fallen state is compounded by his inability to give vent to his prophetic wrath, which further causes him to be separated from the energies of Eternity and thus causes the diminution of heat and light. Blake, using the imagery of humors psychology, has the overheated rage of Los putrefy into melancholy adust,[10] the hard black substance that imprisons him. Like the figure of black Melancholy in Milton's *Il Penseroso*, Los, with ironic literalness, forgets himself to marble:

> Coldness, darkness, obstruction, a Solid
> Without fluctuation, hard as adamant
> Black as marble of Egypt; impenetrable
> Bound in the fierce raging Immortal.
> And the separated fires froze in
> A vast solid without fluctuation,
> Bound in his expanding clear senses.
>
> (4:4-10)

Like Urizen in *The Book of Urizen*, Los becomes imprisoned in the world of formless matter, the "vast rock of eternity" (4:12) that Urizen has formed from his own fall (*Urizen* 4:43).

But Los's wrath revives, this time taking the form of

255

action, the iconoclastic act of "stamping furious to dust"
(4:20) the Rock of Sinai that is the foundation of Urizen's
laws. This act echoes Orc's stamping the stony law to dust
in *A Song of Liberty* and *America*, and it is precisely be-
cause Los assumes this Orc-like role of iconoclast that he
begins to fall again:

> Falling, falling! Los fell & fell
> Sunk precipitant heavy down down
> Times on times, night on night, day on day
> Truth has bounds. Error none: falling, falling.
>
> (4:27-30)

Los is in error because he can only express himself in de-
structive action without the compensatory creation that is
the true function of the Imagination. With the collapse of
the world of solid matter, he falls into the void and cannot
stop this fall until he resumes his creative function and
organizes himself into the vegetative world, which is a step
above the lifeless mineral world in which he and Urizen
had imprisoned themselves. He accomplishes this by em-
bracing contemplative thought:

> wrath subsided
> And contemplative thoughts first arose
> Then aloft his head rear'd in the Abyss
> And his downward-borne fall chang'd oblique.
>
> (4:39-42)

Through the birth of consciousness, his awareness of his
fallen state, Los decides that he must work his way back to
Eternity by re-creating the world of matter into a living
form, and he begins by organizing the world of matter into
four elements and forming the finite inflexible organs that
will be needed to preserve the vegetable world from falling
into chaos.

In Chapter III Blake shows the process by which Los
finally accepts this new prophetic function, however de-

based it may appear, and assumes a form that parodies the spirit of God hovering on the water in Genesis 1:2:

> The Lungs heave incessant, dull and heavy
> For as yet were all other parts formless
> Shiv'ring: clinging around like a cloud
> Dim & glutinous as the white Polypus
> Driv'n by waves & englob'd on the tide.

$$(4{:}54{-}58)$$

Playing upon the Hebrew word "ruach," which the Authorized Version translates as "Spirit," but which also means "breath," Blake renders the breath of divine inspiration in its appropriately material form, a pair of lungs that grotesquely float upon the primeval waters. Los's polypus lungs are thus a parody of the divine inspiration, just as the globe-shaped sun that he later creates is a parody of true illumination.

As Los continues to take on form, he separates the elements and finally recovers some of the divine light from which he became divided. He then perceives the fallen form of Urizen, a serpentine spinal column "Hurtling upon the wind" (5:15), and begins his task of binding Urizen's form, to prevent him from falling into nonentity, and creating the sun to which he binds Urizen. Once Urizen is bound to the "glowing illusion," the divine light departs again and the material light of the sun is obscured by the rock of eternity that is again created, this time from Urizen's brain, and by the four rivers of Eden that flow from Urizen's heart, which are the natural analogues, or the fallen form, of the four desires or "vices" enumerated in Eno's song. The waters of the four rivers represent the quenching of those four desires by materialism and their conversion into abstract virtues, which is Blake's adaptation of Philo's well-known allegorization of the four rivers of Eden as the four virtues.[11] In Blake's poem, the ability of those waters to obscure the sun's illuminating powers suggests the gnostic belief that man was placed in Eden to

keep him in ignorance of his divine nature.¹² The passive
Urizen triumphs through Los's creation of a world that is a
grotesque parody of the freely flowing fires of Eternity.

The central subject of *The Book of Los* is thus the efforts
of the Imagination to repair the damage caused by Rea-
son's attempts to divorce life from its essential energies.
For Blake, the Genesis version of the sun's creation is the
story of a flawed demiurge's attempts to prevent the fallen
world from slipping into nonentity by creating a mechani-
cal analogue of the fires of Eternity. The initial separation
of light and darkness in Genesis is interpreted by Blake as
the precipitation of a crisis that can only be temporarily
resolved through artifice, through the creation of a "Human
Illusion" (5:56). As Jehovah, the anthropomorphic crafts-
man-god of the Genesis J narrative who creates form out
of the matter and infuses that matter with the breath of
divine inspiration, Los is the creator of diurnal light, as
well as the world of time that its movements regulate. He
attempts to set a limit to the errors of that abstract creator
of the Genesis E narrative, the Elohim, represented in
Blake's work as Urizen. Furthermore, the material world
that Los-Jehovah creates is divided between the two deities
of Genesis 1 and 2: Los-Jehovah controls the elements of
air and fire, inspiration and illumination, whereas Urizen-
Elohim is given dominion over earth and water, the Mosaic
rock of abstract law, and the four rivers of the earthly para-
dise. As in *The Book of Urizen*, Urizen-Elohim triumphs
over Los-Jehovah: the mind of fallen man is enclosed in
stone, and the human heart is enclosed in the waters of
materialism, thus completing the human illusion that pre-
vents fallen man from regaining the Eternity that he has
lost.

Thus *The Book of Los* elaborates upon the myth of the
Fall that Blake had begun in *Urizen*, presenting a more
detailed exploration of the Imagination's struggle to rees-
tablish itself as an organizing principle in the fallen world

and to find thereby a means of returning that world to its prelapsarian state. Having explored in *The Book of Ahania* the lesser powers of Fuzon—the Mosaic spirit of legal reform that is elaborated upon in the last four books of the Pentateuch—Blake returns to Genesis in order to detail the workings of genius or Imagination as a liberating force. In this return to a liberating principle that predates the Mosaic reform, Blake continues to follow the biblical pattern that is developed in the books that follow the Pentateuch. The Book of Joshua merely consolidates the failure of the Mosaic dispensation that begins to occur in Deuteronomy, with the possession of the promised land of Canaan being qualified by the fact that Israel never fully achieves that possession, will fall into apostasy, and will be oppressed by the Canaanites just as she had been previously oppressed by Pharaoh. The aging Joshua, who has been an extension of the Mosaic leadership, prophesies: "When ye have transgressed the covenant of the Lord your God, which he commanded you, and have gone and served other gods, and bowed yourselves to them; then shall the anger of the Lord be kindled against you, and ye shall perish quickly from off the good land which he hath given unto you" (Joshua 23:16). The biblical book ends with the reestablishment at Shechem of the covenant, which will continue to be broken. The covenant is embodied in two symbols at the end of the Book of Joshua, a stone and a sacred oak under which it stands (24:26). Blake had represented these in *Ahania* as the Stone of Night lying beneath the Tree of Mystery (*Ahania* 3:55-67); thus he had no need to write a new work that would develop themes that were already incorporated into *The Book of Ahania*.

The Book of Judges, however, begins a new phase in biblical history, showing that although Israel continued to fall into error and suffer oppression, there arose from time to time divinely inspired individuals who attempted to deliver Israel from her Canaanite oppressors:

259

And the children of Israel did evil in the sight of the Lord, and served Baalim. . . .

And the anger of the Lord was hot against Israel, and he delivered them into the hands of the spoilers that spoiled them, and he sold them into the hands of their enemies round about, so that they could not any longer stand before their enemies. . . .

Nevertheless the Lord raised up judges, which delivered them out of the hands of those that spoiled them.

(Judges 2:11, 2:14, 2:16)

As Protestant exegetes understood, the Hebrew word for "judge" as it is used here does not signify a person who delivers legal decisions, but rather means "deliverer" or "vindicator," describing the judge's twofold function of delivering his people from the hands of the oppressor and visiting divine vengeance upon the enemies of God.[13] For Blake, the appearance of these biblical heroes signified the stirrings of the fires of genius that were obscured by the Fall and by Mosaic Law, especially since the imaginative center of the Book of Judges was for him, for Milton, and for many others, the story of Samson—that energetic folkhero whose exuberance threatens to burst beyond the more sober pattern established by the other biblical judges. Through allusions to Samson, the biblical and literary tradition surrounding him, his pagan analogues, as well as allusions to other elements of the Book of Judges, *The Book of Los* interprets that biblical book as an exploration of the ways of the Imagination or genius in the fallen world.

The context of the Book of Judges is immediately established in the preludium to *The Book of Los* by the figure of Eno sitting beneath an oak tree. Although the oak tree suggests the oak at Shechem in the Book of Joshua, and thus the Tree of Mystery, the prophetic female sitting beneath it more precisely parallels the angel sitting beneath the oak of Ophrah who gives Gideon his divine commission in Judges 6:11-24. Eno serves a similar function; her lament over the passing of a time when desire was freely flowing is an implicit call for a deliverer who will return the world to its prelapsarian state. Her song is a libertarian interpretation of the last line of the Book of Judges: "In those days there was no king in Israel: every man did that which was right in his own eyes" (Judges 21:25). The biblical authors intended this description of the anarchistic world in which the judges arose to be looked upon with disapproval, since their obvious intention was to make the Book of Judges an exemplum that would justify the establishment of a monarchy in Israel, as detailed in the books of Samuel and Kings. But for Blake this state in which everyone does what is right in his own eyes would be a world in which the promptings of genius rather than Reason would be the mainspring of human action; thus he inverts the meaning of the biblical line by having Eno lament the passing of that state in which every man followed his energies and by seeing the biblical judges as heroes of genius whose inspiration lies in their doing what is right in their own eyes.

Eno's song suggests one such hero, Samson, using the image of the breaking of locks and bars to describe the beneficial results of the free expression of one particular desire (3:20); this image is an allusion to Samson's breaking the doors of the gate of Gaza in Judges 16:3. The Samson motif is developed more fully throughout the rest of *The Book of Los*, with Los, the would-be deliverer and awakener of the fallen world, made to resemble Samson in many respects. Blake effects this resemblance by employing images and themes not only from the Book of Judges but also from *Samson Agonistes*, Young's *Night Thoughts*, and the biblical traditions that inform these works. Like the blind and imprisoned Samson at the beginning of Milton's drama, Los, in the opening of Blake's poem, finds himself chained in darkness; and the imagery that Blake uses to describe Los's fallen state echoes Milton's descriptions of Samson's

261

condition. Los, like Samson, is self-imprisoned because he is cut off from internal and external light, a point that Milton emphasizes in the speeches of Samson and in the chorus:

> To live a life half dead, a living death,
> And buried; but O yet more miserable!
> Myself my Sepulcher, a moving Grave.
>
> (*SA* 100-102)

> Thou art become (O worst imprisonment!)
> The Dungeon of thyself; thy Soul
> (Which Men enjoying sight oft without cause complain)
> Imprison'd now indeed,
> In real darkness of the body dwells,
> Shut off from outward light
> To incorporate with gloomy night;
> For inward light, alas,
> Puts forth no visual beam.
>
> (*SA* 155-63)

Blake renders this self-imprisonment more literally, with the fires that are separated from Los freezing into a black rock that becomes Los's dungeon; the formation of this black substance from Los's suppressed wrath extends the imagery that Samson uses to describe his own state:

> My griefs not only pain me
> As a ling'ring disease,
> But finding no redress, ferment and rage,
> Nor less than wounds immedicable
> Rankle, and fester, and gangrene,
> To black mortification.
>
> (*SA* 617-22)

This mortification of wrath that can find no vent calls attention to a trait that Los shares with the biblical and Miltonic Samsons: he is a man whose genius expresses itself in wrath, which the Bible interprets as a form of divine inspiration. When Samson slays the lion of Timnath and the thirty men of Ashkelon, these acts are preceded by the statement that the spirit of God came upon him (Judges 14:6, 14:19). Similarly, the anger of Milton's Samson, which Dalila describes as an "Eternal tempest never to be calm'd" (*SA* 964) finally vents itself as the expression of divine wrath against the Philistines.

The binding of the illuminating fires of Eternity into spheres and their freezing into a solid without fluctuation that binds Los's expanding clear senses echo Samson's lament over the finite nature of man's fallen senses:

Since light so necessary is to life,
And almost life itself, if it be true
That light is in the Soul,
She all in every part; why was the sight
To such a tender ball as th'eye confin'd
So obvious and easy to be quench't
And not as feeling through all parts diffus'd
That she might look at will through every pore?

(*SA* 90-97)

Samson thus describes precisely the state from which Los has fallen. And just as Los shares Samson's deprivation of divine light, so too must Los struggle toward a new illumination and revive his fading spirits, laboring—as the chorus tells Samson—with his mind more than with his hands (*SA* 1298-99).

Samson's final act of physical strength is effected through "rousing motions" that take place internally, and is accompanied by a new illumination, as "With inward eyes illuminated / His fiery virtue rous'd" (*SA* 1689-90). Samson's destruction of the Philistine temple finds its parallel in Los's awakening his prophetic wrath to rend the rock of eternity that imprisons him, but unlike Samson, Los at this point possesses no illumination, nor do the labors of his mind cease until he repeats Samson's pattern of flagging and reviving strength a second time. After he falls and then organizes himself into "finite inflexible organs" (4:45), Los rises again and rekindles his prophetic wrath, through which he separates the elements and receives illumination. As he receives this illumination, Los regains his strength, "Upfolding his Fibres together / To a Form of impregnable strength" (5:18-19), and he employs his strength this time in a creative rather than a destructive act, seizing upon the newly arisen light and pounding it into the form of the sun, to which he then binds Urizen. Ironically, the effect of this act is the same as that of his previous resurgence of strength, for the illuminating fires of Eternity are still obscured. After destroying one error, Los creates a new one, in a parodic allusion to Gideon's smashing the altar of Baal only to establish the altar to Yahweh in its place (Judges 6:25-26). Los's success, like Samson's, is at best an internal and temporary one; and Los obviously shares Samson's fate as a failed deliverer and awakener of oppressed Israel.

Like Milton's Samson, Los is a tragic figure, and the nature of this tragedy is defined by exegetical traditions surrounding Samson that had become commonplaces of Protestant thought. Although the Samson of the Old Testament failed to cause a physical regeneration of Israel, he was considered in the New Testament to be a hero of faith, according to the Epistle to the Hebrews 11:4-32. The biblical story of Samson and Milton's *Samson Agonistes*, as Milton indicated in the preface to his drama, are tragedies in the same way that the Book of Revelation, according to Pareus and others, is considered a tragedy. In Pareus' view, as Barbara Lewalski delineates it, Revelation depicts the agon of the Christian Church: "the tragic suffering and agony that she undergoes throughout all ages comprise the burden of Apocalypse."[14] The Church throughout fallen history must undergo "overwhelming suffering and calamity," while at the same time it is "struggling nobly against the forces which oppose and oppress her."[15] Because of the nature of the fallen world, the Church's victories can only be spiritual ones, for the only true victory can be accomplished by Christ at the Apocalypse.

Protestant exegetical tradition regarded Samson and the other Old Testament judges as types of the Christian elect, both in their earthly life of spiritual trial and in their hope ultimately to "judge" the world with Christ at the Apocalypse. Protestant exegetes emphasized "the union of the saints with Christ in the final conquest of the Beast and the Kings of the Earth (Rev. xix. 19-21), and in meting out judgment to the wicked."[16] Psalm 149:7-9 was also interpreted as the outcry of the saints on judgment day: "To execute vengeance upon the heathen, and punishments upon the people; To bind their kings with chains, and their nobles with fetters of iron; To execute upon them the judgment written: this honor have all his saints. Praise ye the Lord."

Because the Philistines and Dagon were interpreted as types of Satan or the Antichrist,[17] Samson's battle with them was seen as a type of that ultimate eschatological battle. Seen in this context, which Milton's drama invokes, the impact of Milton's tragedy lies in its forcing a realization that until the Apocalypse "there is no effective deliverance from external bondage save by death (though there is deliverance from the internal bondage of sin), and that in the fallen world the deliverer whom God raises up achieves no lasting liberation."[18] The tragic effect of Samson's fall is enhanced by our knowledge of the typological relationship between Samson's flawed victory and the perfect victory of Christ and the saints: "By these adumbrations we are made constantly aware of what might have been (without Samson's sin, without the radical sinfulness of us all) and what will be again (at the Apocalypse), and the contrast intensifies our consciousness of the miserable, grief-filled, pain-wracked life that now is."[19]

The same contrast between antitype and the type in which it is adumbrated informs *The Book of Los*, with Los's binding of Urizen in chains of iron echoing the

265

apocalyptic binding of kings and their nobles in Psalm 149, as well as the binding of Satan in Revelation. This apocalyptic image serves to remind the reader of the contrast between Los's forging of the material sun and the dissolution of the sun in Revelation when the New Jerusalem descends: "And the city had no need of the sun, neither of the moon, to shine in it: for the glory of God did lighten it, and the lamb is the light thereof" (Revelation 21:23). Similarly, Eno's song combines the image of Samson bursting the gates of Gaza with the millenarian image of the wrathful lion's companionship with the lamb (3:23-24).[20] For this traditional reading of the Samson story in an apocalyptic context, Blake did not have to pore through seventeenth- or eighteenth-century biblical commentaries. Besides its embodiment in Milton's tragedy, it was more explicitly stated in the closing lines of Edward Young's *Night Thoughts*, which Blake had begun to illustrate at the time he wrote *The Book of Los*. In Young's poem the apocalyptic destruction of time is described through the image of Samson's tearing down the temple of Dagon:

> Awake, then: Thy PHILANDER calls: Awake!
> Thou, who shalt wake, when the Creation sleeps;
> When, like a Taper, all these Suns expire;
> When TIME, like Him of *Gaza* in his Wrath,
> Plucking the Pillars that support the World,
> In NATURE'S ample Ruins lies entomb'd;
> And MIDNIGHT, *Universal* Midnight! reigns.[21]

Young's identification of Samson with Time, along with Blake's depiction, in other illustrations to *Night Thoughts*, of Los as Time, the charioteer of the sun,[22] points to another aspect of the Samson tradition that Blake invokes in *The Book of Los*. As far back as the patristic period, biblical commentators detected in the Samson story traces of a solar myth. This myth is implied in the etymology of Samson's Hebrew name, *Shemshon*, which is derived from *shemesh*, the Hebrew word for sun. This etymology was advanced by St. Jerome and Augustine, and it was the accepted one in the patristic period.[23] It was included in most eighteenth-century biblical commentaries and was certainly well known to Milton,[24] who in *The Reason of Church Government*, likened the state and the king to Samson, whose "sunny locks" represent "the golden beames of Law and Right."[25] This solar association, as scholars have argued, informs Milton's concept of Samson in *Samson Agonistes*, where the imagery of sun, light, darkness, and eclipse creates a pattern that indicates that "the triumph of Milton's Samson is his rising as God's little sun—from 'total eclipse' (*SA* 81)—to his former eminence, his spiritual light regained."[26] Northrop Frye likens the movements of Milton's Samson in his symbolic "subterranean prison" of blindness to the movements of the sun at night: "It is almost as though Samson, or a power guiding Samson, were moving under the world like the sun at night, back to the place of its rising. The action ends abruptly at noon, with the zenith of the Philistine triumph suddenly blown to pieces by the explosion of a dark hidden fire rising like the Phoenix from its ashes."[27]

Milton's biblical source also contains hints of a solar pattern. The seven plaits of Samson's hair are the rays of the sun that are weakened when shorn. Samson's burning the Philistine fields by setting fire to the tails of foxes represents the blighting of the corn by the heat of the sun.[28] The whole biblical narrative of Samson, in fact, can be seen as the cyclical progression of the sun through the days and seasons: "Samson, who has been in his prime vigour in the summer (chapter 15) ends his days in darkness (chapter 16) which suggests winter. He grinds [at the mill], repeating the weary round of daily toil under external compulsion."[29] These are the remarks of a modern biblical scholar, yet in Blake's time Matthew Henry's commentary on the Samson narrative also perceives a solar pattern: Samson, whose name means "little sun" (*sol parvus*), rises brilliantly, "his morning-ray strong and clear," then continues to shine

267

brightly for twenty years, but finally sets "under a cloud, and yet, just in the setting darts forth one strong and glorious beam."[30]

Blake's certain knowledge of this solar aspect of the Samson tradition is clearly shown in his inscription to his painting of "Albion Rose":

> Albion rose from where he labourd at the Mill with
> Slaves
> Giving himself for the Nations he danc'd the dance of
> Eternal Death.

(p. 660)

The picture of the blazing youth with sunny locks is depicted in terms of the regenerated sun, which is liberated from the external compulsion of its daily rounds—the mill at which Samson labored—and takes on a human form rather than the form of a globe. This image of Albion-Samson as the regenerated sun, and thus regenerated Time, is echoed in Blake's illustration to the last page of Young's *Night Thoughts*, where the collapsing pillars represent the pillars of heaven (Job 26:11) and Samson, with open eyes, represents the apocalyptic new sun of inner vision that causes all previous suns to expire. Here Blake interprets Samson's death as symbolizing the role of the true deliverer who gives himself to nations by sacrificing his Selfhood to Eternal Death—an interpretation that contradicts the gloomy conclusion of Young's text.[31]

Although Blake repeats the apocalyptic themes of *Samson Agonistes* and Young's *Night Thoughts* in "Albion Rose" and in the Young illustration, rejecting the tragic implications of those themes by emphasizing Albion-Samson as a symbol of the regenerated sun, in *The Book of Los*, he shows the solar hero Los from a fallen perspective, with Los binding both Urizen and himself to the global sun and thus the cyclical world of time that is represented by the mill at which the imprisoned Samson was compelled to grind. In an ironic answer to Young's apocalyptic imagery,

Blake asserts that it is the creation of the fallen sun, rather than its destruction, that brings about the reign of universal midnight. Milton's tragedy is turned to pure irony, as Blake's poem, instead of moving from eclipse to blazing noon as *Samson Agonistes* does, moves in precisely the opposite direction, portraying Los-Samson as a pathetic figure who fails to redeem the world through physical means. Blake has not forgotten that in the Book of Judges Samson's heroic death does not liberate Israel from the Philistine oppression.[32]

Not only is Los a failed redeemer, but the product of his failure symbolizes the visionary significance of that failure. The sun that Los creates and to which he binds Urizen perfectly objectifies the cyclical vision of time that is the central pattern and concept informing the Book of Judges. The narratives in that book describe a repeated pattern of apostasy, deliverance, and return to apostasy. That this pattern is the shaping vision of the Book of Judges is explicitly established in the second chapter:

> And when the Lord raised them up judges, then the Lord was with the judge, and delivered them out of the hand of their enemies all the days of the judge: for it repented the Lord because of their groanings by reason of them that oppressed them and vexed them. And it came to pass, when the judge was dead, that they returned and corrupted themselves more than their fathers, in following other gods to serve them, and to bow down unto them; they ceased not from their own doings, nor from their stubborn way. (2:18-19)

Given this pattern, it is no wonder that Protestant exegetes seized upon Judges as a paradigm of the "tragedy of the apocalypse" that would be broken only by replacing those imperfect Old Testament deliverers with the apocalyptic Christ as the true deliverer. Los, by establishing rather than breaking this cyclical pattern, bears an ironic relationship not only to the true redeemer and awakener of Revelation but to Milton's Samson as well. Whereas Samson moves from blindness to inner illumination, from a state of eclipse to a fiery rebirth as a phoenix, Los moves in precisely the opposite direction. The fires of Eternity that blaze forth at the opening of the poem gradually diminish and finally withdraw from him. His newly created sun is eclipsed by the rock of eternity and the four rivers of Eden.

Los's failure, unlike that of Milton's Samson, is not tempered by any hint of spiritual victory. The only possible amelioration of his fall lies in the fact that through the creation of the illusory world of time man has been saved from falling into nonentity and that through the cycle of successively appearing imperfect liberators the medium through which a true liberator may appear has been created. But neither the text nor the designs of *The Book of Los* emphasize this theme. Los thus represents the Imagination at its lowest ebb, unable to envision a world beyond the endless cycles of illumination and eclipse but conscious of the pattern and its limitations. The prophetic wrath, as embodied in Samson and Los, serves the paradoxical function of expending its light to reveal the darkness in which fallen man gropes, but it is not sufficient to re-create the lost world of Eternity. It has power to expose and contain error by revealing its form, but it cannot herald the eschaton.

In his adaptation of the Samson myth, Blake neglects one important feature of the biblical story: Samson's temptation and fall at the hands of Delilah. He focuses instead on the struggle that Samson undergoes in the last episode of his life, thus emphasizing the opposition between Samson and the Philistine god, Dagon. As I have already noted, this emphasis upon Samson's function as a queller of tyrants is symbolized by Los's chaining the serpentine form of Urizen, which echoes Christ's victory over Satan in Revelation —the traditional antitype of Samson's victory over Dagon.[33] This heroic struggle that lies at the center of Blake's poem points to a mythic substructure within the poem that connects the biblical myths of the Creation, Samson, and the apocalypse with pagan mythology.

Within the overriding pattern of the Samson myth, Blake also suggests associations with pagan solar mythology. For instance, Los's subduing the snakelike form of Urizen suggests Apollo's victory over Python; and Milton had already linked this myth with the biblical myth of Samson in *The Reason of Church Government*, where he showed an implicit parallel between the "sunny locks" of Samson, the subduer of oppressive prelatry, and the "darts of the sun, the pure and powerful beams of God's word" that destroy Python, the dragon of episcopacy.[34] Similarly, Los's binding of Urizen suggests the chaining of Cerberus and the overcoming of other beasts by Hercules, whose association—if not identification—with Samson had become a commonplace in literature and biblical exegesis. Parallels between Samson and Hercules have been drawn since the time of Eusebius, Philastrus, and Augustine; and acceptance of this relationship has persisted through the Renaissance, the eighteenth century, and our own time as well.[35] Indeed the parallels between the biblical and Greek heroes are so striking that Philastrus asserted that the Greeks stole the concept of Samson from the Old Testament and named it Hercules, a view that became popular in the Renaissance and one with which modern biblical scholars have been generally inclined to agree.[36] Needless to say, Blake, who believed that the Greeks borrowed their mythology from the Bible, would have also concurred.

From among the numerous parallels between Samson and Hercules, we may cite a few. Like Samson, Hercules was the personification of strength and a champion who fought tyranny and oppression. Both men began their careers by slaying a lion; both were brought to ruin through the machinations of women; and both died voluntarily.[37] Also, Hercules, like Samson, was the embodiment of wrath, as he vented his terrible rage upon his enemies. This her-

271

culean wrath was interpreted in the Renaissance as *ira per zelum*, or righteous indignation, a form of divine inspiration.[38] Most importantly, Samson and Hercules both embody solar myths. George Sandys, in his notes to his translation of Ovid's *Metamorphoses*, asserted that some claim that Samson and Hercules were the same man, and he cites Macrobius' identification of Hercules as a solar deity: *"For what signifies Hercules but the Glory of the Aire? and what is the Glory of the aire, but the Suns illumination, which expelleth the Spirit of Darkness?"*[39] This shared solar theme that is only implied in Sandys is stated more explicitly by Simon Patrick in his commentary on Judges, where he reiterates the belief that the Greek figure is derived from the Hebrew hero: "It is a very probable Conjecture of some great Men, that hence the *Greeks* framed the Fable of their *Hercules*; who lived about this time, and whose Name is the same with *Samson's*, if it be derived from *Schemesh* the Sun. For *Hercules* is as much *Or-chol* that which enlightens all, i.e. the *Sun*."[40]

Similarly, modern biblical scholars who attempt to link the myths of Samson and Hercules, tracing their origin to the Phoenician myth of Hercules Melkart, the Egyptian Horus Ra or the Babylonian epic of Gilgamesh, find the common basis of these myths to be their invocation of a solar deity.

> It is difficult quite to dissociate the Samson-cycle from the cult-legend of the shrine of Beth-Shemesh ("the Shrine of the Sun"), $2\frac{1}{2}$ miles SSE. of Zorah, Samson's reputed home. The role of the hero with the sun-name as upholder of God's order against the enemies of his people is reminiscent of the Sun as the protagonist of Cosmos against Chaos, in the Egyptian myth of the sun-god nightly menaced by Apophis, the serpent of darkness. This theme was also known in the sun-mythology of Canaan and is explicitly expressed in a hymn appended to the Baal-myth of Rās Shamra.[41]

This myth of a solar hero who battles a chaos-monster, some modern scholars have theorized, lies beneath the account of the creation in Genesis 1, having been edited out by the priestly redactors of that book. One ground for this theory is the Hebrew word for chaos in Genesis 1, *tehom*, which has been etymologically linked to "Tiamat," the name of a female monster who represents chaos in Babylonian mythology. In this myth, as elaborated in the Babylonian *Enuma Elish* tablets, a solar deity named Marduk engages in battle with Tiamat and her monstrous host, kills her, separates heaven and earth by cutting her carcass in half, and then continues to create the universe.[42]

This theory that the combat between the deity and a chaos-monster lies in the background of the Genesis creation myth has also been educed from the presence of references to similar combats in other parts of the Old Testament,[43] such as Psalm 74:

> For God is my King of old, working salvation in the midst of the earth. Thou didst divide the sea by thy strength: thou brakest the heads of the dragons in the waters. Thou brakest the heads of leviathan in pieces, and gavest him to be meat to the people inhabiting the wilderness . . . The day is thine, the night also is thine: thou hast prepared the light and the sun.
>
> (Psalm 74:12-14, 16)

The currency of this theory was made possible by the unearthing in the late nineteenth century of the Babylonian texts contained in the library of Ashurbanipal at Nineveh.[44] But the general outlines of the Babylonian cosmogony had long been available in a fragment of the writings of Berosus, which had been copied by Polyhistor and Eusebius, and in a passage from Damascius, a Neoplatonic writer of the sixth century.[45] Furthermore, the idea of a battle between deity and monster preceding the Creation persisted in Jewish and Christian thought, although in a different form:

it became transmuted, in the Apocrypha and the patristic writings, into the battle between God and Satan that took place before the events of Genesis 1.[46]

For a poet steeped in biblical tradition and the habits of mind that readily drew parallels between pagan myth and Christian truth, our modern discoveries of biblical syncretism would merely validate what he had already intuited or absorbed from tradition. Milton, in *Paradise Lost* (I.197-202), for instance, could readily link the fall of Satan with the chaining of leviathan and the defeat of the monster Typhon, just as in *The Reason of Church Government* he could connect Apollo's slaying of Python with Samson's defeat of the Philistines and St. George's killing the dragon.[47] And even more than Milton, Blake, who was familiar with the syncretic theories of Jacob Bryant and the other mythographers,[48] could readily perceive the solar mythology that connected Genesis with the Samson story and with the pagan myths of Apollo, Hercules, and other solar heroes.

A central thesis of Bryant's *A New System or an Analysis of Ancient Mythology*, for which Blake designed and engraved a number of plates, was that all pagan religion was simply the worship of the sun and that pagan deities and deified heroes were represented by emblems of the sun and its powers.[49] And while Bryant does not mention the etymology of Samson's name, he provides material with which Blake, who did understand Samson's solar significance, could connect the biblical hero, the Genesis creation myth, and pagan myth. *The Book of Los* contains at least one direct manifestation of Bryant's influence in the image that Blake uses to describe Los's self-imprisonment in mineral form: the rock that binds Los, which is "Black as marble of Egypt" (4:6), is the form in which Thoth, the chief god of Egypt, was worshiped in Petra, "a black, square pillar of stone, without any figure, or representation."[50]

Blake would have also found in Bryant the identification of Hercules as a solar deity and a translation of Berosus' account of the Babylonian cosmogony, in which the solar

274

deity Marduk (called "Belus" in Bryant's text) battles with
and defeats the chaos-monster Tiamat (called "Omorca" in
Bryant), forming the earth and the heaven from her body
and then creating the rest of the universe.[51] Bryant also
suggests that Milton's descriptions of hell and chaos in
Paradise Lost (II.624-28, 891-93) allude to the description
of the primeval chaos in Berosus' Babylonian cosmogony.
Blake adopted and expanded this hint of a link between
Babylonian and biblical myth in his representation of Los
as the solar deity who struggles with the serpentine form of
Urizen, who has created and embodied chaos, and in his
showing the fallen world to be formed out of the defeated
Urizen's body. Los, like the solar heroes of pagan antiquity,
both creates and enacts the same dull round that is symbol-
ized by Samson's grinding at the mill and Hercules' labors
as he passes through the twelve constellations of the zodiac[52]
—the solar hero's perpetual struggle, victory, and defeat,
which continually occur as he makes his diurnal and sea-
sonal rounds. It is the same pattern that appears, on the
spiritual level in The Book of Judges, as the fires or inspira-
tion are awakened with the appearance of each judge, who
battles with the forces that oppose the divine order, and
who then is eclipsed by his own death and by the reappear-
ance of the darkness of apostasy and oppression.

It is in this context of solar myths that Blake develops
another important myth in *The Book of Los*, the myth of
Vulcan (also called Hephaestus and Mulciber), who was
cast out of heaven, either by Zeus or Hera, and fell to earth,
landing on Lemnos, where he established his forge to work
as a fashioner of metals. His marvelous works include the
shields of Achilles and Aeneas, and in Ovid's *Metamor-
phoses* he is the fashioner of the chariot of Apollo (II.105)
and the Palace of the Sun (II.1-31). Thus Vulcan not only
represents excellence in craftsmanship but also has solar
and cosmogonic associations. Jacob Bryant notes that Sui-
das, Cicero, and the author of Clementines identify Vulcan
with Ptha, the Egyptian sun god.[53] He finds that the syn-

cretistic Greeks and Romans also identified Vulcan with the Chaldean god Alorus, "the dispenser of light and every other blessing," and that Herodotus mentions the worship of Vulcan in Heliopolis and Memphis, the latter being called *Ains Shems* or *Shemesh*, "the fountain of the sun."[54] Vulcan's cosmogonic activities include his creation of Pandora, the first woman, and, according to Lucian's *Hermotimus*, the creation of man.

In Lucian, the general admiration with which the classical world regarded the works of the divine artificer is qualified; Lucian relates the story of the judgment of Momus, who criticized Hephaestus' craftsmanship because he made man opaque[55]—a theme with obvious relevance to Blake's ideas about the creation of fallen man. Christian tradition added to this qualification by identifying Vulcan with Cain's son, Tubal-Cain, and thus placing him among the reprobate.[56] Milton takes this tendency to its logical conclusion by associating Mulciber's fall with that of Satan and by making the pagan smith deity the architect of heaven—echoing his building of Apollo's palace in Ovid—who falls and becomes the architect of hell:

> his hand was known
> In Heav'n by many a Tow'red structure high, . . .

> Nor was his name unheard or unador'd
> In ancient *Greece;* and in *Ausonian* land
> Men call'd him *Mulciber;* and how he fell
> From Heav'n, they fabl'd, thrown by angry *Jove*
> Sheer o'er the Crystal Battlements: from Morn
> To Noon he fell, from Noon to dewy Eve,
> A Summer's day; and with the setting Sun
> Dropt from the Zenith like a falling Star,
> On *Lemnos* th' *Aegaean* Isle: thus they relate,
> Erring; for he with this rebellious rout
> Fell long before.

> (*PL* I. 732-33, 738-48)

This passage is the source of Blake's description of Los's fall in *The Book of Los* and of Urizen's casting Orc out of heaven in *A Song of Liberty*.[57] In this earlier poem, Blake uses the myth ironically to subvert the Miltonic as well as the classical interpretations of the Mulciber myth, while at the same time renovating other themes that are contained in that myth. The reprobate Orc is not an artificer, but an iconoclast who stamps Urizen's stony law to dust; and he appears not as a chthonic deity, but rather resumes his solar splendor:

> Where the son of fire in his eastern cloud, while
> the morning plumes her golden breast,
> Spurning the clouds written with curses, stamps
> the stony law to dust, loosing the eternal horses
> from the dens of night, crying
> Empire is no more! and now the lion & wolf shall cease.
>
> (*A Song of Liberty*, lines 19-20)

When we recall that in Virgil Vulcan creates an icon that glorifies empire—Aeneas' shield—the completeness of Blake's ironic reversal is apparent. When Blake transfers the myth of Vulcan from Orc to Los in *The Book of Urizen* and *The Book of Los*, his irony becomes more complex; he invokes both the chthonic and solar interpretations of the myth to create an ambivalent attitude toward Los's activities. In *The Book of Urizen*, Blake articulates Los's fall in terms of the grosser elements of the Vulcan myth, the cuckolded deity's forging a chain to ensnare and thus expose the adultery of Mars and Venus.[58] This chain Blake transmutes into the chain of jealousy that grows around Los's chest at the birth of Orc and that Los uses to bind the infant Orc, an act that alludes to Hephaestus' binding of Prometheus. Blake fuses both of these details from the myth to transform a ribald comedy about jealousy into a bitterly ironic satire, as that jealousy causes Vulcan, who had himself been persecuted by his father, to persecute his own son.

277

In *Urizen*, as in *Paradise Lost*, the fallen artificer's original creative gifts become perverted. Los's creative fires become eclipsed. Blake gives this point visual emphasis through his depiction of the setting sun on plate 21, where the form of Los—which is copied from Michelangelo's Apollo[59]—has rested his hammer and is bound about the chest with the chain of jealousy.

In *The Book of Los* Blake continues to exploit the dark side of the Vulcan myth at the same time that he invokes the solar aspects of that myth. Like Lucian's Hephaestus, Los is an imperfect craftsman, because here, as in *Urizen*, he makes the body of man opaque and thus causes the eclipse of whatever light might emerge from his newly created sun. The sun is also flawed; the nine ages of its creation (5:41) synchronize with the nine days that Vulcan fell from heaven, according to some versions of the myth.[60] The passage describing Los's forging of the sun echoes Hephaestus' forging the shield of Achilles in *The Iliad* and the shield of Aeneas in *The Aeneid*, recalling that like those two circular structures the newly created sun in its circular motions will describe a world of death, war, and empire. By creating this icon, Los, as a solar hero, falls, because he has objectified his inner light or inspiration—and by extension the divine vision of Eternity—by casting it into a finite and abstract form, a demonic parody of the illuminating fires of Eternity that assume human form in "Albion Rose" and in the expansive youth in flames depicted on plate 3 of *Urizen*. He thus creates and falls into idolatry, as Blake shows on plate 5 of *The Book of Los*, where Los kneels before his newly created globe that "Stood self-balanc'd" (5:45).

Los's role as an icon-creator in the last chapter in *The Book of Los* stands in contrast to his role as an iconoclast in the first two chapters of that book. Just as Orc, in *A Song of Liberty*, arises as the sun in its glory to stamp the stony law to dust, the eternal prophet in *The Book of Los* rends the rock of eternity with his prophetic wrath "stamping furious to dust . . . The black marble on high into fragments" (4:20-22). This eruption of Los's wrath is appropriate to Vulcan's role as a volcanic deity. Fusing the Vulcan myth with the myth of Samson destroying the temple of Dagon and Gideon's destruction of the altar of Baal (Judges 6:25), Blake depicts Los, like Orc in *A Song of Liberty*, as a deliverer. Los's work as a deliverer is qualified, however, by the fact that he himself had created the black rock in which he was imprisoned. Furthermore, immediately after he smashed the rock—rather than before, as in the case of Orc—he suffered an Hephaestuslike fall, to arise not as the blazing sun but as a vegetable form, a white polypus. When his fires did revive they were used to create a new icon to replace the old one, just as Gideon builds an altar to Yahweh upon the ruins of the altar of Baal that he had destroyed (Judges 6:24). In *The Book of Los*, the Mosaic rock of the Law, the stone that imprisons Los, is replaced by the sun that Los creates. The sun is an icon of natural religion that symbolizes the worship of the finite world that the sun inscribes and whose materialistic premises once again establish the hegemony of the Law, represented by the eclipse of the sun by the rock of natural law that grows out of Urizen's brain.

Thus the myth of Hephaestus, like the myth of Hercules and the cosmogonic myth, is subsumed under the biblical pattern of Judges, wherein the victory of the would-be champion of light and order over the forces of darkness and chaos is at best an ambiguous one because of the hero's fallen state and because of the flaws in the material that he is compelled to work with. The dialectical pattern of illumination and eclipse upon which the Samson story and all solar myths are based, and which symbolizes the pattern of liberation and repression that organizes the entire Book of Judges, remains unresolved.

Since Los represents, among other things, the Imagination, his situation at the end of *The Book of Los*, one of the last of the Lambeth books and the last of Blake's sequence

279

of comogonic or mythological prophecies, could very well represent Blake's despairing of the Imagination's ability to overcome the effects of the Fall, a position that is understandable in light of the depressing historical events of the time.[61] But perhaps more importantly, *The Book of Los* also contains Blake's retrospective view of the achievement in the Lambeth books and a prospect of the road leading to *Jerusalem*. Los's organization of the material world symbolizes the Imagination's comprehension of error—of the fallen world as illusion and of the ways in which this illusion was established and perpetuated as an ontological truth—but nowhere, either in *The Book of Los* or in the other early prophecies, does Blake dramatize the process whereby this illusion is to be supplanted by true vision. Having abandoned the idea of energy, embodied in Orc, as a means of heralding the eschaton,[62] Blake's emerging concept of the Imagination as a liberating force seeks to subsume the role of Orc and incorporate that role into the larger pattern of the destruction of error and the re-creation of truth. Yet it appears that Blake at this stage in his career can see the Imagination as functioning only ironically, exposing error as a parodic mirror of truth in a fun house vision of biblical and modern history. Whatever vision of a new heaven and a new earth Blake had in mind, he reveals it only through inversion and indirection. The Lambeth books culminate, in *Asia*, with the strife of blood, a struggle analogous but also contrary to the mental wars of Eden that are the true occupation of those dwelling in Eternity. A last judgment appears to be at hand, but whether the beast will be exposed and defeated or slouch toward Bethlehem to be born again is a question that Blake does not resolve at this time.

Thus Blake's Bible of Hell lacks the all-important capstone, Blake's equivalent of the Book of Revelation, which would reiterate and bring to a period the cyclical pattern of illumination and obscurity, liberation and repression that exists both in the Bible and the Lambeth books and that the Book of Judges and *The Book of Los* epitomize. But Blake does intimate, through his ironic handling of the Samson theme, Los's true apocalyptic function, since the human illusion that Los creates is better than the loss of any semblance of humanity altogether. Through Los's forging of the sun in *Asia* and in *The Book of Los*, Blake reveals that he has begun to realize that the road back to Eternity is the road that leads ahead, leading the Imagination further into the demon universe; it must continue to create the human illusion until this illusion has been embodied in all its variety at the same time that it becomes condensed into a single unifying image. Only then, as in Revelation, when the body of error has been completely revealed, will the body of truth reappear, will the heavenly bride descend and meet the bridegroom, and will Blake simultaneously fulfil and annihilate the great code of art.

Notes

Introduction

1. John Thomas Smith, *Nollekens and his Times* (London, 1828), quoted in *Blake Records*, ed. G. E. Bentley, Jr. (Oxford: Clarendon Press, 1969), p. 458; Benjamin Heath Malkin, *A Father's Memoirs of His Child* (London, 1806), quoted in *Blake Records*, p. 426.

2. Henry Crabb Robinson's diary, quoted in *Blake Records*, ed. Bentley, p. 322.

3. Joseph Anthony Mazzeo, "New Wine in Old Bottles: Reflections on Historicity and the Problem of Allegory," in his *Varieties of Interpretation* (Notre Dame, Ind.: Univ. of Notre Dame Press, 1978), p. 63.

4. Boehme's *Mysterium Magnum*, for instance, is an extended commentary on Genesis, in which Boehme, like Paracelsus, gives a spiritual reading of the Bible.

5. Blake, of course, read and annotated Swedenborg's *Heaven and Hell, The Wisdom of Angels, concerning Divine Love and Divine Wisdom*, and *The Wisdom of Angels concerning the Divine Providence* (Blake, *The Poetry and Prose of William Blake*, ed. David V. Erdman, rev. ed [Garden City, N.Y.: Doubleday, 1970], pp. 590-601). Blake's most explicit reference to the cabbala is in his Preface to Chapter II of *Jerusalem*, "To the Jews" (*J* 27), which mentions the cabbalistic tradition of Adam Kadmon, the universal man who "contain in his mighty limbs all things in Heaven & Earth" (See Northrop Frye, *Fearful Symmetry: A Study of William Blake* [Princeton: Princeton Univ. Press, 1947], p. 125).

6. Frederick Tatham, "Life of Blake," quoted in *Blake Records*, ed. Bentley, p. 526; Smith, quoted in *Blake Records*, p. 467; Crabb Robinson's diary, quoted in *Blake Records*, p. 322; Henry Crabb Robinson, "Reminiscences," quoted in *Blake Records*, p. 545.

7. Algernon Charles Swinburne, *William Blake: A Critical Essay* (1868; rpt. ed., Lincoln, Nebr.: Univ. of Nebraska Press, 1970), pp. 96, 149-50, 156, 157, 171, 227, et passim. Swinburne's dependence on Seymour Kirkup is noted in S. Foster Damon, *William Blake: His*

283

NOTES

Philosophy and Symbols (1924; rpt. ed., London: Dawsons, 1969), p. 248.

8. Frye, *Fearful Symmetry*, pp. 108-44.

9. Ibid., pp. 110-11.

10. For instance, Frye's insistence that for Blake "words are of the pattern of the human mind and not of nature" (ibid., p. 114) and that "a poet who has put things into words has lifted 'things' from the barren chaos of nature into the created order of thought" (p. 114) point to the Augustinian idea of biblical style as the direct expression of human thought (see Ruth Wallerstein, *Studies in Seventeenth-Century Poetic* [Madison: Univ. of Wisconsin Press, 1965], pp. 54-55).

11. J. G. Davies, *The Theology of William Blake* (1948; rpt. ed., Hamden, Conn.: Archon, 1966).

12. Milton O. Percival, *William Blake's Circle of Destiny* (New York: Columbia Univ. Press, 1938); Désirée Hirst, *Hidden Riches: Traditional Symbolism from the Renaissance to Blake* (London: Eyre and Spottiswoode, 1964); Kathleen Raine, *Blake and Tradition*, Bollingen Series 35·11, 2 vols. (Princeton: Princeton Univ. Press, 1968); Edwin John Ellis and William Butler Yeats, eds., *The Works of William Blake, Poetical, Symbolic, and Critical*, 3 vols. (London, 1893).

13. Mark Schorer, *William Blake: The Politics of Vision* (New York: Henry Holt, 1946), pp. 93-148; Peter F. Fisher, *The Valley of Vision: Blake as Prophet and Revolutionary*, ed. Northrop Frye (Toronto: Univ. of Toronto Press, 1961), pp. 56-79, 122-43, 173-76; Morton D. Paley, *Energy and the Imagination: A Study of the Development of Blake's Thought* (Oxford: Clarendon Press, 1970).

14. Murray Roston, *Prophet and Poet: The Bible and the Growth of Romanticism* (London: Faber and Faber, 1965); David B. Morris, *The Religious Sublime: Christian Poetry and Critical Tradition in Eighteenth-Century England* (Lexington, Ky.: Univ. Press of Kentucky, 1972); Harold Fisch, *Jerusalem and Albion: The Hebraic Factor in Seventeenth-Century Literature* (New York: Schocken, 1964).

15. M. H. Abrams, *Natural Supernaturalism: Tradition and Revolution in Romantic Literature* (New York: Norton, 1971); Florence Sandler, "The Iconoclastic Enterprise: Blake's Critique of 'Milton's Religion'," *Blake Studies* 5 (1972), 13-57; Joseph Anthony Wittreich, Jr., "Sublime Allegory: Blake's Epic Manifesto and the Milton Tradition," *Blake Studies* 4 (1972), 15-44; Wittreich, "Opening the Seals: Blake's Epics and the Milton Tradition," in *Blake's Sublime Allegory*, ed. Stuart Curran and Joseph Anthony Wittreich, Jr. (Madison: Univ. of Wisconsin Press, 1973), pp. 23-58; Wittreich, *Angel of Apocalypse: Blake's Idea of Milton* (Madison: Univ. of Wisconsin Press, 1975), pp. 147-219; Stuart Curran, "Blake and the Gnostic Hyle: A Double Negative," *Blake Studies* 4 (1972), 117-33.

CHAPTER I: Blake and Biblical Tradition

1. Most modern histories of biblical interpretation are mainly concerned with tracing the growth of the higher criticism. See, for example, George Holley Gilbert, *Interpretation of the Bible: A Short History* (New York: Macmillan, 1908); Emil G. Kraeling, *The Old Testament Since the Reformation* (London: Lutterworth, 1955); Fred Gladstone Bratton, *A History of the Bible: An Introduction to the Historical Method* (Boston: Beacon Press, 1967); W. Neil, "The Criticism and Theological Use of the Bible, 1700-1950," in *The Cambridge History of the Bible*, Vol. III, *The West from the Reformation to the Present Day*, ed. S. L. Greenslade (Cambridge: Cambridge Univ. Press, 1963), 238-255. The varieties of biblical interpretation in eighteenth-century England are suggested, very sketchily, in Frederic Farrar, *A History of Interpretation* (London: Macmillan, 1886), p. 377. A somewhat fuller account can be gleaned from incidental statements about exegesis in Charles J. Abbey and John H. Overton, *The English Church in the Eighteenth Century*, 2 vols. (London: Longmans, 1878); John H. Overton and Frederic Relton, *The English Church from the Accession of George I to the End of the Eighteenth Century* (London: Macmillan, 1906); and Horton Davies, *Worship and Theology in England from Watts and Wesley to Maurice, 1690-1850* (Princeton: Princeton Univ. Press, 1961). More recently there have been attempts to comprehend the complexities of eighteenth-century exegesis in a carefully argued study of the fate of allegorical exegesis in the eighteenth century by Victor Harris, "Allegory to Analogy in the Interpretation of Scriptures," *Philological Quarterly* 45 (Jan. 1966), 1-23; and in a study of the interpretation of the historical narratives in the Bible by Hans Frei, *The Eclipse of Biblical Narrative: A Study in Eighteenth and Nineteenth Century Hermeneutics* (New Haven: Yale Univ. Press, 1974). Both works of course deal with only limited topics, and Frei does not even claim to give a full history of the hermeneutics of biblical narrative in the eighteenth and nineteenth centuries (p. 10).

2. The increasing number of nonconforming sects and societies in London in the second half of the eighteenth century, prompted in large part by the Methodist and evangelical revival, is discussed in George Rudé, *Hanoverian London, 1714-1808* (Berkeley and Los Angeles: Univ. of California Press, 1971), pp. 108-110. The growth of "enthusiasm" on the one hand and the spectre of critical deism on the other were but two causes of the controversial spirit that marked eighteenth-century England, and James Downey was not the first to observe that "for all its reason and common sense the age was one of heated controversy. Pulpits, presses, and coffee-houses reverberated with the sounds of attack and counter-attack" (*The Eighteenth-Cen-*

tury Pulpit, A Study of Butler, Berkeley, Secker, Sterne, Whitefield and Wesley [Oxford: Clarendon Press, 1969], p. 16). See also Overton and Relton, *The English Church*, p. 1; and J. H. Overton, *The Evangelical Revival in the Eighteenth Century* (London: Longmans, 1891), pp. 6-7. To give one example of the enormous proliferation of controversial literature during this time, Voltaire reported that Thomas Woolston's *Discourses on Miracles* (1726-28) sold 30,000 copies and provoked sixty pamphlets written in opposition to it (J. M. Robertson, *A History of Freethought*, 4th ed., rev. and enl. [1936; rpt. ed., London: Dawsons, 1969], II, 727). This kind of controversial literature was a large part of the stock in trade of Joseph Johnson, who, for instance, published not only Priestley's work but also the replies of Priestley's antagonists (Leslie F. Chard, "Bookseller to Publisher: Joseph Johnson and the English Book Trade, 1760 to 1810," *The Library*, 5th ser., 32 [1977], 140).

3. In the eighteenth century the national literacy rate was not very high, especially among the lower classes (see Richard D. Altick, *The English Common Reader: A Social History of the Mass Reading Public 1800-1900* [Chicago: Univ. of Chicago Press, 1957], pp. 30-41).

4. See ibid., pp. 24-25, 33, 38; Rudé, *Hanoverian London*, pp. 115-17.

5. G. E. Bentley, Jr., and Martin K. Nurmi, in *A Blake Bibliography* (Minneapolis: Univ. of Minnesota Press, 1964), p. 93, attest to the profitability of these family Bibles by listing twenty editions bearing the title, *The Royal Universal Family Bible*, published between 1735 and 1800, several of which were issued in parts. Among the numerous Bibles issued in fasciculi, probably the most significant was that annotated by Thomas Scott, which was begun in 1788 and consisted of five thousand copies (Thomas Hartwell Horne, "Bibliographical Appendix" to his *An Introduction to the Critical Study and Knowledge of the Holy Scriptures*, new ed. from the 8th London ed., rev. and enl. [New York: Robert Carter, 1848], II, 111 [separately paginated]). Serial publication of Bibles in the eighteenth century is mentioned in Altick, *The English Common Reader*, pp. 55-56; M. H. Black, "The Printed Bible," in *Cambridge History of the Bible*, III, ed. Greenslade, 463.

6. With the exception of Benjamin Blayney's new chapter headings for his 1769 edition of the Authorized Version, which were adopted for Oxford Bibles and later abandoned in favor of the old headings, most Bibles used the chapter headings of the original 1611 edition (F.H.A. Scrivener, *The Authorized Edition of the English Bible (1611), Its Subsequent Reprints and Modern Representatives* [Cambridge: Cambridge Univ. Press, 1910], pp. 132-33).

7. Comparatively few of the Bibles intended for mass distribution are distinguished by originality of insight or scholarly discovery. Thomas Scott's commentary, which was highly praised for its original-

ity (Horne, "Bibliographical Appendix," in *Introduction*, II, 112), is an exception that proves the rule.

8. Anthony Purver, trans., *A New and Literal Translation of All the Books of the Old and New Testaments*, 2 vols. (London, 1764); Joseph Priestley, *The New Testament in an Improved Version, upon the Basis of Archbishop Newcome's New Translation* (London: Joseph Johnson, 1808). The latter work, the Unitarian Bible, published by Joseph Johnson, was projected by Priestley and his associates as early as 1788, but its completion was evidently delayed by the destruction of the material for it in the Birmingham Riots of 1791 (E. S. Shaffer, *"Kubla Khan" and the Fall of Jerusalem: The Mythological School in Biblical Criticism and Secular Literature, 1770-1880* [Cambridge: Cambridge Univ. Press, 1975], p. 24). It contains very little commentary on the text, but, as Shaffer points out, "the introduction gives a compact but well-informed summary of German textual criticism, information that was disseminated among Priestley's collaborators during the period of preparation" (p. 24), hence the possibility of Blake's receiving some of this information through his contact with Johnson's circle.

9. John Wesley, *Notes on the Old and New Testaments*, 4 vols. (London, 1764). For Wesley's textual scholarship, see Luther A. Weigle, "English Versions Since 1611," in *Cambridge History of the Bible*, III, ed. Greenslade, 368; and for his borrowing from others, see Overton, *The Evangelical Revival*, p. 119.

10. Robert Lowth, trans., *Isaiah: A New Translation with a Preliminary Dissertation, and Notes, Critical, Philological, and Explanatory*, 2 vols. (London, 1778); William Newcome, trans., *An Attempt Towards an Improved Version, a Metrical Arrangement, and an Explanation of the Prophet Ezekiel* (Dublin, 1788); Benjamin Blayney, trans., *Jeremiah, and Lamentations: A New Translation, with Notes, Critical, Philological, and Explanatory* (Oxford, 1784); Thomas Percy, trans., *The Song of Solomon, Newly Translated from the Original Hebrew; with a Commentary and Annotations* (London, 1764).

11. Alexander Geddes, trans., *The Holy Bible, or the Books Accounted Sacred, Otherwise Called the Books of the Old and New Covenants*, 2 vols. (London, 1792 [vol. I] and 1797 [vol. II]). This work, which was never completed, contains Genesis to Chronicles and the Book of Ruth. The project was abandoned apparently because Geddes' radical approach to textual criticism provoked hostility from both orthodox Catholics and Protestants. (See W. Neil, "The Criticism and Theological Use of the Bible, 1700-1950," in *Cambridge History of the Bible*, III, ed. Greenslade, 272).

12. As F. B. Curtis points out, Blake would have had access to "the immense volume of scriptural criticism, writings on prophecy, and

sermons that stocked Johnson's premises in St. Paul's Churchyard" ("The Geddes Bible and the Tent of the Eternals in *The Book of Urizen*," *Blake Newsletter* 6 [1973], 94). See also F. B. Curtis, "Blake and the Booksellers," *Blake Studies* 6 (1975), 167-78.

13. For Fuseli's education, ministry, and continued interest in biblical and theological issues, see John Knowles, *The Life and Writings of Henry Fuseli*, 3 vols. (London, 1831), I, 9-18; Eudo C. Mason, *The Mind of Henry Fuseli: Selections from His Writings with An Introductory Study* (London: Routledge and Kegan Paul, 1951), pp. 14-15, 158-67, 339.

14. Scott's annotated Bible, noted above, went through numerous large editions: the second (1805) consisted of two thousand; the third (1810), two thousand; the fourth (1812), three thousand. Eight other editions, in a total of 25,250 copies were printed in America between 1808 and 1819 (Horne, "Bibliographical Appendix," in *Introduction*, II, 111). Matthew Henry's commentary, *An Exposition of the Old and New Testaments*, 5 vols. (London, 1710) was mainly written for the common people and may well be the most popular commentary ever published, going through numerous editions and revisions way into the present century (see Adam Clarke, general preface, *The Holy Bible*, ed. Adam Clarke, 3rd American ed., 6 vols. [New York, 1820], I, x; Horne, "Bibliographical Appendix," in *Introduction*, II, 110-11; S. L. Greenslade, epilogue to *Cambridge History of the Bible*, III, ed. Greenslade, 493). Although not as popular as Scott and Henry, the commentaries of Simon Patrick (historical and poetical books of the Old Testament), William Lowth (the prophets), Richard Arnald (The Apocrypha), and Daniel Whitby (New Testament) were frequently published separately and in a combined *Commentary upon the Old and New Testaments, with the Apocrypha*, 7 vols. (London, 1727-1760), which went through several editions. The 1809 edition adds Moses Lowman's commentary on Revelation.

15. John Smith [of Cambleton], *A Summary View and Explanation of the Writings of the Prophets* (Edinburgh and London, 1787).

16. In his Introduction to the notes on Revelation, Wesley acknowledges his borrowing from Bengel (*Explanatory Notes upon the New Testament*, 2nd American ed., 2 vols. [New York, 1806], II, 312).

17. *The Christian's Magazine* 8 (1767). This journal, edited by William Dodd, was published in London between 1760 and 1767 (Samuel J. Rogal, "Religious Periodicals in England during the Restoration and Eighteenth Century," *The Journal of the Rutgers University Library* 35 [Dec. 1971], 30). Dodd, incidentally, wrote one of the best biblical commentaries of the period, *A Commentary on the Books of the Old and New Testaments*, 3 vols. (London, 1770), which was originally issued in individual numbers. Drawing heavily upon the

scholarship of Calmet and Houbigant, and the unpublished notes of Clarendon, Waterland, and Locke, Dodd's commentary made these important works accessible to the English reading public. Dodd's commentary was reprinted, without acknowledgement of its author, by Wesley's right-hand man, Thomas Coke, under the title *A Commentary on the Holy Bible* (6 vols. [London, 1801-1803]. See Clarke, general preface, *The Holy Bible*, pp. x-xi). For Blair's summary of Lowth, see the facsimile reproduction of his *Lectures on Rhetoric and Belles Lettres*, ed. Harold F. Harding, 2 vols. (1783; rpt. ed., Carbondale, Ill.: Southern Illinois Univ. Press, 1965), II, 385-405 (Lecture 41). For a bibliography of the numerous editions, adaptations, and abridgments of Blair's *Lectures*, see Robert Morell Schmitz, *Hugh Blair* (New York: King's Crown Press, 1948), pp. 144-45.

18. For Johnson's publication of religious pamphlets, see Chard, "Bookseller to Publisher," p. 140. The circulation of tracts by the Wesleyans, the evangelicals, and the S.P.C.K. is discussed in Overton, *The Evangelical Revival*, pp. 134-35; and Altick, *The English Common Reader*, pp. 37-38, 73-77, 100. For a discussion of the proliferation in the 1790s of interpretations of the prophetic books of the Bible, see Clarke Garrett, *Respectable Folly: Millenarians and the French Revolution in France and England* (Baltimore: Johns Hopkins Univ. Press, 1975), pp. 145-78. Garrett sees the activities of Richard Brothers between 1793 and 1795 as contributing importantly to the intensive interest in examining biblical prophecy (p. 146). This interest and its association with Brothers can be illustrated in an anecdote about Joseph Johnson that Chard relates ("Joseph Johnson: Father of the Book Trade," *BNYPL* 79 [1975], p. 71), wherein Johnson, just previous to his trial for selling a seditious pamphlet, was suddenly detained while walking through Lincoln's Inn by his defense attorney, the eminent Thomas Erskine, who wanted to discuss a matter of import. As Johnson later related to a friend who had been walking with him at that time, the important subject that Erskine wanted to discuss was not the trial at hand but Richard Brothers and a commentary on Revelation that Johnson was considering for publication.

19. See Garrett, *Respectable Folly*, pp. 125-26, 152-53. As Garrett points out (pp. 130, 138), Priestley's writings during this period, which were very popular, cite the works of his scholarly predecessors. Similarly, Edward King's *Remarks on the Signs of the Times* (published thrice in London in 1798 and 1799) and James Bicheno's *The Signs of the Times: or The Overthrow of the Papal Tyranny in France* (London, 1793), which saw five British editions by 1800 and one American edition in 1794, cited and summarized the findings of Mede, Whiston, Newton, and others. In 1794 the sermons on prophecy by John Gill, a Baptist preacher and learned rabbinical scholar, were reprinted

(Garrett, pp. 171, 215); and in the same year the interpretations of prophecy by Bishop Newton and Priestley were included in one of the many collections of prophecies that were published at this time (Garrett, p. 188). For a fuller discussion of the reprinting of commentaries on biblical prophecy in the 1790s, see Garrett, pp. 168-72; and Le Roy Froom, *The Prophetic Faith of Our Fathers* (Washington, D.C.: Review and Herald, 1946-1954), II, 647, 723-30; IV, 108-16.

20. Garrett notes the appearance of eschatological speculations in such "barometers of opinion" as the *European Magazine* and the *Gentleman's Magazine* just previous to the French Revolution (*Respectable Folly*, pp. 162-63), as well as the reprinting and discussion in most of the newspapers and journals in 1793 of Robert Fleming's interpretation of Revelation in his *The Apocalyptical Key, or Prophetic Discourse on the Rise and Fall of Papacy* (London, 1701) (Garrett, p. 168). Fleming built his interpretation on the findings of such earlier exegetes as Joseph Mede, Henry More, and Drue Cressner (Froom, *The Prophetic Faith*, II, 643). Garrett also notes that the issue of biblical prophecy was kept alive in the periodical press by the publication of Richard Brothers' *A Revealed Knowledge of the Prophecies and Times* (London, 1794), which went through four editions in London, one in Dublin (1795), and a translation in Paris (1795): "During the first half of 1795, the book and pamphlet literature it engendered were discussed in all the literary reviews, and *The Monthly Magazine, Gentleman's Magazine*, and *Analytical Review* even set aside sections of their magazines for the subject of 'prophecy' " (Garrett, p. 188). The *Analytical Review*, which took a distinctly Unitarian point of view in matters of religion, was founded and published by Joseph Johnson, as was *The Monthly Magazine*, which was "more explicitly Dissenting in its focus" (Chard, "Joseph Johnson," p. 67). These journals, along with those explicitly devoted to religious matters—such as *The Protestant Dissenter's Magazine*, Joseph Priestley's *Theological Repository* (published by Johnson, 1766-1770), and Wesley's *Arminian Magazine*—either directly or incidentally raise exegetical issues in articles and reviews. (For a bibliography and brief discussion of religious magazines printed during the eighteenth century, see Rogal, "Religious Periodicals," pp. 27-33.) Furthermore, there arose in the 1790s two journals in France, the *Journal prophétique* and the *Journal de Pierre Pontard*, and one in England, *The World's Doom; or Cabinet of Fate Unlocked*, all of which were exclusively devoted to ancient and modern prophecies (Garrett, *Respectable Folly*, pp. 29-30, 53, 57, 63-64, 70, 199).

21. Jean H. Hagstrum, "Blake and the Sister-Arts Tradition," in *Blake's Visionary Forms Dramatic*, ed. David V. Erdman and John E. Grant (Princeton: Princeton Univ. Press, 1970), p. 88.

22. Altick, *The English Common Reader*, p. 56, records that in the

290

middle of the eighteenth century there was a "special vogue" for books issued in installments and that the most popular works issued in numbers included illustrated Bibles, Foxe's *Book of Martyrs*, lives of Christ, and the works of Flavius Josephus. Altick further notes that some of these works "were probably bought quite as much for their pictures as for their text" (p. 56). Blake himself did engravings for such number-publications: *The Protestants Family Bible* (1780-81), *The Royal Universal Family Bible* (1780-83), George Henry Maynard's translation of Josephus (which went through four editions), and Edward Kimpton's *A New and Complete History of the Holy Bible* (?1781) (G. E. Bentley, Jr., *Blake Books* [Oxford: Clarendon Press, 1977], pp. 514-17, 585-91). The impact of prints upon the public was far greater than that of any art that could be found in the churches, since the churches, from the Reformation through the eighteenth century, were generally kept free of paintings, as Altick points out in *The Shows of London* (Cambridge, Mass.: Harvard Univ. Press, 1978), pp. 99-100. Prints, on the other hand, were available for viewing not only in illustrated books but also in the windows of the print shops, which were called "the poor man's picture gallery," and inside the print shops, whose displays became increasingly popular as the century progressed (Altick, *The Shows of London*, pp. 109-10).

23. The painting of biblical subjects in the late eighteenth century was stimulated by Lowth's *Lectures on the Sacred Poetry of the Hebrews* and Edmund Burke's *Philosophical Enquiry into the Origin of our Ideas of the Sublime and the Beautiful* (1757), both of which made the Bible, in matters of sublimity, a serious rival to the classics. (See Anthony Blunt, *The Art of William Blake* [1959; rpt. ed., New York: Harper and Row, 1974], pp. 14-17; and David Irwin, *English Neoclassical Art* [Greenwich, Conn.: New York Graphic Society, 1966], pp. 135-38.) Joshua Reynolds, in his *Discourses*, echoes Jonathan Richardson's recommendation of the Bible as a source of subjects for historical painting (Rudé, *Hanoverian London*, p. 68). For a history of the London art exhibitions, see Altick, *The Shows of London*, pp. 99-116.

24. See G.W.H. Lampe, "The Reasonableness of Typology," in *Essays on Typology*, ed. G.W.H. Lampe and K. J. Woollcombe, Studies in Biblical Theology Series 22 (London: SCM Press, 1957), pp. 13-14.

25. See J. B. Trapp, "The Iconography of the Fall of Man," in *Approaches to Paradise Lost: The York Tercentenary Lectures*, ed. C. A. Patrides (London: Edward Arnold, 1968), pp. 223-26.

26. For this typology and other iconographical issues surrounding illustrations of the Cain and Abel story, see my article, "Blake and the Iconography of Cain," in *Blake in His Time*, ed. Robert N. Essick and Donald Pearce (Bloomington: Indiana Univ. Press, 1978), pp. 23-34.

27. Bo Lindberg, *William Blake's Illustrations to the Book of Job*

(Åbo, Finland: Åbo Akademi, 1973), pp. 125-32. Lindberg points out other iconographic elements in the tradition of Job illustration on pp. 133-49.

28. The young Blake's habit of frequenting the print-dealers' shops and the sales of auctioneers is noted by Malkin, quoted in *Blake Records*, ed. Bentley, p. 422.

29. For instance, both editions of G. Gregory's English translation of Robert Lowth's *De Sacra Poesi Hebraeorum Praelectiones Academicae, Lectures on the Sacred Poetry of the Hebrews* (London, 1787 and 1816) contain translations of the notes that Michaelis had added to the Gottingen edition of Lowth's lectures. Similarly, Newcome's preface to his translation of Ezekiel (pp. xxi-xxvii) quotes very extensively, in English, from Eichhorn's *Einleitung ins Alte Testament* (1779). Alexander Geddes, whose own works gave "the fullest and most widely publicized accounts of recent German Biblical criticism" (Shaffer, *"Kubla Khan,"* p. 26), reported that Henry Maty's *New Review* (10 vols., 1782-1786) "contains the earliest intelligence of foreign publications of every kind; and particularly those that relate to sacred criticism" (Geddes, *Prospectus to a New Translation of the Bible* [Glasgow, 1786], p. 122, n.). Joseph Johnson's *Analytical Review* frequently printed reviews and brief notices of works by or about Lessing, Herder, Eichhorn, and Michaelis. For instance, a review of and extracts from *Introduction to the New Testament, by John David Michaelis . . . Translated from the fourth Edition of the German. By Herbert Marsh*, 3 vols. (London: Joseph Johnson, 1793) appeared in *Analytical Review* 16 (1793), 304-10, 512-14; and a notice of Herder's *On the Gift of Tongues at the First Pentecost* (Riga, 1794) is in vol. 20 (1794), 329-30.

30. See Shaffer, *"Kubla Khan,"* pp. 5-7, 24-25. Fuseli, in a letter to Lavater, indicates his familiarity with Ernesti and Michaelis: "Except for Klopstock, Ernesti and Michaelis, there is not a man of real genius in Germany" (quoted in Mason, *The Mind of Henry Fuseli*, p. 119). Fuseli also knew the works of Herder, including *Ältester Urkinde des Menschengeschlechts* (1774-1776), a study of Genesis, which Lavater sent to Fuseli in 1774 (Mason, p. 360; see also Marcia Allentuck, "Henry Fuseli and J. G. Herder's *Ideen zur Philosophie der Geschichte der Menschheit*: An Unremarked Connection," *Journal of the History of Ideas* 35 [1974], 113-20). Fuseli wrote reviews of Herder and other German writers for Johnson's *Analytical Review* (Allentuck, p. 15; Mason, pp. 18-19, 355-59). Another contributor to Johnson's journal was Alexander Geddes, who reviewed books on biblical subjects. (For a list of works reviewed, see John Mason Good, *Memoirs of the Life and Writings of Alexander Geddes* [London, 1803], pp. 192-94.) Shaffer (p. 27) points out that toward the end of the century Geddes' views became increasingly radical and he became intimate with the Unitar-

ians, who were working on a translation of the New Testament. As Shaffer suggests, Blake's contact with these biblical scholars, through Joseph Johnson, would have made available to him a great deal of information about biblical criticism, particularly the recent work of German biblical scholars (p. 27). For a discussion of the probability of Blake's familiarity with the Geddes Bible and Blake's possible borrowing from that work, see Curtis, "The Geddes Bible," pp. 93-94. The probability that Blake knew Geddes is increased by the fact that Geddes and Henry Fuseli often met at the dinner gatherings that were regularly held at Johnson's house and frequently fell into violent debate (Good, pp. 282-83; Knowles, *The Life and Writings of Henry Fuseli*, I, 73-76). It is not unlikely that Blake, who also dined at Johnson's, may have been present at some of these episodes.

31. Shaffer states that "it is significant that German Biblical criticism was particularly in vogue among the predominantly middle-class Unitarians, while the working-class radicals not only at the time of the Revolution but throughout the nineteenth century continued to take their inspiration from French sources, De La Mettrie, Voltaire, and especially Volney" (*"Kubla Khan,"* p. 25).

32. See Robertson, *A History of Freethought*, pp. 780, 790, 796. William Hamilton Reid, in *The Rise and Dissolution of the Infidel Societies in this Metropolis* (London, 1800), pp. 88-89, complains of the availability of deist works—particularly cheap translations of Voltaire —to the lower classes during the 1770s.

33. See Robertson, *A History of Freethought*, pp. 795-99; Schorer, *William Blake*, p. 203; Reid, *Infidel Societies*, pp. 1-40.

34. In his annotations to Watson's *Apology for the Bible*, Blake does not always agree with Paine's objections to the Bible, but he recognizes the value of Paine's attacks on priestcraft and superstition, stating that "the Holy Ghost . . . in Paine strives with Christendom as in Christ he strove with the Jews" (p. 604). (See Fisher, *The Valley of Vision*, p. 159; Schorer, *William Blake*, p. 205.) Similarly, Blake told Henry Crabb Robinson that Voltaire was sent by God to expose the natural sense of the Bible, that is, the orthodox interpretation of the Bible as natural fact or as a moral allegory that serves the ends of bigotry and State Religion (Crabb Robinson's diary, quoted in *Blake Records*, ed. Bentley, p. 322). The aim of Voltaire's criticism of the Bible was to prevent the Bible from being used as an instrument of intolerance and repression, "to deprive famous doctrines and their myths of authority without yet questioning revelation" (Bertram Eugene Schwartzbach, *Voltaire's Old Testament Criticism* [Geneva: Librairie Droz, 1971], p. 33).

35. In his annotations to Watson's *Apology*, Blake concedes to Paine the possibility that the Pentateuch was not written by Moses, but he

then goes on to say that if this is so, then "it ceases to be history & becomes a Poem of probable impossibilities fabricated for pleasure as moderns say but I say by Inspiration" (p. 606). Spinoza, Voltaire, and Paine maintained that the biblical prophets were essentially poets, a point that Blake asserts in his early tractate, *All Religions are One*, where he says that the Poetic Genius "Is every where call'd the Spirit of Prophecy" (p. 2). As Paley points out, the belief that the biblical prophets were poets was one that Blake shared with Spinoza and Paine; and Anglicans, Dissenters, and deists "could agree on this [belief] though each might draw different conclusions from it" (*Energy and the Imagination*, p. 21, n. 4). Voltaire's understanding of the biblical prophets was conditioned by his reading of Lowth's *Lectures on the Sacred Poetry of the Hebrews* (Schwarzbach, *Voltaire's Old Testament Criticism*, p. 151). Paine's horror at Israel's slaughter of the Canaanites in the name of God, a popular deist point of contention against the inspiration of the Bible, is shared by Blake, who is even more horrified at Watson's defense of such an atrocity. In answer to Paine, however, Blake affirms the inspiration of the Bible by holding that the depiction of such atrocities has a purpose, that "the Jewish Scriptures . . . were written as an example of the possibility of Human Beastliness in all its branches" (*Annotations to Watson*, p. 604).

36. For the influence of deism upon eighteenth-century worship and theology, see Horton Davies, *Worship and Theology*, pp. 53-54, 58, 69, 95-96, 99-100; and Robertson, *A History of Freethought*, pp. 770-75. For the corresponding change in hermeneutics, see Harris, "Allegory to Analogy," pp. 52-54, 66-85.

37. Hutchinson and Dove are discussed in Harris, "Allegory to Analogy" (pp. 16-17); Harris sees the survival of the allegorical heritage, particularly typology, as an important but lesser current in eighteenth-century exegesis (p. 14). George Horne's *A Commentary on the Book of Psalms* (Oxford, 1771), which was very popular and which appeared in many editions (T. H. Horne, "Bibliographical Appendix," in *Introduction*, II, p. 119), presented a typological reading of the psalter. Samuel Horsley's *The Book of Psalms, Translated from the Hebrew, with Notes Explanatory and Critical* (London, 1815) also applied the Psalms to the Messiah. He does the same thing in his sermons, many of which take their text from the Psalms, interpreting, for instance, Psalm 45:3 ("Gird thy sword upon thy thigh, O most mighty") as a description of Christ arming for spiritual war against his enemies (*Sermons*, 2nd ed. [London, 1811], p. 101). In remarks like these, and in the extended defense of the spiritual reading of the Bible in George Horne's preface, we find striking parallels with Blake's understanding of biblical poetry. Horsley, incidentally, was one of

Priestley's "most tenacious antagonists" (Garrett, *Respectable Folly*, p. 212), and Blake may therefore have been familiar with him and/or his work. Swedenborg's doctrines, whose influence was greater than the number of followers he attracted might suggest, "initially attracted much interest among the working classes in manufacturing towns like Birmingham, Manchester, and London" (Garrett, p. 156). For his influence on Blake, see J. G. Davies, *The Theology of William Blake*, pp. 31-53; Fisher, *The Valley of Vision*, passim.; Raine, *Blake and Tradition*, I, 5-6, et passim.

38. For Swedenborg's relation and possible debt to Jacob Boehme, see Hirst, *Hidden Riches*, pp. 204-06. For Law's debt to Boehme, see Hirst, pp. 194-97, 270; and Fisher, *The Valley of Vision*, p. 128. For Jacob Duché's connection with Swedenborg, Law, and Boehme, see Hirst, pp. 10-12, 200, 201, 207-8. For Blake's connection with Law, see Fisher, p. 128; and Paley, *Energy and the Imagination*, passim. For Blake's relation to Duché, see Hirst, pp. 212-14. The Law translation of Boehme, which Blake read and perhaps owned, was *The Works of Jacob Behmen, the Teutonic Theosopher*, ed. G. Ward and T. Langcake, 4 vols. (London, 1764-1781). It was actually translated by a number of writers, whose names were omitted, most notably D. A. Freher and Francis Lee (See Bentley and Nurmi, *A Blake Bibliography*, pp. 198-200; and Hirst, pp. 96, 188-89, 271). For the influence of Boehme on Blake, see Hirst, pp. 95-99; Paley, passim; Raine, *Blake and Tradition*, passim; Serge Hutin, *Les Disciples Anglais de Jacob Boehme aux XVIIᵉ et XVIIIᵉ siècles* (Paris: Éditions Denoel, 1960), pp. 163-70.

39. Boehme, despite the popular image of him as a simple shoemaker, was well read in the areas of science and theology (John Joseph Stoudt, *Sunrise to Eternity: A Study in Jacob Boehme's Life and Thought* [Philadelphia: Univ. of Pennsylvania Press, 1957], p. 93; and Hirst, *Hidden Riches*, pp. 84-87). He learned the cabbala from Balthasar Walther (Stoudt, p. 96), and from Martin Moller, chief Pastor of Gorlitz, he learned the teachings of St. Augustine, Tauler, St. Bernard of Clairvaux, the Victorines, Thomas à Kempis, and others (Hirst, p. 85).

40. Schwartzbach, *Voltaire's Old Testament Criticism*, p. 257, states that Calmet organized and made available to Voltaire "the entire Christian exegetical tradition which otherwise would have been too dispersed to refute effectively." Schwartzbach also cites other sources that Voltaire used, which include Astruc, Bayle, Simon, Huet, Leclerc (p. 257), Bochart (p. 203), Kircher, Warburton (p. 185), and Wagenseil (p. 52). Calmet's *Commentaire Littéral sur tous les Livres de l'Ancien et du Nouveau Testament*, 9 vols. (Paris, 1719-1726), was praised by Adam Clarke as "the best comment on the Sacred Writings ever published either by Catholics or Protestants" (preface to *The*

Holy Bible, p. vii). Its enormous critical apparatus is a compendium of all ancient and modern commentaries, both Catholic and Protestant. This work was scarce and expensive, but a lot of Calmet's material was used in William Dodd's *Commentary* (1770), reprinted as Thomas Coke's *Commentary* (1801-1803); and Calmet produced a *Dictionnaire Historique, Chronologique, Géographique, et Littéral de la Bible* (Paris, 1730), which was made available in England through several translations and inexpensive abridgments and adaptations, including John Brown's *A Dictionary of the Holy Bible, on the Plan of Calmet, but Principally Adapted to Common Readers*, 2 vols. (London, 1769). The fifth edition of this work cost eighteen shillings. For other English editions of Calmet's dictionary, see T. H. Horne, "Bibliographical Appendix," in *Introduction*, II, 154-55.

41. Curran, "Blake and the Gnostic Hyle," p. 122; Paley, *Energy and the Imagination*, pp. 66-67.

42. For Milton's biblical exegesis and his citation of earlier commentators, see Christopher Hill, *Milton and the English Revolution* (New York: Viking, 1978), pp. 242-52, 306-16; H. R. MacCallum, "Milton and the Figurative Interpretation of the Bible," *Univ. of Toronto Quarterly* 31 (April 1962), 397-415; John Paul Pritchard, "The Fathers of the Church in the Works of Milton," *Classical Journal* 33 (1937), 79-87; and C. A. Patrides, *Milton and the Christian Tradition* (Oxford: Clarendon Press, 1966), pp. 1-4, 26-40, et passim.

43. Patrick Hume's *Annotations on Milton's Paradise Lost* (London, 1695), which was incorporated into *The Poetical Works of Mr. John Milton* (London: J. Tonson, 1695), provides a thorough detailing of biblical parallels and contains a great deal of exegetical material taken from the church fathers, the Talmud, and the cabbala. Hume's notes were later borrowed by many of the eighteenth-century commentators on Milton. Francis Peck's *New Memoirs of the Life and Poetical Works of Mr. John Milton* (London, 1740) traces patristic and rabbinical sources in Milton. Thomas Newton's variorum *Paradise Lost*, 2 vols. (London, 1749), and *Paradise Regain'd. A Poem, in Four Books. To which is added Samson Agonistes: and Poems upon Several Occasions* (London, 1752), both of which went through several editions, contain notes taken from Peck and Hume. Charles Dunster's edition of *Paradise Regained* (London, 1795), which is reprinted in facsimile in *Milton's Paradise Regained: Two Eighteenth-Century Critiques, by Richard Meadowcourt and Charles Dunster*, ed. Joseph Anthony Wittreich, Jr. (Gainesville, Fla.: Scholars' Facsimiles and Reprints, 1971), displays Dunster's considerable interest in and knowledge of Milton's ties with biblical tradition. Dunster was also one of the contributors to Henry John Todd's *The Poetical Works of John Milton*, 6 vols. (London: Joseph Johnson, 1801), which contains Todd's investigation

into some of Milton's rabbinical sources. For a fuller discussion of these commentators, to which the above remarks are indebted, see Ants Oras, *Milton's Editors and Commentators from Patrick Hume to Henry John Todd (1695-1801), A Study in Critical Views and Methods* (London: Oxford Univ. Press; Tartu: Univ. of Tartu [Dorpat], 1931).

44. Garrett, *Respectable Folly*, pp. 121, 150-51; 201; E. P. Thompson, *The Making of the English Working Class* (1963; rpt. ed., New York: Vintage-Random House, 1966), pp. 26-54; A. L. Morton, "The Everlasting Gospel," in his *The Matter of Britain: Essays in a Living Culture* (London: Lawrence and Wishart, 1958), p. 99.

45. Reid, *Infidel Societies*, p. 19.

46. Ibid., pp. 91-92.

47. Morton, "The Everlasting Gospel," pp. 98-121; Thompson, *The English Working Class*, pp. 41, 50-52; Hill, *Milton*, pp. 467-69; Abrams, *Natural Supernaturalism*, pp. 51-55.

48. Reid, *Infidel Societies*, p. 91.

49. For a discussion of occultism among the seventeenth-century sects, see Keith Thomas, *Religion and the Decline of Magic* (New York: Scribner, 1971), pp. 270-71, 374-77. For the eighteenth century, see Garrett, *Respectable Folly*, pp. 97-120.

50. See Thomas, *Religion*, pp. 271, 375-76.

51. Garrett, *Respectable Folly*, p. 99.

52. The Avignon Society's existence, activities, and millenarian prophecies and beliefs were publicized by a carpenter named James Wright and a printer named William Bryan, both of whom went to France in 1789 to spend a year with the Avignon Society, returned to London, and later became followers of Richard Brothers; they described the society in pamphlets that they wrote as testimony to Brothers. Bryan, who claimed to be a prophet, was befriended by the engraver and mystic, William Sharp, who taught him the trade of copperplate printing and set him up in business. It is therefore possible that Blake, who probably knew Sharp, was also familiar with Bryan. But even if Blake did not know Sharp, he might have heard about the Avignon Society through his Swedenborgian friends or through his own possible attendance at the meetings at Jacob Duché's house, where Count Grabianka—a millenarian, dabbler in the occult, and leader of the Avignon Society—frequently visited during a year's stay in London in 1786. (The information mentioned above, with the exception of the suggestion that Blake knew Bryan, is taken from ibid., pp. 111-13, 158-62, 176. Garrett suggests similarities between Blake and James Wright on p. 161.)

53. Garrett, *Respectable Folly*, p. 99.

54. Ibid., pp. 99-103.

55. Ibid., pp. 99, 109-10.

56. For Blake's connection with Parcelsus, other alchemists, and other forms of esoteric lore, see Paley, *Energy and the Imagination*; Hirst, *Hidden Riches*; and Raine, *Blake and Tradition*, passim.

57. For a discussion of the moribund nature of eighteenth-century Anglicanism, see Downey, *The Eighteenth-Century Pulpit*, pp. 13-16; Horton Davies, *Worship and Theology*, pp. 52-60; J. G. Davies, *The Theology of William Blake*, pp. 8-21. Norman Sykes, in "The Religion of Protestants," in *Cambridge History of the Bible*, III, ed. Greenslade, 197-98, points out that the church's absorption of natural religion and the church's rationalistic approach to the Bible weakened the authority and popularity of the Scriptures, a condition that was reversed by the evangelical revival.

58. The educational and publishing activities of the Evangelicals and Methodists are detailed in Altick, *The English Common Reader*, pp. 35-38, 57-59, 73-77; and in Overton, *Evangelical Revival*, pp. 98-130, 132-33.

59. Overton, *Evangelical Revival*, pp. 113-18, 123.

60. See Horton Davies, *Worship and Theology*, pp. 146-50, 230-31.

61. Ibid., p. 161.

62. For the enthusiasts' critique of the Anglican church, see ibid., pp. 68-72. The application of the word, "Rabbis," to the Anglicans is Whitefield's (ibid., p. 68). For the contribution of the evangelical revival to biblical studies, see Neil, "Criticism and Theological Use of the Bible," p. 254; and Horton Davies, *Worship and Theology*, pp. 238-39.

63. Horton Davies, *Worship and Theology*, pp. 157, 166, 169-70; Downey, *The Eighteenth-Century Pulpit*, pp. 196-97.

64. Fisher, *The Valley of Vision*, pp. 124-28, discusses Blake's attitudes toward the Methodists. The antirevolutionary nature of Hannah More's works is discussed in Altick, *The English Common Reader*, pp. 73-75. For Blake's championship of enthusiasm, see Fisher, pp. 125-27, 136. In *Jerusalem*, Los wants to subdue the reasoning Spectre so that "Enthusiasm and Life may not cease" (9:31).

65. George P. Landow points out that evangelical Anglicans, Methodists, Baptists, and similar sects were responsible for the revival of the typological reading of the Bible in the late eighteenth and nineteenth centuries ("Moses Striking the Rock: Typological Symbolism in Victorian Poetry," in *Literary Uses of Typology, from the Late Middle Ages to the Present*, ed. Earl Miner [Princeton: Princeton Univ. Press, 1977] pp. 342-43).

66. Horton Davies, *Worship and Theology*, pp. 201-04, 234-36; Roston, *Prophet and Poet*, pp. 74-75, 101-108.

67. See Morris, *The Religious Sublime*, pp. 104-96; Roston, *Prophet and Poet*, pp. 126-59; Murray Roston, *Biblical Drama in England, from*

the Middle Ages to the Present Day (Evanston, Ill.: Northwestern Univ. Press, 1968), pp. 189-97.

68. Roston, *Prophet and Poet*, pp. 143-46; Morris, *The Religious Sublime*, pp. 164-68. Malcolm Laing, in his notes to his edition of *The Poems of Ossian* (Edinburgh, 1805), enumerates parallels between Ossian and Hebrew poetry.

69. See Morris, *The Religious Sublime*, pp. 84-85, 145-50, 152-53, 157-59. As one would expect, Blake's knowledge of the German poets came through his friendship with Fuseli. Gessner was Fuseli's godfather, Bodmer was his mentor, and Klopstock was one of his favorite poets (Knowles, *The Life and Writings of Henry Fuseli*, I, 6, 12, 17-18; Mason, *The Mind of Henry Fuseli*, pp. 15, 87-94). According to Mason (p. 92, n. 1), Blake's "When Klopstock England defied" was based upon what Blake had heard about Klopstock from Fuseli.

70. For Milton's influence on the German writers, see J. H. Tisch, "Milton and the German Mind in the Eighteenth Century," in *Studies in the Eighteenth Century: Papers Presented to the David Nichol Smith Memorial Seminar*, ed. R. F. Brissenden (Toronto: Univ. of Toronto Press, 1968), pp. 205-29. For Milton's influence on Johann Bodmer, who translated *Paradise Lost* into German, see M. H. Abrams, *The Mirror and the Lamp: Romantic Theory and the Critical Tradition* (1953; rpt. ed., New York: Norton, 1958), 276-77; and for Young and Cumberland, see Raymond Dexter Havens, *The Influence of Milton on English Poetry* (1922; rpt. ed., New York: Russell and Russell, 1961), pp. 149-60, 285-87. Byron, in his preface to *Cain*, claims that his drama is derived exclusively from the Genesis text, but then he somewhat grudgingly admits that he had read Milton so frequently when he was younger that he was also influenced by his poetic forebear (*The Works of Lord Byron: Poetry*, ed. E. H. Coleridge, 7 vols. [London: John Murray, 1898-1904], V, 208).

71. See Douglas Bush, *Pagan Myth and Christian Tradition in English Poetry*: Jayne Lectures for 1967 (Philadelphia: American Philosophical Society, 1968); Jean Seznec, *The Survival of the Pagan Gods: Mythological Tradition and Its Place in Renaissance Humanism and Art*, trans. Barbara F. Sessions, Bollingen Series, 38 (New York: Pantheon, 1953); Don Cameron Allen, *Mysteriously Meant: The Rediscovery of Pagan Symbolism and Allegorical Interpretation in the Renaissance* (Baltimore: Johns Hopkins Press, 1970).

72. John Milton, *Areopagitica*, in *Complete Prose Works of John Milton*, ed. Don M. Wolfe et al., 8 vols. (New Haven: Yale Univ. Press, 1953——), II, 508, 517-18. All citations of Milton's prose works are from this edition, henceforth abbreviated as *Yale Milton*.

73. See David Shelley Berkeley, *Inwrought with Figures Dim: A Reading of Milton's 'Lycidas'* (The Hague: Mouton, 1974), pp. 28-29.

NOTES

74. Allen, *Mysteriously Meant*, pp. 33-34, esp. n. 61; Shaffer, *"Kubla Khan,"* p. 311, n. 10.

75. Allen, *Mysteriously Meant*, pp. 65-66.

76. For Voltaire's use of Calmet, see Schwartzbach, *Voltaire's Old Testament Criticism*, pp. 187, 189, 205, 209. For the importance of Wettstein's edition of the New Testament, see Shaffer, *"Kubla Khan,"* p. 311, n. 10; T. H. Horne, "Bibliographical Appendix," in *Introduction*, II, 127.

77. T. H. Horne, "Bibliographical Appendix," in *Introduction*, II, 151. The full title of Wakefield's work is *Silva Critica, sive in Auctores Sacros Profanosque Commentarius Philologus*, 5 vols. (Canterbury, 1789-95). According to T. H. Horne, the work received a great deal of critical notice. It was reviewed by Alexander Geddes in the *Analytical Review* (Good, *Alexander Geddes*, p. 194).

78. Robert Lowth, *Lectures on the Sacred Poetry of the Hebrews*, trans. G. Gregory, 2nd ed., 2 vols. (London, 1816), I, 204-13.

79. For the ideas in my discussion in this paragraph I am indebted to Frye, *Fearful Symmetry*, pp. 168-77; Abrams, *Mirror and the Lamp*, pp. 76-82; Roston, *Prophet and Poet*, pp. 78-93; Morris, *The Religious Sublime*, pp. 1-103, 155-70; Shaffer, *"Kubla Khan,"* pp. 62-144; and Vincent Freimarck, "The Bible and Neo-Classical Views of Style," *JEGP* 51 (1952), 507-26.

80. See Freimarck, "The Bible"; and Shaffer, *"Kubla Khan,"* pp. 66-67.

81. For bibliographical information about these writers, see works cited in n. 68 above. See also the historical survey, excerpts and bibliography in Burton Feldman and Robert D. Richardson, *The Rise of Modern Mythology, 1680-1860* (Bloomington: Indiana Univ. Press, 1972). This work, while not directly concerned with biblical tradition, provides valuable information about syncretism and the growing appreciation of the Bible as myth in Blake's time.

82. See Shaffer, *"Kubla Khan,"* pp. 32, 49, 151-61; Feldman and Richardson, *Modern Mythology*, p. 224.

83. For discussion and bibliography of the eighteenth-century speculative mythologists, see Feldman and Richardson, *Modern Mythology*, Frank Manuel, *The Eighteenth Century Confronts the Gods* (Cambridge, Mass.: Harvard Univ. Press, 1959); and Edward B. Hungerford, *Shores of Darkness* (1941; rpt. ed., Cleveland: Meridian-World, 1963).

84. See Feldman and Richardson for Ramsay's adaptation of typology (*Modern Mythology*, p. 63) and Stukeley's ideas about Druidism (pp. 124-25). Neither Feldman and Richardson, nor A. L. Owen (*The Famous Druids* [Oxford: Clarendon Press, 1962]) relate Stukeley's ideas about England being the site of an ancient patriarchal Christianity to Puritan typology, which identified Christian England with the Jewish

NOTES TO CHAPTER I

patriarchs, who were regarded as proto-Christians living in the age preceding the imposition of the Law. Milton, who favored the patriarchs and cited them to support polygamy, belongs to this typological tradition. (See Boyd Berry, *Process of Speech: Puritan Religious Writing and Paradise Lost* [Baltimore: Johns Hopkins Univ. Press, 1976], pp. 93-96, 124-35, 173-74.) Furthermore, the idea that the patriarchs were Christians was also shared by the Swedenborgians and orthodox Christians, as Lindberg points out (*William Blake's Illustrations to the Book of Job*, p. 127).

85. For example, Shuckford's *The Sacred and Profane History of the World Connected* (1728) saw at least eight editions in England and the United States (Feldman and Richardson, *Modern Mythology*, p. 71); Bryant's *A New System* went through three editions between 1774 and 1807 and was published in abridged form by John Wesley (Feldman and Richardson, p. 241); Dupuis' *Origine des tous les cultes* (1795) was issued in two different formats, epitomized twice, and was refuted by Joseph Priestley and Jean Sylvain Bailly (Feldman and Richardson, p. 276).

86. See Raine, *Blake and Tradition*, passim; Hungerford, *Shores of Darkness*, pp. 35-61; Feldman and Richardson, *Modern Mythology*, pp. 288-90; Owen, *Famous Druids*, pp. 224-36; Ruthven Todd, "William Blake and the Eighteenth-Century Mythologists," in his *Tracks in the Snow* (London: Grey Walls Press, 1946), pp. 29-60; Peter F. Fisher, "Blake and the Druids," *JEGP* 58 (1959), 589-612; reprinted in *Blake: A Collection of Critical Essays*, ed. Northrop Frye (Englewood Cliffs, N.J.: Prentice-Hall, 1966), pp. 156-78; Albert J. Kuhn, "English Deism and the Development of Romantic Mythological Syncretism," *PMLA* 62 (1956), 1094-1116; and Sandler, "The Iconoclastic Enterprise," pp. 13-57.

87. Jacob Bryant, *A New System: or an Analysis of Ancient Mythology*, 3rd ed., 6 vols. (London, 1807), IV, 127-51.

88. James John Garth Wilkinson, preface to his edition of Blake's *Songs of Innocence and of Experience* (1839), in G. E. Bentley, Jr., ed., *William Blake: The Critical Heritage* (London: Routledge and Kegan Paul, 1975), p. 58. Wilkinson and Henry Crabb Robinson, reacting to Blake's syncretism, mistake him for a pantheist. Robinson's remarks are in his "William Blake, Kunstler, Dichter, und Religiöser Schwärmer," *Vaterländisches Museum* 1 (Jan. 1811), 107-31, translated and reprinted in Bentley, *Critical Heritage*, p. 161.

89. See Crabb Robinson's diary, quoted in *Blake Records*, ed. Bentley, p. 316.

90. See Wittreich, "Opening the Seals"; and Wittreich, *Angel of Apocalypse*, pp. 147-219.

301

NOTES

CHAPTER II: Prophetic Form: The "Still Better Order"

1. See Abrams, *Mirror and the Lamp*, pp. 184-95.

2. Roston, *Prophet and Poet*, pp. 22-24.

3. Lowth, *Sacred Poetry of the Hebrews*, II, 24-59.

4. Ibid., p. 64-65.

5. Ibid., p. 69.

6. Ibid., p. 69. Lowth chooses for his examples Isaiah 34 and 35 because of the symmetrical relationship of these two prophecies (II, 70-80).

7. See Abrams, *Mirror and the Lamp*, p. 201.

8. Lowth, *Sacred Poetry of the Hebrews*, II, 60-61, 64.

9. Ibid., pp. 96-99.

10. Ibid., pp. 85-86.

11. Ibid., p. 86; Robert Lowth, *Isaiah: A New Translation* (Albany, 1794), p. 5. The first edition of Lowth's *Isaiah* was published in London, 1778. Lowth, of course, was correct in perceiving Isaiah to be a collection of scattered prophecies collected by redactors, but the age demanded—or, rather, the deists and defensive Christians demanded —that the Bible have intelligible form.

12. Thomas Howes, "Doubts Concerning the Translation and Notes of the Bishop of London to Isaiah, Vindicating Ezekiel, Isaiah, and other Jewish Prophets from Disorder in Arrangment," in his *Critical Observations on Books, Antient and Modern*, 4 vols. (1776-1813; rpt. ed., New York: Garland, 1972), II, 270. All further references to this work appear in the text.

13. See also ibid., pp. 213, 215, 227-28, 259-63, and 269.

14. For a discussion of these theories, see Abrams, *Mirror and the Lamp*, pp. 184-225.

15. See also Howes, "Doubts Concerning . . . Isaiah," pp. 296 and 333.

16. Lowth, *Sacred Poetry of the Hebrews*, I, 50. For eighteenth-century ideas about the Bible as primitivist poetry, see Abrams, *Mirror and the Lamp*, p. 82; and Roston, *Prophet and Poet*, pp. 78-93.

17. William Newcome, *An Attempt Towards an Improved Version, A Metrical Arrangement, and an Explanation of the Prophet Ezekiel* (Dublin, 1788), pp. lxv, 114, 118, 122, 123, 125, 129, 133.

18. In Volume III of *Critical Observations on Books*, Thomas Howes printed "A Discourse on the Abuse of the Talent of Disputation in Religion, Particularly as practiced by Dr. Priestley, Mr. Gibbon, and others of the modern Sect of Philosophic Christians" (pp. 1-36). Priestley responded to this in an appendix to his *Letters to Dr. Horsley*, and Howes answered Priestley's reply in his preface to the fourth volume of *Critical Observations on Books*.

19. Of course there are important differences between Revelation and Old Testament prophecy, the most obvious being the recognizably coherent and schematized structure of Revelation (See Richard Hurd, *An Introduction to the Study of the Prophecies Concerning the Christian Church*, 2nd. ed., Warburtonian Lectures, No. 1 [London, 1772], p. 324). Furthermore, the apocalyptic mode differs from the prophetic mode in some very fundamental ways. But since Revelation grew out of Old Testament prophecy, reshaping its elements and making new additions (See Hurd, pp. 317-23; Newcome, *Ezekiel*, xxvi), there are important structural elements that both modes share.

20. Charles Daubuz, *A Perpetual Commentary on the Revelation of St. John* (London, 1720), p. 103.

21. John Gill, *An Exposition of the Old Testament*, 6 vols. (Philadelphia, 1818), v, iii. The first edition of this work was published in London, 1748-63.

22. François de Salignac de la Mothe Fénelon, *Dialogues on Eloquence in General*, trans. William Stevenson, new ed., rev. and corrected (London, 1808), pp. 96-98.

23. Fénelon, *Dialogues*, pp. 82-83; see also Wilbur Samuel Howell, *Eighteenth-Century British Logic and Rhetoric* (Princeton: Princeton Univ. Press, 1971), p. 511.

24. For Fénelon's relationship to Augustine and the Augustinian rhetorical tradition, see Howell, *Eighteenth-Century British Logic and Rhetoric*, p. 505; and Wallerstein, *Seventeenth-Century Poetic*, pp. 15-17, 54-55. For Milton's relationship to Augustinian rhetoric, see Joseph Anthony Wittreich, Jr., " 'The Crown of Eloquence': The Figure of the Orator in Milton's Prose Works," in *Achievements of the Left Hand: Essays on the Prose of John Milton*, ed. Michael Lieb and John T. Shawcross (Amherst: Univ. of Massachusetts Press, 1974), pp. 3-54.

25. Blake's concept of the "true Orator," who varies his verse to suit his subject (*Jerusalem*, pl. 3), appears to be a direct echo of Fénelon's true orator, who uses a variety of styles in each discourse, adjusting his style to his subject (*Dialogues*, pp. 136-37). Fénelon, in turn, probably derives this idea from Augustine's *Confessions*, in which Augustine says, "I indited verses in which I might not place every foot everywhere, but differently in different metres; nor even in any one metre the self-same foot in all places. Yet the art itself by which I indited, had not different principles in these different cases, but comprised all in one" (quoted in Wallerstein, *Seventeenth-Century Poetic*, p. 36). Blake of course could have read Augustine (Richard Downing, "Blake and Augustine," *TLS*, 18 June 1970, p. 662; J. B. Beer, "Blake and Augustine," *TLS*, 2 July 1970, pp. 726-27), but it is also very likely that he knew Fénelon's *Dialogues*, since Stevenson's translation was

NOTES

reprinted several times (Howell, *Eighteenth-Century British Logic and Rhetoric*, p. 518) and since Blake admired Fénelon enough to identify him as a "Son of Eden" in *Jerusalem* (72:48-50). Whether the source of Blake's concept of the prophet as poet and orator was direct or indirect, the concept is part of the tradition of Augustinian rhetoric, which is ultimately rooted in the Bible (See Erich Auerbach, *Literary Language and Its Public in Late Latin Antiquity and in the Middle Ages*, trans. Ralph Manheim, Bollingen Series 74 [New York: Pantheon, 1965], pp. 50-52).

26. Campegius Vitringa, *Typus Doctrinae Propheticae* (1708), quoted in Gill, *An Exposition of the Old Testament*, V, x-xi.

27. Samuel White, *A Commentary on the Prophet Isaiah* (London, 1709), pp. xxviii-xxxvi.

28. For summaries of Mede's explanation of the synchronic form of Revelation, see Hurd, *Prophecies Concerning the Christian Church*, pp. 332-43; Daubuz, *The Revelation of St. John*, pp. 19-20.

29. Daubuz, *The Revelation of St. John*, pp. 19-20.

30. Wesley, *Explanatory Notes Upon the New Testament*, II, 313.

31. Ralph Cohen, *The Art of Discrimination: Thomson's The Seasons and the Language of Criticism* (London: Routledge and Kegan Paul, 1964), p. 76.

32. Milton, *Apology for Smectymnuus* (Yale Milton, I, 721), quoted and interpreted in Wittreich, "Opening the Seals," p. 52.

33. Shaffer, *"Kubla Khan,"* p. 64.

34. John Mayer, *A Commentary on All the Prophets both Great and Small* (London: 1652), p. 2.

35. Blunt, *Art of William Blake*, p. 17, n. 11.

36. Lowth, *Sacred Poetry of the Hebrews*, II, 60-61, 64.

37. Johann Gottfried Eichhorn, *Introduction to the Old Testament*, quoted in Newcome, *Ezekiel*, p. xxiii.

38. See Joseph Anthony Wittreich, Jr., "'A Poet Amongst Poets': Milton and the Tradition of Prophecy," in *Milton and the Line of Vision*, ed. Wittreich (Madison: Univ. of Wisconsin Press, 1975), pp. 102-103, 113-14

39. Eichhorn, *Introduction to the Old Testament*, quoted in Newcome, *Ezekiel*, p. xxiii.

40. Henry Hammond, *A Paraphrase and Annotations Upon All the Books of the New Testament* (London, 1681), p. 883; Philip Doddridge, *The Family Expositor: or, A Paraphrase and Version of the New Testament*, 6 vols. (London, 1792), VI, 362; Hurd, *Prophecies Concerning the Christian Church*, pp. 340-42; Daubuz, *The Revelation of St. John*, pp. 47-48. For Pareus' ideas about perspectivism in Revelation, see Wittreich, *Angel of Apocalypse*, p. 181.

41. Samuel Horsley, *Critical Disquisitions on the Eighteenth Chapter of Isaiah in a Letter to Edward King, Esq.* (Philadelphia, 1800 [a rpt.

of the 1799 London ed.]), pp. 73-75. Compare Horsley's statement with Frye's idea of the "Bard's Song" in *Milton* as a series of "lifting backdrops" (*Fearful Symmetry*, p. 332).

42. William Kerrigan, *The Prophetic Milton* (Charlottesville: Univ. Press of Virginia, 1974), p. 114.

43. John Smith, *A Discourse on Prophecy*, in *A Collection of Theological Tracts*, ed. Richard Watson, 2nd ed., 6 vols. (London, 1791), IV, 328-29, 361. See also p. 303; and Daubuz, *The Revelation of St. John*, pp. 49, 151, for other examples of the application of the theatre metaphor to prophecy.

44. Milton, *The Reason of Church Government*, in *Yale Milton*, I, 815; preface to *Samson Agonistes*, in *Complete Poems and Major Prose*, ed. Merritt Y. Hughes (New York: Odyssey Press, 1957), p. 549. All future references to Milton's poetry are from the Hughes text. As Michael Fixler notes, while Milton accurately echoes Pareus' insistence upon the principle of dramatic structure in Revelation, Milton inadvertently distorts the particular structural pattern that Pareus perceived. Pareus described Revelation as a "PROPHETICAL DRAMA REVEALED IN SEVEN VISIONS," which were subdivided into visionary acts and choruses (Fixler, "The Apocalypse within *Paradise Lost*," in *New Essays on Paradise Lost*, ed. Thomas Kranidas, [Berkeley: Univ. of California Press, 1971], p. 146). Wittreich insists that Pareus and Milton's use of the word "tragedy" does not refer to our present understanding of the word; rather, the word is used primarily to emphasize the dramatic structure of Revelation ("Opening the Seals," pp. 34-35).

45. Wittreich, " 'Poet Amongst Poets,' " p. 106.

46. Unpaginated translator's note in Joseph Mede, *The Key of the Revelation*, trans. Richard More (London, 1643). Actually, the statement is taken from a letter by a certain Mr. Haydock that the translator quotes.

47. Fénelon, *Dialogues*, p. 96.

48. Karl Kroeber, "Graphic-Poetic Structuring in Blake's *Book of Urizen*," *Blake Studies* 3 (Fall 1970), 9-11. See also W.J.T. Mitchell, "Poetic and Pictorial Imagination in *The Book of Urizen*," in *The Visionary Hand: Essays for the Study of William Blake's Art and Aesthetics*, ed. Robert N. Essick (Los Angeles: Hennessey and Ingalls, 1973), p. 356; and his "Blake's Composite Art," in *Blake's Visionary Forms Dramatic*, ed. David V. Erdman and John E. Grant (Princeton: Princeton Univ. Press, 1970), pp. 58-59.

49. Jean Hagstrum, "Blake and the Sister-Arts Tradition," p. 87.

50. Hagstrum, "Blake and the Sister-Arts Tradition," p. 87; Mitchell, "Blake's Composite Art," pp. 69-70, 72-73; Mitchell, "Poetic and Pictorial Imagination in *Urizen*," p. 354.

51. Eichhorn, *Introduction to the Old Testament*, in Newcome,

Ezekiel, p. xxii; Thomas Newton, *Dissertations on the Prophecies* (Northampton, Mass., 1796 [rpt. of London ed. of 1754]), pp. 467-68. See also Wittreich, "Opening the Seals," p. 43.

52. See Susan Fox, *Poetic Form in Blake's Milton* (Princeton: Princeton Univ. Press, 1976), pp. 10-12.

53. Mitchell, "Poetic and Pictorial Imagination in *Urizen*," p. 353.

54. See Fox, *Poetic Form*, pp. 10-12.

55. Ibid., p. 12.

56. See Mitchell, "Blake's Composite Art," p. 67; Kroeber, "Graphic-Poetic Structuring in *Urizen*," pp. 10-12; Anne Kostelanetz Mellor, *Blake's Human Form Divine* (Berkeley: Univ. of California Press, 1974), p. 134.

57. David V. Erdman, "*America*: New Expanses," in *Blake's Visionary Forms Dramatic*, ed. Erdman and Grant, p. 103.

58. Ibid., p. 109.

59. Ibid., pp. 106-07.

60. See ibid., p. 110.

61. Mitchell, "Blake's Composite Art," pp. 79-80.

62. David V. Erdman, note to *America*, pl. 14, in *The Illuminated Blake*, p. 152.

63. Erdman, "*America*: New Expanses," p. 93.

64. Ibid., p. 95.

65. Wittreich, *Angel of Apocalypse*, p. 181; "Opening the Seals," pp. 42-43.

66. Wittreich, "Opening the Seals," p. 36.

67. See, for instance, Kroeber, "Graphic-Poetic Structuring in *Urizen*," pp. 11-12; Mitchell, "Blake's Composite Art," p. 68; and Alicia Ostriker, *Vision and Verse in William Blake* (Madison: Univ. of Wisconsin Press, 1965), pp. 111-12, 149-50.

68. See Wittreich, " 'Poet Amongst Poets,' " p. 106.

69. Ibid., p. 106.

70. Swinburne, *William Blake*, pp. 188, 194.

71. Ibid., p. 195.

72. George Saintsbury, *A History of English Prosody, from the Twelfth Century to the Present Day*, 3 vols. (London: Macmillan, 1910), III, 27.

73. Ostriker, *Vision and Verse in Blake*, pp. 123-24, 158-70.

74. Ibid., p. 127. Minimizing the effect of the Bible on Blake's concept of structure, Ostriker misses the point that all of those modes that Blake adopts were incorporated into the structure of biblical prophecy.

75. See, for instance, ibid., p. 158; Erdman, "*America*: New Expanses," p. 97; Harold Bloom, *Blake's Apocalypse: A Study in Poetic Argument* (1963; rpt. ed., New York: Anchor-Doubleday, 1965), pp. 127-28.

76. Ostriker, *Vision and Verse in Blake*, pp. 168-69.

77. Ibid., p. 168.

78. Geoffrey Keynes and Edwin Wolf, 2nd, *William Blake's Illuminated Books: A Census* (New York: The Grolier Club, 1953), p. 70.

79. Ostriker, *Vision and Verse in Blake*, p. 164.

80. For ideas in this paragraph I am indebted to the discussion of Blake's variety of pictorial styles in W.J.T. Mitchell, "Style and Iconography in Blake's *Milton*," *Blake Studies* 6 (Fall 1973), 47-71; and the discussion of Blake's multiple etching techniques in Robert N. Essick, "Blake and the Traditions of Reproductive Engraving," *Blake Studies* 5 (Fall 1972), 59-103.

81. Mitchell, "Style and Iconography in Blake's *Milton*," p. 59; Mellor, *Blake's Human Form Divine*, p. 135.

82. See Essick, "Blake and the Traditions of Reproductive Engraving," pp. 67-70.

83. Mitchell, "Style and Iconography in Blake's *Milton*," p. 51, n. 7; Essick, "Blake and the Traditions of Reproductive Engraving," p. 68. Essick identifies the technique of this plate as the "woodcut on copper" described by Blake in his Notebook (p. 672), but Mitchell more correctly identifies the process as engraving, whereby the lines are inscribed with a burin and the ink is applied to the surface of the plate, as in relief etching, thus causing the lines to be white rather than black.

84. Erdman calls these designs "home pictures" (*Illuminated Blake*, p. 208). See also Mitchell, "Poetic and Pictorial Imagination in *Urizen*," pp. 372, 374; and Kroeber, "Graphic-Poetic Structuring in *Urizen*," pp. 13-14.

85. Erdman, *Illuminated Blake*, pp. 159, 160, 169; David V. Erdman, *Blake: Prophet Against Empire*, rev. ed. (Garden City, N.Y.: Anchor-Doubleday, 1969), pp. 213, 218-19, pl. V; Jean Hagstrum, *William Blake: Poet and Painter: An Introduction to the Illuminated Verse* (Chicago: Univ. of Chicago Press, 1964), pp. 102-103.

86. See Jean Hagstrum, *The Sister Arts: The Tradition of Literary Pictorialism and English Poetry from Dryden to Gray* (Chicago: Univ. of Chicago Press, 1958), p. 146; and Mellor, *Blake's Human Form Divine*, pp. 105-10. For a useful summary of the tradition of history painting, see Ronald Paulson, "*The Harlot's Progress* and the Tradition of History Painting," *Eighteenth-Century Studies* 1 (Fall 1967), 69-92.

87. Mellor, *Blake's Human Form Divine*, p. 105.

88. Paulson, "*The Harlot's Progress*," p. 69.

89. See my essay, "Blake and the Iconography of Cain," pp. 25-27.

90. See Irwin, *English Neoclassical Art*, pp. 127-30.

91. This design, bearing the title, *Oberon and Titania*, was issued by Blake as a separate plate (Erdman, *Illuminated Blake*, p. 178).

92. See Erdman, *Illuminated Blake*, p. 173; Robert Rosenblum, *Transformations in Late Eighteenth-Century Art* (Princeton: Princeton Univ. Press, 1967), pp. 14-15 and plates 8-10.

93. See Hagstrum, *Sister Arts*, pp. 147-50; and his *Blake: Poet and Painter*, pp. 48-51, 62-64.

94. Hagstrum, *Blake: Poet and Painter*, p. 102.

95. See Hagstrum, *Sister Arts*, pp. 190-95.

CHAPTER III: The Figurative Language of Scripture and Blake's Composite Art

1. Unpaginated translator's note in Mede, *The Key of the Revelation*.

2. Hammond, *A Paraphrase and Annotations Upon All the Books of the New Testament*, p. 844.

3. Campegius Vitringa, *Commentarius in librum prophetarium Iesaiae* (Leuwarden, 1720) quoted in Samuel Horsley, *Biblical Criticism on the First Fourteen Historical Books of the Old Testament; Also on the First Nine Prophetical Books*, 2nd ed., 2 vols. (London, 1844), II, 262. Vitringa was a celebrated authority on biblical prophecy and was frequently cited by biblical commentators.

4. Fénelon, *Dialogues*, pp. 76, 157.

5. Horsley, *Sermons*, p. 278.

6. See, for example, Daubuz, *The Revelation of St. John*, p. 35. William Lowth, whose *Commentary Upon the Prophets* (1714-26) was frequently reprinted, said that "the far greater part of Prophetical Predictions are couched in symbols and sacred hieroglyphs" (Simon Patrick, William Lowth, Richard Arnald, and Daniel Whitby, *A Commentary Upon the Old and New Testaments, with the Apocrypha*, 7 vols. [London, 1809], IV, ii). George Stanley Faber uses the word "hieroglyphic" and "symbol" synonymously in *A Dissertation on the Prophecies that Have Been Fulfilled, Are Now Fulfilling, or Hereafter Will Be Fulfilled*, 3 vols. (London, 1818), I, 96n., 106.

7. See Liselotte Dieckmann, *Hieroglyphics: The History of a Literary Symbol* (St. Louis: Washington Univ. Press, 1970), pp. 124-66.

8. Warburton's ideas about prophecy and hieroglyphics were disseminated by the various editions and translations of *The Divine Legation of Moses*, by Richard Hurd's Warburtonian Lectures on the biblical prophecies, and by the frequent citation of *The Divine Legation* by other scholars and critics. Warburton's ideas about hieroglyphics also had "a strong influence on both the French Encyclopedists, who exploited it, and on Herder, who strongly attacked it" (Dieckman, *Hieroglyphics*, p. 124).

9. William Warburton, *The Divine Legation of Moses Demonstrated*, 10th ed., rev., 3 vols. (London, 1846), II, 90.

10. Ibid., p. 185.
11. Ibid., p. 185.
12. Ibid., p. 188.
13. Ibid., pp. 190, 216.
14. Ibid., p. 209.
15. Ibid., pp. 224-25.
16. Ibid., p. 227.
17. Hurd, *Prophecies Concerning the Christian Church*, pp. 284-303.
18. Daubuz, *The Revelation of St. John*, p. 13.
19. Ibid., pp. 11-12.
20. Ibid., p. 13.
21. Ibid., p. 483.
22. Ibid., p. 35.
23. Eichhorn, *Introduction to the Old Testament*, quoted in Newcome, *Ezekiel*, p. xxii.
24. Ibid., pp. xxv, xxvi.
25. Ibid., p. xxiii.
26. William Jones, *A Course of Lectures on the Figurative Language of Scripture*, in his *Theological and Miscellaneous Works*, 6 vols. (London, 1826), III, 6. The *Lectures* were first published in 1786 and were republished several times.
27. See Roston, *Prophet and Poet*, pp. 70-72, 78-93; Morris, *The Religious Sublime*, pp. 88-92, 159-66.
28. Jones, *Works*, III, 168.
29. Ibid., p. 189. This idea that the two trees in Eden were the first emblems or devices, through which God first instructed man, was advanced in Henry Estienne's *The Art of Making Devices* (1645), a book on the theory of emblem books (Dieckmann, *Hieroglyphics*, pp. 56-57).
30. Jones, *Works*, III, 183.
31. Ibid., pp. 177-78. For the presence of these ideas in the Augustinian rhetorical tradition, see Wallerstein, *Seventeenth-Century Poetic*, pp. 28-30. For Augustine on the universality of signs, see his *On Christian Doctrine*, trans. D. W. Robertson, Jr. (New York: Library of Liberal Arts, 1958), pp. 36-37.
32. Jones, *Works*, III, 181-82.
33. Ibid., pp. 186-87. See Lowth, *Sacred Poetry of the Hebrews*, I, 280-82.
34. Blair, *Lectures*, II, 398.
35. Daubuz, *The Revelation of St. John*, p. 481.
36. See John M. Steadman, *The Lamb and the Elephant: Ideal Imitation and the Context of Renaissance Allegory* (San Marino, Calif.: Huntington Library, 1974), p. 174; John Milton, *Of Education*, in *Yale Milton*, II, 366-69.

37. Daubuz, *The Revelation of St. John*, p. 35.

38. Augustine, in *On Christian Doctrine*, says, "He is a slave to a sign who uses or worships a significant thing without knowing what it signifies. But he who uses or venerates a useful sign divinely instituted whose signifying force he understands does not venerate what he sees and what passes away but rather that to which all things are to be referred [i.e., Christ]. Such a man is spiritual and free" (pp. 86-87).

39. See Joseph Anthony Mazzeo, "St. Augustine's Rhetoric of Silence: Truth vs. Eloquence and Things vs. Signs," in his *Renaissance and Seventeenth-Century Studies* (New York: Columbia Univ. Press; London: Routledge and Kegan Paul, 1964), pp. 5-7.

40. I borrow this terminology from Steadman, *The Lamb and the Elephant*, p. xxiv.

41. See Wallerstein, *Seventeenth-Century Poetic*, pp. 75-76, 182-83.

42. Jones, *Works*, III, 174. The idea of the Book of Nature was also expressed by Hamann (See Dieckmann, *Hieroglyphics*, pp. 143-45).

43. Mazzeo, "Augustine's Rhetoric of Silence," p. 6. See also Frye, *Fearful Symmetry*, p. 114.

44. Fisher, *The Valley of Vision*, pp. 24-25.

45. For accounts of critical statements and refutations of this idea, see Morris, *The Religious Sublime*, pp. 211-12; Cohen, *The Art of Discrimination*, pp. 140-73, 188-247; and Freimarck, "The Bible," p. 509.

46. Hagstrum, "Blake and the Sister-Arts Tradition," pp. 85-90. In the sentences that follow, I summarize the argument of these pages.

47. Ibid., p. 91.

48. See, for example, Lowth, *Sacred Poetry of the Hebrews*, I, 174-77; Eichhorn, *Introduction to the Old Testament*, quoted in Newcome, *Ezekiel*, pp. xxv, xxvii.

49. Daubuz, *The Revelation of St. John*, p. 36. For a discussion of the prominence of the Shield of Achilles and the Table of Cebes in the sister-arts tradition, see Hagstrum, *Sister Arts*, pp. 19-22, 33-34.

50. W.J.T. Mitchell, *Blake's Composite Art: A Study of the Illuminated Poetry* (Princeton: Princeton Univ. Press, 1978), p. 22.

51. Ibid., p. 22.

52. Ibid., p. 23.

53. Ibid., p. 24. Mitchell's discussion of the doctrine of the imitation of nature in the sister-arts tradition is on pp. 16-18.

54. Eichhorn, *Introduction to the Old Testament*, quoted in Newcome, *Ezekiel*, pp. xxiv-xxvi.

55. Johann David Michaelis, notes to Lowth's *Sacred Poetry of the Hebrews*, II, 89-93.

56. Blair, *Lectures*, II, 399-400. For Murdoch's views of biblical imagery, see Cohen, *The Art of Discrimination*, p. 203.

57. Freimarck, "The Bible," pp. 512-13.

58. Richard Steele, *The Guardian*, No. 86, quoted in Freimarck, "The Bible," p. 514.

59. Freimarck, "The Bible," p. 515.

60. Steele, *The Guardian*, quoted in ibid., p. 514.

61. Freimarck, "The Bible," pp. 515-17.

62. John Husbands, unpaginated preface to *A Miscellany of Poems by Several Hands* (Oxford, 1731).

63. Ibid.

64. Ibid.

65. For Lowth's contribution to the expressive theory of poetry, see Abrams, *Mirror and the Lamp*, pp. 76-78.

66. Lowth, *Sacred Poetry of the Hebrews*, I, 121-22.

67. Ibid., p. 230.

68. Ibid., p. 122.

69. Lowth, *Sacred Poetry of the Hebrews*, II, 81.

70. Ibid., p. 82.

71. Lowth, *Isaiah*, p. 48.

72. Lowth, *Sacred Poetry of the Hebrews*, I, 366-67. See also Vol. II, 68-69; and Paley's discussion of Blake and Lowth, in *Energy and the Imagination*, pp. 20-21.

73. Fénelon, *Dialogues*, p. 158.

74. Husbands, preface to *A Miscellany of Poems*.

75. Lowth, *Sacred Poetry of the Hebrews*, I, 367-69. It is interesting to see the similarity between Lowth's aesthetic and that of mannerism, which held that paintings or poems that apparently violated the laws of probability and verisimilitude "could be defended paradoxically as both probable and verisimilar, insofar as they represented a heightened state of emotion. . . . In art, distorted forms and an unrealistic treatment of space or light and shadow could enhance the visionary quality of the work as a deliberate appeal to the imagination. . . . In literature the same effect could be achieved by hyperbolic and far-fetched imagery and emotionally charged figures" (Steadman, *The Lamb and the Elephant*, p. 155). Furthermore, mannerist theorists such as Lomazzo and Zuccaro defended violations of accepted laws of probability, verisimilitude and decorum by claiming that the divinely inspired painter or poet was "following the Creator of nature and imitating an archetypal idea superior to natural forms" (Steadman, p. 154). Needless to say, these theories have strong affinities with biblical and Blakean aesthetics.

76. See Erdman, "*America*: New Expanses," p. 93; and Harold Bloom, "The Visionary Cinema of Romantic Poetry," in *William Blake: Essays for S. Foster Damon*, ed. Alvin Rosenfeld (Providence: Brown Univ. Press, 1969), pp. 18-35.

77. Augustine, *On Christian Doctrine*, p. 14.

78. Mazzeo, "Augustine's Rhetoric of Silence," pp. 6-7.

79. Jacob Boehme, *Mysterium Magnum*, in *Works*, ed. Ward and Langcake (the William Law translation), II, 193-206 (35:46-36:59). All further references to *Mysterium Magnum* are from this edition and will be cited parenthetically within the text, the numbers indicating chapter and section.

80. Boehme, *The Three Principles of the Divine Essence*, in *Works*, I, 171-73 (18:23-35).

81. St. Augustine, *Enarrations on the Psalms*, 130.6, trans. Edmund Hill, in Henri Marrou, *St. Augustine and His Influence through the Ages*, trans. Patrick Hepburne-Scott, Men of Wisdom Books (New York: Harper; London: Longmans, 1957), p. 118.

82. Boehme, *Aurora*, in *Works*, I, 80 (9:61), 81 (9:66).

83. Ibid., p. 81 (9:67).

84. See Jean Hagstrum, "Christ's Body," in *William Blake: Essays in Honour of Sir Geoffrey Keynes*, ed. Morton D. Paley and Michael Philips (Oxford: Clarendon Press, 1973), pp. 129-56, esp. pp. 145-56.

85. Raine, *Blake and Tradition*, II, 108.

86. J. G. Davies, *The Theology of William Blake*, pp. 35-36.

87. Hagstrum, in "Christ's Body," says that "the process of identification with Christ has always been regarded by the Church as the essence of conversion" (pp. 145-46).

CHAPTER IV: Sublime Allegory: Blake's Use of Typology

1. Frank Kermode, *The Sense of an Ending: Studies in the Theory of Fiction* (New York: Oxford Univ. Press, 1967), p. 47. See also Paul Tillich, "Kairos," in *A Handbook of Christian Theology*, ed. Marvin Halverson and Arthur A. Cohen (New York: Meridian, 1958), pp. 193-97; and Joseph A. Galdon, *Typology and Seventeenth-Century Literature* (The Hague: Mouton, 1975), pp. 62-63.

2. Todd, "Blake and Eighteenth-Century Mythologists," pp. 47-52; Hungerford, *Shores of Darkness*, pp. 66-68.

3. Milton, *Areopagitica*, in *Yale Milton*, II, 552-58. For anachronism and typology in the Puritan conception of history, see Berry, *Process of Speech*, p. 171 et passim. For the relationship of the eighteenth-century mythographers' conception of Druidism to Puritan typology, see Allen, *Mysteriously Meant*, pp. 33-34, esp. n. 61; Shaffer, "Kubla Khan," p. 311, n. 10. And for the relationship of the eighteenth-century mythographers to typological tradition in general, see Paul J. Korshin, "The Development of Abstracted Typology in England, 1650-1820," in *Literary Uses of Typology*, ed. Earl Miner (Princeton: Princeton Univ. Press, 1977), pp. 187-88.

4. See Korshin, "Abstracted Typology," p. 154; and Karl Keller, "Alephs, Zahirs, and the Triumph of Ambiguity: Typology in Nineteenth-Century American Literature," in *Literary Uses of Typology*, ed. Miner, p. 282. For an example of the use of "type" and "prophecy" as synonyms, see Anthony Collins, *A Discourse of the Grounds and Reasons of Christianity* (1724; rpt. ed., New York: Garland, 1976), p. 228.

5. Ursula Brumm, *American Thought and Religious Typology*, trans. John Hoaglund (New Brunswick, N.J.: Rutgers Univ. Press, 1970), p. 23.

6. The Old Testament figure is usually called the type, and its New Testament parallel is often called the antitype; but sometimes antitype is used to describe a negative version of a type or is even applied to the Old Testament figure, and the New Testament figure is sometimes called a type. Thus either term can refer to either the original or the copy (Mazzeo, "New Wine in Old Bottles," p. 159, n. 4; Galdon, *Typology*, p. 20).

7. Erich Auerbach, "Figura," in his *Scenes from the Drama of European Literature* (1959; rpt. ed., Gloucester, Mass.: Peter Smith, 1973), p. 34.

8. Galdon, *Typology*, pp. 41-43; John Jortin, *Remarks on Ecclesiastical History*, 5 vols. (London, 1751), I, 183.

9. Auerbach, "Figura," pp. 41-43.

10. Lampe, "The Reasonableness of Typology," pp. 18-20; Mazzeo, "New Wine in Old Bottles," p. 49; E. Earle Ellis, *Paul's Use of the Old Testament* (London: Oliver and Boyd, 1957), pp. 126-35.

11. Lowth, *Sacred Poetry of the Hebrews*, I, 184-213.

12. Ibid., p. 203.

13. See S. Henley's note in Lowth, *Sacred Poetry of the Hebrews*, II, 247-48. Henley does not use the term "typology," but he emphasizes the prophetic function of the imagery that Lowth is talking about, citing as a parallel Jesus' references to Old Testament events in the Gospel According to St. Matthew.

14. Lowth, *Sacred Poetry of the Hebrews*, I, 195-201.

15. Auerbach, "Figura," p. 50; A. C. Charity, *Events and their Afterlife: The Dialectics of Christian Typology in the Bible and Dante* (Cambridge: Cambridge Univ. Press, 1966), pp. 13-15.

16. Galdon, *Typology*, p. 38; Stephen Manning, "Scriptural Exegesis and the Literary Critic," *Typology and Early American Literature*, ed. Sacvan Bercovitch (Amherst: Univ. of Massachusetts Press, 1972), pp. 48-49.

17. Jean Daniélou, *Origen*, trans. Walter Mitchell (New York: Sheed and Ward, 1955), p. 161, quoted in Galdon, *Typology*, p. 50.

18. Galdon, *Typology*, p. 51.

NOTES

19. Lampe, "The Reasonableness of Typology," p. 34.

20. Ibid., p. 33.

21. Berkeley, *Inwrought with Figures Dim*, pp. 28-32; Galdon, *Typology*, pp. 141-42; Korshin, "Abstracted Typology," p. 155. Pre-eminent among writers who used this kind of syncretic typology was, of course, Milton (see Barbara Kiefer Lewalski, "Typological Symbolism and the 'Progress of the Soul' in Seventeenth-Century Literature," in *Literary Uses of Typology*, ed. Miner, p. 103).

22. Mazzeo, "New Wine in Old Bottles," pp. 48-51; Auerbach, "Figura," p. 36; Beryl Smalley, *The Study of the Bible in the Middle Ages* (1952; rpt. ed., Notre Dame, Ind.: Univ. of Notre Dame Press, 1964), pp. 22-24; Thomas M. Davis, "The Traditions of Puritan Typology," in *Typology and Early American Literature*, ed. Bercovitch, pp. 26-28.

23. Gerald Bonner, "Augustine as Biblical Scholar," in *The Cambridge History of the Bible*, Vol. I: *From the Beginnings to Jerome*, ed. P. R. Ackroyd and C. F. Evans (Cambridge: Cambridge Univ. Press, 1970), pp. 551-55. See also Harris, "Allegory to Analogy," pp. 3-5.

24. Bonner, "Augustine as Biblical Scholar," p. 562. See also Marcia L. Colish, *The Mirror of Language: A Study in the Medieval Theory of Knowledge*, Yale Historical Publications Miscellany, 881 (New Haven: Yale Univ. Press, 1968), pp. 41-42.

25. Auerbach, "Figura," pp. 42-44; Bonner, "Augustine as Biblical Scholar," p. 554.

26. Mazzeo, "New Wine in Old Bottles," pp. 50-51.

27. Ibid., p. 51.

28. Lampe, "The Reasonableness of Typology," pp. 9-14.

29. Davis, "Traditions of Puritan Typology," p. 28; Harris, "Allegory to Analogy," pp. 6-7; Earl Miner, afterword to *Literary Uses of Typology*, ed. Miner, p. 389.

30. Davis, "Traditions of Puritan Typology," pp. 29-42.

31. Berry, *Process of Speech*, pp. 8-9, 79-80 et passim.

32. Steven N. Zwicker, "Politics and Panegyric: The Figural Mode from Marvell to Pope," in *Literary Uses of Typology*, ed. Miner, p. 116, nn. 2, 3. The threefold application of typology to the past, present, and future actually originated with the church fathers (Galdon, *Typology*, pp. 48-49).

33. Lewalski, "Typological Symbolism," p. 82; Brumm, *American Thought and Religious Typology*, pp. 48-53; Roston, *Biblical Drama in England*, pp. 69-78.

34. Berry, *Process of Speech*, pp. 73-74; Brumm, *American Thought and Religious Typology*, pp. 33, 46-48, 79-80; Miner, afterword to *Literary Uses of Typology*, p. 390.

NOTES TO CHAPTER IV

35. Berry, *Process of Speech*, pp. 124-35.

36. Korshin, "Abstracted Typology," pp. 155-56; Galdon, *Typology*, pp. 141-42. Brumm (*American Thought and Religious Typology*, pp. 44-45) notes Cotton Mather's use of types taken from pagan history. Milton's use of pagan typology is mentioned in Berkeley, *Inwrought with Figures Dim*, p. 22; and Lewalski, "Typological Symbolism," p. 103.

37. Zwicker, "Politics and Panegyric," pp. 115-45.

38. Korshin, "Abstracted Typology," pp. 182-83, 189-90; Emery Elliott, "From Father to Son: The Evolution of Typology in Puritan New England," in *Literary Uses of Typology*, ed. Miner, p. 227.

39. Thomas Paine, *The Age of Reason*, in *The Selected Works of Tom Paine and Citizen Tom Paine*, ed. Howard Fast (New York: Modern Library-Random House, 1943), p. 328; Paine, *Common Sense*, in *Selected Works*, ed. Fast, p. 25.

40. Korshin, "Abstracted Typology," pp. 179-97.

41. Ibid., pp. 191-92, 194-97.

42. Ibid., p. 148.

43. Harris, "Allegory to Analogy," p. 8.

44. Ibid., pp. 14-17; Miner, afterword to *Literary Uses of Typology*, pp. 391-92; Landow, "Moses Striking the Rock," pp. 343-44.

45. Korshin, "Abstracted Typology," pp. 161-62, 170-79.

46. Ibid., pp. 152-53.

47. Lowth, *Sacred Poetry of the Hebrews*, I, 202-203.

48. Korshin, "Abstracted Typology," p. 153.

49. Mazzeo, "New Wine in Old Bottles," pp. 64-65. Here Mazzeo is following Augustine in his use of the term "allegory" to denote typology (see p. 49).

50. Keller, "Alephs, Zahirs, and the Triumph of Ambiguity," pp. 287-88.

51. Ibid., p. 287. Brumm (*American Thought and Religious Typology*, p. 53) discusses the early appearance of this looser typology in the works of Cotton Mather.

52. Keller, "Alephs, Zahirs, and the Triumph of Ambiguity," pp. 284-93.

53. Ibid., pp. 295-98.

54. See Korshin, "Abstracted Typology," pp. 148-50.

55. See my article, "Lord Byron in the Wilderness: Biblical Tradition in Byron's *Cain* and Blake's *The Ghost of Abel*," *Modern Philology* 72 (May 1975), 361-63.

56. John Parkhurst, *An Hebrew and English Lexicon, without Points*, 4th ed. (London, 1799), pp. 339-57. Parkhurst's *Lexicon*, which went through four editions and several reprintings, was not an ordinary Hebrew dictionary: Parkhurst was a member of the Hutchinsonians,

NOTES

a sect that shared Blake's dislike of Isaac Newton, and the *Lexicon* contains Hutchinsonian doctrine.

57. Frank Kermode, "Deciphering the Big Book," *The New York Review of Books*, 29 June 1978, pp. 41-42.

58. Ibid., pp. 40-41. Anthony Collins, in *The Grounds and Reasons of Christianity* (pp. 53-61), cites Surenhusius' discoveries of parallels between rabbinic exegesis and the interpretation of the Old Testament by New Testament writers.

59. See Mazzeo, "New Wine in Old Bottles," pp. 64-67. Auerbach notes that figuralism (his term for typology) is "by nature a textual interpretation" ("Figura," p. 57). Austin Farrer differentiates the New Testament apostles from the Old Testament prophets by stating that the apostles took the images of the prophets and transformed them by applying them to the Incarnation (*The Glass of Vision, Bampton Lectures for 1948* [Westminster: Dacre Press, 1948], pp. 132-36). Wittreich, in "Opening the Seals" (pp. 30-41), sees this dual process of interpretation and creation operating in the prophetic books of the Bible, but it is clear that this method also applies to the Bible as a whole.

60. See Galdon, *Typology*, pp. 46-49.

61. See Charity, *Events and Their Afterlife*, pp. 103-11.

62. See Charity's discussion of this idea as it is illustrated by the fourth Gospel (ibid., pp. 155-58).

63. Frye, *Fearful Symmetry*, p. 108.

64. Galdon, *Typology*, pp. 57-59; Charity, *Events and Their Afterlife*, pp. 57-59, 71-72, 80, 159-60.

65. Charity, *Events and Their Afterlife*, pp. 157-58.

66. Ibid., p. 158.

67. Ibid., pp. 21-27.

68. D. W. Robinson, *The Hope of Christ's Coming* (London, 1960), p. 11, quoted in ibid., p. 63.

69. Charity, *Events and Their Afterlife*, pp. 107-108.

70. Ibid., pp. 150-54.

71. Ibid., pp. 160-61.

72. Ibid., p. 72.

73. Ibid., p. 130.

74. These typological parallels are outlined in Northrop Frye, "The Typology of *Paradise Regained*," *Modern Philology* 53 (1956), 227-38; reprinted in *Milton: Modern Essays in Criticism*, ed. Arthur E. Barker (New York: Oxford Univ. Press, 1965), pp. 429-30. As Frye points out, the figure of St. George, as used by Milton and Spenser, is an example of a single type that is employed to invoke all of the other types; but Milton also uses the device of including multiple types, most obviously in the last two books of *Paradise Lost*, where Michael's prophecy describes the appearance of several men of faith who are types of

Christ (Galdon, *Typology*, pp. 83-88). An example of Donne's use of multiple types is given in Galdon, p. 120.

75. Adam and Esau are identified as reprobates in Jacob Duché's *Discourses on Various Subjects* (1779), a copy of which Blake probably owned (Bentley and Nurmi, *A Blake Bibliography*, pp. 204-205). Duché, however, describes these two figures as reprobates in the orthodox sense, as two possessed by "odious passions" (*Discourses on Various Subjects*, 3rd ed., 2 vols. [London, 1790], II, 271-72).

76. Augustine, *On Christian Doctrine*, pp. 86-87.

77. See Blake's *Annotations to Watson*, pp. 601-609. While Blake had his own answers to Paine's criticism of the Bible, Blake considered *The Age of Reason* to be a work of genius and not the product of a "modest enquirer" (p. 603).

78. The location of Paris, three degrees to the east of London, is alluded to in the fourth "Memorable Fancy" (pl. 18), in which the terrifying leviathan originates from that location (Martin K. Nurmi, *Blake's "Marriage of Heaven and Hell": A Critical Study*, Kent State Univ. Bulletin Research Series III [Kent, Ohio: Kent State Univ. Press, 1957], p. 51).

79. See n. 74 above. For Blake's possible knowledge of and meeting with Duché, who was chaplain at the Female Orphan Asylum in Lambeth from 1782 to 1789, see Hirst, *Hidden Riches*, pp. 212-13; and Erdman, *Prophet Against Empire*, pp. 11-12, n. 19; p. 290, n. 18.

80. Duché, *Discourses*, II, 125-36.

81. Duché, *Discourses*, I, 182-93.

82. Ibid., p. 33.

83. Ibid., p. 131.

84. Ibid., p. 27.

85. Ibid., p. 25.

86. Ibid., p. 29.

87. Duché, *Discourses*, II, 161.

88. Charity, *Events and Their Afterlife*, pp. 157-58.

89. Duché, *Discourses*, I, 287-88.

90. Duché, *Discourses*, II, 397.

91. Ibid., p. 161.

92. "To Thomas Butts," 6 July 1803, letter 33, *The Letters of William Blake*, ed. Geoffrey Keynes (Cambridge, Mass.: Harvard Univ. Press, 1968), p. 69; Lowth, *Sacred Poetry of the Hebrews*, I, 203.

93. I borrow this last expression from the title of David G. Halliburton's article, "Blake's *French Revolution*: The *Figura* and Yesterday's News," *Studies in Romanticism* 5 (Summer 1966), 158-68.

94. See Mitchell, *Blake's Composite Art*, p. 127.

95. For a discussion of the concept of corporate personality in biblical figuralism, see Charity, *Events and Their Afterlife*, p. 48.

96. Mazzeo, "New Wine in Old Bottles," p. 51.

NOTES

97. Augustine, *On Christian Doctrine*, p. 132.
98. "To Dr. Trusler," 23 August 1799, letter 6, *Letters of Blake*, ed. Keynes, p. 29.
99. For the following discussion of these qualities of typological form, I am indebted to Mazzeo, "New Wine in Old Bottles," pp. 64-66.
100. Berry, *Process of Speech*, pp. 32, 81-83, 121.
101. Ibid., p. 224.
102. Mitchell, "Blake's Composite Art," p. 349.
103. Mazzeo, "New Wine in Old Bottles," p. 65.
104. Collins, *A Discourse*, p. 21.
105. Jerome J. McGann, "The Aim of Blake's Prophecies and the Uses of Blake Criticism," in *Blake's Sublime Allegory*, ed. Curran and Wittreich (Madison: Univ. of Wisconsin Press, 1973), p. 5.
106. Charity, *Events and Their Afterlife*, pp. 167-68.
107. Ibid., p. 221.
108. Duché, *Discourses*, II, 107, 117-18.

CHAPTER V: *America*: "The Doors of Marriage Are Open"

1. See Erdman, *Prophet Against Empire*, p. 209, n. 21; Bloom, *Blake's Apocalypse*, p. 75. Lowth points out the balanced contrasts between Isaiah 34 and 35 (*Sacred Poetry of the Hebrews*, II, 70-80), showing the principle of contraries that Blake obviously had in mind when he cited those two chapters.
2. Lowth, *Sacred Poetry of the Hebrews*, II, 70-74; Simon Patrick, *A Commentary Upon the Old Testament*, 3rd ed., 4 vols. (London, 1727), IV, 119; Matthew Henry, *An Exposition of the Old and New Testaments*, 7th ed., 6 vols. in 5 (Edinburgh, 1767), IV, 135.
3. Lowth, *Sacred Poetry of the Hebrews*, II, 73, n. 8.
4. Derek Kidner, "Isaiah," in *The New Bible Commentary: Revised*, ed. D. Guthrie and J. A. Motyer, 3rd ed., rev. (Grand Rapids, Michigan: Eerdmans, 1970), p. 609.
5. See, for example, Matthew Poole, *A Commentary on the Holy Bible* (1685; rpt. ed., London: Banner of Truth Trust, 1962), II, 477; Patrick, *Commentary Upon the Old Testament*, IV, 119.
6. Madeleine S. Miller and J. Lane Miller, *Harper's Bible Dictionary*, 7th ed. (New York: Harper, 1961), p. 149; Lowth, *Sacred Poetry of the Hebrews*, II, 352.
7. See also Deuteronomy 33:2 and Habbakuk 3:3.
8. Raine, *Blake and Tradition*, I, 338. See Emanuel Swedenborg, *Arcana Coelestia*, rev. and ed. John Faulkner Potts, 12 vols. (New York: American Swedenborg Printing and Publishing Society, 1915-1937), IV, 480-81; VI, 323.
9. Raine, *Blake and Tradition*, I, 338.
10. Erdman, *Prophet Against Empire*, p. 209.

318

11. Stanley Stewart, *The Enclosed Garden: The Tradition and the Image in Seventeenth-Century Poetry* (Madison: Univ. of Wisconsin Press, 1966), pp. 47-48. The breach in the wall is also used as an image in Lamentations 2:8-9, indicating the breach between God and Israel.

12. W. Graham Robertson, in his edition of Alexander Gilchrist's *Life of William Blake* (London: Bodley Head, 1906), p. 471, notes the affinity between this design in "The Preludium" and Blake's "The Body of Abel Found by Adam and Eve, with Cain Fleeing."

13. The source of this typological interpretation of Abel is Hebrews 11:4. For Blake's use of typological and iconographic traditions surrounding Cain and Abel, see my essays, "Blake and the Iconography of Cain"; and "Lord Byron in the Wilderness," pp. 350-64.

14. John Caspar Lavater, *Essays on Physiognomy*, trans. Henry Hunter (London: John Murray, 1792), II, 286. This design is reproduced in Essick and Pearce, eds., *Blake in His Time*, pl. 34.

15. Francis Lee, "A Dissertation Upon the Second Book of Esdras," in his *Dissertations, Theological, Mathematical and Physical* (London: Alexander Stratham, 1752), I, 28. Here Blake may be synthesizing two traditional ideas that were revived by contemporary mythographers: that America is the Atlantis described in ancient legend and that the ten lost tribes of Israel mentioned in II Esdras settled in America (see Hungerford, *Shores of Darkness*, pp. 79-88).

16. Summaries of the major Jewish and Christian interpretations of The Song of Songs may be found in Christian D. Ginsburg, *The Song of Songs and Coheleth* (first published separately, 1857 and 1861; rpt. ed., New York: Ktav, 1970), pp. 20-102; and in H. H. Rowley, "The Interpretation of the Song of Songs," in his *The Servant of the Lord and Other Essays on the Old Testament* (London: Lutterworth Press, 1952), pp. 189-234.

17. Jean Daniélou, *The Bible and the Liturgy* (Notre Dame, Ind.: Univ. of Notre Dame Press, 1956), p. 191. Abrams points out the use of the marriage metaphor in Isaiah 54:5 and 62:2-5 (*Natural Supernaturalism*, pp. 43-44).

18. Abrams, *Natural Supernaturalism*, p. 46.

19. Stewart, *The Enclosed Garden*, p. 29. See also Abrams' discussion of the apocalyptic marriage in *Natural Supernaturalism*, pp. 37-46. Abrams notes that the marriage metaphor was even extended to the Passion, as "commentators early inaugurated the tradition that Christ's words on the cross (*'consummatum est'* in the Vulgate, John 19:30) signified that Christ mounted the cross as a bed on which to consummate the marriage with humanity inaugurated at the Incarnation, in the supreme act of sacrifice which both certified and prefigured His apocalyptic marriage at the end of time" (p. 45).

20. Ginsburg, *The Song of Songs and Coheleth*, pp. 28-29.

21. Ibid., pp. 34-36, 44-45, 57-58.

22. Ibid., pp. 67-69.

23. *Opera Cocceii, Tom. viii. fol. Amstel. Tom. ii. Synopsis et Medulla prophet. Cantici.*; Thomas Brightman, *A Commentary on the Canticles* (Amsterdam, 1644). Both are summarized by Ginsburg, *The Song of Songs and Coheleth,* pp. 70-73, 76-77. Ginsburg also mentions John Cotton's historico-prophetic interpretation (in *A Brief Exposition of the Whole Book of Canticles* [London, 1648]) on pp. 77-78.

24. These allusions are cited by Morris Jastrow in his introduction to *The Song of Songs,* tr. Morris Jastrow, Jr. (Philadelphia and London: Lippincott, 1921), p. 73. See also Marvin H. Pope, trans. and ed., *Song of Songs, A New Translation with Introduction and Commentary,* The Anchor Bible (Garden City, N.Y.: Doubleday, 1977), p. 92.

25. Robert Lowth, following Grotius and Bossuet, interprets the Song of Songs as primarily a celebration of Solomon's marriage to Pharaoh's daughter; but he also cautiously allows an allegorical reading of the work (*Sacred Poetry of the Hebrews,* II, 298-305, 309-31). While Bishop Percy, Thomas Harmer, J. T. Jacobi, and Herder advocated a literal reading of the text, the still dominant allegorical reading was endorsed by Wesley (see Ginsburg, *The Song of Songs and Coheleth,* pp. 83-92) and continued to be promulgated in such popular works as Matthew Henry's *An Exposition of the Old and New Testaments.*

26. John Bland, *A Grammatical Version from the Original Hebrew of the Song of Solomon, Into Blank Verse* (1750; rpt. ed., New York: Readex Microprint [Three Centuries of Drama: English 1751-1800], 1954), p. xi.

27. Milton, *The Reason of Church Government,* in *Yale Milton,* I, 815.

28. Milton, *Tetrachordon,* in *Yale Milton,* II, 597.

29. Stewart, speaking of the seventeenth century poetic tradition surrounding the Canticles, provides an important critical caveat:

> Unless we see the full power of the erotic language in the tradition of the Canticles, we miss an important aspect of Renaissance poetic culture. Poets did not, as some critics would have us believe, simply polarize lust and love. The latter word, until placed in a proper context, is too passive to describe the passion sung by Solomon. The Song of Songs dealt in no uncertain terms with the fever-burn of lust. (*The Enclosed Garden,* p. 27.)

30. Frye, *Fearful Symmetry,* p. 276.

31. Abrams describes the appearance of the apocalyptic marriage

in the works of Blake and his contemporaries as a "prominent period metaphor," which embodies "a complex of ideas concerning the history and destiny of man and the role of the visionary poet as both herald and inaugurator of a supremely better world" (p. 31) in *Natural Supernaturalism*, esp. pp. 29-31.

32. See ibid., pp. 50-51.

33. Reproduced in Geoffrey Keynes, *William Blake's Illustrations to the Bible* (London: Blake Trust, 1957), frontispiece; and in Ruthven Todd, *William Blake the Artist* (London: Dutton, 1971), p. 141.

34. Stewart, *The Enclosed Garden*, p. 73.

35. Erdman, *The Illuminated Blake*, p. 152.

36. Ibid., p. 152.

37. Raine, *Blake and Tradition*, I, 191-92.

CHAPTER VI: *Europe*: The Bride and the Harlot

1. See Michael J. Tolley, "*Europe*: 'to those ychained in sleep,'" in *Blake's Visionary Forms Dramatic*, ed. Erdman and Grant (Princeton: Princeton Univ. Press, 1970), pp. 115-45. Tolley, hitherto the only one to attempt an extended study of the biblical and Miltonic contexts of *Europe*, maintains that "*Europe* is primarily a reworking of Milton's poem to fit Blake's understanding of the events Milton celebrated" (p. 119). He does not see the extended structural parallels between both works, however, and his emphasis differs from mine. Similarly, our interests in biblical patterns differ, although I believe that they complement each other, particularly with regard to his concern with allusions to the Song of Solomon. Needless to say, I am indebted to this valuable study, as I have indicated below.

2. See ibid., p. 120.

3. See Tolley's close analysis of the rhetorical parallels between these two sections of Blake and Milton's poems (ibid., pp. 120-21).

4. William John Roscelli, "The Metaphysical Milton," *Texas Studies in Literature and Language* 8 (Winter 1967), 478-79.

5. Roscelli, "The Metaphysical Milton," p. 479.

6. Boehme, *Three Principles of the Divine Essence*, in *Works*, I, 285-86 (26:21-27). Boehme says that for these Christians "Christ in them (from whence the Holy Ghost goes forth, which drives and leads Men, and who at first had begotten them with Power and Miracles) must now be nothing but a History, and they became but historical Christians" (26:21).

7. Lily B. Campbell, *Divine Poetry and Drama in Sixteenth-Century England* (Cambridge at the University Press; and Berkeley and Los Angeles: Univ. of California Press, 1961), p. 77.

8. See Spenser's *Teares of the Muses*, lines 499-522, in the Oxford

NOTES

Standard Authors edition of *The Poetical Works of Edmund Spenser*, ed. J. C. Smith and E. de Selincourt (New York: Oxford Univ. Press, 1912), p. 485. All citations of Spenser's works are from this edition.

9. Milton's reluctant farewell to the "yellow-skirted Fays," whose attractiveness is all too evident in the poem, has been noted in Cleanth Brooks and John E. Hardy, eds., *Poems of Mr. John Milton: The 1645 Edition with Essays in Analysis* (New York: Harcourt, Brace, 1951), pp. 102-103.

10. Blake's use of the biblical images of the ark and the tabernacle as sexual metaphors is discussed at length in Paul Miner, "William Blake's 'Divine Analogy'," *Criticism* 3 (Winter 1961), 46-61.

11. Tolley notes that "Superficially, the nameless shadowy female in *Europe* and the shadowy daughter of Urthona in *America* are not identical" ("*Europe*," p. 121, n. 4). The biblical allusions surrounding the figure in *Europe* suggest that these differences are not superficial, however.

12. As Michael Tolley points out, the fairy's song on plate iii of *Europe* suggests that "Enitharmon in *Europe* also has affinities with the 'foolish woman' of Prov. 9:13-18" and that by alluding to Proverbs 9:17 the fairy shows "the bait by which fallen man has been caught" ("Blake's Songs of Spring," in *Essays in Honour of Sir Geoffrey Keynes*, p. 112, n. 35). Since the guests of the foolish woman in Proverbs are "in the depths of hell" (Proverbs 9:18), we can only conclude that here folly is the cloak of knavery and that this foolish woman is the harlot mentioned in other sections of Proverbs, an interpretation advanced by biblical commentators (see Patrick, *Commentary Upon the Old Testament*, III, 305).

13. As Tolley points out, this secret place is the place of generation ("*Europe*," p. 121).

14. See Erdman, *Prophet Against Empire*, p. 264.

15. Fixler convincingly argues that in the *Nativity Ode* Milton has not yet achieved any real prophetic strain ("Apocalypse in *Paradise Lost*," pp. 49, 54-58).

16. Tolley, "*Europe*," p. 127.

17. *Ovid's Metamorphoses, in Fifteen Books. Translated by the most Eminent Hands* [John Dryden et al.], ed. Samuel Garth, 4th ed., 2 vols. (London, 1773), I, 14.

18. Ovid, *Metamorphoses*, ed. Garth, I, 9. In George Sandys' translation, this division of the earth is described as the snaring of the ground by "limit-Giving Geometry" (*Ovid's Metamorphosis, Englished, Mythologized, and Represented in Figures by George Sandys* [1632 ed.], ed. Karl K. Hulley and Stanley T. Vandersall [Lincoln, Nebr.: Univ. of Nebraska Press, 1970], p. 29).

19. Frye, *Fearful Symmetry*, p. 263.

20. Peter F. Fisher, "Blake's Attacks on the Classical Tradition," *Philological Quarterly* 40 (January 1961), 17.

21. Milton, *Apology for Smectymnuus*, in *Yale Milton*, I, 890.

22. Ibid., pp. 890-91.

23. John Milton, *Poems upon Several Occasions, English, Italian, and Latin, with Translations*, ed. Thomas Warton (London, 1785), p. 479.

24. A.S.P. Woodhouse and Douglas Bush, eds., *The Minor English Poems*, in *A Variorum Commentary on The Poems of John Milton*, ed. Merritt Y. Hughes (New York: Columbia Univ. Press, 1970———), II, Part I, 24.

25. Sandler, "The Iconoclastic Enterprise," p. 32.

26. Ibid., pp. 28-30.

27. Ibid., p. 33.

28. Brooks and Hardy, *Poems of Milton*, pp. 102-103.

29. Frye, *Fearful Symmetry*, pp. 132, 171.

30. See Patrick, *Commentary Upon the Old Testament*, IV, 468; Samuel Humphreys, *The Sacred Books of the Old and New Testament . . . with Critical and Explanatory Annotations, Carefully Compiled from the Commentaries and Other Writings of Grotius, Lightfoot, Pool, Calmet, Patrick, Le Clerc, Lock, Burkitt, Henry, Pearce*, 3 vols. (London, 1735-1739), II, 2142. Humphreys' Bible contains many engravings by Isaac Basire, James Basire's father, and Blake's engraving master may well have owned a copy of this work.

31. William Collins, "Ode on the Poetical Character," in *The Poems of Thomas Gray, William Collins, Oliver Goldsmith*, ed. Roger Lonsdale (London: Longmans, 1969), pp. 427-35. All citations of Collins' poem are from this edition.

32. Milton, *Tetrachordon*, in *Yale Milton*, II, 596-97.

33. Wittreich, *Angel of Apocalypse*, pp. 123-28.

34. Thomas Gray, "The Bard, a Pindaric Ode," in *Poems of Gray, Collins, Goldsmith*, ed. Lonsdale, p. 198, line 127.

35. Irene Tayler, *Blake's Illustrations to the Poems of Gray* (Princeton: Princeton Univ. Press, 1971), p. 104.

36. Frye, *Fearful Symmetry*, pp. 168-72.

37. Ibid., pp. 168-69.

38. A number of modern scholars have noted Milton's aesthetic distance and the abstract qualities of his picture of Christ in the *Nativity Ode*. Brooks and Hardy speak of Milton's "remoteness and tranced deliberation" (*Poems of Milton*, p. 104). James Holly Hanford observes that Milton's tone in the *Nativity Ode* is characterized by "an austere intellectualized emotion stirred in him by the idea of its [the Nativity's] moral significance" ("The Youth of Milton, An Interpretation of His Early Development," in his *Studies in Shakespeare, Milton, and Donne* [New York: Macmillan, 1925], pp. 122-24). According to

Malcolm Ross, the Christ in Milton's poem is an abstract symbol, and in Milton's description of the ways of divine providence "Man is the passive spectator (and astonished beneficiary) of an abstract and remote performance" (*Poetry and Dogma: The Transfiguration of Eucharistic Symbols in Seventeenth Century English Poetry* [New Brunswick, N.J.: Rutgers Univ. Press, 1954], pp. 188, 191).

39. See Arthur E. Barker. "The Pattern of Milton's *Nativity Ode*," *University of Toronto Quarterly* 10 (1941), 168-81.

40. See Woodhouse and Bush, *The Minor English Poems*, pp. 39-40.

41. Sandler, "The Iconoclastic Enterprise," p. 15, observes that the Book of Revelation "is structured around the successive 'unveilings' and apotheoses of the components of the Anti-Christ (the Beasts, the Dragon, the Whore who is the False City) and then those of the Christ and his Bride, the True City, Jerusalem."

42. Erdman perceives Enitharmon to be an archetypal Queen, representing in part the Queen of France (*Prophet Against Empire*, pp. 223, 267).

43. Poole, *Commentary on the Holy Bible*, II, 960.

44. See John Albert Bengel, *Gnomon of the New Testament*, trans. Charlton T. Lewis and Marvin R. Vincent, 2 vols. (Philadelphia and New York, 1864), II, 315; James Bicheno, *The Signs of the Times* (London, 1799), p. 112.

CHAPTER VII: *The Song of Los*: Enslavement to the Elements

1. Erdman, *Illuminated Blake*, p. 176.

2. John Beer, in *Blake's Humanism* (Manchester: Manchester Univ. Press; New York: Barnes and Noble, 1968), p. 133, observes, "Where *America* and *Europe* contained sizeable segments of human history, this further book, though brief in compass, comes nearer to an account of human history as a whole."

3. See Henry, *Exposition of Old and New Testaments*, VI, 285.

4. See Schwartzbach, *Voltaire's Old Testament Criticism*, pp. 183-85; Allen, *Mysteriously Meant*, pp. 36-38.

5. All citations of William Warburton's *The Divine Legation of Moses Demonstrated* are from the 10th edition, rev. (London, 1846), 3 vols. This edition is a reprint of the quarto edition edited by Richard Hurd in 1788, except in the very few instances in which the latter differs, in matters of orthography, from the octavo edition of 1766 and from that of 1811.

6. Ovid, *Metamorphoses*, bk. III, ed. Garth, I, 90.

7. See Sandys' commentary in his translation of *Metamorphoses*, p. 148. As Allen points out, Sandys' commentary on Ovid "is actually a

great variorum of adjusted and acceptable symbolism and allegory" (*Mysteriously Meant*, p. 193).

8. Ovid, *Metamorphoses*, trans. Sandys, p. 149.

9. Ibid., p. 149.

10. Garth, in the preface to his edition of *Metamorphoses*, reads Ovid's poem as a moral allegory (I, xlii-xlvii).

11. *The Book of Enoch*, ed. R. H. Charles, in *The Apocrypha and Pseudepigrapha of the Old Testament*, ed. R. H. Charles (Oxford: Clarendon Press, 1912), II, 191-92. Blake read the Book of Enoch, but he could not have seen it before 1821, when an English translation by Richard Laurence was published. However, the apocryphal book is cited in Jude 6, 14-15 and perhaps in 2 Peter 2:4-5, which juxtaposes the punishment of the fallen angels with the Flood. The Book of Enoch was also cited in other apocryphal works and in the writings of the early fathers (see G. E. Bentley, Jr., "A Jewel in an Ethiop's Ear: The Book of Enoch as Inspiration for William Blake, John Flaxman, Thomas Moore, and Richard Westall," in *Blake in His Time*, ed. Essick and Pearce, pp. 213-15; H. J. Lawlor, "Early Citations from the Book of Enoch," *Journal of Philology* 25 [1897], 164-225). Thomas Blackwell cites the Book of Enoch in *Letters concerning Mythology* (London, 1748), p. 404n. Also, Patrick points out that some of the ancients took the "sons of God" in Genesis 6:2 to be angels and that the Septuagint translates the biblical phrase as "Angels of God" (*Commentary Upon the Old Testament*, I, 32).

12. Patrick, *Commentary Upon the Old Testament*, I, 56.

13. Ibid., p. 56.

14. Milton mentions Thammuz and Adonis, two dying gods of Lebanon, in *Paradise Lost* I.446-54.

15. See also 2 Kings 19:25.

16. Ovid, *Metamorphoses*, bk. III, ed. Garth, I, 87.

17. Poole, *Commentary on the Holy Bible*, III, 292.

18. Pierluigi de Vecchi, notes to *The Complete Paintings of Raphael*, ed. Richard Cocke (New York: Abrams, 1966), p. 101.

19. Erdman, *Illuminated Blake*, p. 181.

20. Ibid., pp. 174, 181.

21. Erdman suggests the comparison with Blake's illustration of *The Sacrifice of Noah* (ibid., p. 174).

22. Ibid., p. 181.

23. See *Jerusalem* 95:17-20.

CHAPTER VIII: *The Book of Urizen*: Blake's Inverted Genesis

1. Some of the pictorial motifs in the Genesis manuscript echo Blake's earlier treatment of Genesis. The two title pages of the manuscript are

reproduced in C. H. Collins Baker, *Catalogue of William Blake's Drawings and Paintings in the Huntington Library*, enl. and rev. R. R. Wark (San Marino, Calif.: Huntington Library, 1957), plates XXXII and XXXIII. In both of these title pages, the figure of the Holy Ghost at the top of the page is the same running youth that appears on plate 3 of *Urizen*, though in the Genesis manuscript the figure is running in the opposite direction. S. Foster Damon observes that at the end of chapter ii of the Genesis manuscript there is a picture of Adam sleeping with a girdle around his chest. This echoes the girdle around Los's chest described in *Urizen* (20:8-17) and illustrated on plate 21 (*A Blake Dictionary: The Ideas and Symbols of William Blake* [1965; rpt. ed., New York: Dutton, 1971], p. 152).

2. The tree on the title page is the Tree of Mystery, whose growth is described in *The Book of Ahania* (3:55-67; 4:2-4). The tree's aerial roots create a dark wood of error, an "endless labyrinth of woe" (*Ahania* 4:4), the enclosed world of the fallen senses. The tree is directly alluded to twice in the text of *Urizen*: in Urizen's "vast forests" (3:23) and in the "garden of fruits" that Urizen plants (20:41). But the tree is also indirectly evoked in visual and verbal images. As a Daphne figure, Enitharmon echoes the tree. Her arching form in the illustration on plate 19 parallels the form of the tree on the title page. The formation of Urizen's fallen body is described in images that reflect the tree on the title page. Urizen's spine shoots "pain'd / Ribs, like a bending cavern" (10:38-39). His heart and his brain also shoot branches (11:6, 10-12). His ears "Shot spiring out and petrified / As they grew" (11:23-24).

3. The figure in flames is an allusion to Ezekiel 8:2:

> Then I beheld, and lo a likeness as the appearance of fire: from the appearance of his loins even downward, fire; and from his loins even upward, as the appearance of brightness, as the colour of amber.

This is Ezekiel's spiritual guide, who brings him "in the visions of God to Jerusalem" (Ezekiel 8:3). For Blake the figure thus represents inspiration, the expansion of the senses, the "unquenchable burnings" (4:13) of Eternity that Urizen opposes.

4. Frye, *Fearful Symmetry*, p. 41. See also J. M. Evans, *"Paradise Lost" and the Genesis Tradition* (Oxford: Clarendon Press, 1968), pp. 62-70.

5. Evans, *"Paradise Lost,"* pp. 40, 94-95.

6. Bratton, *History of the Bible*, p. 106. This discovery was made by Robert Simon in his *Critical History of the Old Testament* (1678).

7. Bratton, *History of the Bible*, p. 107. This distinction was first pointed out by Jean Astruc, physician to Louis XV.

8. Evans, *"Paradise Lost,"* p. 11.

9. Ibid., pp. 11, 14.

10. Ibid., pp. 12, 14.

11. Crabb Robinson, in his "Reminiscences," recalls the following conversation with Blake:

> On my obtaining from him the declaration that the Bible was the work of God, I referred to the commencem^t of Genesis—In the beginning God created the Heaven & the Earth—But I gained nothing by this for I was triumphantly told that this God was not Jehovah, but the Elohim, and the doctrine of the Gnostics repeated with sufficient consistency to silence one so unlearned as myself.
>
> (quoted in *Blake Records*, ed. Bentley, p. 545)

Blake's print, "Elohim Creating Adam," is reproduced in Martin Butlin, *William Blake, A Complete Catalogue of the Works in the Tate Gallery*, rev. ed. (London: Tate Gallery, 1971), p. 35.

12. Evans, *"Paradise Lost,"* pp. 232-33. See also Hope Traver, *The Four Daughters of God: A Study of the Versions of this Allegory* (Philadelphia: John C. Winston, 1907); and Samuel C. Chew, *The Virtues Reconciled, An Iconographic Study* (Toronto: Univ. of Toronto Press, 1947), esp. pp. 35-68.

13. Evans, *"Paradise Lost,"* p. 236.

14. Chew, *Virtues Reconciled*, pp. 59-60. The quotation of the Cambridge Manuscript is from *The Works of John Milton*, ed. Frank Allen Patterson, et al. (New York: Columbia Univ. Press, 1931-1938), XVIII, 229.

15. Thomas Birch reproduces almost the entire Cambridge Manuscript in "An Historical and Critical Account of the Life and Writings of Mr. John Milton," in *The Works of John Milton, Historical, Political, and Miscellaneous*, ed. Thomas Birch, 2nd ed. (London, 1753), I, xlviii-lxxii. The first three versions of Milton's projected drama are on pp. xlviii-lxxii, and "Adam unparadiz'd" is on pp. liv-lv. These four drafts were also reprinted in Francis Peck, *New Memoirs of the Life and Poetical Works of Mr. John Milton* (London, 1740), pp. 38-41; *The Poetical Works of John Milton*, ed. Thomas Newton (London, 1761), III, 581-82, 586; and Samuel Johnson, "Life of Milton," in his *The Lives of the Most Eminent English Poets; with Critical Observations of Their Works* (London, 1781), I, 170-76.

16. See my essay, "Lord Byron in the Wilderness," pp. 358-59.

17. S. H. Hooke, "Genesis," in *Peake's Commentary on the Bible*, ed. Matthew Black and H. H. Rowley (London: Nelson, 1962), p. 194 [161c].

18. Damon, *Blake Dictionary*, pp. 116, 204.

19. There are three paintings and one drawing of this subject. See

Keynes, *Blake's Illustrations to the Bible*, p. 2; and Butlin, *Tate Gallery Catalogue*, p. 62. Two copies of the painting are reproduced in Keynes, plates 15a and 15b. The third painting, in Keynes's collection, is a miniature version of 15b. Butlin reproduces the Tate copy. The preliminary sketch for these paintings, now in the British Museum, is reproduced in Keynes, *Drawings of William Blake: 92 Pencil Studies* (New York: Dover, 1970), pl. 47. In this sketch Cain does not have flames streaming behind him.

20. Sin is identified as a "great ban-dog ready to pull out the throat of thy soul" in the gloss on this verse in John Trapp, *A Clavis to the Bible, or a New Comment upon the Pentateuch or Five Books of Moses* (London, 1650), p. 48.

21. The theme of self-destructive pity and the image of the dog at the wintry door were originally incorporated in the Notebook fragments called the "Fayette" stanzas:

O who would smile on the wintry seas
& Pity the stormy roar
Or who will exchange his new born child
For the dog at the wintry door.
("Who will exchange his own fire side," lines 9-12)

Like Fayette's pity for the captive King and Queen of France, Los's pity for the chained Urizen is totally misplaced. Fayette and Los fail to see that the tyrant is self-imprisoned. By pitying the tyrant they capitulate to the forces of tyranny. They sacrifice their human potential for a bestial mode of existence.

22. In *The Song of Los* (1795), when Urizen gave his law to the nations, "Abram fled in fires from Chaldea" (3:16). Like Fuzon, Abram flees from Urizen's dominion. For Blake, Abram marks the end of the Druidical age in which "human sacrifice would have depopulated the earth" (*Descriptive Catalogue*, p. 533). See Damon, *Blake Dictionary*, pp. 3-4.

23. Peter Allix, *Reflexions upon the Books of the Holy Scripture, to establish the Truth of Christian Religion* (London, 1688), reprinted in Watson's *Tracts*, I, 319. For Allix's tracing of the pattern of division by jealousy in Genesis, see pp. 252-63. Watson (p. v) notes that Allix's *Reflexions* was held in high repute, going through a number of translations and editions.

24. Abraham J. Heschel, *The Prophets* (1962; rpt. ed., New York: Harper Torchbooks, 1971), II, 218.

25. *Song of Songs Rabba*, iii.7, quoted in Evans, "*Paradise Lost*," p. 51.

26. John Skinner, *A Critical and Exegetical Commentary on Genesis* (New York: Scribner, 1910), p. 20.

27. See Jerome Rothenberg, ed., *Technicians of the Sacred: A Range*

of *Poetries from Africa, America, Asia, & Oceania* (Garden City, N.Y.: Doubleday, 1968), pp. 7, 385, 392-93.

28. Evans, "*Paradise Lost*," pp. 40, 94-95.

29. The book in the center, Urizen's book of brass, also appears in the design on plate 5 and is called, in Blake's inscription to that picture in the *Small Book of Designs*, "The Book of my Remembrance" (p. 662). This inscription has been identified as an allusion to Malachi 3:16 in Paul Miner, "Visions in the Darksom Air: Aspects of Blake's Biblical Symbolism," in *Essays for S. Foster Damon*, ed. Rosenfeld (Providence: Brown Univ. Press, 1969), p. 264. Malachi, in his prophecy of the Last Judgment, proclaims that God has drawn up "a book of remembrance" by which he will judge men in the future. The motif of the three books appears in Blake's illustration of "The Last Judgment" from Blair's *Grave* (1806) and in all of Blake's versions of *A Vision of the Last Judgment*. In his letter of February 1808 to Ozias Humphry (p. 543) and in his Notebook description of the painting (p. 551), Blake identifies the three books as the books of Life, Death, and Judgment.

30. Each of the figures in *The Book of Urizen* ironically inverts the meaning of its counterpart in Michelangelo's painting. The figures on plates 9, 15, and 24 are literally reversed, mirror images of their sources. The figure of Urizen on plate 9 and that of Grodna on plate 24 are derived from the knee-raising figure that is emerging from the grave on the bottom left side of *The Last Judgment*. The figure of Urizen is a more exact likeness, though his head is facing forward instead of to the right. The figure in Michelangelo is among the resurrected who are ascending to heaven. Rather than rising from the dead, Urizen has buried himself and has created death. Grodna's resurrection is an ascent into the fallen world rather than into heaven. The figure of the Eternal with the downward extending left arm on plate 15 is the reversed form of Michelangelo's figure of an angel on the left side of *The Last Judgment*. In Michelangelo the angel is lifting up one of the elect into heaven. In *Urizen* the Eternal is spreading the tent of Science, closing the fallen world off from Eternity. The falling figure on the right in plate 6 of Urizen is an inversion of the figure that the angel is lifting up. In his adaptation Blake makes the ecstatic expression of this figure appear ludicrous by changing the position of the arms to express the strokes of a swimmer. The "heaven" to which Urizen is ascending in such ecstasy is the world of matter, the "wide world of solid obstruction" (4:23). See my essay, "Transformations of Michelangelo in William Blake's *The Book of Urizen*," *Colby Library Quarterly* 16 (1980), 21-43.

31. S. H. Hooke, "Genesis," p. 175 [143a].

32. Ibid., p. 175 [143b].

CHAPTER IX: *The Book of Ahania*: Moses Fell and Asia Arose

1. Frye, in *Fearful Symmetry*, p. 214, observes, "When the Israelites got from the wilderness into the garden of God which had been promised them, the revolutionary vigor of their revolt against Egypt had collapsed, and all they got was another Egypt, from which imagination and desire were excluded as dangerous intruders. "

2. For a brief summary and bibliography of these findings, see John H. Hayes, *Introduction to the Bible* (Philadelphia: Westminster Press, 1971), pp. 88-95. Sandler shows that "it was all too evident in Blake's day that Judaism and Christianity throughout their history had been entangled in Canaanite ideas and practices" ("The Iconoclastic Enterprise," p. 55).

3. Milton, *An Apology for Smectymnuus*, in *Yale Milton*, I, 900.

4. See Judges 2:13, 10:6.

5. Joseph Priestley maintains that the period of time between Israel's settlement in Canaan and the decline of Israel was not quite five hundred years ("Observations on the Prophets of the Old Testament," in his *Theological Repository* [Birmingham: Joseph Johnson, 1784], IV, 119-20).

6. See Albert S. Roe, "The Thunder of Egypt," in *Essays for S. Foster Damon*, ed. Rosenfeld (Providence: Brown Univ. Press, 1969), pp. 159-63. In this rather thorough detailing of Blake's use of symbolism and imagery associated with Egypt, Roe does not include a discussion of the appearance of Egyptian themes in *Ahania*.

7. *The Life and Works of Flavius Josephus*, trans. William Whiston (1737; rpt. ed. Philadelphia: John C. Winston, n.d.), p. 78.

8. William Lowth, in his continuation of Patrick's *Commentary*, notes that the Bible uses the symbols of the dragon, the serpent, and leviathan interchangeably as "Instruments and types of Satan" (Patrick, *Commentary Upon the Old Testament*, IV, 53).

9. See Patrick, *Commentary Upon the Old Testament*, IV, 53; Henry, *Exposition of Old and New Testaments*, III, 244.

10. Exodus 4:21, 7:3, 9:12, 10:1, 10:20, 11:10, 14:4, 14:8, 14:17. The idea that God deliberately hardens Pharaoh's heart, so that He "might inflect greater punishments upon him," Humphreys finds to be "so extremely shocking to all right reason, and so utterly inconsistent with the graceful disposition of the mercifull creator of mankind, that we reject it with horror as a bold imputation on the divine attributes" (*The Sacred Books*, I, 162).

11. See Warburton, *The Divine Legation*, I, 193-94. *The Divine Legation*, as well as Pierre Jurieu's *Histoire critique des dogmes et des cultes* (1704), was influenced by the theories of the Egyptian origin of Hebrew

ceremonial law developed by John Spencer and John Marsham (see Allen, *Mysteriously Meant*, pp. 36-37).

12. The close association—often an exact identification—of the Tree of Knowledge and the cross was a popular Christian tradition that appears in the works of such writers as John Donne and Joseph Beaumont (Stewart, *The Enclosed Garden*, p. 75).

13. See, for example, Raine, *Blake and Tradition*, II. 35-36; Frye, *Fearful Symmetry*, p. 136.

14. See Exodus 34:13; Deuteronomy 7:5, 12:3, 16:21.

15. Bloom identifies the crucified Fuzon with the brazen serpent in *Blake's Apocalypse*, p. 193.

16. Sandler, "The Iconoclastic Enterprise," p. 55. Sandler also records the contribution of the *philosophes*, such as Dupuis and Boulanger, to this awareness of the Jewish and Christian inheritance of Canaanite beliefs and practices (p. 55).

17. Whiston, in a note to Josephus' paraphrase of Moses' farewell speech, maintains that Josephus epitomizes Moses' long oration with the sentence, "O children of Israel! there is but one source of happiness for all mankind, the favour of God." (*The Life and Works of Flavius Josephus*, p. 129).

18. See Henry, *Exposition of Old and New Testaments*, I, 453; Patrick, *Commentary Upon the Old Testament*, I, 836.

19. Fisher, *Valley of Vision*, p. 195; Bloom, *Blake's Apocalypse*, p. 195.

20. See Song of Solomon 2:8, 2:17, 6:11. Bloom mentions that the imagery of Ahania's lament is taken from The Song of Solomon (*Blake's Apocalypse*, p. 194), but he does not specify the particular images that Blake uses.

21. See also Deuteronomy 31:17-18, 32:20.

22. See also Deuteronomy 31:20.

23. Blake's pejorative association of the tabernacle of Exodus with the generative organs is detailed in Paul Miner, "William Blake's 'Divine Analogy,' " pp. 50-52.

24. The biblical basis of this tradition is Hebrews 8:5, which states that the priestly sacrifices were a "shadow of heavenly things." See Duché, *Discourses*, I, 25; Horsley, *Sermons*, p. 134.

25. Henley, in a note to Lowth, discusses Michaelis' observations on the resemblance between Psalm 19 and the myth of Aurora (*Sacred Poetry of the Hebrews*, I, 204-205, n. 22).

26. Samuel Sandmel, *The Hebrew Scriptures: An Introduction to Their Literature and Religious Ideas* (New York: Knopf, 1963), p. 393; *The Life and Works of Flavius Josephus*, p. 131.

27. See Erich Auerbach, *Mimesis: The Representation of Reality in Western Literature*, trans. Willard R. Trask (Princeton: Princeton Univ. Press, 1953), pp. 3-7. For my discussion of the form of *Ahania*, I am indebted to the first chapter of Auerbach (pp. 3-23).

NOTES

CHAPTER X: *The Book of Los*: Los Agonistes

1. Frye, *Fearful Symmetry*, p. 254.
2. Voltaire, *Philosophical Dictionary*, trans. Peter Gay, 2 vols. (New York: Basic Books, 1962), I, 286.
3. Arnold Williams, *The Common Expositor, An Account of the Commentaries on Genesis, 1527-1633* (Chapel Hill: Univ. of North Carolina Press, 1948), p. 53.
4. See *Paradise Lost* III.1-12, VII.243-52 and n.; Williams, *The Common Expositor*; pp. 52-53; Don Cameron Allen, *The Harmonious Vision: Studies in Milton's Poetry*, enl. ed. (Baltimore and London: Johns Hopkins Univ. Press, 1970), pp. 100-102.
5. See Williams, *The Common Expositor*, p. 53; Kester Svendson, *Milton and Science* (Cambridge, Mass.: Harvard Univ. Press, 1965), p. 64.
6. Williams, *The Common Expositor*, p. 53.
7. Donald D. Ault, *Visionary Physics: Blake's Response to Newton* (Chicago: Univ. of Chicago Press, 1974), p. 152.
8. Allen, *Harmonious Vision*, p. 102.
9. For this pairing of vices with their contrary virtues, see Chaucer's "Parson's Tale," in F. N. Robinson, ed., *The Works of Geoffrey Chaucer*, 2nd ed. (Boston: Houghton Mifflin, 1957), pp. 242-49, 251-54, 255-60; Dante's *Purgatorio*, XIII (Envy and *Caritas*), XVI (Meekness and Wrath), XX (Avarice and Generosity), XXV (Lust and Chastity); and Morton Bloomfield, *The Seven Deadly Sins* (1952; rpt. ed., East Lansing: Michigan State Univ. Press, 1967), p. 67 and passim.
10. For a discussion of the significance of melancholy adust in humors psychology, see Lily B. Campbell, *Shakespeare's Tragic Heroes, Slaves of Passion* (1930; rpt. ed., New York: Barnes and Noble, 1968), pp. 73-78; Lawrence Babb, "The Background of 'Il Penseroso,'" *Studies in Philology* 37 (1940), 257-60, 266, 272, n. 72.
11. This allegory is mentioned in the third of Voltaire's *Homelies prononcées à Londres en 1765* (Schwartzbach, *Voltaire's Old Testament Criticism*, p. 173). In Eno's song, however, Blake does not follow Philo's interpretation exactly, since the virtues that Eno alludes to are not the four cardinal virtues (prudence, temperance, fortitude, and justice).
12. Evans, *"Parade Lost,"* p. 64.
13. See Humphreys, *The Sacred Books*, I, 679; Patrick, *Commentary Upon the Old Testament*, II, 89; Barbara K. Lewalski, "*Samson Agonistes* and the 'Tragedy' of the Apocalypse," *PMLA* 85 (Oct. 1970), 1056-57.
14. Lewalski, "*Samson Agonistes* and Apocalypse," p. 1052. My discussion of the apocalyptic significance of Samson, as it was delineated in Protestant exegesis, is drawn from Lewalski's account of this tradition.

15. Ibid., p. 1051.

16. Ibid., p. 1052.

17. Matthew Henry interprets Samson's pulling down of Dagon's temple as a type of Christ's destruction of the devil's kingdom (*Exposition of the Old and New Testaments*, II, 103). Humphreys interprets the Philistines as "the declared enemies of the Church of God" (*The Sacred Books*, I, 738).

18. Lewalski, "*Samson Agonistes* and Apocalypse," p. 1061.

19. Ibid., p. 1062.

20. See Isaiah 11:6, 65:25.

21. Edward Young, *The Complaint: or, Night Thoughts on Life, Death and Immortality* (London: R. Dodsley, 1742-1745), "Night the Ninth." This quotation is taken from the page of that edition (p. 119) that is inlaid, with line numbers cut away, on the drawing paper of Illustration 537 of Blake's watercolor designs to *Night Thoughts*, which are in the Print Room of the British Museum. The design and text are reproduced in Wittreich, *Angel of Apocalypse*, pl. 22; and Thomas H. Helmstadter, "Blake and Religion: Iconographical Themes in *Night Thoughts*," *Studies in Romanticism* 10 (Spring 1971), 199-212.

22. Morton D. Paley, "Blake's *Night Thoughts*: An Exploration of the Fallen World," in *Essays for S. Foster Damon*, ed. Rosenfeld (Providence: Brown Univ. Press, 1969), p. 145.

23. F. Michael Krouse, *Milton's Samson and the Christian Tradition* (1949; rpt. ed., New York: Octagon, 1974), p. 43.

24. Among the commentaries published in the eighteenth century that explain the etymology of Samson's name are Patrick (*Commentary Upon the Old Testament*, II, 154), Henry (*Exposition of the Old and New Testaments*, II, 103) and Humphreys (*The Sacred Books*, I, 726).

25. Milton, *The Reason of Church Government*, in *Yale Milton*, I, 859.

26. Barbara Carson, "Milton's Samson as *Parvus Sol*," *English Language Notes* 5 (March 1968), p. 174. The solar mythology and imagery in *Samson Agonistes* is also discussed at length in Kenneth Fell, "From Myth to Martyrdom: Towards a View of Milton's *Samson Agonistes*," *English Studies* 34 (1953), 145-55.

27. Northrop Frye, "Agon and Logos: Revolution and Revelation," in *The Prison and the Pinnacle: Papers to Commemorate the Tercentenary of "Paradise Regained" and "Samson Agonistes" 1671-1971*, ed. Balachandra Rajan (Toronto: Univ. of Toronto Press, 1973), p. 145.

28. Fell, "From Myth to Martyrdom," p. 146, recapitulates these points from A. Smythe Palmer, *The Samson Saga and Its Place in Comparative Religion* (London: I. Pitman, 1913).

29. John Gray, ed., *Joshua, Judges and Ruth* [*The Century Bible*, new ed.] (London: Nelson, 1967), p. 234; see also George Foot Moore,

A Critical and Exegetical Commentary on Judges [*The International Critical Commentary*] (New York: Scribner, 1901), p. 365.

30. Henry, *Exposition of the Old and New Testaments*, II, 108.

31. See Helmstadter, "Blake and Religion," pp. 211-12.

32. Gray, *Joshua, Judges, and Ruth*, p. 233, emphasizes that "Samson did not liberate Israel from the Philistine forty years' oppression (13:1) which lasted for twenty years after his death (15:20, 16:31), when the Philistines were very much in the ascendant, and continued so throughout the time of Saul until David finally broke their power in the interior and confined them strictly to the coastal plain after his victory at Baal-perazim by Jerusalem." Matthew Henry makes the same point (*Exposition of the Old and New Testaments*, II, 101).

33. See Lewalski, "*Samson Agonistes* and Apocalypse," pp. 1059-60.

34. Milton, *The Reason of Church Government*, in *Yale Milton*, I, 858-59.

35. Sandys, in a note to Book VIII of Ovid's *Metamorphoses*, observed that Samson and Hercules are "supposed by some to be the same man" (p. 435). Similarly, Krouse notes the widespread linking of the two heroes in the patristic period and the Renaissance (*Milton's Samson and the Christian Tradition*, pp. 44-45, 78), observing that in the exegetical, homiletic, and literary works of both periods few writers mentioned one hero without being reminded of the other. In Blake's time the similarities between these two heroes were even discussed in biblical commentaries (Patrick, *Commentary Upon the Old Testament*, II, 165; Clarke, *The Holy Bible*, II [notes to Judges 16]). For examples of modern discussion of the relationship of Samson to Hercules, see Moore, *Commentary on Judges*, pp. 364-65 (which includes a bibliography) and C. F. Burney, ed., *The Book of Judges, with Introduction and Notes* (1903; rpt. ed. [with *Notes on the Hebrew Text of the Books of Kings*], New York: Ktav, 1970), p. 391.

36. See Krouse, *Milton's Samson*, pp. 44, 78; and Burney, *Book of Judges*, p. 391.

37. See Moore, *Commentary on Judges*, pp. 364-65; and Krouse, *Milton's Samson*, pp. 44-45. Anthony Low traces the parallels between Milton's Samson and the Hercules of classical drama in *The Blaze of Noon, a Reading of Samson Agonistes* (New York and London: Columbia Univ. Press, 1974), pp. 176-79.

38. See Eugene M. Waith, *The Herculean Hero in Marlowe, Chapman, Shakespeare and Dryden* (New York: Columbia Univ. Press; London: Chatto and Windus 1962), pp. 44-45, 206 n. 18; and Raymond B. Waddington, "Melancholy Against Melancholy: *Samson Agonistes* as Renaissance Tragedy," in *Calm of Mind: Tercentenary Essays on Paradise Regained and Samson Agonistes in Honor of John S. Diekhoff*, ed. Joseph Anthony Wittreich, Jr. (Cleveland and London: Press of Case Western Univ., 1971), p. 279.

39. Ovid, *Metamorphoses*, trans. Sandys, p. 440; Sandys notes the traditional association of Samson and Hercules on p. 435.

40. Patrick, *Commentary Upon the Old Testament*, II, 165.

41. Gray, *Joshua, Judges, and Ruth*, p. 234. See also Moore, *Commentary on Judges*, pp. 364-65; and Burney, *Book of Judges*, p. 391.

42. Skinner, *Commentary on Genesis*, pp. 41-47. For a translation of the Babylonian *Enuma Elish* tablets and other texts containing cognate creation myths, see James B. Pritchard, ed., *Ancient Near Eastern Texts Relating to the Old Testament* (Princeton: Princeton Univ. Press, 1955), esp. pp. 6-7, 11-12 and 60-72.

43. Job 7:12, 26:12-13; Isaiah 27:1, 51:9-10; and Ezekiel 29:3, 32:2 have been cited for containing traces of this tradition. See Skinner, *Commentary on Genesis*, p. 48; and Evans, *Paradise Lost*, p. 12.

44. Bratton, *History of the Bible*, p. 26; Skinner, *Commentary on Genesis*, p. 41.

45. Skinner, *Commentary on Genesis*, p. 41.

46. Evans, "*Paradise Lost*," pp. 12-13.

47. Milton, *The Reason of Church Government*, in *Yale Milton*, I, 857-59.

48. See Todd, "Blake and Eighteenth-Century Mythologists," pp. 29-60; Hungerford, *Shores of Darkness*, esp. pp. 35-61.

49. Bryant, *A New System*, I, xlii, 2.

50. Ibid., p. 14.

51. Bryant, *A New System*, IV, 130-33; he identifies Hercules as a solar deity in I, 47.

52. The interpretation of Hercules as a solar hero whose twelve labors represent the sun's journey through the twelve signs of the zodiac is advanced in Charles Dupuis, *Origine de tous les cultes, ou religion universelle*, 7 vols. (Paris, 1795). (See the English translation of Dupuis' epitome of this work, *The Origin of all religious worship* [New Orleans, 1872], pp. 86-98. These pages are reprinted in Feldman and Richardson, *Modern Mythology*, pp. 280-86.) The idea goes back as far as Porphyry, however, as Sandys points out in his notes to his translation of Ovid's *Metamorphoses* (p. 440).

53. Bryant, *A New System*, I, 73.

54. Bryant, *A New System*, VI, 117-18, 120.

55. Lucian, *Hermotimus*, 20, in *Lucian: Selected Works*, trans. Bryan P. Reardon, The Library of Liberal Arts (New York: Bobbs-Merrill, 1965), pp. 123-24.

56. Ovid, *Metamorphoses*, trans. Sandys, p. 203; Bryant, *A New System*, I, 174.

57. W. H. Stevenson, note to *The Book of Los* 4:81, in *The Poems of William Blake*, ed. Stevenson (London: Longmans, 1971; and New York: Norton, 1972), p. 282.

58. See Ovid, *Metamorphoses*, trans. Sandys, IV. 169-87 (p. 176).

59. See my essay, "Transformations of Michelangelo in William Blake's *The Book of Urizen*," pp. 43-48.

60. John Lemprière, *Classical Dictionary of Proper Names mentioned in Ancient Authors*, rev. and enl. F. A. Wright (London: Routledge and Kegan Paul, 1949), p. 665 (*s.v.* "Vulcanus"). Lemprière's *Dictionary* was first published in 1788.

61. See Erdman, *Prophet Against Empire*, pp. 283-87.

62. See Paley, *Energy and the Imagination*, pp. 61-88; E. J. Rose, "Goodbye to Orc and All That," *Blake Studies* 4 (Spring 1972), 135-51.

Bibliography

Abbey, Charles J., and John H. Overton. *The English Church in the Eighteenth Century.* 2 vols. London: Longmans, 1878.

Abrams, M. H. *The Mirror and the Lamp: Romantic Theory and the Critical Tradition.* 1953. Reprint. New York: Norton, 1958.

———. *Natural Supernaturalism: Tradition and Revolution in Romantic Literature.* New York: Norton, 1971.

Allen, Don Cameron. *The Harmonious Vision: Studies in Milton's Poetry.* Enl. ed. Baltimore and London: Johns Hopkins Univ. Press, 1970.

———. *Mysteriously Meant: The Rediscovery of Pagan Symbolism and Allegorical Interpretation in the Renaissance.* Baltimore: Johns Hopkins Univ. Press, 1970.

Allentuck, Marcia. "Henry Fuseli and J. G. Herder's *Ideen zur Philosophie der Geschichte der Menschheit*: An Unremarked Connection." *Journal of the History of Ideas* 35 (1974), 113-20.

Allix, Peter. *Reflexions upon the Books of the Holy Scripture, to establish the Truth of Christian Religion.* 1688. Reprint in *A Collection of Theological Tracts,* ed. Richard Watson. London, 1791. I, 217-504.

Altick, Richard D. *The English Common Reader: A Social History of the Mass Reading Public, 1800-1900.* Chicago: Univ. of Chicago Press, 1957.

———. *The Shows of London.* Cambridge, Mass.: Harvard Univ. Press, 1978.

Auerbach, Erich. "Figura." In his *Scenes from the Drama of European Literature.* 1959. Reprint. Gloucester, Mass.: Peter Smith, 1973.

Auerbach, Erich. *Literary Language and Its Public in Late Latin Antiquity and in the Middle Ages*, trans. Ralph Manheim. Bollingen Series 74. New York: Pantheon, 1965.

———. *Mimesis: The Representation of Reality in Western Literature*, trans. Willard R. Trask. Princeton: Princeton Univ. Press, 1953.

Augustine, St. *On Christian Doctrine*, trans. D. W. Robertson, Jr. New York: Library of Liberal Arts, 1958.

Ault, Donald. *Visionary Physics: Blake's Response to Newton*. Chicago: Univ. of Chicago Press, 1974.

Babb, Lawrence. "The Background of 'Il Penseroso.'" *Studies in Philology* 37 (1940), 257-73.

Baker, C. H. Collins. *Catalogue of William Blake's Drawings and Paintings in the Huntington Library*, enl. and rev. R. R. Wark. San Marino, Calif.: Huntington Library, 1957.

Barker, Arthur E. "The Pattern of Milton's *Nativity Ode*." *University of Toronto Quarterly* 10 (1941), 167-81.

Beer, John B. "Blake and Augustine." *TLS*, 2 July 1970, pp. 726-27.

———. *Blake's Humanism*. Manchester: Manchester Univ. Press; New York: Barnes and Noble, 1968.

Bengel, John Albert [Johann Albrecht]. *Gnomon of the New Testament*, trans. Charlton T. Lewis and Marvin R. Vincent. 2 vols. Philadelphia and New York, 1864.

Bentley, G. E., Jr. *Blake Books*. Oxford: Clarendon Press, 1977.

———. *Blake Records*. Oxford: Clarendon Press, 1969.

———. "A Jewel in an Ethiop's Ear: The Book of Enoch as Inspiration for William Blake, John Flaxman, Thomas Moore, and Richard Westall." In *Blake in His Time*, ed. Robert N. Essick and Donald Pearce. Bloomington: Indiana Univ. Press, 1978, pp. 213-40.

———, ed. *William Blake: The Critical Heritage*. London: Routledge and Kegan Paul, 1975.

———, and Martin K. Nurmi. *A Blake Bibliography*. Minneapolis: Univ. of Minnesota Press, 1964.

Bercovitch, Sacvan, ed. *Typology and Early American Literature*. Amherst: Univ. of Massachusetts Press, 1972.

Berkeley, David Shelley. *Inwrought with Figures Dim: A Reading of Milton's "Lycidas."* The Hague: Mouton, 1974.

Berry, Boyd. *Process of Speech: Puritan Religious Writing and Paradise Lost*. Baltimore: Johns Hopkins Univ. Press, 1976.

Bicheno, James. *The Signs of the Times: or The Overthrow of the Papal Tyranny in France*. London, 1799.

Black, M. H. "The Printed Bible." In *The Cambridge History of the Bible*, Vol. III, *The West from the Reformation to the Present Day*, ed. S. L. Greenslade. Cambridge: Cambridge Univ. Press, 1963, pp. 408-75.

Blackwell, Thomas. *Letters concerning Mythology*. London, 1748.

Blair, Hugh. *Lectures on Rhetoric and Belles Lettres*, ed. Harold F. Harding. Vol. II. 1783. Reprint. Carbondale, Ill.: Southern Illinois Univ. Press, 1965.

Blake, William. *The Illuminated Blake*, ed. David V. Erdman. Garden City, N.Y.: Doubleday, 1974.

———. *The Letters of William Blake*, ed. Geoffrey Keynes. Cambridge, Mass.: Harvard Univ. Press, 1968.

———. *The Poems of William Blake*, ed. W. H. Stevenson. London: Longmans, 1971; New York: Norton, 1972.

———. *The Poetry and Prose of William Blake*, ed. David V. Erdman. Rev. ed. Garden City, N.Y.: Doubleday, 1970.

Bland, John. *A Grammatical Version from the Original Hebrew of the Song of Solomon, Into Blank Verse*. 1750. Reprint. New York: Readex Microprint [Three Centuries of Drama: English, 1751-1800], 1954.

Blayney, Benjamin, trans. *Jeremiah, and Lamentations: A New Translation, with Notes, Critical, Philological, and Explanatory*. Oxford, 1784.

Bloom, Harold. *Blake's Apocalypse: A Study in Poetic Argument*. 1963. Reprint. New York: Anchor-Doubleday, 1965.

Bloom, Harold. "The Visionary Cinema of Romantic Poetry." In *William Blake: Essays for S. Foster Damon*, ed. Alvin Rosenfeld, Providence: Brown Univ. Press, 1969, pp. 18-35.

Bloomfield, Morton W. *The Seven Deadly Sins*. 1952. Reprint. East Lansing: Michigan State Univ. Press, 1967.

Blunt, Anthony. *The Art of William Blake*. 1959. Reprint. New York: Harper and Row, 1974.

Boehme, Jacob. *The Works of Jacob Behmen, the Teutonic Philosopher*, ed. G. Ward and T. Langcake. 4 vols. London, 1764-1781.

Bonner, Gerald. "Augustine as Biblical Scholar." In *The Cambridge History of the Bible*, Vol. I, *From the Beginnings to Jerome*, ed. P. R. Ackroyd and C. F. Evans. Cambridge: Cambridge Univ. Press, 1970, pp. 541-63.

Bratton, Fred Gladstone. *A History of the Bible: An Introduction to the Historical Method*. Boston: Beacon Press, 1967.

Brightman, Thomas. *A Commentary on the Canticles*. Amsterdam, 1644.

Brooks, Cleanth, and John E. Hardy, eds. *Poems of Mr. John Milton: The 1645 Edition with Essays in Analysis*. New York: Harcourt, Brace, 1951.

Brown, John. *A Dictionary of the Holy Bible, on the Plan of Calmet, but Principally Adapted to Common Readers*. 2 vols. London, 1769.

Brumm, Ursula. *American Thought and Religious Typology*, trans. John Hoaglund. New Brunswick, N.J.: Rutgers Univ. Press, 1970.

Bryant, Jacob. *A New System: or an Analysis of Ancient Mythology*. 3rd ed. 6 vols. London, 1807.

Burney, C. F., ed. *The Book of Judges, with Introduction and Notes*. 1903. Reprint [with *Notes on the Hebrew Text of the Books of Kings*]. New York: Ktav, 1970.

Bush, Douglas. *Pagan Myth and Christian Tradition in English Poetry*: Jayne Lectures for 1967. Philadelphia: American Philosophical Society, 1968.

Butlin, Martin. *William Blake, A Complete Catalogue of the Works in the Tate Gallery.* Rev. ed. London: Tate Gallery, 1971.

Byron, George Gordon, Lord. *The Works of Lord Byron: Poetry,* ed. E. H. Coleridge. Vol. V. London: John Murray, 1898-1904.

Calmet, Dom Augustine. *Commentaire Littéral sur tous les livres de l'Ancien et du Nouveau Testament.* 9 vols. Paris, 1719-1726.

———. *Dictionnaire Historique, Chronologique, Géographique, et Littéral de la Bible.* Paris, 1730.

Campbell, Lily B. *Divine Poetry and Drama in Sixteenth-Century England.* Cambridge: Cambridge Univ. Press; Berkeley and Los Angeles: Univ. of California Press, 1961.

———. *Shakespeare's Tragic Heroes, Slaves of Passion.* 1930. Reprint. New York: Barnes and Noble, 1968.

Carson, Barbara. "Milton's Samson as *Parvus Sol.*" *English Language Notes* 5 (March 1968), 171-76.

Chard, Leslie F. "Bookseller to Publisher: Joseph Johnson and the English Book Trade, 1760 to 1810." *The Library,* 5th series, 32 (1977), 138-54.

———. "Joseph Johnson: Father of the Book Trade." *BNYPL* 79 (1975), 51-82.

Charity, A. C. *Events and Their Afterlife: The Dialectics of Christian Typology in the Bible and Dante.* Cambridge: Cambridge Univ. Press, 1966.

Charles, R. H., ed. *The Book of Enoch.* In *The Apocrypha and Pseudepigrapha of the Old Testament,* ed. R. H. Charles. Vol. II. Oxford: Clarendon Press, 1912, pp. 163-277.

Chaucer, Geoffrey. *The Works of Geoffrey Chaucer,* ed. F. N. Robinson. 2nd ed. Boston: Houghton Mifflin, 1957.

Chew, Samuel C. *The Virtues Reconciled, An Iconographic Study.* Toronto: Univ. of Toronto Press, 1947.

Clarke, Adam, ed. *The Holy Bible.* 3rd American ed. 6 vols. New York, 1820.

Cocke, Richard, ed. *The Complete Paintings of Raphael.* New York: Abrams, 1966.

Cohen, Ralph. *The Art of Discrimination: Thomson's The Seasons and the Language of Criticism.* London: Routledge and Kegan Paul, 1964.

Coke, Thomas. *A Commentary on the Holy Bible.* 6 vols. London, 1801-1803.

Colish, Marcia L. *The Mirror of Language: A Study in the Medieval Theory of Knowledge.* Yale Historical Publications Miscellany, 881. New Haven: Yale Univ. Press, 1968.

Collins, Anthony. *A Discourse of the Grounds and Reasons of Christianity.* 1724. Reprint. New York: Garland, 1976.

Cotton, John. *A Brief Exposition of the Whole Book of Canticles.* London, 1648.

Curran, Stuart. "Blake and the Gnostic Hyle: A Double Negative." *Blake Studies* 4 (1972), 117-33.

———, and Joseph Anthony Wittreich, Jr., eds. *Blake's Sublime Allegory: Essays on The Four Zoas, Milton, Jerusalem.* Madison: Univ. of Wisconsin Press, 1973.

Curtis, F. B. "Blake and the Booksellers." *Blake Studies* 6 (1975), 167-78.

———. "The Geddes Bible and the Tent of the Eternals in *The Book of Urizen.*" *Blake Newsletter* 6 (1973), 93-94.

Damon, S. Foster. *A Blake Dictionary: The Ideas and Symbols of William Blake.* 1965. Reprint. New York: Dutton, 1971.

———. *William Blake: His Philosophy and Symbols.* 1924. Reprint. London: Dawsons, 1969.

Daniélou, Jean. *The Bible and the Liturgy.* Notre Dame, Ind.: Univ. of Notre Dame Press, 1956.

Daubuz, Charles. *A Perpetual Commentary on the Revelation of St. John.* London, 1720.

Davies, Horton. *Worship and Theology in England from Watts and Wesley to Maurice, 1690-1850.* Princeton: Princeton Univ. Press, 1961.

342

Davies, J. G. *The Theology of William Blake*. 1948. Reprint. Hamden, Conn.: Archon, 1966.

Davis, Thomas M. "The Traditions of Puritan Typology." In *Typology and Early American Literature*, ed. Sacvan Bercovitch. Amherst: Univ. of Massachusetts Press, 1972, pp. 11-45.

Dieckmann, Liselotte. *Hieroglyphics: The History of a Literary Symbol*. St. Louis, Mo.: Washington Univ. Press, 1970.

Dodd, William. *A Commentary on the Books of the Old and New Testaments*. 3 vols. London, 1770.

Doddridge, Philip. *The Family Expositor: or, A Paraphrase and Version of the New Testament*. 6 vols. London, 1792.

Downey, James. *The Eighteenth-Century Pulpit, A Study of Butler, Berkeley, Secker, Sterne, Whitefield and Wesley*. Oxford: Clarendon Press, 1969.

Downing, Richard. "Blake and Augustine." *TLS*, 18 June 1970, p. 662.

Duché, Jacob. *Discourses on Various Subjects*. 3rd ed. 2 vols. London, 1790.

Dupuis, Charles. *The Origin of all religious worship*. New Orleans, La., 1872.

Elliott, Emory. "From Father to Son: The Evolution of Typology in Puritan New England." In *Literary Uses of Typology*, ed. Earl Miner. Princeton: Princeton University Press, 1977, pp. 204-27.

Ellis, E. Earle. *Paul's Use of the Old Testament*. London: Oliver and Boyd, 1957.

Ellis, Edwin John, and William Butler Yeats, eds. *The Works of William Blake, Poetical, Symbolic, and Critical* 3 vols. London, 1893.

Erdman, David V. "*America*: New Expanses." In *Blake's Visionary Forms Dramatic*, ed. David V. Erdman and John E. Grant. Princeton: Princeton Univ. Press, 1970, pp. 92-114.

———. *Blake: Prophet Against Empire*. Rev. ed. Garden City, N.Y.: Anchor-Doubleday, 1969.

Erdman, David V. and John E. Grant, eds. *Blake's Visionary Forms Dramatic.* Princeton: Princeton Univ. Press, 1970.

Essick, Robert N. "Blake and the Traditions of Reproductive Engraving." *Blake Studies* 5 (1972), 59-103.

————, and Donald Pearce, eds. *Blake in His Time.* Bloomington: Indiana Univ. Press, 1978.

Evans, J. M. *"Paradise Lost" and the Genesis Tradition.* Oxford: Clarendon Press, 1968.

Faber, George Stanley. *A Dissertation on the Prophecies that Have Been Fulfilled, Are Now Fulfilling, or Hereafter Will Be Fulfilled.* 3 vols. London, 1818.

Farrar, Frederic. *A History of Interpretation.* London: Macmillan, 1886.

Farrer, Austin. *The Glass of Vision, Bampton Lectures for 1948.* Westminster: Dacre Press, 1948.

Feldman, Burton, and Robert D. Richardson. *The Rise of Modern Mythology, 1680-1860.* Bloomington: Indiana Univ. Press, 1972.

Fell, Kenneth. "From Myth to Martyrdom: Towards a View of Milton's *Samson Agonistes.*" *English Studies* 34 (1953), 145-55.

Fénelon, François de Salignac de la Mothe. *Dialogues on Eloquence in General,* trans. William Stevenson. New ed., rev. and corrected. London, 1808.

Fisch, Harold. *Jerusalem and Albion: The Hebraic Factor in Seventeenth-Century Literature.* New York: Schocken, 1964.

Fisher, Peter F. "Blake and the Druids." *JEGP* 58 (1959), 589-612. Reprinted in *Blake: A Collection of Critical Essays,* ed. Northrop Frye. Englewood Cliffs, N.J.: Prentice-Hall, 1966, pp. 156-78.

————. "Blake's Attacks on the Classical Tradition." *Philological Quarterly* 40 (January 1961), 1-18.

————. *The Valley of Vision: Blake as Prophet and Revolutionary,* ed. Northrop Frye. Toronto: Univ. of Toronto Press, 1961.

Fixler, Michael. "The Apocalypse within *Paradise Lost*." In *New Essays on Paradise Lost*, ed. Thomas Kranidas. Berkeley: Univ. of California Press, 1971, pp. 131-78.

Fox, Susan. *Poetic Form in Blake's Milton*. Princeton: Princeton Univ. Press, 1976.

Frei, Hans. *The Eclipse of Biblical Narrative: A Study in Eighteenth and Nineteenth Century Hermeneutics*. New Haven: Yale Univ. Press, 1974.

Freimarck, Vincent. "The Bible and Neo-Classical Views of Style." *JEGP* 51 (1952), 507-26.

Froom, Le Roy. *The Prophetic Faith of Our Fathers*. Vols. II and IV. Washington, D.C.: Review and Herald, 1946-1954.

Frye, Northrop. "Agon and Logos: Revolution and Revelation." In *The Prison and the Pinnacle: Papers to Commemorate the Tercentenary of "Paradise Regained" and "Samson Agonistes" 1671-1971*, ed. Balachandra Rajan. Toronto: Univ. of Toronto Press, 1973, pp. 135-63.

———. *Fearful Symmetry: A Study of William Blake*. Princeton: Princeton Univ. Press, 1947.

———. "The Typology of *Paradise Regained*." *Modern Philology* 53 (1956), 227-38. Reprinted in *Milton: Modern Essays in Criticism*, ed. Arthur E. Barker. New York: Oxford Univ. Press, 1965, pp. 429-46.

Galdon, Joseph A. *Typology and Seventeenth-Century Literature*. The Hague: Mouton, 1975.

Garrett, Clarke. *Respectable Folly: Millenarians and the French Revolution in France and England*. Baltimore: Johns Hopkins Univ. Press, 1975.

Geddes, Alexander, trans. *The Holy Bible, or the Books Accounted Sacred, Otherwise Called the Books of the Old and New Covenants*. London, 1792 (Vol. I) and 1797 (Vol. II).

———. *Prospectus to a New Translation of the Bible*. Glasgow, 1786.

Gilbert, George Holley. *Interpretation of the Bible: A Short History*. New York: Macmillan, 1908.

345

Gilchrist, Alexander. *Life of William Blake*, ed. W. Graham Robertson. London: Bodley Head, 1906.

Gill, John. *An Exposition of the Old Testament*. 6 vols. 1748-1763. Reprinted Philadelphia, 1818.

Ginsburg, Christian D. *The Song of Songs and Coheleth*. First published separately, 1857 and 1861. Reprint. New York: Ktav, 1970.

Good, John Mason. *Memoirs of the Life and Writings of Alexander Geddes*. London, 1803.

Gray, John, ed. *Joshua, Judges and Ruth. The New Century Bible*. New ed. London: Nelson, 1967.

Greenslade, S. L., ed. *The Cambridge History of the Bible*, Vol. III, *The West from the Reformation to the Present Day*. Cambridge: Cambridge Univ. Press, 1963.

Hagstrum, Jean. "Blake and the Sister-Arts Tradition." In *Blake's Visionary Forms Dramatic*, ed. David V. Erdman and Jóhn E. Grant. Princeton: Princeton Univ. Press, 1970, pp. 82-91.

———. "Christ's Body." In *William Blake: Essays in Honour of Sir Geoffrey Keynes*, ed. Morton D. Paley and Michael Philips. Oxford: Clarendon Press, 1973, pp. 129-56.

———. *The Sister Arts: The Tradition of Literary Pictorialism and English Poetry from Dryden to Gray*. Chicago: Univ. of Chicago Press, 1958.

———. *William Blake: Poet and Painter: An Introduction to the Illuminated Verse*. Chicago: Univ. of Chicago Press, 1964.

Halliburton, David G. "Blake's French Revolution: The *Figura* and Yesterday's News." *Studies in Romanticism* 5 (Summer 1966), 158-68.

Hammond, Henry. *A Paraphrase and Annotations Upon All the Books of the New Testament*. London, 1681.

Hanford, James Holly. "The Youth of Milton, An Interpretation of His Early Development." In his *Studies in Shakespeare, Milton, and Donne*. New York: Macmillan, 1925, pp. 89-163.

Harris, Victor. "Allegory to Analogy in the Interpretation of Scriptures." *Philological Quarterly* 45 (Jan. 1966), 1-23.

Havens, Raymond Dexter. *The Influence of Milton on English Poetry.* 1922. Reprint. New York: Russell and Russell, 1961.

Hayes, John H. *Introduction to the Bible.* Philadelphia: Westminster Press, 1971.

Helmstadter, Thomas H. "Blake and Religion: Iconographical Themes in *Night Thoughts.*" *Studies in Romanticism* 10 (Spring 1971), 199-212.

Henry, Matthew. *An Exposition of the Old and New Testaments.* 7th ed. 6 vols. in 5. Edinburgh, 1767.

Heschel, Abraham J. *The Prophets.* 2 vols. 1962. Reprint. New York: Harper Torchbooks, 1971.

Hill, Christopher. *Milton and the English Revolution.* New York: Viking, 1978.

Hirst, Désirée. *Hidden Riches: Traditional Symbolism from the Renaissance to Blake.* London: Eyre and Spottiswoode, 1964.

Hooke, S. H. "Genesis." In *Peake's Commentary on the Bible,* ed. Matthew Black and H. H. Rowley. London: Nelson, 1962.

Horne, George. *A Commentary on the Book of Psalms.* Oxford, 1771.

Horne, Thomas Hartwell. "Bibliographical Appendix." In his *An Introduction to the Critical Study and Knowledge of the Holy Scriptures.* Vol. II. New ed. from the 8th London ed., rev. and enl. New York: Robert Carter, 1848.

Horsley, Samuel. *Biblical Criticism on the First Fourteen Historical Books of the Old Testament; Also on the First Nine Prophetical Books.* 2nd ed. 2 vols. London, 1844.

———. *The Book of Psalms, Translated from the Hebrew, with Notes Explanatory and Critical.* London, 1815.

———. *Critical Disquisitions on the Eighteenth Chapter of*

Isaiah in a Letter to Edward King, Esq. 1799. Reprint. Philadelphia, 1800.

————. *Sermons.* 2nd ed. London, 1811.

Howell, Wilbur Samuel. *Eighteenth-Century British Logic and Rhetoric.* Princeton: Princeton Univ. Press, 1971.

Howes, Thomas. "Doubts Concerning the Translation and Notes of the Bishop of London to Isaiah, Vindicating Ezekiel, Isaiah, and other Jewish Prophets from Disorder in Arrangement." In his *Critical Observations on Books, Antient and Modern.* Vol. II. 1776-1813. Reprint. New York: Garland, 1972, pp. 109-449.

Hume, Patrick. *Annotations to Milton's Paradise Lost.* London, 1695.

Humphreys, Samuel. *The Sacred Books of the Old and New Testament . . . with Critical and Explanatory Annotations, Carefully Compiled from the Commentaries and Other Writings of Grotius, Lightfoot, Pool, Calmet, Patrick, Le Clerc, Lock, Burkitt, Henry, Pearce.* 3 vols. London, 1735-1739.

Hungerford, Edward B. *Shores of Darkness.* 1941. Reprint. Cleveland: Meridian-World, 1963.

Hurd, Richard. *An Introduction to the Study of the Prophecies Concerning the Christian Church.* 2nd ed. Warburtonian Lectures, No. 1. London, 1772.

Husbands, John. Preface to his *A Miscellany of Poems by Several Hands.* Oxford, 1731.

Hutin, Serge. *Les Disciples Anglais de Jacob Boehme aux XVIIe et XVIIIe siècles.* Paris: Editions Denoel, 1960.

Irwin, David. *English Neoclassical Art: Studies in Inspiration and Taste.* Greenwich, Conn.: New York Graphic Society, 1966.

Jastrow, Morris, trans. *The Song of Songs.* Philadelphia and London: Lippincott, 1921.

Johnson, Samuel. "Life of Milton." In his *The Lives of the Most Eminent English Poets; with Critical Observations of Their Works.* Vol. I. London, 1781, pp. 123-268.

Jones, William. *A Course of Lectures on the Figurative Language of Scriptures.* In his *Theological and Miscellaneous Works.* Vol. III. London, 1826.

Jortin, John. *Remarks on Ecclesiastical History.* 5 vols. London, 1751.

Josephus, Flavius. *The Life and Works of Flavius Josephus,* trans. William Whiston. 1737. Reprint. Philadelphia: John C. Winston, n.d.

Keller, Karl. "Alephs, Zahirs, and the Triumph of Ambiguity: Typology in Nineteenth-Century American Literature." In *Literary Uses of Typology,* ed. Earl Miner. Princeton: Princeton Univ. Press, 1977, pp. 274-315.

Kermode, Frank. "Deciphering the Big Book." *The New York Review of Books,* 29 June 1978, pp. 39-42.

————. *The Sense of an Ending: Studies in the Theory of Fiction.* New York: Oxford Univ. Press, 1967.

Kerrigan, William. *The Prophetic Milton.* Charlottesville: Univ. Press of Virginia, 1974.

Keynes, Geoffrey. *Drawings of William Blake: 92 Pencil Studies.* New York: Dover, 1970.

————. *William Blake's Illustrations to the Bible.* London: Blake Trust, 1957.

————, and Edwin Wolf, 2nd. *William Blake's Illuminated Books: A Census.* New York: The Grolier Club, 1953.

Kidner, Derek. "Isaiah." In *The New Bible Commentary: Revised,* ed. D. Guthrie and J. A. Motyer. 3rd rev. ed. Grand Rapids, Mich.: Eerdmans, 1970, pp. 588-625.

King, Edward. *Remarks on the Signs of the Times.* London, 1798.

Knowles, John. *The Life and Writings of Henry Fuseli.* 3 vols. London, 1831.

Korshin, Paul J. "The Development of Abstracted Typology in England, 1650-1820." In *Literary Uses of Typology,* ed. Earl Miner. Princeton: Princeton Univ. Press, 1977, pp. 147-203.

Kraeling, Emil G. *The Old Testament Since the Reformation.* London: Lutterworth, 1955.

349

Kroeber, Karl. "Graphic-Poetic Structuring in Blake's *Book of Urizen.*" *Blake Studies* 3 (1970), 7-18.

Krouse, F. Michael. *Milton's Samson and the Christian Tradition.* 1949. Reprint. New York: Octagon, 1974.

Kuhn, Albert J. "English Deism and the Development of Romantic Mythological Syncretism." *PMLA* 62 (1956), 1094-1116.

Lampe, G.W.H. "The Reasonableness of Typology." In *Essays on Typology,* ed. G.W.H. Lampe and K. J. Woollcombe. Studies in Biblical Theology Series, 22. London: SCM Press, 1957, pp. 9-38.

Landow, George P. "Moses Striking the Rock: Typological Symbolism in Victorian Poetry." In *Literary Uses of Typology,* ed. Earl Miner. Princeton: Princeton Univ. Press, 1977, pp. 315-44.

Lavater, John Caspar. *Essays on Physiognomy,* trans. Henry Hunter. Vol. II. London: John Murray, 1972.

Lawlor, H. J. "Early Citations from the Book of Enoch." *Journal of Philology* 25 (1897), 164-225.

Lee, Francis. "A Dissertation Upon the Second Book of Esdras." In his *Dissertations, Theological, Mathematical and Physical.* Vol. I. London: Alexander Stratham, 1752, pp. 13-171.

Lemprière, John. *Classical Dictionary of Proper Names Mentioned in Ancient Authors,* rev. and enl. F. A. Wright. London: Routledge and Kegan Paul, 1949.

Lewalski, Barbara K. "*Samson Agonistes* and the 'Tragedy' of the Apocalypse." *PMLA* 85 (1970), 1050-1062.

———. "Typological Symbolism and the 'Progress of the Soul' in Seventeenth-Century Literature." In *Literary Uses of Typology,* ed. Earl Miner. Princeton: Princeton Univ. Press, 1977, pp. 79-114.

Lindberg, Bo. *William Blake's Illustrations to the Book of Job.* Acta Academiae Aboensis, Ser. A: Humaniora: Humanistika Vetenskaper, Socialvetenskaper och Juridik, Teologi, Vol. xlvi. Abo, Finland: Abo Akademi, 1973.

Lonsdale, Roger, ed. *The Poems of Thomas Gray, William Collins, Oliver Goldsmith.* London: Longmans, 1969.

Low, Anthony. *The Blaze of Noon, A Reading of Samson Agonistes.* New York and London: Columbia Univ. Press, 1974.

Lowth, Robert. *Lectures on the Sacred Poetry of the Hebrews,* trans. G. Gregory. 2nd ed. 2 vols. London, 1816.

———, trans. *Isaiah: A New Translation with a Preliminary Dissertation, and Notes, Critical, Philological, and Explanatory.* 1778. Reprint. Albany, N.Y., 1794.

Lucian. *Lucian: Selected Works,* trans. Bryan P. Reardon. Library of Liberal Arts. New York: Bobbs-Merrill, 1965.

MacCallum, H. R. "Milton and the Figurative Interpretation of the Bible." *University of Toronto Quarterly* 31 (April 1962), 397-415.

McGann, Jerome J. "The Aim of Blake's Prophecies and the Uses of Blake Criticism." In *Blake's Sublime Allegory,* ed. Curran and Wittreich, pp. 3-21.

Macpherson, James. *The Poems of Ossian,* ed. Macolm Laing. Edinburgh, 1805.

Malkin, Benjamin Heath. *A Father's Memoirs of His Child.* In *Blake Records,* ed. G. E. Bentley, Jr. Oxford: Clarendon Press, 1969, pp. 421-31.

Manning, Stephen. "Scriptural Exegesis and the Literary Critic." In *Typology and Early American Literature,* ed. Sacvan Bercovitch. Amherst: Univ. of Massachusetts Press, 1972, pp. 46-66.

Manuel, Frank. *The Eighteenth Century Confronts the Gods.* Cambridge, Mass.: Harvard Univ. Press, 1959.

Marrou, Henri. *St. Augustine and His Influence through the Ages,* trans. Patrick Hepburne-Scott. Men of Wisdom Books. New York: Harper; London: Longmans, 1957.

Mason, Eudo C. *The Mind of Henry Fuseli: Selections from His Writings with An Introductory Study.* London: Routledge and Kegan Paul, 1951.

351

Mayer, John. *A Commentary on All the Prophets both Great and Small.* London, 1652.

Mazzeo, Joseph Anthony. "New Wine in Old Bottles: Reflections on Historicity and the Problem of Allegory." In his *Varieties of Interpretation.* Notre Dame, Ind.: Univ. of Notre Dame Press, 1978, pp. 47-69.

————. "St. Augustine's Rhetoric of Silence: Truth vs. Eloquence and Things vs. Signs." In his *Renaissance and Seventeenth-Century Studies.* New York: Columbia Univ. Press; London: Routledge and Kegan Paul, 1964, pp. 1-28.

Mede, Joseph. *The Key of the Revelation,* trans. Richard More. London, 1643.

Mellor, Anne Kostelanetz. *Blake's Human Form Divine.* Berkeley: Univ. of California Press, 1974.

Miller, Madeleine S., and J. Lane Miller. *Harper's Bible Dictionary.* 7th ed. New York: Harper, 1961.

Milton, John. *Complete Poems and Major Prose,* ed. Merritt Y. Hughes. New York: Odyssey Press, 1957.

————. *Complete Prose Works of John Milton,* ed. Don M. Wolfe et al. 8 vols. New Haven: Yale Univ. Press, 1953————.

————. *Paradise Lost,* ed. Thomas Newton. 2 vols. London, 1749.

————. *Paradise Regained,* ed. Charles Dunster. London, 1795.

————. *Paradise Regain'd. A Poem, in Four Books. To which is added Samson Agonistes: and Poems upon Several Occasions,* ed. Thomas Newton. London, 1752.

————. *Poems upon Several Occasions, English, Italian, and Latin, with Translations,* ed. Thomas Warton. London, 1785.

————. *The Poetical Works of John Milton,* ed. Thomas Newton. Vol. III. London, 1761.

————. *The Poetical Works of John Milton,* ed. Henry John Todd. 6 vols. London: Joseph Johnson, 1801.

————. *The Poetical Works of Mr. John Milton*. London: J. Tonson, 1695.

————. *The Works of John Milton*, ed. Frank Allen Patterson et al. Vol. XVIII. New York: Columbia Univ. Press, 1931-1938.

————. *The Works of John Milton, Historical, Political, and Miscellaneous*, ed. Thomas Birch. Vol. I. 2nd ed. London, 1753.

Miner, Earl. Afterword to *Literary Uses of Typology*, ed. Miner. Princeton: Princeton Univ. Press, 1977, pp. 370-94.

————, ed. *Literary Uses of Typology, from the Late Middle Ages to the Present*. Princeton: Princeton Univ. Press, 1977.

Miner, Paul. "Visions in the Darksom Air: Aspects of Blake's Biblical Symbolism." In *William Blake: Essays for S. Foster Damon*, ed. Alvin Rosenfeld, Providence: Brown Univ. Press, 1969, pp. 256-92.

————. "William Blake's 'Divine Analogy.'" *Criticism* 3 (Winter 1961), 46-61.

Mitchell, W.J.T. "Blake's Composite Art." In *Blake's Visionary Forms Dramatic*, ed. David V. Erdman and John E. Grant. Princeton: Princeton Univ. Press, 1970, pp. 57-81.

————. *Blake's Composite Art: A Study of the Illuminated Poetry*. Princeton: Princeton Univ. Press, 1978.

————. "Poetic and Pictorial Imagination in *The Book of Urizen*." In *The Visionary Hand: Essays for the Study of William Blake's Art and Aesthetics*, ed. Robert N. Essick. Los Angeles: Hennessey and Ingalls, 1973, pp. 337-80.

————. "Style and Iconography in Blake's *Milton*." *Blake Studies* 6 (1973), 47-71.

Moore, George Foot. *A Critical and Exegetical Commentary on Judges. The International Critical Commentary*. New York: Scribner, 1901.

Morris, David B. *The Religious Sublime: Christian Poetry*

and Critical Tradition in Eighteenth-Century England. Lexington, Ky.: Univ. Press of Kentucky, 1972.

Morton, A. L. "The Everlasting Gospel." In his *The Matter of Britain: Essays in a Living Culture.* London: Lawrence and Wishart, 1958, pp. 83-121.

Neil, W. "The Criticism and Theological Use of the Bible, 1700-1950." In *The Cambridge History of the Bible,* Vol. III, *The West from the Reformation to the Present Day,* ed. S. L. Greenslade. Cambridge: Cambridge Univ. Press, 1963, pp. 238-93.

Newcome, William, trans. *An Attempt Towards an Improved Version, a Metrical Arrangement, and an Explanation of the Prophet Ezekiel.* Dublin, 1788.

Newton, Thomas. *Dissertations on the Prophecies.* 1754. Reprint. Northampton, Mass., 1796.

Nurmi, Martin K. *Blake's "Marriage of Heaven and Hell": A Critical Study.* Kent State Univ. Bulletin Research Series III. Kent, Ohio: Kent State Univ. Press, 1957.

Oras, Ants. *Milton's Editors and Commentators from Patrick Hume to Henry John Todd (1695-1801), A Study in Critical Views and Methods.* London: Oxford Univ. Press; Tartu: Univ. of Tartu [Dorpat], 1931.

Ostriker, Alicia. *Vision and Verse in William Blake.* Madison: Univ. of Wisconsin Press, 1965.

Overton, John H. *The Evangelical Revival in the Eighteenth Century.* London: Longmans, 1891.

———, and Frederic Relton. *The English Church from the Accession of George I to the End of the Eighteenth Century.* London: Macmillan, 1906.

Ovid. *Ovid's Metamorphosis, Englished, Mythologized, and Represented in Figures by George Sandys [1632 ed],* ed. Karl K. Hulley and Stanley T. Vandersall. Lincoln, Nebr.: Univ. of Nebraska Press, 1970.

———. *Ovid's Metamorphoses, in Fifteen Books, Translated by the most Eminent Hands* [John Dryden et al.], ed. Samuel Garth. 4th ed. 2 vols. London, 1773.

Owen, A. L. *The Famous Druids*. Oxford: Clarendon Press, 1962.

Paine, Thomas. *The Selected Works of Tom Paine and Citizen Tom Paine*, ed. Howard Fast. New York: Modern Library-Random House, 1943.

Paley, Morton D. "Blake's *Night Thoughts*: An Exploration of the Fallen World." In *William Blake: Essays for S. Foster Damon*, ed. Alvin Rosenfeld. Providence: Brown Univ. Press, 1969, pp. 131-57.

————. *Energy and the Imagination: A Study of the Development of Blake's Thought*. Oxford: Clarendon Press, 1970.

————, and Michael Philips, eds. *William Blake: Essays in Honour of Sir Geoffrey Keynes*. Oxford: Clarendon Press, 1973.

Palmer, A. Smythe. *The Samson Saga and Its Place in Comparative Religion*. London: I. Pitman, 1913.

Parkhurst, John. *An Hebrew and English Lexicon, without Points*. 4th ed. London, 1799.

Patrick, Simon. *A Commentary Upon the Old Testament*. 3rd ed. 4 vols. London, 1727.

————, William Lowth, Richard Arnald, and Daniel Whitby. *A Commentary Upon the Old and New Testaments, with the Apocrypha*. 7 vols. 1727-1760. Reprint. London, 1809 [with Moses Lowman's commentary on Revelation].

Patrides, C. A. *Milton and the Christian Tradition*. Oxford: Clarendon Press, 1966.

Paulson, Ronald. "*The Harlot's Progress* and the Tradition of History Painting." *Eighteenth-Century Studies* 1 (Fall 1967), 69-92.

Peck, Francis. *New Memoirs of the Life and Poetical Works of Mr. John Milton*. London, 1740.

Percival, Milton O. *William Blake's Circle of Destiny*. New York: Columbia Univ. Press, 1938.

Percy, Thomas, trans. *The Song of Solomon, Newly Trans-*

lated from the Original Hebrew; with a Commentary and Annotations. London, 1764.

Poole, Matthew. *A Commentary on the Holy Bible.* Vols. II and III. 1685. Reprint. London: Banner of Truth Trust, 1962.

Pope, Marvin H., trans. *Song of Songs, A New Translation with Introduction and Commentary.* The Anchor Bible. Garden City, N.Y.: Doubleday, 1977.

Priestley, Joseph. "Observations on the Prophets of the Old Testament." In his *Theological Repository.* Vol. IV. Birmingham: Joseph Johnson, 1784, pp. 97-122.

―――― et al., trans. *The New Testament in an Improved Version, upon the Basis of Archbishop Newcome's New Translation.* London: Joseph Johnson, 1808.

Pritchard, James B. *Ancient Near Eastern Texts Relating to the Old Testament.* Princeton: Princeton Univ. Press, 1955.

Pritchard, John Paul. "The Fathers of the Church in the Works of Milton." *Classical Journal* 33 (1937), 79-87.

Purver, Anthony, trans. *A New and Literal Translation of All the Books of the Old and New Testaments.* 2 vols. London, 1764.

Raine, Kathleen. *Blake and Tradition.* Bollingen Series 35.11. 2 vols. Princeton: Princeton Univ. Press, 1968.

Reid, William Hamilton. *The Rise and Dissolution of the Infidel Societies in this Metropolis.* London, 1800.

Robertson, J. M. *A History of Freethought.* Vol. II. 4th ed., rev. and enl. 1936. Reprint. London: Dawsons, 1969.

Robinson, Henry Crabb. "Reminiscences." In *Blake Records,* ed. G. E. Bentley, Jr. Oxford: Clarendon Press, 1969, pp. 535-49.

―――――. "William Blake, Kunstler, Dichter, und Religiöser Schwärmer." *Vaterländisches Museum* 1 (Jan. 1811), 107-31. Translated and reprinted in *William Blake: The Critical Heritage,* ed. G. E. Bentley, Jr. London: Routledge and Kegan Paul, 1975, pp. 156-64.

Roe, Albert S. "The Thunder of Egypt." In *William Blake:*

Essays for S. Foster Damon, ed. Alvin Rosenfeld. Providence: Brown Univ. Press, 1969, pp. 158-95.

Rogal, Samuel J. "Religious Periodicals in England during the Restoration and Eighteenth Century." *Journal of the Rutgers University Library* 35 (Dec. 1971), 27-33.

Roscelli, William John. "The Metaphysical Milton." *Texas Studies in Literature and Language* 8 (Winter 1967), 463-84.

Rose, E. J. "Goodbye to Orc and All That." *Blake Studies* 4 (1972), 135-51.

Rosenblum, Robert. *Transformations in Late Eighteenth Century Art.* Princeton: Princeton Univ. Press, 1967.

Rosenfeld, Alvin, ed. *William Blake: Essays for S. Foster Damon.* Providence: Brown Univ. Press, 1969.

Ross, Malcolm. *Poetry and Dogma: The Transfiguration of Eucharistic Symbols in Seventeenth-Century English Poetry.* New Brunswick, N.J.: Rutgers Univ. Press, 1954.

Roston, Murray. *Biblical Drama in England, from the Middle Ages to the Present Day.* Evanston, Ill.: Northwestern Univ. Press, 1968.

——. *Prophet and Poet: The Bible and the Growth of Romanticism.* London: Faber and Faber, 1965.

Rothenberg, Jerome, ed. *Technicians of the Sacred: A Range of Poetries from Africa, America, Asia, & Oceania.* Garden City, N.Y.: Doubleday, 1968.

Rowley, H. H. "The Interpretation of the Song of Songs." In his *The Servant of the Lord and Other Essays on the Old Testament.* London: Lutterworth Press, 1952, pp. 189-234.

Rudé, George. *Hanoverian London, 1714-1808.* Berkeley and Los Angeles: Univ. of California Press, 1971.

Saintsbury, George. *A History of English Prosody, from the Twelfth Century to the Present Day.* Vol. III. London: Macmillan, 1910.

Sandler, Florence. "The Iconoclastic Enterprise: Blake's Critique of 'Milton's Religion.'" *Blake Studies* 5 (1972), 13-57.

357

Sandmel, Samuel. *The Hebrew Scriptures: An Introduction to Their Literature and Religious Ideas*. New York: Knopf, 1963.

Schmitz, Robert Morell. *Hugh Blair*. New York: King's Crown Press, 1948.

Schorer, Mark. *William Blake: The Politics of Vision*. New York: Henry Holt, 1946.

Schwartzbach, Bertram Eugene. *Voltaire's Old Testament Criticism*. Geneva: Librairie Droz, 1971.

Scrivener, F.H.A. *The Authorized Edition of the English Bible (1611), Its Subsequent Reprints and Modern Representatives*. Cambridge: Cambridge Univ. Press, 1910.

Seznec, Jean. *The Survival of the Pagan Gods: Mythological Tradition and Its Place in Renaissance Humanism and Art*, trans. Barbara F. Sessions. Bollingen Series 38. New York: Pantheon, 1953.

Shaffer, E. S. *"Kubla Khan" and the Fall of Jerusalem: The Mythological School in Biblical Criticism and Secular Literature, 1770-1880*. Cambridge: Cambridge Univ. Press, 1975.

Skinner, John. *A Critical and Exegetical Commentary on Genesis*. New York: Scribner, 1910.

Smalley, Beryl. *The Study of the Bible in the Middle Ages*. 1952. Reprint. Notre Dame, Ind.: Univ. of Notre Dame Press, 1964.

Smith, John. *A Discourse on Prophecy*. 1660. Reprinted in *A Collection of Theological Tracts*, ed. Richard Watson. London, 1791. IV, 297-362.

Smith, John [of Cambleton]. *A Summary View and Explanation of the Writings of the Prophets*. Edinburgh and London, 1787.

Smith, John Thomas. *Nollekens and his Times*. In *Blake Records*, ed. G. E. Bentley, Jr. Oxford: Clarendon Press, 1969, pp. 455-76.

Spenser, Edmund. *The Poetical Works of Edmund Spenser*, ed. J. C. Smith and E. de Selincourt. New York: Oxford Univ. Press, 1912.

Steadman, John M. *The Lamb and the Elephant: Ideal Imitation and the Context of Renaissance Allegory.* San Marino, Calif.: Huntington Library, 1974,

Stewart, Stanley. *The Enclosed Garden: The Tradition and the Image in Seventeenth-Century Poetry.* Madison: Univ. of Wisconsin Press, 1966.

Stoudt, John Joseph. *Sunrise to Eternity: A Study in Jacob Boehme's Life and Thought.* Philadelphia: Univ. of Pennsylvania Press, 1957.

Svendson, Kester. *Milton and Science.* Cambridge, Mass.: Harvard Univ. Press, 1965.

Swedenborg, Emanuel. *Arcana Coelestia*, rev. and ed. John Faulkner Potts. 12 vols. New York: American Swedenborg Printing and Publishing Society, 1915-1937.

Swinburne, Algernon Charles. *William Blake: A Critical Essay.* 1868. Reprint. Lincoln, Nebr.: Univ. of Nebraska Press, 1970.

Sykes, Norman. "The Religion of Protestants." In *The Cambridge History of the Bible*, Vol. III, *The West from the Reformation to the Present Day*, ed. S. L. Greenslade. Cambridge: Cambridge Univ. Press, 1963, pp. 175-98.

Tannenbaum, Leslie. "Blake and the Iconography of Cain." In *Blake in His Time*, ed. Robert N. Essick and Donald Pearce. Bloomington: Indiana Univ. Press, 1978, pp. 23-34.

———. "Lord Byron in the Wilderness: Biblical Tradition in Byron's *Cain* and Blake's *The Ghost of Abel*." *Modern Philology* 72 (May 1975), 350-64.

———. "Transformations of Michelangelo in William Blake's *The Book of Urizen*." *Colby Library Quarterly* 16 (1980), 19-50.

Tatham, Frederick. "Life of Blake." In *Blake Records*, ed. G. E. Bentley, Jr. Oxford: Clarendon Press, 1969, pp. 507-35.

Tayler, Irene. *Blake's Illustrations to the Poems of Gray.* Princeton: Princeton Univ. Press, 1971.

Thomas, Keith. *Religion and the Decline of Magic*. New York: Scribner, 1971.

Thompson, E. P. *The Making of the English Working Class*. 1963. Reprint. New York: Vintage-Random House, 1966.

Tillich, Paul. "Kairos." In *A Handbook of Christian Theology*, ed. Marvin Halverson and Arthur A. Cohen. New York: Meridian, 1958, pp. 193-97.

Tisch, J. H. "Milton and the German Mind in the Eighteenth Century." In *Studies in the Eighteenth Century: Papers Presented to the David Nichol Smith Memorial Seminar*, ed. R. F. Brissenden. Toronto: Univ. of Toronto Press, 1968, pp. 205-29.

Todd, Ruthven. "William Blake and the Eighteenth-Century Mythologists." In his *Tracks in the Snow*. London: Gray Walls Press, 1946, pp. 29-60.

——. *William Blake the Artist*. London: Dutton, 1971.

Tolley, Michael J. "Blake's Songs of Spring." In *William Blake: Essays in Honour of Sir Geoffrey Keynes*, ed. Morton D. Paley and Michael Philips. Oxford: Clarendon Press, 1973, pp. 96-128.

——. "*Europe*: 'to those ychained in sleep.'" In *Blake's Visionary Forms Dramatic*, ed. David V. Erdman and John E. Grant. Princeton: Princeton Univ. Press, 1970, pp. 115-45.

Trapp, J. B. "The Iconography of the Fall of Man." In *Approaches to Paradise Lost: The York Centenary Lectures*, ed. C. A. Patrides. London: Edward Arnold, 1968, pp. 223-65.

Trapp, John. *A Clavis to the Bible, or a New Comment upon the Pentateuch or Five Books of Moses*. London, 1650.

Traver, Hope. *The Four Daughters of God: A Study of the Versions of this Allegory*. Philadelphia: John C. Winston, 1907.

Voltaire, François Marie Arouet de. *Philosophical Dictionary*, trans. Peter Gay. 2 vols. New York: Basic Books, 1962.

Waddington, Raymond B. "Melancholy Against Melancholy: *Samson Agonistes* as Renaissance Tragedy." In *Calm of Mind: Tercentenary Essays on Paradise Regained and Samson Agonistes in Honor of John S. Diekhoff*, ed. Joseph Anthony Wittreich, Jr. Cleveland and London: Press of Case Western Reserve Univ., 1971, pp. 259-87.

Waith, Eugene M. *The Herculean Hero in Marlowe, Chapman, Shakespeare and Dryden*. New York: Columbia Univ. Press; London: Chatto and Windus, 1962.

Wakefield, Gilbert. *Silva Critica, sive in Auctores Sacros Profanosque Commentarius Philologus*. 5 vols. Canterbury, 1789-1795.

Wallerstein, Ruth. *Studies in Seventeenth-Century Poetic*. Madison: Univ. of Wisconsin Press, 1965.

Warburton, William. *The Divine Legation of Moses Demonstrated*. 10th rev. ed. 3 vols. London, 1846.

Watson, Richard, ed. *A Collection of Theological Tracts*. 2nd ed. 6 vols. London, 1791.

Weigle, Luther A. "English Versions Since 1611." In *The Cambridge History of the Bible*, Vol. III, *The West from the Reformation to the Present Day*, ed. S. L. Greenslade, Cambridge: Cambridge Univ. Press, 1963, pp. 361-82.

Wesley, John. *Explanatory Notes Upon the New Testament*. 2nd American ed. 2 vols. New York, 1806.

————. *Notes on the Old and New Testaments*. 4 vols. London, 1764.

White, Samuel. *A Commentary on the Prophet Isaiah*. London, 1709.

Wilkinson, James John Garth. Preface to his edition of Blake's *Songs of Innocence and of Experience* (1839). Reprinted in *William Blake: The Critical Heritage*, ed. G. E. Bentley, Jr. London: Routledge and Kegan Paul, 1975, pp. 57-61.

Williams, Arnold. *The Common Expositor, An Account of the Commentaries on Genesis, 1527-1633*. Chapel Hill: Univ. of North Carolina Press, 1948.

Wittreich, Joseph Anthony, Jr. *Angel of Apocalypse: Blake's Idea of Milton.* Madison: Univ. of Wisconsin Press, 1975.

————. " 'The Crown of Eloquence': The Figure of the Orator in Milton's Prose Works." In *Achievements of the Left Hand: Essays on the Prose of John Milton,* ed. Michael Lieb and John T. Shawcross. Amherst: Univ. of Massachusetts Press, 1974, pp. 3-54.

————. "Opening the Seals: Blake's Epics and the Milton Tradition." In *Blake's Sublime Allegory,* ed. Stuart Curran and Joseph Anthony Wittreich, Jr. Madison: Univ. of Wisconsin Press, 1973, pp. 23-58.

————. " 'A Poet Amongst Poets': Milton and the Tradition of Prophecy." In *Milton and the Line of Vision,* ed. Wittreich. Madison: Univ. of Wisconsin Press, 1975, pp. 97-142.

————. "Sublime Allegory: Blake's Epic Manifesto and the Milton Tradition." *Blake Studies* 4 (1972), 15-44.

————, ed. *Milton's Paradise Regained: Two Eighteenth-Century Critiques, by Richard Meadowcourt and Charles Dunster.* Gainesville, Fla.: Scholars' Facsimiles and Reprints, 1971.

Woodhouse, A.S.P. and Douglas Bush, eds. *The Minor English Poems.* In *A Variorum Commentary on the Poems of John Milton,* ed. Merritt Y. Hughes. Vol. II, Part I. New York: Columbia Univ. Press, 1970————.

Young, Edward. *The Complaint: or, Night Thoughts on Life, Death and Immortality.* London: R. Dodsley, 1742-45.

Zwicker, Stephen N. "Politics and Panegyric: The Figural Mode from Marvell to Pope." In *Literary Uses of Typology,* ed. Earl Miner. Princeton: Princeton Univ. Press, 1977, pp. 115-46.

Index

Aaron, 236

Abel: finding of his body by Adam and Eve, 12, 53, 134; in *Ghost of Abel*, 209, 213, 214; as type of Christ, 12, 99, 135; in *Urizen*, 211, 212, 215. *See also* Cain and Abel myth.

Abraham, 211, 214, 215, 223

Abrams, M. H., 6, 16, 319 n19, 320-21

Achilles, shield of, 64, 65, 275, 278

Acts of the Apostles, The, 106

Adam, 59, 94, 109, 110, 196, 202, 206-207, 218, 219

Aeneas, 173; shield of, 275, 277, 278

Aeschylus, 49

Africa: commentary, 186-93; prophetic form in, 44, 45, 46, 50

Ahania, 230, 239-47, 242, 243-44

Ahania, The Book of: commentary, 225-50; form of, 248-50; prophetic form in, 45-47, 51

Albion, 23, 87

"Albion Rose," 268, 278

allegory, distinguished from typology, 91, 94, 101, 107-108, 110

Allen, Don Cameron, 20

Allix, Peter, 215

All Religions are One, 63, 75, 79, 294 n35

Altick, Richard D., 290-91 n22

America, 120, 196, 256; commentary, 124-51; prophetic form in, 43, 45, 46, 47-48, 50, 51-52, 53

Amos, Book of, 245

Ancient Britons, The, 86, 87

Ancient Deists of Hoxton, 16

Anglican Church, 14, 18, 19, 294 n35

Annet, Peter, 14

antinomianism, 16

Apocalypse, the: beast of, 123, 184; imagery of in *America*, 124, 126-27, 148; and the Nativity Ode, 165-66; in *Song of Los*, 193, 198; as tragedy, 264-65; in *Urizen*, 222

Apollo, 180, 271, 274, 275, 276

Apology for Smectymnuus, 171, 228

Aponius, 144

Aquinas, Thomas, 42

Areopagitica, 20, 88

Aristotle, 35, 39, 70, 73

Arsareth, 137

art, biblical, 11-13, 291 n22

Arthur, 87

Ashtaroth, 230

Asia: in *Ahania*, 225, 239, 248; biblical significance of, 185-86; kings of, 193-96

Asia: commentary, 193-200; prophetic form in, 46, 50

Assyria, 185, 192, 194, 196, 241

Atlantis, 137, 191-92

Atonement, the: in *Ahania*, 234-

363

INDEX

Egypt, 101, 185, 231; Israel's bondage in, 224, 225, 230; as name of fallen world, 211, 221; origin of abstract law and philosophy in, 185; origin of figurative language in, 56, 57, 58; origin of state religion in, 187-88, 192, 193, 200; and serpent symbolism, 231-32

Eichhorn, Johann Gottfried, 13, 22, 40, 41, 58, 66

Elijah, 84, 113, 116

Ellis, Edwin John, 5

Elohim, the, 203, 204, 206, 212, 213-14, 258, 327 n11

"Elohim Creating Adam," 206

Elohist creation account, 203, 204-205, 206, 251, 258

emblem books, 58

Enitharmon: crystal palace of, 182, 183; as harlot, 153, 176, 182; as Milton's wisest Fate, 176; as mistress of chivalry, 170; as Queen of Heaven, 167, 175; as Venus, 53; as woman clothed with the sun, 133

Eno, 254, 257, 260-61, 266

Enoch, Book of, 191, 325 n11

Enuma Elish tablets, 273

epic, 7, 32, 34, 49, 53

Erasmus, Desiderius, 190

Erdman, David, 47, 48, 73, 150, 185, 199, 200

Ernesti, Johann, 13

Erskine, Thomas, 289 n18

Esau, 109-110, 117-18, 127-33, 140, 212, 215. *See also* Edom.

Esau and Jacob myth, 109-110, 124, 127-33, 211-13, 215

Esdras, Second Book of, 50, 124, 125, 134-41, 145, 198, 319 n15

Europe, 117, 216-17; commentary, 152-84; nameless shadowy female in, 153, 161-63; prophetic

form in, 43, 45, 46, 50, 51, 52, 53

Eusebius, 20, 273

Evangelicals, 10, 11, 18

Eve, 202, 203, 207, 249

Exodus, Book of, 65, 192-93, 211, 225, 227, 229, 235-36

Ezekiel, 43, 63, 223, 228

Ezekiel, Book of, 50, 194, 195, 198, 229, 232, 326 n3; atemporality in, 44-45, 119; multiple perspectives in, 41; Newcome's translation of, 9, 36; pictorial nature of, 58, 65, 66; significative actions in, 56, 74, 112

Ezra, 166

Fall, the, 12, 61, 80, 110, 150, 155, 193, 201, 209-210, 217-18, 254

fancy, 177-80

Farrer, Austin, 316 n59

"Fayette" stanzas, 328 n21

Fénelon, François de Salignac de la Mothe, 37, 43, 55, 71, 303-304

firstborn, sacrifice of, 235-37

Fisch, Harold, 6

Fisher, Peter F., 6

Fixler, Michael, 305 n44

Flaxman, John, 53, 124

Flood, the, 190-92, 216-18

Four Zoas, The, 7

Fox, Susan, 46

Freemasonry, 17

freethinkers, 13, 21, 28, 29. *See also* deists.

Freimarck, Vincent, 67-68

French Revolution, 6, 11, 13, 16, 95, 192, 196, 198-99

Frye, Northrop, 5, 47-48, 104, 146, 251, 267, 284 n10, 316-17, 330 n1

Fuseli, Henry, 10, 13, 135, 293 n30

Fuzon, 211, 226-29, 259

Library of Congress Cataloging in Publication Data

Tannenbaum, Leslie, 1945-
  Biblical tradition in Blake's early prophecies.

  Bibliography: p.
  Includes index.
    1. Blake, William, 1757-1827—Religion and
ethics.   2. Bible in literature.   3. Bible—
Criticism, interpretation, etc.—History—19th
century.   I. Title.
PR4148.B52T3   821'.7   81-47158
ISBN 0-601-06490-3   AACR2